Han Suyin is the daughte
father who, a Mandarin a al
Academy, had chosen in on
a scholarship to Europe.

She was moved by the poverty and sickness her
to take up medicine. She studied Chinese classics and
mathematics while waiting for a place at Yenching University.
Then, after completing her pre-medical education, she travelled
across Siberia to Europe on a scholarship and continued her
studies at the University of Brussels. In 1938 she returned to
China, married an ex-Sandhurst Chinese officer, who later
became a general in Chiang Kai Shek's army, and practised
midwifery in the interior during the Sino-Japanese War. From
this experience she wrote her first book, *Destination Chungking*,
in 1940. In 1942 she came to London, where her husband had
been appointed military attache. Three years later he returned to
active service in China, leaving Han Suyin to complete her
medical studies in London. After her husband was killed in 1947,
she spent a year as a house surgeon at the Royal Free Hospital
before accepting a doctor's post in Hong Kong. There she wrote
the Eurasian love story (her own) that brought her international
acclaim and success as a writer. The Sunday Times described *A
Many-Splendoured Thing* as 'an astounding love story . . .
brilliantly topical, but far more than that, for she handles an
eternal theme with power, insight and unfailing artistry.'

Since that time she has written numerous books, both novels
and non-fiction. Her combined autobiography and history of
China in five volumes, has been hailed as an important
contribution to international understanding. Bertrand Russell
said of the first volume, *The Crippled Tree*, 'during the many
hours I spent reading it, I learned more about China than I did
in a whole year spent in that country'.

By the same author

Autobiography, History

A Mortal Flower
Birdless Summer
My House Has Two Doors
Phoenix Harvest

Novels

A Many-Splendoured Thing
Destination Chungking
. . . And the Rain My Drink
The Mountain is Young
Cast But One Shadow and *Winter Love*
Two Loves
The Four Faces

Non-Fiction

China in the Year 2001
Asia Today
Lhasa, The Open City
The Morning Deluge: Mao Tsetung and the
  Chinese Revolution 1893–1953
Wind in the Tower: Mao Tsetung and the
  Chinese Revolution 1949–1975

HAN SUYIN

The Crippled Tree

China: Autobiography, History, Book 1

TRIAD
GRAFTON BOOKS

LONDON GLASGOW
TORONTO SYDNEY AUCKLAND

Triad
Grafton Books
8 Grafton Street, London W1X 3LA

Published by Triad Grafton 1982
Reprinted 1984, 1985, 1986

Triad Paperbacks Ltd is an imprint of
Chatto, Bodley Head & Jonathan Cape Ltd and
Grafton Books, A Division of the Collins Publishing Group

First published in Great Britain by
Jonathan Cape Ltd 1965

Copyright © Han Suyin 1965

ISBN 0-586-03836-1

Printed and bound in Great Britain by
Collins, Glasgow

Set in Linotype Times

The characters in this book are not fictional, neither are the events. So far as research can make it so, historical accuracy has been maintained. Here and there however minor characters have had their names changed in deference to their feelings.

The name 'Son of the Ocean' is a poetic figure of speech given to the Great River or Yangtse River of China, it is not a translation of the river's name.

To all my Chinese, Belgian, English, French and other friends of various nationalities who have helped me, I give my thanks.

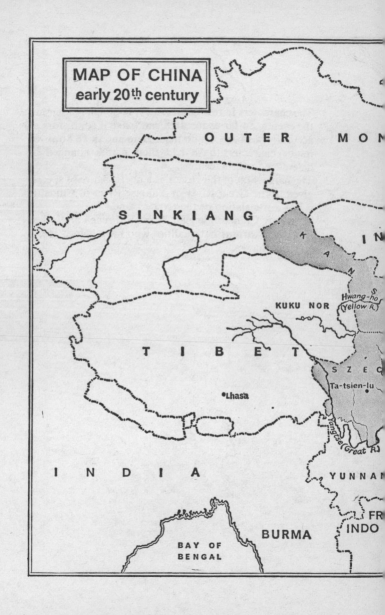

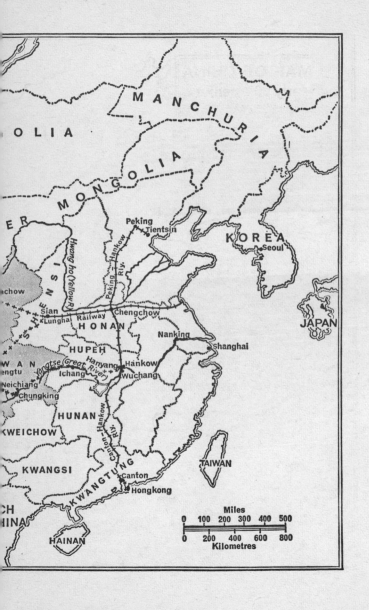

Part One (1885-1913)

ONE

Dear Papa, dear Mama,

Today I shall not have time to write you a very long letter, because the bandits were here last night, and the cook has been decapitated. His head is in the garden, so I have shut the window. The little one is crying with prickly heat, but I cannot get any talcum powder so please send me two dozen tins, it is easy to get in England. I have had to give up my corsets too, and you would not recognize me, I drag myself in slippers all day long.

The pen caught the residue in the inkwell, streaked a hair across the sloping handwriting, defacing the last word. Marguerite broke down.

"Enough, enough," she screamed aloud, "I have had enough!" She pushed back the chair, brought both her hands to her forehead, squeezing upon her temples. The tears, as if squeezed out, ran down her almost lashless eyes on to her thin cheeks. She paced the room, racked by sobs. "Enough, it is enough. My God, I cannot stand any more. I pack, and I go."

It was a formula she had repeated so often, so many times through the years, would repeat so often. And yet she went on, she had gone on, she would go on living in China, unable to tear herself away, until thirty years later a final cataclysm made the choice for her.

Round her the dirty plaster of the walls, the mat ceiling which dropped blobs of dry earth when the rats frolicked above it at night, the earthen floor with its rotting carpet laid in front of the sagging iron bed, the cot with the wailing child, gave back a heavy somnolent indifference, the enormous indifference of the enormous, strange land around her, an indifference more suffocating than any enmity, more void than any vacuum, making of the whole populous land a desert where she turned on herself, imprisoned among crowds, imprisoned in indifference, in dirt, in squalor, an enormous rat-cage without beginning or end that she paced, a rat-cage she had walked into led by what had once been love and was now the wail of a child, another child in her belly, the cook's head, on a pike outside the shut window, buzzing its flies above the tomatoes her husband had planted two months ago.

11

And the tomatoes were already dropping small tight green heads in clusters.

"Enough, enough. I pack, I go. This time it's the end." And she had so wanted to eat fresh tomatoes.

She went to the bed, drew the leather suitcase from under it. Dust pricked her hands. Dust, dust, always dust. Everything always dirty, one could not get away from dirt. She opened the lid, then left the suitcase yawning as a grave upon the carpet. "To go, to go," She bent over the wailing child. "Stop it, do you hear me? Stop it, or I . . ." The next moment she had picked it up, kissed it wildly. "My baby, my baby." Her hands left their grime upon the woollen shawl, the child's white woollen dress so difficult to wash.

There was laughter coming from the garden.

"They are there. Again. May God damn them. Again."

Outside, beyond the pickets of the fence surrounding the small garden where now the sentinel head watched, the usual crowd was standing, laughing, pointing at the house where lived the foreign woman, at the head: the women, hair grey with dust, tight buns low in the neck, the children, standing or being carried, clouds of flies hovering round the women, an old man, two or three younger men; all, all in that ubiquitous, nerve-racking blue cloth, a blue of infinite variegation but still menacing as a uniform; all laughing, pointing at the head like a standard above the tomatoes, at the house where the foreign woman lived, and now that she appeared laughter rose like an explosion.

"Laugh, laugh . . . they would laugh if you disembowelled them. Brutes. Brutes." She started shouting, holding on to the door she had opened. "Brutes, imbeciles, you'll all have you heads cut off. Idiots." She made the gesture of a head being chopped off, slammed the door shut, and the ceiling dropped gravel and the scurry of a rat sounded briefly above her.

Outside the laughter, stopped while she shouted, resounded again, this time directed towards her, no longer shared by the cauliflower head on its pike.

"Foreign devil, foreign devil, foreign devil."

All the children shouted this, laughing, imitating her head-cutting gesture, hopping up and down in the dust, pressing their faces to the fence, hoping for the door to open once again, for the incomprehensible woman to erupt, shouting incomprehensible things. It was a jack-in-the-box act they never tired of. Throughout the day children lingered by the garden fence hopefully.

Marguerite sprang back to the table, her pen scratched the paper again. The writing sloped, rode downwards, and when she came to the end of the sheet half an inch was blank on the left side of the paper while at the right the words had reached bottom.

... I cannot stand their laughter any more. They laugh when I cry, they laugh when people are executed, they are not human. I am coming back ... I shall force him to let me leave today, I do not wish to be killed too.

There was a scuffle. It was the crowd, making way. The garden gate clicked, the steps of her husband paused before the shut door, then he was in the room. Her husband. Her fury, the splendid energy she wasted in fury, in screams, pacing the rat-infested room,. cowering behind closed windows, hating, wanting to be loved, to be accepted, yet always rejected, leapt at him.

"Yentung, I have decided. I am going away today. Now."

He sighed, sat down on the bed, pushing the open suitcase away with his foot, and started to unlace his boots.

"You hear me? Do you hear me? I cannot endure any more."

"Marguerite, you are too nervous."

"Nervous? That's all you can say, I am nervous? You go off and leave me alone with that" – she pointed windowwards – "who would not be nervous? After the night we had? I thought we were coming to a civilized land ... but you are primitive, uncivilized. Listen to them laugh ... You lied to me, you got me here by lying to me."

"I have obtained another cook," said her husband, who had now unlaced his boots (he tramped the new railway line, and the leeches and an occasional snake forced him to wear boots though the hard leather broke his toe nails). "He is coming this afternoon. He has cooked for a Belgian family, the Tardiens."

"I am leaving. You can stay with your cook, I am going. I insist that you get me a passage on the next boat, do you hear? I insist."

"You know, Marguerite, the railway line is cut, the warlords shot twelve workers at Fengtai last night. Besides," he added, "there's war in your country too. The Germans. You can't go back. No boats until the war is over."

Trapped. She was trapped everywhere, by everything. Marguerite threw herself back on her chair weeping. The foolscap she used for her letters received her tears. Later she would continue the letter upon the tear-stained paper, describing the scene:

Now they have come for the head, at last, with drummers who are the village rascals beating in front. The widow comes behind lamenting loudly, but I know she does not feel anything because she does not weep; and when she sees me, she stops, stares, puts her hand to her mouth not to laugh. They are not human, I tell you dear Papa and Mama, and I will not stay. As soon as the war is over I shall be back.

"That is the only one, then?" I said.

It was 1958, cold early summer. My brother Tzechun, Son of Spring, and I sat in the café of the Montparnasse Station in Paris, and I folded the letter paper on which the past had lived again so brusquely. Who was the whining child in the cradle? Perhaps me. What was the year? 1917? 1918? Even earlier? The letter was dated March 17th, but no year was indicated. All that was certain was that it must have been one of the years of the First World War. The letter was from my mother, addressed to her parents, then war refugees in England with my brother Son of Spring.

Now Son of Spring was an olding man, very myopic, with a crew-cut and shabby clothes, and he sat opposite me at a table in a railway station café in Paris. And he had just handed me this letter, from the past. It was the only one. Son of Spring himself had burnt all his mother's letters, all of them except this one.

"You understand, I never dreamt *you* would need them, one day . . ."

There had been a trunk full. A whole trunk. Son of Spring gestured dimensionally over the coffee cups. "If I had known that you wanted them, Little Sister, of course I would have kept them. But at that time you were still a child – how did I know you would want them?"

"It does not matter."

Another search into the past had ended. It's harvest was this one letter, no more. Why had this one been kept? Perhaps as a symbolic reminder of the burning, like a pinch of ash, a lock of hair, kept out of wholesale cremation. Perhaps a satisfaction out of our mother's suffering, screaming at us now out of the angular writing, hitting us as her words used to hit out, at my brother, at myself, when we were young.

"It's time for your train. I would have liked you to stay much longer."

I looked at him. We had always loved each other, my brother and I, in spite of everyone, in spite of everything. We understood each other, he said. That was not true, I think, for he certainly did not know what I was capable of. And I could never understand the life he had chosen, the narrow, restricted life; I would ponder for years on the puzzle of his failure. "And you are happy?"

"Yes, I have made myself reasons ... I am happy. I am useful. I tell myself I am useful."

We went out on to the station platform, the trains herded like bovines in a stable, complacently dirty; the acrid smell of the station was at me.

Son of Spring said: "Trains, trains, trains ... do the trains run on time in China now?"

"Yes, now they do."

"I am so glad, so glad. Remember how worried Father was about his trains? Father must have been happy these last few years. His whole life was the railways, the iron road as it is called in Chinese, is it not? Sometimes I felt the iron road came first with him, before any of us, certainly before me, his son. He never had time for anything else, did he?"

Son of Spring stood planted outside the train window, waving regularly as the carriages slid one by one away from him. His glasses soon turned blind and I thought of the cook's head. The letter was in my bag. The only one that remained of a whole trunk full of my mother's letters.

Sitting down on the filthy seat (why were all provincial trains in Europe so dirty now, far more dirty than in China today?), I felt irritation, compassion, both futile, towards my brother Son of Spring. Burning all those letters, my mother's letters, when I needed them so much. Letters covering the whole of her life in China, from 1913 to God knows when, at least till her father, to whom they were addressed, died in 1940. How long had Mother continued writing those immense epistles of hers, first to her parents, then when her mother died to her father alone? My earliest recollection of my mother as a person consciously separate from myself was of her sitting crouched over a table, and I could still hear the rustle of the sheets she stirred. That was when I had asked: "Mama, Mama, what is writing? How does the person who gets the letter know what you mean?" And I had got the usual answer: "Leave me alone. You will know this when you are bigger ..."

My brother had burnt all her letters, and no one else in her family (and I went to all of them, in Antwerp and Brussels and Louvain, and they gave me memories, their own personal remembrance, but no letters) had any. The stupid man, the poor stupid boy. The hurt child, hurting back ... But he had always been like that, cutting himself off definitely from all that hurt him, trying to escape. And there was no escape, except in facing facts. That was my quality, and mine alone. Son of Spring did not have it. Neither did so many others in the world. So many spent their years running away from facts.

"But why don't you ask your mother to tell you her life? She could tell you herself." Thus my aunt, Lucy Denis, wheeling her paralysed husband in the gravel alleys of the Bois in Brussels. The invalid in the chair drooled, moved a hand. The sun was cold, and a single swan upon the lacquer-green pond (which Aunt Lucy, like everyone in Brussels, called a lake) was immobile as wood. The invalid had been a general, Henri Denis, Minister of Defence of the Kingdom of Belgium, my mother's cousin.

"She hasn't talked to me for thirty years. And she would remember not to speak to me, if she saw me. You know what the Denis are like."

Aunt Lucy gave her usual glow-glow-glow chirrup; she was always a plump, Spanish-looking woman. "Yes, Marguerite was like that. I remember being told how she kicked a hole in the door when her father shut her up because she went out to see a Chinese ... such a thick door, yet she managed to escape. I was only seven then, but I never forgot the story of the hole in the door."

I wanted to write a book about my father and mother and about China, and one day the idea took shape in action, and then it grew, as such seeds do, sprouting and then straightening into a distant shape, a tree of many branches; and as I too lived through years full of change and revolution, I too had to look back, look homeward, and write about that earth-changing time which took place in our generation. I did not know where to begin, how to start. China to me was of course my father and mother, and all I myself knew of China. To separate them from me would be to denude my story.

Inextricably, the tree of my book grew, an odd growth, yet more true than all the ideal books written about China.

It was impossible to isolate either my father or my mother from history itself, the history of their period in China. As impossible as it was for Proust, writing about himself, to cut himself and his characters from the period in which they lived and the events to which they reacted. We are all products of our time, vulnerable to history. I was born because there had been, in China, a Boxer Rebellion (as the Europeans called it) in 1900, and because of this event, which the Chinese call the Uprising of the Righteous Fists, my Chinese father, instead of becoming a classical scholar, perhaps a Hanling Academician, married my Belgian mother. The tree is known by its roots. I had to go back to the roots.

And then there was the iron road, as the Chinese call it, an exact translation of the French *chemin de fer,* a railway. Railways meant a lot to my father, and they were also part of the climate of my growth since my childhood was spent in small or large railway stations. Even now, whenever I hear the siren hoot of an engine, my childhood comes cantering back to me.

After the Revolution of 1949, which in China is called Liberation, I went back year after year, searching for people, facts, memories. I also went to Belgium, tracing the past. For years I gathered what I could, interviewing retired scholars in Szechuan, missionaries in Canada, great-aunts in Ostend.

I was born in a China now past, and the Communist Revolution of 1949 was as frightening to me as to many people of my class and education, who have never been Communists, and can never become Communist because they have passed the age at which they believe strongly enough in anything to man the barricades and die with triumphal shouts on their lips. But mine could be the objective truthful voice of those neither committed to resuscitate the past, nor committed to action in the present. The world needs the artist who records, with dispassionate compassion, more than the missionary who proclaims with virulence unreal crusades against reality, especially those who want to put the clock back to an ideal past that never was.

I could not, as my brother had done, cut myself away, live in a myth of Golden Age, fantasy mummified, preserved from the destroying and creating winds of today. The future begins yesterday, for the tree as well as for man.

"I don't understand you, I don't understand you," cried a friend, a girl like myself, Chinese father, European mother, and now gone away from China, turning her back on its present which she abhorred. "How *can* you go back every year to China, when nothing in China is as it was? I couldn't do it. To find my childhood memories gone, everything destroyed, in the Peking that I loved . . ."

"To begin with, not everything is destroyed. And nobody can live sheltered in the perfection of childhood. *Your* childhood may have been happy, but many other childhoods were not happy in China of the past."

"But they're *my* memories," she said. "And I don't want to go back and find everything changed." She is the daughter of a once-prominent Chinese doctor who lived in Peking, that lovely and haunting city. She is homesick for the China she knew, but stays in Hongkong, at the gates, waiting for the past to return, which of course it will never do. And she keeps everything as it used to be. In her house she uses Chinese furniture and carpets, she eats Chinese food, as if by establishing this ritual she could keep reality shut out of her front door. "My memories are mine, I don't want them changed. I prefer to dream of the past as it was."

I do not blame her. We each choose our horizon, delimit the stretch of our minds.

How many are like her, I do not know. Perhaps they cannot do otherwise than choose to remain with their familiar childhood held close to them, close like a well-loved spectre, a wolfing shadow whose penumbra dims the present. Perhaps they cannot reassemble, make a continuity where there appears to be only cleavage. But I had to do it, to live with myself, to be myself, and to continue growing, where others had stopped. I would not be a crippled tree, marring the landscape with its own malady. At least I would greet the tomorrow I had not made, even if it killed me.

Indeed it is suffering, to go on growing, to hold to what is, to try to understand, to knock down one's own preconceptions. To find one's memories ravaged by time and revolution, one's intimate illusions ripped up, laughter for one's own private desolation the only answer; to realize how difficult, agonizing, is the process of understanding, and how long it takes.

And so I am writing this book, having achieved one thing all Asians will understand, and I think many Europeans too:

a continuity between what was and what is, a sense of destiny fulfilled, not by some Higher Power, nor by mystic concatenation of stars, but by the relentless logic of each day lived with courage, within the enormous scope that the word day implies.

In this book all the records are authentic, the facts as accurate as research could make them. I set them down, since the time may come when it is impossible for such as I to write.

TWO

A MAN'S life begins with his ancestors and is continued in his descendants. My father's life, and after my father my own life, begins with the Family. To describe the Family I must go back into time past and tell how the progenitors came to the land where they settled. For they were Hakkas, the Guest People, wanderers within the continent that is China.

A fertile oasis of red earth, eighty thousand square miles in extent, with mountain ramparts hedging it from the great plains of China, that is Szechuan, the region of Four Streams. On its west, like guarding walls, rise the cliffs of Tibet, the Snow Mountains and the Cold Mountains, ice-peaked and panda-roamed. Until the present road was built after the Revolution, only pathways wound up and down those parallel ranges barring the way to Lhasa, and along these paths one hundred thousand tea-carriers from Szechuan plodded, each with a four-hundred-pound load of brick tea, climbing the passes three miles above sea level to the Tibetan plateau. North of Szechuan are the massive Tapa and Chin Ling mountain blocks, with a single pass winding to the loess plains of the Yellow River. More ranges fret and curve in pleated folds eastwards, to hem Szechuan in, closing the access to the spreading plains of Middle China. Through this confusion of cliffs the Great River Yangtse, Son of the Ocean, hacks a turbulent zigzag through eight hundred miles of contorted limestone before it cuts loose from the whimsical evolution of primeval rock to run a course of fifteen hundred miles to the ocean. South of Szechuan are more mountains, looped in and out in a dense stifle, as if mashed together when still in the doughy stage some millions of years ago. Through these a few passes lead to Kueichow, the Precious Province, and to Yunnan, the Land South of the Clouds. Szechuan thus is a kingdom apart, the silted, dried bed of an old, enormous

inland sea of the days before the Flood. And from Szechuan,
rising higher and higher like a giant's stairs, the plateaux of
Central Asia vault upwards to Tibet, highest of them all.

The four headwaters of the Great River Yangtse give Szechuan province its name. They rise in Tibet as torrents, and
tumble across Szechuan towards the sprawling Chinese vastness. One of these headwaters is called the River of Golden
Sands, since gold is found in its silt. Another is named the
Mien, and two thousand years ago was tamed by Li Ping the
engineer, made to serve man when he settled to plant and
reap the red earth basin of Szechuan; its once impetuous
waters now diverge into nine hundred thousand man-dug
canals, a web of water intricate as the body's capillary system,
nourishing the seabed silt into the best rice-growing earth of
China.

And here in the plain, called sea-on-land because of its
waterworks, lies Chengtu, the capital city of Szechuan. Eight
miles west of Chengtu is a small townlet called Pihsien, where
the family ancestors settled between 1682 and 1710.

The seventeenth century saw the end of the Ming dynasty,
when the Mandate of Heaven passed from the Imperial House
in turbulence and misery, incompetence and the usual massive peasant revolts which accompany each change of rule. At
that time rose to armed might many a peasant, fighting against
tyranny, and one of them was a carpenter named Chang
Hsienchung. Born in 1600 in the semi-desertic province of
Shensi, north of Szechuan, of massive build, sallow complex-
ion and heavy chin, he was nicknamed the Yellow Tiger. In
1628 a famine occurred in Shensi, and hungry bands of peasants roamed the northern plains, forming brigand brotherhoods, and giving themselves fanciful names such as Lord of
the Mountain or King of the Plain. Chang Hsienchung the
carpenter became leader of such a band, and went plundering
across the wide loess marches of the North, where on the
imperial roads stretched the million skeletons of those dead
of hunger. He took the title of Eighth Great King, crossed
the Yellow River to swoop upon the middle provinces where
there was abundance of water, and rice to eat. He occupied a
part of Hupeh province, which is berthed astride the Great
River and its overflow lakes in mid-course, and there set up
an overlordship, killing, and confiscating wealth from the rich,
and giving it to the poor.

The Ming Emperors had been fighting the Manchus in the

north since 1622, and were unable to put down the peasant insurrections which erupted everywhere. Portuguese Jesuits helped the dynasty to cast cannon and to buy firearms, but it was of little use. The Manchus swept in, helped by dissident generals.

Meanwhile, in March of 1635, Chang first entered Szechuan, following the River westwards, and conquered the city of Chengtu. He met with much local resistance, and turned northwards again, back to Shensi, his native place. In 1640, having formed an alliance with other peasant leaders, he again left Shensi, re-asserted his rule over twenty-one districts in Hupeh, marching his armies the same westward journey to Szechuan, and captured Chengtu again; and it is said, such was his savagery, he put all the inhabitants to the sword.

Thus write the historians of the succeeding Manchu dynasty, quoting Chang the Yellow Tiger's words against him: "Heaven is bounteous to man; but man turns against Heaven. Kill kill kill kill kill kill kill." It was the custom, when a town was sacked by a victorious general's troops, to allow the soldiers their will over the helpless citizens only for the length of time it took an incense stick to burn; but it is said that Chang Hsienchung lit a great taper that burnt seven days and nights during the sack of Chengtu.

Chang enthroned himself in Chengtu as King of the West, to rule in Szechuan, and from there defied the invading Manchus. Hence Chang is known as a patriot, despite his notorious cruelty. In 1644 a Manchu Emperor reigned in Peking, the first of the Manchu dynasty. Chang Hsienchung proclaimed his loyalty to the Ming descendants and prepared to recruit forces in Szechuan and Shensi, to turn these provinces into a fortress stronghold against the Manchus. But the Manchu cavalry were too swift. The Manchu bannermen entered Szechuan, and there defeated and killed the Yellow Tiger in the autumn of 1645 Again Chengtu was sacked, and this time with utmost ferocity.

More killing went on during the next fifty years, and these recurrent massacres unpeopled the Chengtu plain. It is not known how many died, but the census held in 1710 showed the population of the plain at under one hundred and twenty thousand; it had been reckoned at two million in the previous century. Those who survived fled to the mountains, lived in trees as apes, or became troglodytes in the rock caves that pit the cliffs along the Great River.

In the public park of Chengtu, where Chang reigned so briefly as King of the West, there stood until 1949 a monument of granite called the Seven Kill Stone. On it the word "Kill" was engraved seven times. All the children of Szechuan were taught that it was Chang's stone, and that he had slain the population. I believed this tale until 1963, when in a museum at Hangchow I came across the opposite and now current view, that Chang was actually a patriotic brigand, a super-scale Robin Hood. His cruelty was not denied, but it was not he who depopulated Szechuan, since forty years after Chang's death pockets of resistance to the Manchus still existed, and slaughter still went on. In fact the mountain people of Szechuan's hinterland, the Miaos and the Lolos, never gave up their sporadic revolts against Manchu rule. And with these long-drawn massacres must have come famine and disease, murdering their millions. Today the Seven Kill Stone has been removed from the park, and Chang Hsienchung's reputation, submitted to the grave scrutiny of historians in the University of Chengtu, has undergone historical redemption.

I have told this story because it was due to Szechuan's depopulation that the Guest People, the Hakkas, from whom our family descends, came to settle in the province; and until thirty years ago entire villages in Szechuan still spoke Hakka. Today still the potters of Anfuchen and the weavers of ramie cloth along the water courses are Hakkas.

Long, voluminous and weighty are the books and records about the Hakkas, written both by Chinese and non-Chinese. Their origin is Honan province, in the Yellow River loess plains of North China. Five centuries before Christ, in the time of the great philosophers, this was the centre of Han culture. But the Han people of the northern plains were for ever subject to pressures from invaders, galloping in from the Siberian steppes on their horses, Tartars and Mongols of various names and tribes. Great migrations of the Han people took place, until the almost empty luxuriant middle and south of China were also peopled by northern migrants. The trek of the Guest People, the Hakkas, was one of many such peasant migrations which must have taken place again and again in the course of the centuries, always greatly intensified in times of wars and during famines due to drought or floods. The fact that the silt-loaded Yellow River overflowed its rising bed and changed its course nine times during the last two thousand years, each time ravaging areas as large as England, must also have led to large peasant displacements.

Every change of dynasty was heralded by peasant risings, a shifting into gigantic Long Marches of millions of the dispossessed and the hungry, and these are now recorded in the Museum of History in Peking, for they belong to history, they were the upheavals of a people looking for a way out of the long feudalism which ended only yesterday.

The word Hakka does not denote a racial group, for the Hakkas are Han People, Chinese people. It was a word applied to all displaced peasants, and only after the tenth century came to designate a special group. Moving *en masse* these refugees from misery were "people who sought a roof", hence called "Guest People" which was more courteous than calling them displaced persons or refugees. A code of regulations was formulated for dealing with such immigrants into new districts, to provide for their welfare and their resettling in lands where tillers were needed, and to avoid conflicts with older settlers.

The Hakkas themselves claim that they moved five times within recorded history. In their first migration, dating about A.D. 311, they crossed the Yangtse River and settled in the provinces of Kiangsi and Anhwei. Some of their historians claim that they already had their own folklore, traditions, customs and dialect, but this is doubtful. A second migration took place from A.D. 874, during the decades of turbulence which saw the end of the Tang dynasty. A third migration, started after A.D. 1276, was due to the Mongols, when Genghis Khan's hordes came riding in from the steppes of Siberia. In this migration the Hakkas were at a disadvantage, for by that time the provinces of Middle and South China were in great part settled, the jungles curbed, the best fields tilled. The Hakkas were driven farther south, or to mountainous, poor areas. They entered Fukien, Kuangtung, Formosa and what is now North Vietnam, settled on the poorer lands, survived and multiplied.

Because of their mobility, hardihood and fierceness, the dynasties began to regard the Hakkas as potential pioneers, good for resettling in sub-populated areas.

The Hakkas spread in the middle and south provinces, building villages which they often fortified. They multiplied exceedingly, which made them more land-hungry; and since the barren districts were their portion, they engaged in feuds with older settlers on more fertile land, raided their villages and were in turn raided; they erected gates and watch towers and locked themselves in their villages at night, as they still do in the British colony of Hongkong where there are many Hakka villages.

Circumstance thus defined their group character: clannish, thrifty, loyal to each other, bad neighbours and ready fighters, the name Hakka stuck to them and they became proud of it.

The fourth migration of the Guest People took place after the Manchus came to power. Between 1680 and 1720 the Manchu Emperor Kanghsi, in his peregrinations through the land, sought to rally the hearts of the people of the south, and to resettle the Hakkas in Szechuan and other regions. The Imperial Office paid eight ounces of silver per man, four ounces per woman or child, to the migrants. In this way many Hakkas came to Szechuan, and among them were the ancestors of my family.

The fifth and last migration of Hakkas occurred at the end of the Taiping rising, one of the many enormous peasant revolts which have characterized the history of China, important because the present Revolution looks upon the Taiping as its precursor.

To the Hakkas the Taiping is their most glorious epic, for the leader was a Hakka named Hung Hsiuchuan. Hung raised the standard of revolt against the Manchus in 1850. Millions flocked to his standard, marched to the Great River and captured Nanking, which Hung renamed the Heavenly City, capital of the Heavenly Kingdom.

Hung proclaimed social justice for all; throughout his hundred-millioned domain the feet of women were unbound, land redistributed, taxes lightened, and the pigtail, emblem of Manchu servitude, abolished.

At first the Western Powers favoured the Taiping, but later this attitude changed, and the Manchu dynasty received help from the West. General Gordon was hired to lead the imperial armies against the Taiping. Fresh from the loot of the Summer Palace in Peking, Gordon now served the dynasty which he had helped to pillage, and was rewarded with high rank in the mandarinate and much gold. He refused the latter, misliking the slaughter, for when Nanking had fallen after two years of gruelling siege not one of the forty thousand remaining inhabitants surrendered, and all were killed. Hung, the Heavenly King, died by self-administered poison.

In 1964 I visited Hung's village, near the city of Canton. It is now a commune, prosperous since the dam built four years ago. After the Taiping failed, in 1864, the Manchus put all men, women and children named Hung to the sword, to extirpate the breed; many fled, or changed their names. A century later, in the small village of three hundred families where the Hung clan lived, two hundred and eighty-six were named Hung.

Because of these massacres many Hakkas migrated to south-east Asia, or were inveigled by the boat-load to become indentured labourers on railways and canals in the East Indies, Malaya, the United States, and as far as Panama, Brazil and Africa. Today the settlers of Chinese descent in Sarawak claim to be one hundred per cent Hakkas.

The Hakkas say they are the true people of Han, and that they have escaped degenerate habits brought by foreign rule. They are proud of their singularity as the Guest People, especially among the Overseas Chinese, where their clans are prosperous and strong. But they also gave many leaders to peasant risings, and supplied many heroes in the Revolutions. Their love songs date back to the Han dynasty, their speech is a mixture of South and North dialects, and when they move to a new settlement they carry their ancestors' bones with them in jars upon their backs. In past migrations each family went to its fields or burial ground to disinter a forefather, placing his bones in a clay jar called a golden urn, to be carried by the men of the family, the women being loaded with every other belonging.

The records of a Hakka family named Tsung, of the district of Meihsien in Kuangtung province, describe how the great-grandfather's bones were exhumed, cleaned without water, placed in the golden urn which was then tied to the back of the eldest grandson. When the Tsung family reached the land to resettle, which in the Hakka dialect is called New Mountain, the urn was placed under some trees so that the ancestor might rest at ease. Meanwhile a suitable spot for a new grave was found, and the ancestor reburied; after which the living proceeded to build a house for themselves. A descendant of the Tsung family told me this in Peking in 1962. The date of the recorded move was 1708.

In their marches to new land the Hakkas often fought their way through hostile villages. It is said that they left on the road those too weak to walk; but that happens with any migratory group. Hakkas in the past did not tolerate crippled or defective babies and left these to die at birth, as did the Greeks.

At times the Hakkas could not find their ancestral graves, especially if there had been much fighting and burial grounds had been disturbed. One of the ways in which village vendettas were carried out was the digging up and scattering of buried ancestors, considered a desecration worse than the extermination of the living. When they left in too much of a hurry to take their progenitors along, or where no bones were available, they would carry the clothes of the ancestor and bury them in a grave called a clothes grave. When no clothes or other possessions were available, a small tablet of silver or of wood, with the name and dates of birth and death of the ancestor engraved upon it, was buried when the New Mountain was reached, after calling the spirit of the dead by name in the appropriate compass direction and enticing it with food and tea laid under some shady tree, under the guidance of a Taoist wind-and-water geomancer. When the spirit had taken possession of the tablet, it was then laid in the prepared grave. Often trees were planted near the new burial site, from seeds or cuttings brought from the original home, to keep the dread wind off the bones.

Perhaps this custom of taking along an ancestor's bones was founded on land acquisition, like flag-planting, in order to stake a claim to the new settlement. It gave validity to ownership. It certainly made for a feeling of attachment to the land.

Many other customs of the Hakkas have equally practical explanations. Their claim that their history was made by their women's feet is strict truth. Hakka women do not bind their feet, nor their breasts, do not hire wet nurses for their children, and do not become prostitutes. The custom of footbinding, so long associated with Chinese pulchritude, began probably in the eleventh century, and by the twelfth reached even the peasantry. No young woman was considered desirable unless she had small feet. The binding of breasts seems to have started later, and only in the cities, until the twentieth century; a good many of my schoolmates in the 1930s wore tight cloth straps round their chests.

The reason for the Hakka women's freedom from such corsetry was their function. The women worked in the fields, at building houses, at porterage, while the men, cutlass or spear in hand, watched for enemies or went out fighting. Since many of the Hakka villages were poor, the men shipped off to the South Seas, or went away as pedlars. And since the Guest People moved frequently, hired themselves out to labour or to war, they could not afford to have women unable to work and to walk. Tall, big-boned, not renowned for good looks, in manner direct, in later life quarrelsome and garrulous, the Hakka woman went chest- and foot-free, and consequently tongue-free. What necessity had dictated was continued and cherished as a proud tradition, and the unglamourous Hakka maid was praised for her thrift, hard work, clean life, and lively retort. She raised sons on her own milk, despised artifices to beauty, and when necessary fought like a man. She was not in demand by connoisseurs in the cities, who relished the fragility of two-inch golden lotus feet, and other devices to please, and of this also the Hakkas are proud.

It is not surprising, with this background, to find the Guest People taking an active part in uprisings of the last centuries; the men proud of their energy, strong with the knowledge of their prowess, and cunning at outwitting enemies, the women proud of their working ability, both deeply conscious of social injustice, both ready to fight for their beliefs and for their rights. Hakkas claim that the regiments which fought against the Mongols were recruited from among them; that the men who followed Coxinga, the loyal Ming general, to Formosa to resist the Manchus, were Hakkas; Hung Hsiuchuan, as well as many other leaders of the Taiping uprising, were Hakka; Hung's sister fought and won a pitched battle against the Manchu soldiery, and unbound the feet of thousands of women in the regions under Taiping rule.

Mao Tsetung in his military writings also referred to the Hakkas when he wrote of the rift between the native inhabitants and the "settlers whose forefathers came from the north several hundred years ago". He observed that the settlers, numbering several million in a zone across several provinces, lived in the hilly regions and had been oppressed by the native inhabitants.

How many Hakkas are there in China proper and among the Overseas Chinese? No one knows for certain. Some say twenty million, some say fifty. In Hongkong alone there are one million (out of a total population of three and a half million). But today in China the distinction between Hakka and non-Hakka has gone, as has village feuding, and the feudal system which pitted one group against another in the great hunger of China is also going as the Revolution comes of age.

My ancestors, named Chou, came from Meihsien in the province of Kuangtung, a purely Hakka district. The Meihsien area was until recently a poor, barren place, with unproductive land, many hills devoid of trees, only pathways, and a badly arranged irrigation system. On the patchy fields one only saw women working, and they outnumbered men by six to one because the men left home. I visited the place recently, and now it is quite different, with water reservoirs, canals, schools, and afforestation; but this has only happened in the last decade.

My ancestors had settled in Meihsien in the thirteenth century, and the migration to Szechuan took place most probably between 1682 and 1710. In our family records it is stated that the first ancestor to reach Szechuan arrived as an itinerant pedlar. His manner of travel was not mentioned. Did he walk, across his shoulder a pole, at both ends the baskets that pedlars swing as they walk, and what did he sell? – Southern goods, sweetmeats, carved objects of wood which may have fetched a good price? The family gravestones are only certain on one point: that the ancestor was a pedlar, and very poor.

I found in the National Library in Peking, among a collection of Hakka love songs dating back to the sixteenth century, the following chant:

> My loved one is going, going up to Szechuan.
> At the Salt Point he boards the salt boat to Chieh An.
> A hundred, a thousand riches I gladly forsake,
> But how can I leave my heart, my loved one?

The salt gondolas, with their slanted prows, sailed up the inland river and canal system from the salt pans in Kuangtung province to Chieh An in Kiangsi province, at that time a big entrepôt city for the salt. Until some years ago they were still in use, and one of my Chinese writer friends, Han Behping, told me only the other month of his sailing on them, disguised as a worker, during the Sino-Japanese war.

The new settlers seeded themselves all over Szechuan province, chiefly along the Great River and its tributaries, all the way from Chungking, up the Mien River to Chengtu, and in the plain of Chengtu, the most fertile sea-on-land plain. And because there was little opposition, no feuding, much to eat, they assimilated in great part, intermarried with the local inhabitants. By the end of the nineteenth century only traces of the original Hakka dialect lingered among the older members of the family, my father's generation no longer spoke it.

After his arrival in Szechuan, the first ancestor, the pedlar, became a land-tiller, first a hired hand, then later a small tenant-farmer. That was at Pihsien, west of Chengtu, where in 250 B.C. Li Ping, governor of the region, but also an engineer, carried out a complex operation upon the Mien River as it descended steeply from the Tibetan ranges to hurtle at vast speed across the plain, dragging frightful boulders, and flooding the shallow basin every three years. At Kuanhsien, where the Mien River left the foothills, Li Ping redirected its waters by cutting a gorge forty metres deep through the solid rock of the cliffs, thus dividing the river into two forks, and by means of dams and barriers, still kept up today, controlling the water flow. The strong current out of this artificial gorge was then divided and subdivided, twisted and curbed by stone revetments, the water grooved into innumerable canals and streams which latticed the plain and transformed it into a garden fair and beautiful in all its corners. Pihsien was reputed one of the best corners, the first district after Kuanhsien to receive the now domesticated and harmonious waters.

In such a well chosen spot the ancestors prospered, and soon acquired more land, and moved up the feudal hierarchy of China, accumulating estate and property, becoming educated, and thus attaining the top echelon, the scholar-official-administrator class. They became landed gentry; began to wear silk and read literature; soon their sons were competing in the provincial examinations. No longer did they marry large-footed hard-working women from the ancestral district of Meihsien; their brides were small, pale, had bound feet, and seldom left the house. They erected ancestors' sanctuaries and halls with fields attached for their upkeep and for the collective education of their sons. They kept the Book of Generations filled with the names of new sons; they planted groves of the lanmu tree, that exellent fine-whorled wood for coffins in which the body does not rot, so that their heirs might be well provided for, from birth to beyond death.

They multiplied, and held the family property in joint ownership; family councils decided on the careers of the sons, the alliances to be contracted through marriages, the buying and selling of land. Soon there were too many of them, and they had to subdivide, both the property and the families into local branches, some remaining in Pihsien, others settling in other towns of Szechuan, in spite of their efforts to live up to the motto Five Generations Under One Roof.

They must have quarrelled, and there must have been family scandals, but not a word of these was ever recorded. It is not propitious to record lapses. What affected the Family as a whole is recorded, the final, authoritative decision is inscribed on paper, or even carved on stone if weighty enough; but the transient concern of an individual member, a wayward and aberrant effusion soon terminated, finds no place here; as in the feudal families of Europe with their alliances based on self-interest, there was no place for the individual choice. The tenor of continuity, an invisible but relentless heart, beats its steady pulsation, propelling the Family forward into its own destiny through these two centuries, the seventeenth to the nineteenth. Only a harmony unceasingly displayed could sustain this relentless holding together, nonconformism and disunity were erased from memory lest they maintain or suscitate discord.

I possess a copy of the Family Book of Generations, prefaced by my Third Uncle, my father's younger brother, the only one of his generation devoted to genealogical research. Perhaps that is why when I went to Szechuan in 1939, Third Uncle and I got on so well, and I wrote about him in two of my books. Of all my family, including my own father, Third Uncle and I resemble each other most in this matter of inquisitiveness. I share with him this curiosity, this wonder for understanding, the hall-mark of the writer, God's spy. In him this desire for scrutiny is perhaps more limited than in myself. He stuck to the Family, while I have pushed with passion beyond the precincts of a family, trying to grasp the motivation, the social and economic background of a whole era: to understand, through one family, the long feudal millenniums of China; through her yesterday made explicit to grasp her wholeness in her new day.

Third Uncle's preface gives compendiously the Confucian moral structure which propped the feudal gentry family in its social and economic framework.

All things under heaven have their rise and fall; and these occur beyond our intercession; only resolution and uprightness, virtues bequeathed by our ancestors, can transform ruin into resurgence. That is why a family erects its ancestral sanctuaries, to maintain the veneration due to progenitors and the remembrance of its own humble beginnings. Hence the necessity for filial virtue to accomplish the rites due to the spirits of predecessors; hence forbearance among members of a household, to remember one's responsibilities, to strengthen the clan and the breed, to inspire sacrifice of self for the common good. In these ways our Chou clan, remembering and holding fast to virtue, has risen once again. From the seventh generation, when ancestor Chienhsi entered into the southern province of Kuangtung (after the Mongol ravages) till the fifteenth generation, when ancestor Mofah moved from thence to Szechuan, these filial rites were followed. Loyal and upright, practising agriculture, and industriously learning, our family held together, in spite of manifold disasters. In the seventeenth generation our ancestor Hsinghua first established himself in Chengtu at the Street Si Fu Nan, where he acquired a piece of land for building. In the eighteenth generation ancestor Chaochung and his younger brothers, on that piece of land, erected a Sanctuary for the veneration of soul tablets, and also built a habitation and dedicated it to the ancestor Hsinghua, calling it the Hsinghua Branch Sanctuary. Here now, at the Branch Sanctuary, we offered ritual sacrifice, from generation to generation, continuing until our present twenty-third generation. Thus the Family was not parted, but remained together, acquiring merit by fulfilling the ideal of five generations under one roof.

In the twenty-sixth year of the Republic (1937) the Japanese invaded our country. Due to the upheavals and the destruction by the Kuomintang troops being quartered in many temples and sanctuaries in Szechuan, our sanctuaries fell into decay. Today we, the twenty-third generation, have decided to rebuild these in order to continue the traditions, to maintain the links between the various branches of our family which are continually increasing, that they may not grow scattered and lost to each other.

A better exposé of the meaning of ancestor veneration, its utilization in terms of curbing the property-dissipating tendency of individual members, its usefulness in shaping joint-family solidarity to maintain and expand collective wealth and influence, can seldom be quoted. As in feudal Europe, with its laws of entail connected with the retention of land and power, the Confucian code reinforced land ownership and therefore feudal power in feudal China, and led to the conservation of families such as mine, the landed gentry, from which the scholar-official-administrator class was chiefly drawn.

From 1720 to about 1820 the Chou clan in Meihsien received formal visits from representatives of the branch in Szechuan. Births of sons, deaths, marriage contracts, establishments of sanctuaries, extensions of commerce, successful competitions in examinations, were announced in the ancestors' hall to the soul tablets there. Then came the Opium Wars, and after that the Taiping rising, and the connection ceased. Impoverishment, dislocation of travel, the exile of many Hakkas now suspect, put a stop to it. By now the Family in Szechuan had become local landed gentry, staunchly loyal to the established order. They no longer worked their own land, but rented their fields to tenant-farmers, and took half the crop in payment of rent. Possibly they loaned money to the poorer peasants at the usual thirty-six per cent interest per year, as was the benign custom.

Several times during these decades, due to the increase in sons, divisions of property occurred, of real estate and capital assets and fields. All such contracts drawn up, and now incomprehensible to the new generation growing up in China, were couched in the usual euphemisms of divisions of responsibility in the care of shrines, ancestral sanctuaries and graves.

Third Uncle in his probings into familiana came against certain discrepancies when he compared the records of the family in Szechuan with those of the "root" clan of the Chous still resident in the district of Meihsien in Kuangtung. He recorded these in an appendix to the Book of Generations:

From ancestor Mofah [the one who left Meihsien to come to Szechuan in 1690 or thereabouts] to the present, nine generations have passed, fifteenth to twenty-third. From ancestor Jenteh to ancestor Chienhsi there are six generations. It seems we should add six generations between Mofah and Chienhsi [the seventh-generation head of the clan who fled from the Mongols after A.D. 1276]. Ancestor Mofah should be the twenty-first progenitor, not the fifteenth.

Who was ancestor Jenteh? According to the records, another founder of the Meihsien clan. To make a complicated story simple, our Szechuan records had mislaid six generations. Third Uncle at one time worried a good deal about those strayed six generations. Where, and how, had the mistake happened? He went to Sikang, in the west of Szechuan, to consult another branch of the clan there established, and reported his findings:

Venerable Great-Uncle Yichieh tells me that he is the twenty-fifth generation after Chienhsi. According to my original record, he was the nineteenth generation.

Venerable Great-Uncle Yichieh was eighty-seven years old in 1932. I never met him, he had become a soul tablet by the time I reached Szechuan in 1939. But here were two branches of the same clan differing in their records. Obviously a serious matter. My uncle made further research; then came the Second World War, which for China lasted from 1937 to 1945. After that came the Civil War, and then the last Great

Revolution of 1949, and after that everything was changed, and there was a lot more work to do than to worry over family genealogies. At Land Reform the fields were divided, the large burial grounds had their graves removed since some of the best fields were taken up by them; our family graves were not spared. A letter from Third Uncle in Szechuan to my father in Peking, in March 1952, made this clear:

We have just undergone Land Reform. I was not there, being busy with the Bank at Chungking, where as a Bank Director I had to be present while the government went into a strict check of all banking matters. I was absent nine months, and during this time Fourth Daughter-in-Law stood in my place; she endured the ordeal [of Land Reform] many months with fortitude; the peasants came with grievances of the past, and these were checked. It is good that we had not spilt blood or been grievously unjust, and that we were not great landowners, only rich farmers. Thus we were spared and pardoned, though the fields were removed from us. I have now been notified that our graves and sanctuaries are occupying precious land, and that the coffins must be removed to one of the public cemeteries, to be buried along with many others. But our family has always kept profound veneration for the Sanctuaries and the graves, since our whole prosperity depended on them. I have had rubbings made of the gravestones before they were removed, and I am sending you one copy, wrapped in oilpaper. I have also written my will, and therein directed that when the time comes I should be cremated, for I do not wish to lie in close company with a thousand strangers. Thus are old customs changed. It is hard for me to express myself on these matters.

It was hard indeed, one could see that. Third Uncle, so prone to the past, addicted to tradition, ancestor veneration, the preservation of rites, must have found it searing, at least for a time. But later, in his autobiography, he wrote that he knew the burial grounds were productive fields, that ancestral sanctuaries were selected for investment purposes and ways of consolidating the property system; and that this business of veneration, selecting propitious spots in accordance with the wind and water diviner, was actually a functional way of acquiring land and of evading some of the more onerous agrarian and house taxes.

I saw Third Uncle again, in 1956, in 1958, in 1960, in 1962. He was sprightly of spirit, though he now moved stiffly with a cane; his talk was of the rubbings he had made of the gravestones, and he was concerned that my father might have lost the copy he had posted in 1952. He had done well, all banking matters cleared, and was drawing from the government a fixed interest rate of eight per cent on the capital he had previously invested in the bank, and nine per cent on capital invested in other companies in the pre-Revolution days, all of this tax free. I had found the rubbings, had them with me. Thus was Third Uncle satisfied, though still wondering about the lost six generations. He was preparing for death, he told me, though no lanmu coffin had been purchased since he wanted cremation, but he had wisely consoled himself, saying he now knew the value of earth, and would not take up good land which might grow food for generations to come. In 1964 he was still alive, though stiffer in the knee-joints. He had now given up worrying about the six generations that could not be traced, and turned over to me the last photographs and all the letters in his possession.

"For your book," he said. He knew none of the others in the younger generation cared much about these old relics; there were so many new things to care for.

In the new peace, order and security come to China today, scrupulous historians were delving into family records, and everyone I knew was either writing or compiling memoirs, from the ex-Emperor to the Eighth Route Army old soldiers For the first time in a hundred and fifty years, there had been fifteen years of peace, and all was being classified and recorded, studied and investigated, for many were now eager to relate the past to the present, not because the past was good, but because no one can afford to forget the yesterday which gave birth to today.

I remember going to Pihsien in 1941, where the family fields lay, though much reduced in extent, round the Ancestral Sanctuary. I was with Third Aunt, it was spring, the fields bright yellow with flower of rape, young trees a jade shimmer, water glistening in the small canals. We were there to sweep the graves, to give food to the ancestors; but actually to see to the hiring of farm hands, and to assess the condition of the crops. It did not strike me as odd at the time. We placed food and drink at the graves, and these were their fields, our fields, it seemed so natural. The fields were so beautiful, the oil crop promised to be excellent.

Third Aunt sighed. "The taxes, the taxes." But then she was always unhappy about the taxes.

In the evening came an old peasant, a tenant-farmer of ours, to tell us that his son had been taken away, dragged away, to be made into a soldier, taken while working in the fields, taken by the Kuomintang, and who was to help him harvest the crop? My aunt gave him a dollar, and told him to hire someone. Only now, more than twenty years later, does the tragedy suddenly hit me in the chest. Only now do I see, in the mind's eye, the old peasant, very bent, very polite, not daring to be sad because his son was kidnapped for the army while working. I see Aunt and myself sitting at a table laid out for three, but where only two ate. For these were Grandmother's fields, and her place was set, though she was dead many years. I hear Third Aunt call out: "Mother, please eat your rice." All this comes back, as today again. There has been a Revolution since, and peasants no longer lose their sons to kidnappers; and today I feel the brutality we accepted as normal, and the shame of having accepted as normal and common what was so much injustice, burns in me. Today the dollar my Third Aunt gave the old man burns in my eye, although it did not do so in 1941.

And today we have no fields, and no Ancestors' Sanctuaries with fields about them. In spring we visit the graves at the public cemetery, and this is as it should be.

Due to the propitious disposal of burial grounds, the Family owned land, fertile good fields, in the plain of Chengtu and chiefly in Pihsien, holdings later divided as collateral branches sprang up and settled in other parts of the province, fields disposed of when the Family's fortunes ebbed, as they did during the First World War.

More important as a source of revenue to the Family was their commerce in tobacco, which started in 1795, and went on till 1917, about one hundred and twenty years, when this also went bankrupt.

Tobacco came to China with the Dutch, from Luzon in the Philippines, and by 1530 the habit had spread widely, to men and women alike. In Szechuan tobacco was never smoked in the form of cheroots, but shredded, and put in a pipe, either the ordinary pipe of varying lengths, or the water-pipe. Today the cigarette has displaced all pipes, and their jade mouthpieces, as well as the pewter or chased and engraved silver water-pipes, are on sale as old curios in the secondhand shops of the cities.

The name of the tobacco company operated by the family was Kuang Hsing, the word Kuang being the same as that for Kuangtung province, to indicate the Meihsien district origin. The main tobacco shop was in East Main Street, the main shopping street of Chengtu. According to Third Uncle, the shop was well known for its reliability, the tobacco being of best quality, the weights accurate, the apprentices courteous and swift. The sign on the shop front was a large slab of lacquered black wood with carved and gilt characters. All over Szechuan, branch shops operated in the main cities, and Kuang Hsing was a trade-mark for good tobacco.

Tobacco was grown in Pihsien, and the big bundles of leaves of first-grade tobacco brought into the city for processing and selling. But Kuang Hsing also bought the finest tobacco from Yunnan. It was the cultivation of opium, the taxes on native tobacco, the road-toll taxes, and the competition from the British–American Tobacco Company which totally ruined the native tobacco industry, and Kuang Hsing, in the early twentieth century.

Next door to the tobacco shop, now destroyed, was one selling medicines, and this was auspicious, for those who came to buy black hens' feet, tiger-bone wine, sliced antlers of young deer, and rhubarb, would stop by to scan the tobacco in lacquered wood trays, in jars. The first-grade tobacco, of the leaf that would not shrivel, was used for smoking in the water-pipe. Before the advent of the cigarette most of the well-to-do in Szechuan smoked the water-pipe. The very fine shredded tobacco it needs was kept in special pewter boxes.

Tobacco requires much manure, spraying with manure being done every five days in April and May when the plants grow. The good earth of Szechuan, moist and replete and rich, glistening as with oil, is nourished with human and pig excrement, treated for some days in pits. It is only now, after the Revolution, that chemical ferilizer plants are being built, but today man and pig are still the main providers of manure. And therefore in the city of Chengtu in the nineteenth century, and up to 1949, some of the wealthiest families were those owning the public cloacae and selling extrement to the countryside.

I remember Third Uncle on this subject, which rendered him prolix, for he was always aware of the earth, the sowing and planting and reaping of it: "Three things are necessary, water, earth and manure. Water from the sky, soil of the earth, and manure of man and animal; the excremental waste confirms the harmonious cycle of life, since out of waste comes renewal."

In an agricultural society dung has its function and natural dignity; and even today, I can become engrossed in the relative merits of "green lush" or "brown gold".

Besides the tobacco shops, the Kuang Hsing Company also engaged retail pedlars, who sold tobacco at street corners or in the smaller villages. Their stalls were often set opposite a public privy, which led a wag of those days to write a semi-scurrilous essay on the trade:

No moment is more propitious for selling a man fresh tobacco for his water-pipe than when, having relieved himself, he feels that lightness and good temper about him which comes from the accomplishment of a natural function, a generosity which demands the expenditure of a few coins as its issue. He stops to inhale the better air, nostrils perceiving the aromas of the streets with a new keenness, due to their pinched restraint during his time in the privy. The pedlar stands at the street corner, enticingly; here is no stench, but faint scent of the leaf, reinforced by a stick of burning incense. The man feels for his water-pipe at his belt, finds his tobacco pouch depleted, and buys fine shredded to refill it. Thus do some wealthy tobacco merchants prosper.

The Family's interest in cloacae was not coprophilia, but economics.

There must have been six hundred large and small public cloacae in Chengtu while I was there between 1939 and 1942, and in the houses of the rich servants sold the household nightsoil by the bucket in the early mornig to collectors, who resold it to the farmers. The collectors of manure formed a guild, under a "manure head" who was important, being also a Secret Society member, of which more later. The poor took their own excreta out to sell. At reaping time the hired share-croppers were always shacked on the fields, for the landlords of Szechuan insisted that they should defecate in the manure pits provided, so as to get back some of the value of the food they ate. This led to a saying among the hired hands: "They take your sweat, your breath, your spit, your work, your wife, and your shit!" The wife part is not an exaggeration, for in Szechuan the poor were so frightfully poor that they often resorted to wife-sale or wife-renting to "endure the days". This also has stopped since 1949.

In spring in Szechuan the first laying on of manure in the fields becomes almost a ceremony, almost as significant as the first furrow ploughed by the Emperor at the Spring Solstice to break the earth from its winter death into life. For this life-giving spraying of the fields the women put on embroidered clothes, the young girls on the communes tie ribbons in their hair and swing the pails of dung to the fields, singing all the way.

I remember one day in Chengtu during the war, when Third Uncle in one of his walks stopped at a street corner where a public convenience, derelict assemblage of bamboo matting with coir roof and a half-wall of brick to give it semi-privacy, advertised itself. Through the apertures I could see the stone-lined pits straddled by planks. Thoughtfully Third Uncle told me: "This one makes sixteen hundred dollars a week." Of course there was inflation at that time, but sixteen hundred dollars a week was still three times the nominal salary of an army colonel per month, and I was married to an army colonel then. Battles between servants, belonging to rival wealthy houses, used to occur, each accusing the other of manure stealing. In the nineteenth century certain members of the Family owned some interest in two public cloacae, but they never went into the business in a big way. Later the cloacae were all monopolized by the big warlords, and dung, as well as opium, financed their mutual strife till the Great Change.

Another source of income for Kuang Hsing was the paper spill. The paper spill was brought to the Family by an apprentice named Ma, bought by the Family after some calamity or other a hundred years ago or more, no one knows and the records do not tell. The nineteenth century was replete with wars, surfeited with floods, droughts, famine, massacres and such, and especially wars made upon China by the colonial Powers. Dispossessed peasants wandered about selling their children and their wives to provide them with food and shelter. Families such as ours bought children, they needed maids, servants, and sometimes they also "adopted" boys as apprentices, the brightest and sturdiest male children from six to eight years old.

The apprentice system was also prevalent in medieval Europe, and was also then a part of the feudal system where the fiction of family relationships was extended to include into spurious kinship all servants and dependants, linking them solidly to the interests of the feudal family by ties of regard and gratitude, a hierarchy based on heaven's will, whereas in the industrial society it is based on money's worth.

I remember seeing the apprentices in the silk shops, boys and girls of twelve or so bent on their needles, fourteen hours a day, threading the shaded pink, pale-blue, pepper-red, or yellow satin thread of the embroidered bedspread covers for which Chengtu is famous. Many became blind by the age of twenty-five, then went begging on the streets.

Apprentices served twelve years, received no money the first eight years since they were supposed to be "adopted children", had two meals a day, a new suit and two pairs of cloth shoes every year, and a haircut once a month. After eight years they received a string of cash a month (about one shilling), and sat at the feast of the three great festivals of the year. They slept in the shop, or inside the main gates of the house, wrapped in quilted cotton, with the sedan chair carriers, on long rows of benches along the walls. After twelve years they were supposed to have learnt the trade, gave their master a "parting feast", and were free.

Ma was a clever boy; he was therefore educated, at first by accident when, accompanying the sons of the family to their classes with the house tutor, he began to trace the characters with his wetted finger on the courtyard stones. He was put to work in the Kuang Hsing shop, and there one day began to roll thin rice-paper sideways into a spill, which burnt admirably and for a long time like an incense stick. This paper spill was cheaper than the incense stick, or the pine silver with sulphur head used as matches. Soon the paper spill became a part of the tobacco-shop trade, and twelve apprentices were kept rolling paper spills all day. One spill in twelve was theirs to sell and keep the money thereof, as an incentive to more spill-rolling.

The paper spill solved the problem of a constant source of fire for smokers in a land where fuel is scarce and expensive and the people thrifty by necessity as well as by inclination (the inclination born of necessity). One piece of charcoal, one ounce of oil, all counted in the growing poverty which was China's in the nineteenth century; and even wealthy people, like my family, were chary of spending except at stated occasions, and ostentation in Szechuan was always considered heinous. Hence the paper spill sold extremely well all over the province. One piece of straw paper could make seven spills, and seven spills were sold for one copper *fen*, which was one-thousandth part of a silver dollar in the 1890s.

When Ma grew up he was put in charge of the Kuang Hsing Company accounting. He never married, for his life was given to the Family. He could do sums in his head, and when he died was commemorated, a small soul tablet being placed at one side in the ancestral hall, that his spirit might also partake, though modestly, of the reverence due to the progenitors.

Thus did the Chou Family foster its rise, after a pedlar's migration, by acquisition of fields, and later the toil of peasants tilling the soil for them; on the exertion of apprentices such as Ma in the commerce of tobacco; and, having climbed the ladder rungs to the gentry class, upon the continued exertions, this time military and intellectual, of its sons as officials-scholars.

As each village and town in a feudal society is nearly self-sufficient, so the Family strove for self-sufficiency. It had its own craftsmen. Clothes and shoes, household utensils, were made for the joint-family unit by not so gifted relatives, under the supervision of the more energetic and commandeering matriarchs. Much of the food eaten was from the family fields.

In this society little money circulated, payment being in kind on a credit and barter system. Many transactions also depended upon invisible accounts of services rendered, blood ties, mutual help, guild associations; all relationships not based on money, but as prescribed by a social order, authoritarian and static, which remained valid until very recently.

The system that fostered my family was the Chinese feudal system, similar in many respects to the West, different in other respects. Government in China was not by aristocracy of blood, but by a non-hereditary officialdom, picked by examinations; so that merit and intellect were, in theory, the passport to becoming a member of the upper class, and not a mythical blueness of the blood. Slavery, except sporadically in wealthy families buying maidservants, was small compared to the wholesale slavery of the American plantations in the eighteenth and nineteenth centuries. Serfdom, with the corvee system, did not exist as a system, though the impositions upon the peasants were equally dreadful. Chinese feudalism continued for two millenniums possibly because of the elaborate development of irrigation, making for a stable village economy, except when the irrigation was neglected, and floods and drought harrassed the land, which occurred in times of war or governmental inefficiency. In the nineteenth century this system finally broke down; the disastrous wars with the West, with their levies of indemnities, and the inroads of industrial capitalism, destroyed the native handicrafts, transport and commerce. To this destruction entailing starvation for millions was added increasing corruption and inefficiency of the ruling class and therefore increased exactions by the landlord-gentry-official upon the peasant.

From this breakdown emerged China in revolution, a long process of turbulence moulding the China of today. And all this happened within the memory of men still living. It transformed all of us, transformed such feudal families as mine, the Chou family; catapulting all of us into the modern age at a pace not of our making.

THREE

THE rubbings from the gravestones are on silk paper, slowly decaying. Some of these gravestones date from the seventeenth generation but were erected by the nineteenth, when the Family became prosperous and remained well off for over a hundred years. The nineteenth generation is that of my great-grandfather, Chou Taohung, who died in 1912 at the age of ninety-two. Of his generation were eight males, the sons of three brothers of the eighteenth generation, and of these eight males three were still alive, aged eighty-nine, eighty-seven and eighty-two respectively in 1907 when a photograph was taken, a great event. I have this photograph, showing the three old men wrapped in golden monkey fur gowns, with peaches of longevity in a dish on one side and a large French clock on the other, and laudatory scrolls hung on the walls behind them. One of these reads: "O future generations, see this, and remember to stay united." In front of the three old men is a row of flowers in pots, emblematic of thrift and endurance and tenacity, plum blossom, narcissi and chrysanthemums. There are also flat dishes with stones of strange shape, miniature trees, and formal miniature landscapes, such as the Chinese love and collect in their passion for the abstract beauty of stone and wood and leaf.

My great-grandfather Taohung was a rather magnificent character. His gravestone is abundantly explicit, and moreover two more stone inscriptions, composed by eulogious friends, celebrate his merits. He was born in Chengtu, but brought up and spent part of his life in Lingchow, a salt-producing city in Kansu province on the north-western

borders of China where his father was a military and administrative official. The post itself was not an enviable one, except
that as salt-collector perhaps some unofficial money might be
made from the government salt monopoly. But great-great-
grandfather, and his son Taohung, never made "salt money".
Taohung was renowned as a scholar, obtaining the provincial
examination degree of Tsujen, and later, after a military career, serving as the Supervisor of Chinkiang Academy, a neo-
Confucianist school for the training of administrative personnel, later a military institution.

Out of the encomiums on his character and especially on
his loyalty, one fact emerges: it was through military exploit
rather than as an administrator that Chou Taohung obtained
the prestige and influence he wielded at the time. He was no
languid stooped scholar in long robe. He rode a lot on horseback, and fought in Kansu and in the arid north-west to maintain the Manchu dynasty and put down the peasant risings,
which from 1840 onwards never really stopped until 1949. The
scholar, literate class cumulated all functions, civil, military,
educative, and this official bureaucracy was picked by public
examinations which, though open to all irrespective of wealth,
were nevertheless attempted only by the literate; though in
principle the poorest, meanest peasant could compete on equal
terms with the Emperor's children, the years of study required
to attempt the test confined the choice to the more wealthy,
the landlord-gentry class, those who could afford the time and
the expense. In some villages, such as the Hakka ones, an
entire village would pay for the brightest, most intelligent boy
to study, so that there were exceptions; some of China's greatest scholars and statesmen came from very poor families. Even
today one meets some engineer or doctor whose education is
due to the collective effort of forty or sixty village families.
But in the past the system did in practice tend to confirm all
official, administrative, economic and political activities in the
hands of one class. To this class great-grandfather's father had
acceded, and his son was shrewd enough to realize that military prowess was as essential as academic ability, a judgment
to be later substantially confirmed.

Until the Taiping rose in 1850 the military power of China
was entirely held by the Manchus, who were not desirous of
arming their conquered peoples. The Manchu garrison in each
city was divided into banners or clans, fed and paid at public expense all their lives, so that by the mid-nineteenth cen-

tury they were useless; as also useless were the Green banner-men, Chinese recruits officered by Manchus and numbering about five hundred thousand. The Manchu troops carried fans and opium pipes to battle, and were famous for their speed at running away. When the Taiping conquered seventeen provinces and threatened to overthrow the Manchus, the dynasty resorted to the Chinese gentry to organize levies of Chinese provincial militiamen to fight their own countrymen and put the Taiping down. Once before, in 1840, the people of Kuang-tung province had organized a militia and fought the British, encouraged to do so by Lin Tzehsu, the commissioner who burnt the British opium; the dynasty, though it punished Lin and disbanded the militia, remembered however that they could fight.

And though every effort was made to disband these militia and retire, if not actually banish or otherwise amputate their leaders' prestige, there were so many revolts – on an average two per year from 1840 onwards – that militia-raising became almost a permanency, though not reported to the Court so as not to upset the digestion of the Emperor.

When the Taiping swept onward to Nanking to establish their Heavenly Kingdom, Tseng Kuofan, a Chinese vice-minister of the Board of Ceremonies, on two-year leave to mourn his mother's death, was ordered by the Emperor to raise militia in Hunan, his native province. Overnight Chinese scholars turned into military commanders, Hanling Academicians sweated years and battles in deserts and swamps. Tseng, whatever his defects (and he is now considered a traitor, since he was serving a Manchu ruler against his own people), trained an army instead of only a militia, possibly more by accident than by design. He knew that to get people to fight they must have something to fight for, and paid his soldiers four times as much as the prevailing rates. He had never had any military training, being a writer of moral essays, classical poems, a student of ancient philology, and a rigid Confucianist. His career I shall not relate. His brother Kuochuan, later a viceroy, was as corrupt as he himself was honest in money matters. Both were Confucianists, and pitiless in their slaughter of peasants and the inhabitants of conquered cities.

Due to Tseng's exertions militia were raised, and out of the scholar-gentry came forth the military officers and commanders. In Szechuan my great-grandfather Chou Taohung was one of these commanders, and though he did not fight the

Taiping, the insurrections he helped to put down were related to the great Taiping rising. The Hueis, the Muslims of
Kansu, rose in revolt time and time again in sympathy with
the Taiping. So did the Niens, whose risings lasted from 1852
to 1868. Taohung fought both the Niens and the Hueis as a
commander of militia, and on his gravestone is credited with
having saved Chengtu from the Niens, though details are lack-
ing. The Nien never reached Szechuan, according to the historians who have studied this equally enormous revolt. But
a remnant of the Taiping did, reaching the western borders
of Szechuan, where they were exterminated while trying to
cross the Tatu River to escape into Tibet, in 1868.

The word Nien means "rolling", and it was because the
peasants of the Northern provinces rolled straw torches dipped in fat, lit them and marched in mile-long processions,
that they were called Nien. The Niens were true guerrillas,
with no fixed name, abode or organization. Like locusts fer-
ried by the wind, they swept upon the provinces, killing officials and distributing the landlords' hoards of grain. Peasants
gone into massive, many-millioned revolt, they became consummate guerrilla warriors on horseback. The surprise raid,
the ambuscade, the night attack, the feint, the feigned defeat,
the circling exhaustion, the psychological use of noise (they
blew lugubrious sounds through huge conch shells at night
near the enemy encampments), the sneak dawn raid: not one
of the guerrilla tactics employed today did the Nien not know
or use. They were finally vanquished after sixteen years and
(reportedly) twenty million dead, as many as the Taiping.

Chou Taohung, when he retired from active command,
wrote an essay about the Niens which was preserved in the
family, until it disappeared some twenty years ago. In it he
discoursed of the counter-guerrilla measures that the imperial troops adopted, and these too are surprisingly modern:
scorched earth, deprivation of cover, strategic fortified hamlets, all these were used, and also the economic blockade.
"To clean up the Nien bandits, the price of salt must be stand-
ardized, and smuggling punished." Taking away all the iron
pans from the peasants, punishing anyone found with iron,
is also mentioned by Taohung as effective to prevent the Nien
obtaining weapons from the people.

Actually, between the years 1860 and 1870, when Taohung
was engaged in warfare on behalf of the dynasty, no less than
five large uprisings were going on at the same time: the Niens

in Anhwei, Shantung, Honan, Hupeh and Shensi; the Hueis in Shensi and Kansu; the Hueis in Yunnan; the Miaos in Kueichow; and the Chiangs in Szechuan. In these epics of peasant revolt, upheavals subsiding, simmering and again spewing forth, inchoate, fluid, elusive but tenacious and never ending, here, there and everywhere, three generations, great-grandfather Taohung, his father before him, and his son my grandfather, were to participate. True to their class, loyal to their Emperor, they fought against their own people, and put them down. At that time they were considered praiseworthy. Today they are not so regarded. And if I record their deeds, it is detachedly. They fought on the wrong side, the judgment is history's.

The Huei or Muslim risings were part of the great turmoil of Central Asia, and the tussle between England, Russia and China for its control. In 1862 the Hueis of Kansu cut off the roads to Chinese Turkistan, and the whole of the enormous border region fell into chaos. An adventurer from Kokand, Yakub Bey, allegedly paid by England to organize an independent region under British influence, and also paid by the Russians to create a kingdom for himself under their protection, now reigned in this area, and this East Turkistan fabrication lasted twelve years, from 1865 to 1877. Of it the historian Alastair Lamb says candidly: "Many observers, both Russian and British, thought this situation would be permanent." But they were wrong.

The Manchus were stupid, timorous and weak, but the rising Chinese landlord-gentry-scholar-official class was now armed and militarily competent. They had tasted blood fighting their own peasant revolts. They now also destroyed Yakub Bey's kingdom, and consolidated the western borders of the Empire. They knew their own power, had a new confidence, a new desire for armed might. Had they also been wiser, more patriotic, not imbued with Confucian gentry and class notions, not blinded by pseudo-loyalty to the dynasty, the Manchus would have gone earlier. But they were also frightened at the revelation of their own peoples' talent for fighting, and fell back upon upholding the dynasty.

Great-grandfather also appears to have served for a while under Tso Tsungtang, the man who pacified the border regions and confirmed Chinese Tukistan, now named Sinkiang, as a Chinese province.

Not only my great-grandfather on the paternal side, but

also my great-grandfather on the maternal side, the Lord Hung, took part in these military consolidations of territory threatened by Russia and England. Lord Hung was a great friend of Tseng Kuofan; and the Confucianism of Tseng Kuofan, through Lord Hung and through his daughter, my grandmother, subsequently influenced the Family so that they became even more conservative.

After Chou Taohung came back from the wars, it became customary for the Family to dedicate at least one son to a military career. Military power, removed from the Chinese by the Manchus for nearly three centuries, had now returned to them, and this was not forgotten in Szechuan. With the whole of Central Asia at its back door, Szechuan the main gate for the passage of armies, its fertile rice-growing plains the main source of food, equipment and money for the garrisons stationed on the frontiers with Russia and British India, it became impossible for the dynasty to disregard the Szechuan militias. And this rise of Chinese military talent helped to weaken the central rule of the Manchus by reinforcing the autonomy of the provinces in military and financial matters against the Court in Peking; it gradually loosened the bonds of loyalty to this far-distant alien Emperor, and established the seeds of the warlord armies which in the next period were to fight up and down the land for power.

Taohung retired in the 1880s, to reign over the Family, to enjoy his great reputation as a scholar. He was honoured and visited by notables. Hundreds of scholar-officials acknowledged him their teacher. Many scrolls written by contemporaries, laudatory verse written by callers, were dedicated to him, full of bombast and moralizing.

Taohung also wrote much, though nothing was very original in what he wrote. Again and again he wrote that land alone is not wealth enough, that power is the most untrustworthy weapon of survival, and riches the great corruptor. Only by staying united, by co-operative effort, can the solid bedrock of survival be kept solid. "Loyalty, filial duty, to continue the family." On his gravestone he enjoined his posterity: "Remember your humble beginnings, remember the hardships of your ancestors; be filial and thrifty, be frugal and upright."

Lacquered on wood boards, hanging above doors, on the walls, I found when I went to Chengtu, Great-Grandfather's calligraphy exhorting the descendants to moral rectitude. I rediscovered these precepts on the photographs of these scrolls, sententious hangings which decorated the rooms, so thoughtfully preserved by Third Uncle, when in 1939 I returned to Szechuan and to the Family; the originals have gone. A world of moral maxims, beleaguering the Family in its impregnable feudal fortress, has gone for ever. And I am glad I spent five years at that world's end, in Szechuan, during the Second World War.

Because of his busy life, Taohung married late and only bred two sons, the elder being my grandfather, Chiehyu.

My grandfather Chiehyu was exceedingly different from Taohung. His portrait shows a sensitive, longish face, mournful and haunted. He was much weaker than his father, for he died aged forty-seven in 1910, two years before his own father's death in 1912.

Chiehyu was not a dominating person. He did not resemble Taohung, either physically or mentally. He seems to have been a much more compassionate man, and reading his epitaph one has a feeling that he had a social conscience, that he was not, as his father was, a guardian of Confucian morality, a conservative ready to put to the sword a thousand hungry peasants, nor was he imbued with loyalty for the dynasty. He was uneasy and tormented in his life, but he could not escape it.

Grandfather also became an official in Kansu, the first time in 1884, returning about 1890, the second time about 1896, returning in the 1900s. He appears to have held the same post as his father and grandfather before him, both civil and military at once, and in charge of the supervision of salt. Salt in China was already a government monopoly in the second century A.D., and one of the main sources of revenue to the state. It was taxed at every stage, when manufactured, transported, sold in bulk, retailed. It came from three main areas: the sea marshes of the South, the Szechuan salt mines at Tzeliuching, and the salt pans of Kansu. The collecting and conveyance of salt was part of a district magistrate's duties, and its production, distribution and retailing was farmed out under special licence to salt merchants. Our family for a time held such a licence; and hence the official post in Kansu must have been of great financial benefit to the Family.

Chiehyu was stationed as district magistrate at Lingchow, a frontier territory formally incorporated into the boundaries of the Chinese Empire in the fifteenth century. It was rich salt country, with man-dug waterways, so that the salt could be moved away in barges, and a road connected with the Silk Road on which salt went by camel caravans across the Ordos Desert to Peking.

The Huei risings, the post-revolt exterminations, epidemics and famine, had devastated the area. The poverty was appalling, and Chiehyu was not happy. So says the gravestone, which cannot lie, but seeks to soften. Great indeed his unhappiness, that it should be memoried in stone after death. His character changed during his years in Kansu. He found the people's living conditions extremely difficult, and sought to alleviate them. His many hardships explained his later seclusion and infirm condition, is the glib explanation given posthumously; here again tragedy lies sleeping, for he seems to have done all he could to relieve the poverty round him, and found no rest nor surcease, and died at forty-seven before his own father, leaving this photograph of a face, long, sad, unsmiling, with haunted mouth and eyes.

We further learn that he excelled in scholarship, studied history, and gained judgment above the ordinary. Because of the requirements of the time, he had to go through the matriculation examinations, "but he himself was indifferent to all honours".

Taohung, the successful warrior, the unbending loyal servant of a corrupt and despotic throne, must have found his son very disappointing. Grandfather returned once to Chengtu, and wanted to retire; but he was persuaded to go on, and returned to Kansu. No sooner there, another Muslim revolt took place. "This added to his anxiety and his responsibilities, in having to devise defence, and the maintenance of law and order. He had to work day and night, and still give time to attend to court and legal matters. His health broke down under the strain."

The amount of work extracted from an official in a border post was enormous. He was everything at once: health inspector, tax collector, military commander, magistrate, school supervisor. Grandfather put down the rebellions, repaired the dykes, collected the salt, wrote reports, organized levies, fought bandits, opened schools, managed to accomplish in a surprisingly short time the work of pacification and rehabilitation. But it was against his character to tolerate the routine of an official life, says the gravestone, seeking desperately the apt euphemism, and though his administrative ability was widely recognized, he finally resigned from public service and returned once again to Chengtu, where he became a doctor and gave aid to all who came.

The time he returned was 1902, and now he felt the new currents of thought, and reacted to them. "When the dynasty was ending, the movement for change of the political and social order led the younger generation to a state of confusion. To them he gave guidance, inspiring their vision to reach for new horizons, to free themselves of their own shackles and prejudices, to broaden their field of knowledge and appreciate humanity." Thus the epitaph.

Grandfather would probably now be called a liberal, or a reformist; but he was also a very sick man, with little influence, a compassionate man in a pitiless age. We shall never know what he really thought, for nothing except a pedestrian essay in praise of railway travel has reached me from his writing brush.

My grandmother, his wife the Lady Hung, daughter of the Lord Hung, friend and follower of the illustrious Tseng Kuofan, was utterly different from her husband. Her gravestone epitaph is more enthusiastic than the one above her husband's body for he was the aberrant type, the failure, whereas she was the ideal: the ideal lady, the ideal mother, daughter-in-law, wife, and matriarch; ideal for the gentry class, progenitor, sustainer, conservator, nourished on and nourishing a great dislike of change. No one could have found a more typical example of all the virtues that were extolled by the Confucian rigidists than grandmother, the Lady Hung. "The Lady Hung's father being a follower of Lord Tseng, she received a family discipline patterned after the Tseng family, and her character was therefore a result of conscientious bringing up."

In order to understand her character, I read the life of Tseng Kuofan, which I had anyway been made to read by my first husband when he was aide-de-camp to Generalissimo Chiang Kaishek in 1938. Chiang Kaishek revered Tseng Kuofan, and therefore Pao, my husband, thought it good for our moral fibre, his and mine (but especially mine, of course), to read Tseng's life and writings.

Tseng was certainly admired by many Englishmen of the 1860s, though he did not get on too well with the English officer Gordon, to be known as Chinese Gordon, or Gordon of Khartoum, who helped him to put down the Taiping.

Tseng kept copious diaries for posterity, and in them

describes everything, his campaigns as well as his ringworm and failing sight. He always refused to consult a western doctor as his principles were against it, though he wrote that "we must learn from the West what is useful, reject what is unrighteous and destructive of our own high moral values", a sentiment generally concurred to by the then ruling class, including Chiang Kaishek in a later age.

One longed, reading Tseng, for some relief from his dour, humourless, utterly righteous pontification. I can find only one frolicsome phrase in Tseng's diaries, and it is about deportment when with Westerners: "In your association with the foreigners, be not too lofty; cultivate a slightly confused, casual aspect. Let their insults, deceitfulness, arrogance, contempt for everything they do not understand, glide over you; try to look somewhat stupid; this is a good way of facing a difficult situation . . ."

In all things he sought to live as prescribed by the Rites. It is said that before cohabiting with his wife, he first bathed, lighting the great red candles of wedding night, and burnt incense, performing obeisance to Heaven and Earth before entering the lady's apartment. There is something touching and grandiose about this respect for the sex act, but I do not know whether the story is true.

In this very perfect gentleman, with his perfect, rigid code, there was none of the humanity of my grandfather. And I stare at my grandmother's photographs, who was trained in the same principles, and wonder. Her photographs show a square-jawed, strong face, thoughtful eyes, a broad calm brow. The two families had the same background, shared the same circle of influential friends among the rising Chinese gentry. Great-grandfather Taohung probably knew he was getting an exceptional daughter-in-law for his not entirely satisfactory elder son. I can imagine the shrewd, unscrupulous old gentleman planning it, planning his daughter-in-law as a strong fortress to contain his son's weakness. But, of course, not a word of this was said; only some talk about her pickle-making, which was superb. For in those days the making of pickles was a sign of good breeding, and no woman of the gentry remained inefficient in this art.

Grandmother's eulogy in stone is rhapsodic. She was married at seventeen, and when her husband was transferred to Kansu Taohung ordered his daughter-in-law to join her husband there, a seldom done thing, for Chinese women of the gentry did not go off to wild border regions. In those days it was quite a journey, many weeks by sedan chair through very wild and dangerous country. She left her first son with Great-Grandfather, and two more sons were born in Lingchow, one of them being my father.

"The wheat diet did not agree with her husband. Better and varied rations were only available to the very rich. The Lady-Hung was both thrifty and industrious, and served her husband with every care; thus he was made more comfortable."

Grandfather and Grandmother were both rice-eaters, wheras in Kansu no rice grows, only barley and millet. There were no vegetables, and only mutton and horseflesh to eat, and she could not stand the smell of mutton. As for company, they had none, save for the incursions of bands of hungry peasants, the restless, resentful Hueis around them, always ready to revolt again. One episode which is not on the gravestone but which was told me by both Third Uncle and my mother, was of the night when such a band of Muslims on horseback attacked the magistracy in Lingchow. Grandmother, with such servants, retainers and guards as were about, held them off, while she made Grandfather flee, vaulting over the wall at the back. She secured the heavy doors, which had been shut, by pushing all the furniture in the house against them. Finally the Hueis left. The gravestone does not mention this incident out of modesty: it was not becoming to a woman to be brave. Thus her epitaph:

Historians regard virtuous women not necessarily for their excellent or outstanding conduct, but for the observance of virtue, for being able to overcome adversity, and keep to a life of exemplary behaviour by diligence and frugality, by family tradition and instruction. A great lady like the Lady Hung fulfilled all her duties; on account of her, her children grew up of gentlemanly character; she maintained her extreme humility even in aristocratic surroundings in her latter days. Although in relatively well-to-do conditions at the end of her life, she kept up her thrift and industry, and thus guided her children. Her balance and sense of proportion and her sociability were virtues to be exalted. Indeed, words cannot fully describe the wonderful character of this lady.

She was survived by four sons, eleven grandsons, eleven granddaughters, and two great-grandsons.*

Respectfully, her sons petition a commemorative essay in their mother's memory, singling out her great deeds for emulation and eulogy, with necessary omissions.

Alas, the long-living now comes to her rest, as conscientious at the end as she was at the beginning. Neither abundance nor want

---

*This count does *not* include her three daughters, nor their children, otherwise it would have added another twenty grandchildren.

could alter the beauty of the Lady Hung's spirit, and she becomes a tradition for ever reflected in her children.

Such as the design of a tapestry, with a reigning figure surrounded by fauna and flora in unity and harmony, such was the life of Lady Hung. By the dragons high in the clouds, Heaven shower its blessings on this noblest of families.

Thus the Matriarch's life, the guiding spirit of the feudal family, is retained in memorial stone; and now the stone has gone, only decaying silk paper and the photographs remain. Side by side they stare, the sad, sick man, troubled with questions, the strong, calm woman, so sure of her duties and her place in society.

Of all her sons, my father was the Lady Hung's favourite, and of course it was my father who made her suffer the most. It was my father's children, though so different, whom she desired round her and inquired about. The only two of these alien grandchildren who ever saw her do not remember her. One of them was my sister Marianne, who crossed through the Japanese lines to Chengtu in 1938, a feat of enormous daring and one few men would have attempted. My grandmother loved her, but Marianne was impatient of the old lady and could not bend herself to family discipline, and the day my grandmother died she had gone out, with flowers in her hair, to meet a young man at the university. The other was my brother, and he does not remember her either, though when he was a small boy she held him tightly while he bowed to his ancestors. But grief and sorrow are necessary omissions in the pattern of a life, and Grandmother would not have liked more to be carved in stone about her.

Grandmother died of cancer in 1937. To the end she refused to consult a western doctor, possibly following the example of Tseng Kuofan, more likely because she did not believe in western medicine, but took potions of Chinese medicine, a brew of wine, herbs and ground pearls.

FOUR

My father wrote the story of his life three times altogether, and all after Liberation in 1949, twice because he had to, once on his own account. I have all three in my files. The first two are more or less catalogues of events in his life. The third is an autobiography, detailed, personal and incomplete, for he died before he had finished it.

When the Communist government took over in 1949, people such as my father who did not run away, were of many kinds. Actually few people, comparitively speaking, did go away, and they were chiefly from the westernized upper class. Others, like my father, were so heartily sick of the Kuomintang that, though apprehensive of the Communists, anything seemed better than Chiang Kaishek. Engineers, physicians, professors, civil servants, with little or no interest in politics, they had had enough of the corruption, the inefficiency, the squalid methods and the police terror; most of them wanted an end to civil war, the country set on its feet, and they themselves able to work in security, in peace. There were also among them some with no such simple motives. There were still thousands of officials and military men who had gone over to the Communists in the last few months because they could see that the Communist armies were winning, but who had also served under the Kuomintang. How many of these docile intellectuals and bureaucrats, now apparently enthusiastic, were actually secret agents, planted there by the Kuomintang, who would bide their time and seek to corrupt the system from within?

Between 1951 and 1953, and again in 1954, my father twice wrote an autobiography, as everyone employed by the government was required to do. They are not very long, covering about six to eight pages. This material was checked and counter-checked, a security measure understandable in the circumstances. Every government keeps files on its civil servants, especially those engaged in work of some importance, material collected by secret police, or through investigation, and this in all the democracies is now routine. In China this was done by collecting the self-descriptions of people such as my father, and comparing them with whatever records there were, and with the facts as known. In doubtful cases, of corruption in the past, of black-market traffic, of hidden money – and there were many, for corruption was almost a normal state of affairs during the last fifteen years of Chiang Kaishek – in cases suspect of maintaining affiliations with enemy groups in Formosa or elsewhere, such autobiographies were scrutinized and possibly re-written three or four times, with requests for clarification on this or that obscure or ambiguous point.

It was best to make a clean breast of past misdeeds, to give a truthful account of lapses, for the chances of forgiveness, without more punishment than a telling-off, were then about one hundred per cent. But infractions kept hidden were likely to bring one into great trouble.

I myself, returning to China in 1956 and every year after that, met and talked with dozens of people whom I had known when my husband was a general of the Kuomintang. I met some of his military colleagues, at one time serving Chiang Kaishek, and now employed by the Communist government. They were alive, healthy, useful, rallied to New China. What astonished me most was the small number of political casualties among them. Among such people now in Peking, working or in sinecures because of age, are quite a handful of old warlords, with the blood of hundreds of Communist revolutionaries, decapitated or tortured, on their executioners knives ... yet there they were, unhurt, in Peking. But then, that is China; that is why the Chinese Revolution is different from any other, and why so many like my father rallied to it; it did not slaughter out of hand, there was forgiveness for those who showed repentance and told the truth; there was a place for everyone, even for an ex-Manchu Emperor,* in this Revolution.

With my father, the only explanation required of him, which made him re-write some parts, was his brief conversion to Catholicism in 1929. A note in the margin of his diary reads: "To explain this point verbally." He seems otherwise to have had little trouble.

Third Uncle wrote voluntarily his life deeds, copiously elaborating on all his financial deals, his warlord affiliations, the opium eradication racket of which he had been in charge, and listing all the companies he had founded, twenty-seven in all. He was classified as native capitalist, served on a financial committee, and is now retired, living on the interest of his invested capital.

I found by accident, returning to Peking in 1958 after my father's death to take over the ownership of the four houses he had left me, among old books and notebooks in a trunk, his unofficial, fragmentary memories. They were among bunches of letters, heaped photographs, old bills, Father's poems, his marriage certificate and engineering diplomas, a gold ingot, and my mother's old watch with its lattice grid, which I remembered well for it gave the dial a jailed aspect

*See Aisin Gioro Pu Yi: *From Emperor to Citizen* (Foreign Languages Press, Peking, 1964).

and made me think of the incarcerated days I spent fretting in the house because I was not allowed to go on studying; I had nightmares about that watch till I saw it again in the trunk. There was also Father's penknife and his fountain-pen, which he always carried about him. They must have been placed in the trunk after he died, for safe keeping by the servant. Father had something of the innovator in him, he was for ever noticing and writing down observations, chiefly on engineering techniques, whenever they came to him; anywhere, in a bus, in a train, while walking, he would take his fountain-pen, which was stubby and black and filled by lifting a small lever, extract a notebook from the outer pocket of his cotton jacket in summer, or if it was winter the lower pocket of the camel-hair waistcoats he wore, and write.

It was he who first drew some plans for the large water reservoir which, after Liberation in 1949, was built near the Ming tombs in Peking. He had drawn a sketch of it in 1928, but nothing was done till in 1957 a hundred and eighty thousand volunteers went and built it in six weeks, and it made Father very happy. He also drew up plans for enlarging the city's sewers.

These drawings, sketches, trigonometrical and mathematical formulae, daily expenses, names of friends, addresses, all went into notebooks. Into the notebooks too, on thin silk paper, went his memories, and also his poems. For he was, like many a Chinese trained in the classical scholarship, also something of a poet.

I reproduce the first fragment I found, not because it begins at the beginning, but because it was the first one I found. It took me four years to collect the whole lot, for some he had sent to my Third Uncle, his younger brother, and these I was only given in October 1964, the day after China exploded her first atom bomb.

I had a stroke two months before Liberation*, and the blood froze in my head and my left side became useless. As I lay on my bed, unable to move, I could see them pack, my wife and my Second Daughter, hastily picking up things all through the house and flinging them into their suitcases. They were going away. I knew they were frightened, frightened because the Communists were coming. But I was not frightened.

---

*Liberation: 1949, when Chiang Kaishek was beaten, and the Communists formed the present government of China.

I had been expecting them for so long, so long ... In fear and hope, in doubt and wonder, for nothing could be worse than what we had undergone, yet who knew what the new era would bring?

At last they were coming, and because they were coming my wife and my daughter were leaving, and so I was left alone. I was looked after, I became well again, and I have been working. And though I often disagree with them, yet they have treated me well, and certainly many things have been done which needed to be done. Comrade Lu, who is in charge of the Department where I work, has always been respectful to me, though we have argued, each one holding to his own viewpoint, until a few months ago. Because he is a peasant, a soldier of the Eighth Route Army, thus neither an intellectual nor a scholar, and I and my colleagues are classified as high-grade intellectuals, at first we made fun of him secretly, insulted him smoothly in many ways, calling each other loudly "Comrade" in front of him, aping his talk, his humility. But now I have changed, or has he changed, or have we both changed? The change came when he said to me:

"Comrade Chou, why do you not write down your life in full? It would be precious teaching for us, young ones with no experience. Certainly valuable material to add to our knowledge, and enable us to avoid mistakes, to correct our shortcomings."

That is their style of speech – self-depreciatory, almost impossibly modest, all the more annoying to someone like myself because it seems to make fun of our own pompous modesty, our own tricks of speech. And people like Comrade Lu have power, which makes their humility all the more galling to us. But Comrade Lu says he wishes to learn from us, he wishes to understand science, to become in a way an engineer. He has had little schooling, being an illiterate boy of fourteen when he joined the Red Army. He has fought twenty years of war and has had five years of administration, looking after the running of our Engineering and Design Department, its finances, our welfare, and our souls. Every night the lamp glows in the small cubby-hole where he sits, without fire in the winter, a muffler round his neck; in his cotton underpants in the summer, fanning himself; poring over the engineering books he borrows. He is studying. He will know as much as we do, we the intellectuals, the engineers, one day.

We all resented him, resented his political lectures, his telling us to read political books; he the coarse peasant who scarcely knew how to read, now put in charge of us, so many of us graduates of western universities, the élite of China. Our vanity was unbearably hurt, we were humiliated, and prophesied disaster. The Party cadres had no regard for us, for our learning, we the intellectuals. And Lu was so slow, so slow to understand us, so stupid the first two years ... but in the last three he has begun to know; he follows our work, he put himself to school with us. In the last year he has been particularly zealous to learn from me, and now I am forgetting that I disliked his ways, and we have begun to talk, and I think I must have told him of my dreams, of episodes in the past when I was young, of my life on the railways ... Perhaps that is why he suggests that I should write a book about myself. Yet he is younger than my own son. And so, when he suggests my writing down my life, "I'm busy with some plans for water reservoirs," I reply.

"Yes, Comrade Chou, I know that. But think about it. We feel that you have so much experience of life which we lack, we need to remember the past in order to be wise for the future."

Four months ago I would have suspected Comrade Lu of wanting once again to clarify past events, of wanting to find out what I really thought. I would have wondered whether anything new had turned up, anything important which I had ommitted to mention; for what may not appear important to us, these events of our past, are material to be scrutinized and compared, time and again, till all that is insidious, carrying the seed of future evil, comes forth in plain sight.

At the end of each year for the first four years, and after each Great Movement, we have written down our thoughts, held meetings at which we spoke our feelings about our work, voiced our criticisms of the Party, of Comrade Lu, who has pilloried himself for what he calls shortcomings or faults in the Department. To this I have been hostile, calling it an ample waste of time. But being old, and having some achievement behind me, no one has tried to change me, or is it perhaps that they truly value sincerity? We have learnt to reappraise and criticize our own conduct, and we have also been taught not to backbite or gossip but to criticize each other openly.

This time, I have no feeling of hostility, no reflex at being snared. I suddenly *want* to write down my life, to write down everything that happened. Many of us now have this urge, for we feel we have lived through a great change. For a Revolution is not impersonal events moving helpless human beings about. It is made by man, and it also is an inner process, it changes us. I feel as a pond that has been dredged, mud gone, bottom stone seen. As I left my Department that day, spring had begun.

Spring has begun, and spring hurts, for there is Marguerite, still, though she has left me. And the children. Lu knows about them; therefore he never asks, for his heart is polite even if his manners are coarse. And suddenly he is my friend, thinking of me as a friend, wishing me to release myself into the time to be remembered. And it is so true that now we have peace, and the days have come when memories, reminiscences, can be remembered in tranquillity and stored, for our young generation will need to know the past as it was for us, they will need also to remember the long, long and hard road we have come.

As one looks back after a long and terrible ascent at the slopes left behind; as the embroiderer, having put each stitch into place after hours and days bent upon his frame, rubs his eyes and looks at the whole pattern at last understood; so must I now look at myself, whole, in the clear light of spring that has come back.

*

Thus wrote Father in 1955, released from silence. He had always been a silent man, so much so that Mother called him *Le Muet*, the Dumb One, when she was in one of her raging moods. His silence had nearly suffocated me. It had left us, his children, with no adequate counterpoise to fight the torrent of words with which our mother wore down her children's lives.

Father never did write down his life connectedly, gathering his experiences as others did into a cogent wholeness, through wars and revolutions, the Empire's fall and the rise of the war-lords, chaos and desolation and civil war and war, and war until the final overwhelming battle. Even Puyi, the last Manchu Emperor of China, now a man of fifty-eight, had written his memoirs, a wholeness covering approximately the same span of years as my father's. I do not think my father expected to be published. He wrote for himself. Paradoxically, it was my return to China to see him in 1956 which stopped his pen, so that he wrote practically nothing of what happened after 1925. But here other material turned up: his voluminous correspondence with my Third Uncle, letters in which he recorded all that his silence withheld from his children.

The paper on which he wrote was loose sheet hand-made silk paper, folded carefully into four, and then eight small squares. He placed these sheets between pages in his various notebooks. Father made paper birds and frogs, crickets and fish, as do the men of Szechuan to amuse their children, and I was not astonished when I found a portion of his life shaped as a squatting frog, for he excelled particularly at them; they could be blown into fatness through a hole at the back, and these rotund frogs, which could be sent bounding through air, enchanted my childhood which destroyed them without caring. I have never learnt how to make them, and regret it.

My mother was not so inhibited. She talked and talked, of what she felt and suffered and thought, the universe cast in her own image. She talked especially to me, the child she disliked, burdening me with the weight of her passionate hates and loves till I became allergic to such effusions. The more verbose she was, the more my father retreated into a silent watching of his roses and carnations, into a pruning of lilac trees and vine rampage. This enormous silence of his was my chief torment when I yearned to love him, and he was unget-at-able, in muteness shrouded, preserved from us, his all-too-vigorous, savage, alien offspring. And were it not for the accident of Comrade Lu, the Communist cadre in charge of my father's Department during the years 1950 to 1958, I would know much less about my father than about Third Uncle.

Father became physically younger, happier, more active, after I returned, turned towards the future, a future in which I was by his side, or in which I returned year after year to see him. He bought things for me so that I might settle down in Peking near him: "You can write here, in peace." He collected furniture, installed a new flush toilet in the house, kept cuttings out of the newspapers, started to ask for his house at the sea-side which had been confiscated some years back because it belonged technically to my sister and she was an American citizen and had not claimed it; he had received monetary compensation for it from the government, but now he wanted the house back, for me. "You can write here, in peace." And so he gave up writing, overtaken by the vision of a future in which he was no longer lonely, in which the incisive image of his wife and other daughter hastily packing, flinging objects into trunks, of my mother lifting the crucifix from the wall above the big double bed in which he lay (its whiter outline is still visible on the wall, which has not been whitewashed for twenty years), would one day leave his mind.

•   FIVE

I WAS born in 1886, the year after the war with France, in Lingchow, Kansu, where my father was district magistrate. At the time of my birth my mother was very unhappy because her niece had died, in circumstances I must relate for they affected my life, in the curious way things have of returning to their origin; a full cycle, unpremeditated, inexorable as the tide's return.

Towards Christianity my family bore the agnostic indifference of Confucianism; veneration of ancestors being sufficient for the rational discipline of the civilized, why fill the clear landscape of reason with ghosts and devils, with fatuous gods* and supernatural no-sense? Morning and evening the eldest son struck the bell and re-fuelled with oil the lamp kept burning in front of the soul tablets. Funerals and marriages were arranged according to the augurs, which were material phenomena of stars and dependent on the harmonies of universal motion. This was enough.

But this aloofness, tinged with contempt, turned to active hostility before I was born. This had nothing to do with the spiritual content, but with the temporal encroachments of the Christian sects.

In the case of my family, we had no active aversion until 1885, the year of war with France, when she took Annam. The French had been for decades active in Asia, where they were countered by the British almost everywhere, except in Indo-China. France occupied Hanoi, and to stop her Britain took Upper Burma. Both were hypnotized by China's reported wealth, by the trade of Central Asia and Tibet, and Szechuan was the key to Tibet. The British then thought of a swift war, annexing the whole of the Great River basin up to Szechuan, to stop the French; the French began an invasion of China through Yumman; we were the victims of this greedy rivalry.

*To the Chinese the Christian veneration of saints and of the Mother of God appears equal to the worship given to the Deity.

In London and Paris, an Anglo-French war was in the offing.

In Szechuan the agitation was intense, demanding that the dynasty protect our provinces and raise militia. In North Annam bands of peasants formed themselves into the Black Flag guerrillas, fought the French, and beat them. The French resorted to what they called intelligent destruction by bombing Formosa, destroying our coastline shipyards and blockading the Great River ports; their fleet made land forays and massacred the inhabitants of the sea-coast villages.

Although the Black Flags had won a victory at Langson, the Court in Peking was not apprised of it, and when apprised took no heed. Sir Robert Hart, the British Superintendent of Chinese Customs since 1860 when, to pay indemnities since the Opium Wars, Chinese Customs revenue passed under foreign control, promoted himself mediator; he feared the Black Flags might start another militant uprising, like the Taiping. In London and Paris the fear of another wholesale rising in China led to an *entente* at our expense: France would have Annam, England would have Burma; to get an expeditious agreement the meditating Sir Robert stopped the boats bearing the grain tribute up the Grand Canal from the Middle provinces to the Court, so that the ignoble Manchu noblemen, the bannermen, the Manchu population of about two million in Peking, all living on perpetual subsidies, pensions in silver, free rations of grain and meal and meat, cotton cloth and silk and furs, were pressured into accepting the terms dictated by the powers. France was given suzerainty over Annam, railway concessions and two ports. She also received by treaty a further extension of powers and privileges for her Roman Catholic missionaries. This led, in Szechuan and elsewhere, to an outburst of hatred against the Christians, which the latter did nothing to assuage, and which culminated in the uprising of 1900, the Boxers.

Actually, every treaty since the Opium Wars, imposed by the Western powers extorting indemnities, privileges from China, also contained its missionary clauses demanding concessions for these holy men of which even the commercial foreign firms complained.

Szechuan was the main bastion of Roman Catholic missionary endeavour into Central Asia. From Chengtu French priests went on long treks into Tibet and Mongolia. Their courage and ability to endure hardship might have been praiseworthy had it not been only too clear that the religious garb covered most unreligious actions. Catholic priests and bishops bought up whole villages in times of flood and famine, demanded and obtained on threat of military action the best land in cities for their churches, after evicting the inhabitants and paying no compensation. Catholic priests formed militia bands of their own, and claimed to rank higher than our own magistrates. Bishops were invested with the pomp and power of governor-generals. They used sedan chairs with eight carriers, a drummer going in front, and everyone in the street where they passed had to stop work, stand up, and unroll their headbands in obeisance to the Catholic bishop, on pain of being beaten with the "heavy bamboo".

No one dared go to law against a priest, or one of the converts; the priests were immune, like diplomats, and the converts claimed the same immunity; protected by the Church, the converts could do anything they pleased, and escape the due process of ordinary law, for they always asked protection from the Church against what they called "pagan customs". In the law courts the Catholic converts did not have to kneel, as did everyone else. They called themselves people of the Christian teaching, not subject to Chinese law. They were so strong that people said: "An egg does not stand up against a stone," and did not dare to raise cases against Christian converts. Many books are filled with the evil deeds of such holy men.

So in 1885 and 1886 there were riots against the Catholics in may parts of Szechuan, and in the cities the genty now became involved in this too. Our family also became involved.

My mother's niece-by-affection was the only daughter of a merchant named Lee; the father had made money as a small middle-man to the foreign firms when the Great River ports were opened to foreigners. His wife and my mother had sworn to be sisters for ever, and to look on each other's children as their own.

Among the more influential merchants trafficking with foreign firms was a man named Tu, a Catholic convert. Tu was despised by the others for having "eaten religion", but they were afraid of him. He bought houses and land for the missionaries, arranged for interpreters and servants, getting a commission on each transaction; it was said that even the gardeners of the foreigners paid him his rake-off. Whenever there was a law case against a convert, Tu arranged matters, threatening or bribing the magistrates, with the power of the

Bishop behind him, so that the saying in Szechuan at the time was: "Become a Christian sheep, and the judge will do obeisance to your dung."

Middleman Tu wanted a bride for his son, and thought of Lee's daughter. The latter at first refused, having previously agreed to a match with a young man of the Hung clan, my mother's clan. This marriage had been planned by my mother and her friend, Lee's wife. Our gentry families were kept related to each other by bonds of common interest, shared affection, so that we all called each other brother or cousin, and our aunts and uncles were legion. But Lee was afraid that Tu might ruin him, and delayed the marriage to the Hung clan. When friends reproved him, he replied: "even the Dragon Throne quakes when a foreigner shouts," for he knew that no magistrate would dare to protect him against the Catholic bishop. Great with borrowed power Tu rode the foreign wind to influence and wealth, and officials were timourous and easily browbeaten. Actually, due to the extra-territoriality clauses in the treaties concluded between China and the Western Powers after the wars, no foreigner could ever be brought to justice, whatever he did in China; and this now extended also to Chinese converts.

Finally Lee broke the contract made with the Hungs, wearing mourning to soften their resentment, and taking to his bed. "If I refuse my daughter, Tu will bring foreign soldiers to kill me and to rape my womenfolk, as has been done in certain places. He will take my daughter as his son's concubine."

The case was brought to court and lost.

On an auspicious day the bride-to-be, supported by female relatives, and veiled in red, was placed in the red satin bridal chair, to be taken to the Tu residence for the wedding rites, Chinese and then Catholic. It was reported that the Bishop himself would officiate. She went into the conveyance weeping and reluctant, as was only proper. She had flower shoes on her small feet, the shoes that each bride sews and embroiders for herself, and which male guests peep at covertly, for it is the only thing one sees of a bride, and the perfection of the embroidery, the tinyness of the foot, procured them pleasure, vicarious enchantment.

The cymbals clashed. In front went the gong-beaters, behind the carriers with gifts. The sedan chair, closed by satin hangings, carried by two bearers, was set down in the inner courtyard of the Tu mansion, while crackers exploded. When

their spitting had stopped the go-between from the bride-
groom's side advanced, fan in hand, to lift the curtains and
help the bride out of the chair. But the bride was dead, having strangled herself with the veil covering her face; only her
feet, jutting straight out, were seen before the hangings dropped as the go-between started to scream.

That a girl of seventeen chose to die rather than to break a
promise made by her clan aroused the most violent, passionate
feelings among the gentry. Unmoved by millions of dead
peasants, indifferent to a thousand peasant girls sold, cynical
at the bankruptcy of the country and the ruin of their people,
they were touched to the quick by the chaste virtue of the
Lee daughter. For in those days so different from today, and
which I too have known, family pride, family honour, counted
greatly. This death put us all to shame.

But it did more. It made my mother so ill, when she heard
of it in far off Lingchow, that I was born a month too early.
And later she heard that her best friend, the mother of the
dead girl, also committed suicide.

Big and small, involving whole districts, for the next few
years over one thousand anti-missionary risings took place in
Szechuan. They were savagely put down, in one instance a
thousand peasants being decapitated. Our gentry were not
spared; they openly incited the peasantry against the Christians; some were caught leading local revolts, and put to death.
Aming them was the young man of the Hung clan, the bride-
groom-to-be, who now led peasant bands against the
churches.

My grandfather Taohung wrote: "If your son becomes a
Christian, kill him, for he will desecrate the graves." I learnt
this maxim almost as soon as I could read.

This affliction of hatred could not be healed as long as the
missionaries behaved as they did. My childhood games, as
those of many another child of the gentry in Szechuan, were
to draw pictures of goats, sheep and pigs, representing
Christians, and stick darts into them, and to drown rats, of
which Szechuan had an appalling number, calling them
Christians. Some of the children even crucified the rats before drowning them. Our cook would chop their heads off
with his chopper, calling them foreign devils.

It was only later that we understood it was not Christianity
as such, but those who used Christianity to rob us, who were
to blame. All these years, knowing how the missionaries be-

haved, I yet bore with Marguerite's religion, so staunchly exhibited. But always the dolorous face of the Christ hanging over my bed reminded me, with unease, of the face of an opium-smoker.

When I left Szechuan, my mother made me swear that I would never become converted to the Christian religion. But I married the religion, and brought it home to the Family, and all my children were to become Catholics. How this must have hurt my mother, especially from the one born too early, born in her sadness; but never was a word said in the family against Marguerite's faith when she returned with me. It is, however, because of her religion that I have been abandoned by Marguerite, and that no son of mine is by me in my old age.

On the narrowing horizon of my old man's mind my happy childhood lingers, a sunrise frolic in a heaven of gregarious shouts. Magnolias, crickets, a moon tangled in transparent trees, lacquer, incense, thousands of yesterdays glitter with bright chips of joy. My happiness had company, always some brother, cousin or friend, protecting, cherishing. It centred round my mother. It had approval, for I did most things well.

Even in the midst of a babble of relatives, I could shut eyes and ears, abstract myself. No one minded inattention in a young scholar; much was forgiven me, because I was brilliant. Grandfather taught me the classics himself, and showed my early poems to his friends.

Because of childhood happiness I wronged my wife, for when I met her and told her of China, it was of this China, the China seen on Delft porcelain, a China of palaces and bridges, of satins and gardens, of mountains and rivers wildly beautiful, of obedient servants and benevolent kinsmen, which I described to her. I was only describing my prosperous, secure family. I thought it China. She had read novels on Cathay, fashionable at the time; the cruel and stupid Manchu Dowager Empress, Tze Hsi, was represented as a gracious, sweet old lady, benevolently taking tea with the wives of British and French and American diplomats; China was a land of exotic beauty, ancient traditions, and the restless minds of Europeans hankered for the imagined order and serenity of a China that did not exist. They deluded themselves. I helped to delude Marguerite.

I forgot, or perhaps I never knew well until today, my

country, the tumultuous, angry and starving land, where millions died of famine, where blood flowed so readily, where there had been revolt every year for nearly a hundred years, where Revolution was building its hurricanes, and where her people, my wife's people the Whites, had come to fulfil their rapacity, their greed for possession of lands not theirs, their wealth built upon our disastrous misery.

I wronged her by not telling her any of this; my only excuse is that I did not know it myself, or rather that I never thought of it. I was of my class, the gentry, and childhood betrayed me.

Childhood was the New Year, all of fifteen days long, and the city of Chengtu smothered in flowers; they burst out of the courtyards, the pink and yellow prunus, the translucent bell flower, the white narcissus. All day within the rooms with their lacquered floors and satin embroidered hangings was the murmur of silks as men moved about in their long gowns. The heavy black satin of the women's skirts gave a slight rasp, like young cicadas trying their wings, when they sat on the blackwood carved chairs in my mother's rooms. The cry of the announcer as sedan chairs stopped in the outer courtyard, the hum of congratulations, the laughter, obligatory at a time of happiness, all confirmed that all was well. My knees tired with kneeling to my elders, Mother held me by the hand.

I went with her in her sedan chair to call upon relatives, and peeped through the bamboo woven screen of the small window, such fine mesh I could see the road through a slight blur like rain.

At the New Year the four gates of the city were thrown open, throngs of people sauntered in and out of the walls to go walking in the fields, to visit the temple of Chuko Liang outside the south gate. The streets were clean with new sand, and in the west city, the Manchu section, the panoplied bannermen on horseback went by, spurring their steeds with embroidered boots, and the peacock feathers of their hats stirred in their canter. Manchu women, with high stiff butterfly headgear, walked primly about, their faces covered in rouge. We did not stare at them, for they were Manchus, and stayed apart, forbidden to intermarry with us. And though the bannermen looked proud with their cloaks and plumes and boots, we knew they could not fight; but they were arrogant, and whipped anyone in their way, and no one could touch a Manchu.

Tibetans crowded the market, their thread caps hung with

strings of coral and turquoise which drooped upon their shoulders and curtained their cheeks. The men had one coat sleeve empty, slapping their backs, and sashes of bright satin girdled their fur robes.

Children like myself went about, never segregated, always in groups, to bow and kneel to uncles and aunts, to tutors and teachers and to Grandfather's noble friends. Suddenly I became tired and wept aloud and screamed, and there was a hush, for it was not auspicious to weep on a happy day. The next day I had toothache, and a fever. After that I had my teeth lacquered black to preserve them; a custom possibly adopted from Annam, where this is still done.

There was the Lantern Festival, on the eighth day of the first moon. The ancestral halls were decked in red satin; the incense ash was thick in the burners, we scooped handfuls of it to watch its grey silver sink into the water of the small lotus pond in the garden. For a week the city people walked the streets under flower-arches. In the evening everyone went out, holding lanterns in their hands, children and adults alike, walking about; all the shop-fronts were hung with lanterns, four or more to each shop, making the streets light as in daytime. There was always much competition as to which shop, which house, would set up the best lanterns. Some of these were painted by great masters, and worth hundreds of ounces of silver.

One year I went about carrying a huge fish with glass eyes, the paper scales so deftly knit with thin wire that they moved as I walked, the fish swaying from side to side appeared to swim in air. Another year I had a great bird, a flying crane, the feathers of painted silk paper, each one separate, a whole plumage under my hand, warm, tender and tremulous as a live bird.

In the din of the firecrackers, which did not stop till the fifteenth of the first moon, we walked the East Main street where our family shop, Kuang Hsing, was situated. The street was a mile in length. All the shop counters, and the boards of the shops which at night were put up to close the fronts, were varnished with Szechuan lacquer, a thick blackness with an inner purple glow, used also for floors and lasting fifty years. The sandstone street was broad enough for three sedan chairs of eight carriers each to walk abreast without jostling. The sidewalks were covered with rugs and carpets, each shop bringing them out of its treasure store.

On such days frugality seemed forgotten, and all was profligate beauty. Children were given money to spend, buying puff-cakes and sesame seed cakes, sweet dumplings and almonds and preserved fruits. I delighted in the velvet beancurd, served in transparent porcelain bowls; it was prepared and sold by the Tso family, and was so renowned that from all parts of Szechuan people came to eat the beancurd at the Tso Family Beancurd Shop. The flavour and texture of the beancurd, slipping on my tongue, down my gullet, made me sigh with pleasure.

On the last three nights stalls were set up with beautiful things for sale: painted scrolls, lacquer and ivory screens, porcelain cups and vases from the famous kilns of Kintechen, bales of silk, fine sticks of ink with precious stones ground into them, embroidered coats and kingfisher brooches and turquoise beads and jade sealstones and incense holders of pink crystal; sandalwood boxes and rare spices of Turkistan; Sinkiang seedless raisins for festival dumplings, pummeloes and scented orchids from the north; furs of golden monkey, snow leopard and Himalayan bears from the Tibetan ranges, and fine muslin and nankeens from the eastern provinces down the River.

Later I learnt that these stalls were the means of selling family heirlooms. Aready we were becoming poorer, our handicraft enterprises going bankrupt as a great swelling tide of opium and western manufactured goods, the constant war indemnities and the ruinous taxes, broke our economy. To pay their debts families would sell their lacquer coffers, fur-lined robes, jewels, scrolls, furniture, books and paintings. I did not know that these years were to be the last of our own wealth, and that one day my mother too would pawn her jewellery and her furs in order to provide a welcome for my wife.

At seven my calligraphy was extolled by friends, but Grandfather pretended to scold me and called me lazy, lest I became too proud. Then sorrow: my mother left again, to return to Kansu and to my father. I remained in Chengtu. When she and Father returned it was the Sino-Japanese War and I was nine years old, Chinese fashion, which adds a year to age, the womb-time period.

My mother was the centre of my world, a world of gentleness, in which all things went from her and returned to her, her presence a warm sweetness, enhancing the colour and

savour of my joys. She did all things well, my grandfather
esteemed her, she was honoured by all. She did not have a
perfect face according to Szechuan standards, not the peach-
like contour, the flying-moth eyebrows, the fine-bridged small
nose. But she had very fine, steady eyes, was low-voiced and
patient. Her dark hair shone so much that it was said "a fly's
feet would skid on its surface"; she oiled it with jasmine oil in
which fragrant wood shavings had been dipped.

My father was a man often ill; that is how I remember him,
when he returned from Kansu and lay under quilts in the stifling summer, shivering with fever. Every day the family doctor
came to take his several pulses (a Chinese has twelve pulses);
and though Grandfather frowned at superstition, the Taoist
diviner from the Ram temple sought to alter the fates and
mend his failing health with characters written upon silk paper
and pasted in front of his room. An aunt who thought it fit
to propitiate strange gods took my elder brother and myself
to the many Buddhist shrines of the city, and we burnt paper
money and made offerings, but were too small to understand
what we were doing, kneeling and knocking clappers to call
the spirits and beseech our father's recovery.

I remember peeping at my father from the bamboo screen
which shadowed the bedroom doorway. The mosquito-net
curtains of figured silk were hooked back on both sides of the
carved four-poster lacquer bed. On the bed was stretched a
leopard fur, and on it lay my father, his thin face glistening
with sweat, his eyelids half-closed, the whites of his eyes showing. I was much afraid and avoided him after that, shrinking
from him and the sad odour of medicine that was about his
garments.

I was with my mother more than is usual for a boy, especially
from the age of ten to twelve, when for some months I followed her about. She had returned from Kansu, and would
not go back, I hoped. We often were together in the kitchen,
for there I was most at ease, loving her in unshackled exuberance, perhaps because I felt childhood slipping from me,
abandoning me to an unforecast adolescence. Not in the inner
courtyard, where among the teacups and the sweetmeats out-
spread in their lacquer trays she served the lady visitors, and
prepared the water-pipes of silver or pewter, deftly picking
the blond shredded tobacco with silver tweezers and filling
the small pipe-bowl before lighting it with a smouldering
paper spill; nor at the mahjong tables, with their regular, un-

stopping clatter, where she would play all night, untiring in deference, and continue to stand about all day, looking to the conforts of the elders; in the kitchen she was wholly unshared by others, and even today I can cook many dishes, having learnt with her.

In the kitchen my mother sat at the flat, smooth slab of polished hard stone which ran along one side, a great smoothness under our hands. The cook sliced the new spring vegetables with his finger nail, as did my mother (iron would vitiate the flavour); we washed them in moving mountain water brought from the Pure True Mountains, rolled them in crystal salt, and with a fine needle of bamboo strung them like beads on a cotton thread; then we hung them to dry in the clear sun for a day.

In our class, pickles were a sign of breeding and eligibility, as important to a girl's marriage chances as a royal ancestor in other lands; education was not for women, though Cheng-tu had a tradition of poetess-courtesans; it was improper to speak of physical beauty; family connections were understood and unmentioned.

Many a husband fell in love with his wife after marriage because of her pickle-making, and the daughters of a mother who made excellent pickles were sought out, for it was assumed that the special recipes would be passed on to them. As a good general does not have weak soldiers, a good mother does not have awkward daughters who cannot make pickles. Like the embroidered shoes of the bride, the pickles' flavour was held by connoisseurs to denote a woman's refinement and delicacy of mind.

At the end of banquets, after the last dishes, with the small bowl of rice which denotes the finish of a feast, pickles made by the lady of the house would appear. Pickles were part of the wedding dowry, taken by the bride to her husband's home, along with headpins and rings, necklaces, lacquer boxes, cushions, bed-hangings, embroidered quilts, bolts of silk and satin, furs, morning and evening mirrors, clocks, fans and personal maidservants. The bridal boxes, carried two by two on lacquered poles with silver hooks, also contained jars of pickles, reputedly made by the bride. Among the maidservants the bride took with her for her service in her new home would be one who had learnt the art and would discreetly supplement the deficiencies of her young mistress.

Mother taught me how to listen to a jar, on a dry afternoon

when the shopkeeper brought dozens of jars, placing them in
neat rows in the outer courtyard; she went slowly by, inspecting them, and I followed her, looking at their rotund, glistening brownness which sent back the sun into my eyes. A pickle
jar must be chosen by its sound, a smooth, steady hum, like
a bee poised above desirable blossom.

In Kansu Mother had started planting vegetables and making pickles to improve my father's appetite, and also a flower
garden and some trees, for she liked to grow things and to
make things live.

Yellow wine, white wine, glutinous rice-water, red sugar,
red chilli dried in the wind, pepper in seed, gingko fruit, mush-
rooms, parsley and chives, and cassia and lotus seeds; all, all
her talk and her doing was of curing and salting, pickling and
preserving, sowing and planting, and she knew better than any
man what the soil was doing, and what field produced the best
rice.

She spoke with the cooks, the tailors and the carpenters and
the cleaners, the farmers and the accountants and the stew-
ards, the great and complex machinery of service and sub-
service, based on the intricate, part-emotional bondage of a
feudal household. All her news came to her secondhand, since
she went outside the gates only in a closely shuttered sedan
chair: the planting of rice and the sowing of beans, the best
seed oil and the abundance of oranges, whether the shallots of
such-and-such a place were not a day past their prime, and
what the tobacco price would be next autumn, and which
junks had sunk in the river and how it would affect us; all this
she knew.

She never wasted anything. She would look through the furs
in summer, dole out the oil for the lamps, trim the wicks;
nothing too small or mean for her to control and bend to her
iron-smooth will. Sometimes she would take, from the embroidered purse that hung by the side of her skirt upon a silver
chain, a small coin. A servant's child would be summoned to
run outside the city wall to a field where the best cabbage grew,
to buy one for a dish; thus she would save a little money, yet
get the most fresh cabbage.

She brought the whole growing sap-rich juice-full earth of
Szechuan into the house, and without her I felt sterile, unsure,
as if bereft of solidity.

And then, so swiftly, we were no longer together. I was

thirteen years old, Mother had seven more children. I was to take the district examinations within a year or two. She suddenly changed, urging me to study, distant, scolding me if I played or shouted with my younger brother in the courtyards. Never again did I sit next to her, to watch her smile, to hear the rustle of her skirt, that sound most comforting, reminiscent of her lap, the universe of childhood which began and ended in the folds of her dress.

As the eternal rhythm of the soft wind upon the Chengtu plain I was to remember her, as the stillness, the feathery rain of autumn; and not as the old woman, old with weeping, tugging at my sleeve, whom I left to follow a stranger.

In this still, enclosed world of my childhood the word "change" was frowned upon, though all was changing. The wars, the defeats, the steady-growing poverty, assaults kept outside the even gloss of our harmony, never mentioned in calligraphic injunctions, erupted upon us, and we could no longer keep out their harsh invasion. And now as I grew older Mother would be stern, and sad, and remind me of her sorrow at my birth, the beheading of a relative, the ruinous injustice practised upon us by the foreigners. One day, suddenly, our house kept its gates shut, and we went about, quiet, reticent ... for punishment extended to kin and clan, and we feigned ignorance. I forget why it was that we were frightened. Thus we learnt not to speak our thoughts fully, for therein lurked danger.

As long as we were mindful of the maxims inscribed in all their gold upon the large lacquer boards, we would be safe, safe from time and from change. Thus the elders asserted, and spoke largely of virtue and tradition. I grew fearful of upsetting time and place and thereby ensuing a catastrophic turn of events by any originality of my own; around me the punishments for rebellion were too ferocious. A mental discipline subordinated desires to the family good: it was called classical education, and it stultified us. It was devised to maintain all things as they were, in immutable hierarchy.

There was, in the complex of relationships in which we lived, a pyramid of authority, not only of people, but of rooms and courtyards, trees and flowers, servants and sedan chairs. My father and my mother were always completely dressed as if for an official call when visiting my grandfather in his room in the same house. Awesome in dignity, he granted us, his grandchildren, a morning audience of ten minutes; we changed our clothes, washed our face and hands to bow to him and wish him good day. The golden chrysanthemums in their pots, the specially honourable ones, on both sides of my grandfather's room door, were part of his person. He tended them personally, their splendour undissociated from his presence. To have picked one would have been almost irreverence, hard to forgive.

Black lacquer gates with a high threshold, stone lions on both sides, opened into the first courtyard with its spirit screen of carved brick. There the sedan chairs were set down, their hangings changed with the seasons. My grandfather's four-bearer chair, with skins of golden monkey, sovereign against bone pains, occupied the place of honour; then came my father's chair, and then the common and the women's chairs. The servants' lodgings were on one side, the apprentices' on the other. In the second courtyard, with an entrance to the first garden, for guests, the appropriate flower-pots were ranged in the reception rooms. Into the third courtyard came the relatives, and there the Family began, in a succession of single rooms arranged four-square round small courtyards; on the east side lived the eldest son and his family, the younger ones on the west; in the middle the parents' room. The innermost courtyard had its well, its hall with soul tablets if it was also a sanctuary house, and immediately behind was the dining room for the family, the kitchen with its servants' quarters, courtyard and a well for ordinary water. Refuse was taken out by the western side back door.

At one time seventy-five of us lived together in the house of my childhood, without counting the servants and serving maids. Then it became impossible to stay together, the over-crowding taxed even my mother's forbearance.

I remember the scrolls, folded in their camphor chests, taken out and duly hung in the correct places according to the seasons, divided into landscapes of summer and winter, spring festival and autumn moon, ordinary days and feast days. There were my grandfather's fans, morning fans and after-noon fans, courtesy fans and those for ceremony, of scented wood inlaid with ivory and ebony, fans when he received im-portant guests, fans for business meetings, fans for pleasure. He owned fifty-six fans. My father had twenty-seven.

In this peopled furnished domain, kin and clan dovetail finely as fine woodwork; not beings as themselves, but beings in re-lation to the common structure to which we belonged, which we owned and which owned us; we were taught our responsibility towards its maintenance. That was the order, seemingly Heaven-ordained, of our medieval society.

The magnolia of spring flowered at the appointed time, and was duly praised with verse. An uncle would stop to inquire of a farmer where he could have some cuttings, for his magnolia was better than ours, and what was the secret of the strength and beauty of his tree? The farmer would produce shoots, and a poem would be written to remember this encounter (but not the farmer's name) and the beginning of a new tree, new beauty in our garden.

A wonderfully shaped stone had been discovered, which had been described in the Sung dynasty eight hundred years previously, then lost in the wars. From a hundred miles scholars came to see it and to write poetry about it, and a feast was given to commemorate the finding of the stone.

All, the mountains, the clouds, the fields, the river going its long journey to the sea, all was matter for literature, all had been matter for history. Every spot had its actual event and also its legend, its appropriate verse, its place in the knowledge of the generations past and those to come. All had been done, commemorated, commented on. Hence at times the real was the calligraphy, and not what really happened; the maxims on the wall were alive, not the revolts and the humiliations, the defeats and the hatred. There was always escape, one could escape from hideousness, into a painted landscape on the wall.

I should have known, for around me was misery enough, tangible, unavoidable. But I had been taught not to think, not to act in any way that would bring admonition; wrongdoing was not individual guilt, but a collective mishap, since we were mutually responsible for each other. When I was scolded by Grandfather, my mother immediately accused herself: "Your unfilial daughter does not know how to bring up children."

Already the system was crumbling, the predatory West within our gates, feeding on our decay. Already all had changed, below the lacquer of our floors the wood had rotted, but we tried hard not to pronounce the word: *change*.

Our world was changing, faster and faster, a great wind would blow down upon us, sweep away these structures, denude us of the apparel of ceremony, render our classical education useless. A new world would be born, in pain and suffering. I knew it not, but one thing also saved me in the end: my mother's deep, tenacious passion for the earth, for this our soil, for the things that grow in this earth of ours, this universe of poverty, torment and despair which was to be reborn, remade one day into something human and good.

And that is why when Liberation came, and some of my friends committed suicide and others died because they could not change, they could not understand, they went madly on, plotting to restore the terrible yesterdays, I needed no such stubbornness, craved no other heaven or earth than to see once again the fields grow their rice, the magnolia flower in its spring, and the brown sun of a pickle jar's belly was sun enough for me. There was much that was new, strange and painful to learn, but had I not, all my life, suffered these wrenchings? I watched my carnations grow in their pots, the lilac in my garden blew mauve and white in the spring, and the vine I planted yielded grapes; the autumn chrysanthemums I grew, though only half as large as those which stood guard at my grandfather's door, were good enough.

So I remained, while the stranger, my love, left me, taking away the crucifix that had hung its sad narcotic visage above me all those years.

And all this was part of the Big Change that had been in preparation even before my birth.

SIX

I READ my father's cramped, sedulous calligraphy, and feel as if I were looking at the landscape painted by a Taoist artist upon a temple wall; it was so excellent, that as its maker stepped back to view his work, he longed to visit the hills and rest under the trees by the side of the cool river he had created upon blank space. So he entered his own painting, and was lost to the material world for ever. Taoist stories are often thus contrived, to make us doubt the reality of the real; Chuangtze dreamed himself a butterfly, Laotze knew the paradox of action. What was truly existent, the painted landscape entered by the longing of the priest, or the true world of hills and shade, rivers and solid soil, left beyond the wall?

My father sometimes confronts me with such a Taoist landscape, a dream-syllabled evocation of his cornered heart upon a small heap of silk paper. Too often, I feel, he tended to reject the solid world round him. As the autumn leaf falls to the tree's root, he went back to his childhood; an old man worn in the panoply of living, he returned to what was no longer in existence. But who shall say it was not also valid?

But there is Third Uncle, my father's brother, and not only deep love, but also their utterly different characters united them strongly throughout their lives. There was about eighteen months difference in age between them. Father was the second son, Third Uncle the third; two more sons died at an early age, a last, Sixth Uncle, is still alive. An older brother was born three years before my father, but his younger brothers did not achieve any closeness with him. When I met him in 1939 I also found him difficult to talk to, unlike my loquacious and extrovert Third Uncle.

In Third Uncle all is collected, retained and classified, in a tradition of verbal and written handing down, punctilious and learned. Third Uncle is the story-teller, the family bard, reciter of ancestral saga, resuscitator of dead bones to make them live in words. But he is also an exact keeper of duly labelled letters, photographs and files. He possesses a veritable frenzy for exact knowledge on all subjects, and an astonishing memory. Nearly twenty-five years ago, he and I talked one afternoon of skin pigmentation. Chungking had been duly flattened into rubble by Japanese bombs; I had been walking quite a lot in the sun, after the bombings, my face had darkened and freckled, and the mole removers, of whom there were so many about, wanted to remove my nefarious moles with acid. Third Uncle asked me to explain the mechanism of tanning, while the moleman took away some freckles. In October 1964, twenty-four years later, he remembered this conversation of ours. "I am now asking you," he said, "to explain to me the formation of moles in old age, as I am having an argument with my doctor about it." Third Uncle was growing some pigmented spots; and the doctor who saw him twice a week and still held notions of auspicious and malefic moles, wished them removed. Third Uncle, always sceptical of metaphysics, desired a scientific answer before submitting to the moleman's acid.

This desire to comprehend has led him to understand the Revolution better perhaps than my father did; he, the capitalist, the banker, not only accepted the inevitability of events, he was convinced that no other answer was possible. "That is because I know economics. Your father was ever a poet, the motions of his heart high and noble." Third Uncle's motions of the mind are concrete and almost too thorough. To broach any topic with him is to be instructed on the subject from its inception, be it in palaeolithic times, to the present day.

How much this nourishing, kindly Great River of words, questioning, weighing, philosophizing, groping for knowledge, imparted solace, repaired the so deep maim to my emotions of Father's taciturnity, how much it did to heal me, Third Uncle will never know. And when, in the end, he gave me all the letters he had received from my father over a span of forty years, this was the eloquent, final gesture, accepting that we might not see each other again, for he was seventy-six years old and did not wish to leave the earth with anything undone. I would continue the quest, in words, and thus keep alive the story of our epoch, even if restricted to one Family, our own. And this was well, this was the only tangible immortality man could accomplish, a prolongation beyond actual existence by some act, some thought, some purpose, of benefit to all. A continuity.

It is due to Third Uncle that the photographs of the ancestors' paintings were duly taken, for the original silk has been corroded by time and dampness. They stare out of the past, these men and women, inhabitants of another era, valid because recorded. Great-Grandfather Taohung, photographed at eighty-seven, my grandfather and the muted questioning in his eyes, my grandfather's brother, Second Great-Uncle, who in 1951, the year of Land Reform, threw himself down a well because he could not bear to face his peasant tenants (he was then seventy-nine, had eighteen children, and was very tough physically, doing exercises every morning and cracking walnuts open with his entire and perfect teeth) ... all of them are with me now. They do not want laudation, suave as a mountain stream. They want the truth, within that immense continuum which is China.

"Your Second Great-Uncle should not have chosen the watery end for his spirit," says Third Uncle, discoursing of this demise, and avoiding the unpleasing taboo word death.

"Of course the peasants did justice on so many landlords, and there were the people's courts."

He does not argue against this uprooting of the feudal countryside. After all, this is Revolution, no child's game; and we have all lived with revolution all our lives, even when we did not recognize its processes. It has eaten and drunk with us, bedded us, and has killed some of us. But then we also killed, and so many more than revolution ever did, our hard hearts untouched in spite of all our talk of righteousness and morality. No one as intelligent as Third Uncle is silly enough to want back what is no more. He feels that Second Great-Uncle was too hasty in ending his life so abruptly.

"He could not bear the loss of face, could not submit to criticism and blame."

Third Uncle was more supple, more teachable.

"We needed a revolution. Now at last our country is our own, we have thrown out all exploiters. No one will shit on our heads any more."

That is the way he feels it, which is the way so many like him feel it. No revolutionary, no Communist, no firebrand, only an old capitalist living off his income, but patriotic and therefore content to see things put to right. And so he rummages in his packed bookshelves, searching for letters and photographs or anything else which I may need.

"You must write it down exactly, for future generations to read, and to know all, the evil and the good. To know the Great Change."

Actions follow each other, and only exist in relation to each other, and the actions of men are consecutive and indivisible. In time and in space, all that we are belongs to everyone else, those that went before us and those who will come after us. And decade-pacing time, now vaulting the centuries, still binds grave and womb into oneness; yesterday has prepared tomorrow, and there is no escape, even if the landscape is painted on the wall.

The time is 1940. The place, Chungking at war. An implacable night heat, relentless, coming down from the sky, rising from the rock, after the bombing routine by the Japanese planes. Third Uncle has borrowed this large house on a hill, which belongs to a friend and where I am staying to recover from malignant malaria. From here we can watch Chungking being bombed, Chungking burning. The house is safe, far enough from the city. There is also a small dug-out shelter below it.

Third Uncle is fanning himself, his loose white silk trousers, his white silk waistcoat, his black cloth shoes. He tries another brand of tea, for he is a tea connoisseur. He has lined up four different boxes, each containing a different leaf, and pours tea of four different tastes in fine eggshell porcelain cups. We sip. He speaks.

"Japanese devils, Japanese devils. Rain down your Japanese devil-eggs, but you cannot conquer us. I, Chou Kiensan of Chengtu, I am telling you so."

Japanese eggs are the bombs, looking so small, like inoffensive pellets, as they drop.

This is Third Uncle's prelude to discourse. I sit and drink noiselessly, honoured, being asked to drink with him. My husband has no such patience; besides, he prefers coffee, and coffee is not to be had, it is too expensive in Chungking. It only comes for the foreigners, at the Correspondents' Club, in the embassies. Tonight my husband is away, on guard on the Generalissimo, Chiang Kaishek, who is giving a big dinner to the German military adviser, von Falkenhausen.

"Even the Germans don't like the Japanese," I say helpfully, "they will turn against them one day. He says so."

"He" means my husband, Pao. With Third Uncle I can only call Pao "he": it would be immodest to call him by name; neither can I call him "my husband", which is not done; in fact, the only way I can refer to him is to say "my son's father", but this I am precluded from doing since I have not borne a son. "He" is explicit enough.

Third Uncle snorts. "The Germans say it to blind us. All of them are the same. All foreigners, ghouls, vampires, waiting to suck our blood." He leans back. "I remember, the first time they fought us, the Japanese, way back in 1894, in the nineteenth year of Emperor Kuanghsu.

"In 1894 I was seven, your father nearly nine. It was early morning in the second month of the year, a mild spring. I had finished eating the morning rice, when your Second Great-Uncle, who had been to the magistracy to read the *Imperial Gazette* which came to us by courier from Peking, walked into the courtyard, and he was screaming and waving his arms: 'They have beaten us, they have beaten us. The Japanese devils have beaten us.' You see, even in those days, so long ago, your Second Great-Uncle was hasty and impulsive.

"It was your great-grandfather Taohung's seventy-fourth year; our parents were back from Kansu, but no one rejoiced. Great-Grandfather made us wear mourning because of the defeat. I remember how we felt, because we had admired the Japanese so much. We had not believed Japan would try her newly acquired ferocity upon us. We were so much alike, Japanese and Chinese, sharing the same culture. Often since then I have asked myself, why did they do this? I sometimes thought: always Japan will imitate someone. First it was us.

Then England and Germany. Next time, it may be America. Always this thirst for military power. The uncivilized heart, despite the politeness.

"Japan had indeed learnt well. Having successfully massacred her Christian missionaries and persecuted her converts (who were asked to walk on the cross or themselves be crucified), she was left in her scorpion peace, being much poorer than China, and not worth the trouble. Then she made her Industrial Revolution in double-quick time, by the simple device of confiscation of lands from her feudal lords, and the driving of underpaid peasants into her factories. She became thus, in a short time, a capitalist power, and such a power has to look for markets; she knew she would have to compete against the West one day. But her first step must be the seizure of territories for raw material, and that meant China.

"From her island bastion she watched the hacking up of China by the Western powers, and decided the time had come to take her share. Already in 1854 Yoshida Shoin, a Japanese reformist, had written: 'We should be strong militarily ... we must have more territory ... Manchuria, Formosa, Luzon, other islands in the south ... We must annex the weak, attack the stupid, seize Korea, conquer China. What we have lost to Russia and the United States can be made up by Korea and Manchuria ...' By 1854 Japan had already lost some islands in the Pacific to America, and part of Sakhalin to Russia.

"Japan watched, and saw England and France and Russia, and their handiwork in China. She observed the United States march eastward, extending her frontiers across the Pacific, which she would turn into her *mare nostrum,* to Asia. She decided the best defence for herself was aggression. 'Make the world tremble before Great Japan!'

"So she put herself to school with the West and worked hard, and had three advantages over China: she was small, no one was afraid of her, everyone laughed at her; she was not quagmired in the rigidity of a moral code, nor handicapped by the perpetuation of a proud historic past of three millenniums; more importantly, she had a native, nationalistic ruling power, Japanese ruling their own people, not a foreign, self-centred dynasty, cowardly and corrupt, verminous with eunuchs, entirely concerned with safeguarding itself, gladly selling great morsels of their possessions to maintain their state."

Today in 1964 some historians aver that if China had had a

native dynasty at the time, she might have taken her place in the modern world more rapidly; and the sense of injury that was to be carried forward into the twentieth century might have been dispelled, and there would have been a capitalistic China, not a Communist Revolution. But is it of any use to soliloquize on what might have been? I do not believe it could have been different. The last thing the West wanted was a strong China, capitalistic, or not. If we are not capitalistic today, it is because the West broke our native capitalism very early on, or rather never allowed it to grow. But it was never so worried about Japan, knowing her small, not all-sufficient to herself like China, and therefore vulnerable; a follower, not a leader among the nations, however hard she may try.

"From the time of her victory over us," said Third Uncle, "Japan came to be regarded as almost equal to the white Powers. Had she not proved herself equal, winning her spurs in the world's banditry? There was no stopping her. 'Who conquers China, conquers the world,' wrote Japanese military experts. And for the next half-century, she would try to conquer China."

The indemnity Japan got from the war of 1895 was to finance her further industrial Great Leap Forward for twenty years. But China in 1895 could not pay. Two hundred million ounces of silver was too much, more than the revenue available to her after having paid all she owed the Western powers for the previous wars they had waged upon her. And there were the Manchus, only three million of them in five hundred million people, but they consumed one-third of the accredited revenue of the land.

The state bankers of Shansi, who had always managed the silver bullion finances of the Empire, proclaimed their inability to find money to pay the Japanese war indemnity. A loan was contracted, the largest of a series of crushing loans, and it was England who arranged the loan. Within forty months, fifty-five million pounds in foreign loans were contracted for; the French, the Germans and the Russians quarrelled over who would lend money to China. Britain won the largest portion of the loan.

It was the five per cent loan of 1895, to pay the war indemnity of Japan, which really ruined the Empire. China had to pay twelve hundred millions of francs; the repayment of interest on loans, even at the moderate rate of five per cent, required sixty million francs per year, and this indemnity added to the previous loans in arrears came to about seventy million francs. But the total customs receipts of the country were only eighty million francs (customs were under foreign control) in silver. And as silver at the time was depreciating, the Powers were only willing to give a loan if the interest could be paid in gold, and gold had to be purchased, its price not under Chinese control.

In order to guarantee this loan the West asked for mortgages and concessions in land, in mines, in natural resources, in factories, in import goods, and in railways.

Then started the terrible years, the years of accelerated wholesale, headlong plunder. China's weakness exposed, the Powers rallied to dismember the foundering land. Britain took control of the whole of the Great River basin, from Shanghai to Szechuan. In the words of Archibald J. Little:* "A region to China, what the valley of the Mississippi is to North America, what the valley of the Amazon is to South America; the heart of a continent, comprising six hundred thousand square miles, one hundred and eighty million of the most industrious and peaceful people on the world's surface; a magnificent prospect."

Russia took Manchuria and Mongolia as her dependencies, building railways there to move her troops into China. France again marshalled her forces for an invasion of Yunnan. America evolved the Open Door Policy, which meant that no goods from any country were to be taxed more than any other country's goods, when imported into China. Japan began to prepare for another war. Not to be outdone, Kaiser Wilhelm II of Germany suddenly proclaimed China the Yellow Peril; when she was at her weakest, with a fine flourish of drama he announced himself leader of Christendom and the White Race in a crusade against the coloured and the yellow, and seized the province of Shantung; all because he had not done well in the quartering of Africa, and wanted his share of the spoils in China. Who would have thought that the forgotten little man with a withered arm would yet have left his lunatic mark upon the world in this phrase? Perhaps because he was one of the first in giving voice to the myth of Aryan, white superiority, which still finds exponents today?

"For me," said Third Uncle, fanning away the brooding heat thickening the night, "1895 is when the Revolution began.

*Archibald J. Little, *The British Sphere of Influence*, Oriental Club, London, October 1898.

If you get to the point where you have nothing to lose, then you get up and make a revolution. But a revolution is not made only by the people who are exploited, it is also prepared by those who exploit them. That is the paradox of history. The Japanese, the West, all of them helped to bring about the Revolution of 1911, and who knows but that after this big War another Revolution may come?"

The time was 1940; already we both knew, knew in our silent hearts, that another revolution might not be too far distant. At the time both of us hoped that it would not happen, for we had much to lose.

"After 1895 our Family also began its slide to ruin," continued Third Uncle. "I knew, because I was always at home, in Szechuan. Ever since the Taiping, the Nien and the Huei revolts, which our forefathers helped to put down, the land tax was collected two or three times a year; and every year it increased, and now taxes were collected at every level, district, county, province, as well as state. Taxes on buildings, ground rent, land sales, on salt, iron, levies for militia support, for relief of bandit-infested areas. But none broke the back of our native industry and commerce more effectively than the *likin* or road-toll taxes. Previously there was no tax barrier between city and countryside, or along the roads and rivers. But in 1860 the toll tax was imposed to pay for the Taiping wars. All overland and river trade, traffic between town and countryside, province and province, all goods were taxed in transport, and so our commerce was paralysed with taxation, especially in and out of Szechuan. We paid fourteen to twenty taxes on a distance of seventy miles, so that a load of tobacco from Chengtu, by the time it reached Chungking, was taxed twenty-five times and was four times its original price. And after 1895 the taxes were almost doubled. But the revenue decreased, because the bulk of revenue was earmarked to discharge the interest on war indemnities and loans contracted with the West.

"Our tobacco commerce shrank instead of growing. And now a flood of foreign goods came in, for there was one exception to the imposition of taxes: and these were foreign goods. They came in under a 'transit pass', totally exempt by the treaties imposed upon us through wars, and thus paid one tax only, varying from five to seven-and-a-half per cent *ad volorem,* and no more. And so all our native industries were ruined.

"Our merchants, to save themselves, refused their own manufacturers' native goods, bought British and Japanese goods in Shanghai, transported them into Szechuan under transit pass, and thus made a profit while those who kept to native industries lost out. Those who wanted to create Chinese factories and start any industries without foreign participation were thus doomed in advance. In these conditions it was impossible for China to modernize and to industrialize. Finally, by treaty, our own native produce, such as raw cotton, could be brought out from the interior on a transit pass by foreign company, and travelled exempt from the *likin* tax, while our Chinese merchants had to pay the *likin* tax to take the same material out! Timber or oil, opium and tobacco, was thus bought and taken by Western companies at one-fifth of the cost to a Chinese merchant company. How could there be independent large native capitalists? To survive, a Chinese merchant must become a middleman to a foreign company, reducing himself to the role of employee, of servant, to the Western merchant.

"Our tobacco trade was strangled, and later tobacco became a monopoly in the hands of the British–American Tobacco Company in Middle and South China, while in North China it fell into the hands of the Japanese; it was exported on an outward transit pass, not taxable, taken to the foreign cigarette factories erected in Shanghai, Hankow and Tientsin, in the foreign concession territories, enclaves of Western territory on our soil, and then re-sold to us in the form of cigarettes.

"Handloom textiles were exterminated by the import of cotton goods, first from Lancashire, later made in India where British companies benefited from cheaper native labour. Later still the Japanese built factories in China's treaty ports, flooded the market with textiles, and annihilated the British textile market. And the Chinese labour was just as cheap as Indian labour, and even more hard-working.

"Taxes were levied on Chinese junks and boats plying the rivers, but never on the foreign steamer companies which now started to go up and down the Great River after 1895.

"And so the provinces began to go bankrupt, and to save themselves kept back a larger share of the taxes, instead of paying it to the centre, to offset the ruinous losses. The more the Manchu dynasty needed money, the more reluctant the provinces became to remit it, the more money remained glued to the local officials' hands.

"But your father never paid attention to economics," said Third Uncle. "He was a scholar, believing in education and reform. Scholars are afraid of violence, afraid to fight, afraid to kill. But change is not an even river, gently flowing. It cannot be held to the sedate pace of an official sedan chair. And because of this war with Japan in 1895 there came a great clamour for change, chiefly from the scholars. A Reform Movement under the scholar Kang Yuwei came to prominence, but only for a short while. Its downfall was swift and bloody, and it affected your father very much, I think, though we never discussed it. Though I was young at the time, something in me scoffed at all the talk of democracy, which the Reformists liked so much. Obscurely I knew that true authority resided elsewhere, that power could only come through armed might. Only when we were strong would people respect us, as the Whites began to respect Japan after 1895 because they were strong. Your father was a gentle poet. He hated violence when all around was violence.

"Now there is another war, with Japan. And who knows what will happen after this war?"

The night of 1940 thickened, the pall of heat would not lift. Tomorrow the Japanese would bomb us again. Third Uncle and I sipped and fanned, and waited for the coolness of dawn.

SEVEN

My father, Chou Yentung of Chengtu, wrote:

The land that is my country, China, wields a quality of hugeness, a magnitude about her rivers and plains, mountains and deserts, her history and her people. All these seem of a size, a longevity, multitude, mass and abundance which exalt the spirit. Undaunted she stands, weathering the ages in tranquil, elemental massiveness. The machine will one day make her gigantic terms manageable, harness her rivers, cleave her mountains; but before the machine, Man in his ingenuity, with his toil and in his numbers, did what he could with hands and mind, and he did a great deal. He came to terms with the land and its enormous caprices. He loved it, cherished it, ploughed and planted it, and painted it and sang it and especially he wrote of it, carving his words in stone whenever he could, trying to midget into writing her greatness, to encompass her vastness with man-made poem, to extol her serenity and her sorrows. He carved sentences on the slopes of her every mountain, in every cave, above every spring, ascribed to each valley and summit a legend, a name and a spirit. He rode her mighty rivers at his peril, and sang to those dangers which imperilled him. And thus he conquered his own land, made it fertile and beautiful to his eyes, and was content. And in the blind country of the word, he sometimes believed that he understood her altogether, and was master of her eternity.

Thus when I was thirteen years old, ascending the towered walls that watch the water above the Nine-Eyed Bridge where the junks leave for the precarious voyage down the Great River, I would splay out my hand to grip the landscape, to knead a thousand miles within my finger-stretch. Into me, intake of my breath, entered the lovely plain, and its thousand spring exhilarations. I would possess the spring, the oriole in the tree staking its territory call, the thrushes easy to cajole into song, the mulberry agleam with leaf above its mirroring shade. With apt quotation I possessed them, syllables on silk paper, for had I not been taught to bewitch the real world into a word shape more lasting than the transient reality where all things flowed and flowered to elude us? All the poetry of two thousand years, the classics, were in stone, indelible, a forest of polished granite, sentences in the temple of Confucius at Sian,* the Word preserved through the ages. And all this was at my call, for I was a scholar-to-be, one of the privileged of the land.

The shrewd winter morning frost, intruding like a murderer on the run, had given place to clear sunlight. Ascending light-bodied, furs discarded, I felt like entering the blue sky, so clear the air, free of that fertile dankness, that grey canopy of mist and mildew and sousing rain which encloses the fruitful plain and keeps it green despite the winter, so that the swallow never really leaves.

My friend – the one I loved and who loved me, Liu Tachun – and I thus climbed to seek the spring high on the city towers, and reaching far out with our eyes, out to the great snow

*At Sian all the classics of China are engraved on 1,816 stone tablets, 9 ft. by 3 ft. by 2 ft., called the Stone Forest.

mountains of Tibet, sought what was visible only a few spring days each year. And this spring of 1898 we espied it, floating above the grey-jade substance of the earth, the shimmering triangular white peak of Miniaganka, the unconquered mountain. My heart leapt, but immediately my lips said: "Oh, how shall I ride the snow goose of ambition?" Tachun squeezed my hand, looking but mute. Above his brows drawn as with painting brush, the clear spread of his forehead was no lesser brightness.

At thirteen my song of life was written for me, out of the massive accumulation of past sayings, past sententiousness, phrases and formulas, of great poets and mean ones. Here lay the fresh-born earth, the wide-laid plain, its edges drawn and measured as by a foot-rule, vanishing into a moth-coloured horizon. New irises grew on the water's edge, young water, colour of the sky, in a million splinters soaked the earth; rilled into minute channels, it wound a thousand million coils into unnumbered small fields, symmetrical, hand-turned, smooth edged; in them the growing rice was green and the rape began its pale-gold magic carpet. And yet all was divested of the sudden shock of discovery, since all had been described.

I sought a frenzy of new words which would be mine alone, thought and wrought by me. But the sleight of hand of previous lore divested mine of sweetness.

Green and gold, the fields stretched beyond our footfall to mount the hill slopes, looping the slopes in crescent curves, turned by hand, made by hand, as far as eye could reach. Here and there magnolia burst in a rash of white poised birds. Snowfalls of plum flowers scattered the ground.

Harsh are the ways to Szechuan, a paradise enclosed, sang the poets. But many poets had trod these harsh and perilous ways; and painters had drawn the mountains which barred from us the rampaging winds of the steppes, and softened their gauntness to cocoon us in misty bloom. I no longer saw the mountains' wizardry because of these paintings. Yet no one had painted Miniaganka, rising from the earth, visible from city of Chengtu. This was our discovery, my friend Tachun and I. Ours alone.

Four-square and moated city, gates older than Peking and a history of three thousand years, Chengtu basked and dawdled in the plain. In and around her the epic feats of the Three Kingdoms had been enacted, and we knew them all. At ease she ungirdled her small fields about her, sure with age, arrogant in her learning, her guilds and her crafts, her books and her scholars. All legend was history as history became legend about her. Along her river and about her plain and far beyond, her fortresses and tumuli, temples and shrines, her trees over a thousand years old, were witness of battles fought, phrases said, stragagems of war and politics; all was in place, known, written and recorded. Was there nothing left to discover?

In that spring of 1898 Tachun and I were preparing for the district examination. He was two years older than I, less studious; he loved to wander in the fields outside the walls, and together we roamed many hours. Yet we were but following custom and precedent, for as young scholars it was right to taste the spring and return home to write a new verse about it, and nothing new.

By the river women in coarse blue dipped the long narrow ramie cloth in the flowing water which tightened its web, and in their hovels the soft click of the weavers' looms beat time. Hakka potters squeezed wet clay, oily as the manured earth of our fields, making spring water jars, to dry quickly in sunny weather. And all was as in *The Book of Songs*, where by the river the hemp is steeped and the reeds float, the young men loiter, their laughter light as the pebbles boys skim upon a water surface.

A twinkle of butterflies, in sudden gale, pelted above the young bean fields, and we went home to find silken words about this spring episode. The aroma* of our ink tablets mingled with the fragrance of our desk orchids.

All was recorded; nothing forgotten?

At night, in the young leaves a glow-worm was snared. The drowsy plain filled with the sleepy whimper of water and the stir of a million insects. Tachun and I nearly wept; words did not come. Next day my emotion evaded my brush.

All day and half the night, bent over the fertile earth, the short thickset people of the plain, pale and stubby, worked the earth by hand, turned each mote of it by hand, plastered each ditch by hand, ploughed with men to pull the wooden plough, their feet and their legs sinking in the dung-thick, wet, oily soil. Carrying and planting, hoeing and banking, hauling water, treading the treadmill wheel, all day and half the night at an enormous treadmill of toil went on by hand, by hand, all by hand. We saw it not.

*In China, ink tablets *smelt* good, and had ground pearls and gold in them.

Treading the mud, treading the wheel, planting and ploughing and manuring, bent over the earth in constant service, as
if they owed it to the fat earth basking in its dampness; but to
us this terrible toil was part of the landscape, almost its due,
at least due to us, as we lounged about, looking for a felicitous
phrase.

On the slopes, replacing the wheat which had once grown
there, the poppy nodded, white flowers sleek, wide-eyed.
When our chair-bearers lifted us on to their shoulders and
trotted to the hills in the summer, they had to stop and smoke
every four hours, otherwise they could not carry us. All
around us was spread a lavish death: too much work, too little
to eat, and opium. The parchment skin, yellow tarred, sticking
to the cheekbones, the film-like white muslin on the eye, the
skeleton, flesh-denuded, protruding through the skin: opium
did this, but only to those who did not eat enough. For us of
the gentry, a pipe gentled post-prandial flatulence into
pleasant dreams. But no poem had been written about this,
and I did not see it. Tachun became at times moody, looking
round him, but my eyes were not his, and I never knew whether
he saw it then, as in my memory's eye I see it now.

By Chengtu's south-west wall stands the Temple of the Ram,
twelve hundred years old, and there every spring the greatest
fair of all is held, to which hundreds of thousands come, and
it is called the Show of Flowers. The temple is Taoist, and
Laotze's birthday is celebrated there, from the fifteenth of
the second month till the middle of the third month, during
which four weeks the great fair runs a joyous riot of blossom,
and all things under heaven are spread on stalls for all to see,
to enjoy, and to buy.

Facing the temple gates, a flight of five stone bridges humps
over the moat. Beyond run the narrow streets, where the rice
and livestock markets are held and the main bargaining in
crops is done. Here are live pigs, hens, ducks and pigeons, as
well as one hundred and eighty-six sorts of vegetables,
mountainous piles of mouth-watering freshness piled along a
mile of stalls, with men and women sloshing pails of clear
water upon their green and pink and yellow and white and
red. Within the gates of the temple, in an octagonal pavilion
with yellow glazed roof, Laotze, old philosopher with the
tremendous forehead and the childish smile, sits on a black
ox on his way out to Nowhere which is Everywhere.

In the main building are two bronze rams, both sacred, both

magical, dissimilar. The one on the left is truly of sheepfold stuff; the one on the right has claws like a tiger, a tail like a lion, the body of a deer and only one horn, for this ram was actually an incense burner dating back four hundred years, bought by a cabinet minister in the market in Peking, later brought by him to Chengtu and given to the temple. The Taoist priests proclaimed a miracle, and told the tale of a miraculous animal sent by Laotze to the temple. Thousands came, and the sick were cured, rubbing the ram's unique horn. But a sceptic scholar examined the ram, and found on its chest the seal of the shop in Peking which had sold it, and which the Taoist priests had not been able to erase altogether. However, more thousands believed in the power of the ram, and crowded round it and rubbed its horn and face and whispered in its ears. For it is said that those who want revenge against an enemy need only tell the ram his name and their story, because this ram is also a militant avenger of wrongs. At night in a dream the ram leaves the temple and goes to butt the evildoer, who thereupon falls sick and occasionally dies. Anyone with any sickness had but to touch the rams, either one, to be healed. Gradually both the rams' surfaces are worn with rubbing, but the coffers of the temple always bulge with money. Neither Tachun nor I believed in the rams, but the fair was a wonderful thing to see.

And the fair was also a festival for women, one of the few when ladies of good family, walking the spring in its delightfulness, would come to the temple gardens, attended by their maidservants, and show off their new clothes, like azure peacocks ambling. They came to taste the weather and to view the flowers, but actually they were there to be looked at.

And this was also the one great occasion for lovers to meet and to exchange letters, or handkerchiefs embroidered with their names. Young men, matched to girls they had never seen and would not otherwise see before they both sat on the bridal bed after the wedding evening cup of wine, would try to arrange, by bribing the matchmaker, a swift passing glance at the face of their intended as she swayed, frail in the delicate air, scented and soft in the soft spring wind, apparently all unknowing.

Great ladies and courtesans were there, and also country girls with their mothers, carrying in their aprons a clutch of eggs or a young duck, the older women worn with work and child-bearing, limping on bound feet, and for a walking-stick they cut a length of purple sugar cane; strolling among the flowers made their faces young again.

Hand in hand Tachun and I sauntered among the cages of painted-eyebrow songsters, thrushes, jackdaws and magpies, parrots and pheasants, young eagles from the Cool Mountains and hawks from the south, the cages of precious cats and the ivory-lidded gourds of fighting crickets. Tachun loved birds and had a great collection of them in beautiful cages, with porcelain bowls for food and rattles to amuse them, fine wands of rosewood and ivory shaped as boughs to take his birds out for walks, cage-free, so that they might fly about at will for exercise and pleasure, before returning to perch on their master's finger.

Here were Manchus too, buying young hawks for wearing on their wrists, a habit, though they had largely given up hunting and riding.

Here were all the flowers of the world, with no cold to frighten them, a feast to gladden the heart of spring. And all the peoples of Szechuan came here. Not only the Han people, like ourselves, but also the Miaos, sturdy and tall and beautiful, who live in the mountains, eat buckwheat cakes baked in ash, and sing to each other from valley to valley with the clearest voices; they came down from their high places to the fair, in embroidered clothes, their women with silver bangles round their necks and their ankles, and silver earrings cascading down their cheeks. Also the Tibetans, with pelts of bears and snow leopards, their guns and their prayer mills, their fur hats askew, walking in their own redolence of yak's butter; and the Lolos, surly and distant, from the Cool Mountains, mostly the landlords' sons with fox fur round their hats; and the Yis, the Hueis, the Mosi, and many another of our diverse peoples of Szechuan, who live in the untouched forests and the ranges between the plain and Tibet.

And in the fair's time our families would change the hangings and carpets and cushions in the houses, and all the furs would lie in the sun of the courtyards, to be stored later in camphor-wood chests till the next cold weather.

But the fair of 1898 at the Ram Temple was not only flowers and birds, pale-skinned maidens burning devotion incense, young scholars ogling them in search of unspoiled passion. It was also a time of unease, hidden dread. Every year since 1892 there had been flood, or drought, in one or other province in our land, and insurrection everywhere; since the Opium Wars not a year had passed without a rising. In spite of the enchantment of the fair and flowers, beneath the perfume of blossom and incense we could smell the smell of trouble.

Among the crowds went Taoist doctor-priests in grey, with their long hair in a topknot, Brothers of the Robe, secret society men belonging to the Kelao, the Society of Brothers. The Kelao was one of the many brotherhoods founded centuries ago; they claimed descendance from the first brotherhood of all, that of the time of the Three Kingdoms. There were many secret societies, taking various names, Heaven and Earth, White Lotus, Triad, and in all of them there was some element of Taoism, giving a spiritual and mystic depth to their fraternity. The Kelao were of Szechuan, and claimed as their patron saint the first Ming emperor, Chu Yuenchang; since resistance to the Manchus had continued for decades in Szechuan, they as well as all the other secret societies were anti-Manchu and pro-Ming. They had been proscribed and driven underground, and degenerated as such brotherhoods do when there is nothing noble to fight for, so that many of these Kelao ran brothels and opium houses, and hired themselves out to the landlords to extort rent from poor peasants. Nevertheless, when the time came for a rising, the Kelao of Szechuan as well as the other sects became again hostile to the Manchus, and this was now evident. Disguised as Taoist medicine men, they travelled carrying messages, acting as liaison among the provinces. The brotherhoods have their own passwords, gestures, slang; no one is allowed to know these who is not initiate, and who reveals them dies.

At night the walls of Chengtu were plastered with antidynastic as well as anti-missionary posters, put up by the followers of Yu the Hothead, a rebel against the dynasty, who had led some villagers to beat up a French priest who had two Chinese wives and extorted money from the peasants. The Kelao supported Yu. And the people were stirred with whispers of insurrection in other provinces, with tales of resistance to the foreigners, unbearable in their extortions. It was openly said that the Manchus were selling out to the foreigners, that a hundred thousand people had been slaughtered in a rising in Kuangtung, the executioners beheading them at the rate of five hundred a day, and that another rising must take place.

As we walked among the flowers and heard the muttered

phrases, I sometimes smelt blood and was seized with fear, for I dreaded bloodshed, and desired lofty visions in men, brought by natural virtue and wise concord, thinking them possible by moderation and virtue alone. I knew not then that men are both noble and vile, that nothing is begot but through pain and action; that man swims a sea of pain harsher than granite, and that he must swim it to save himself. I saw the beauty of the plain, but not its heart-searching toil; joyed in the speckle and glint of water, and knew not each furrow turned on its life-giving mud fertilized not only with water and manure but also with the blood of men. How much blood through the centuries had been spilt in the beautiful plain, how much would still have to be spilt? A great river of blood sped by me, I stood on its grassy bank, looked away, and quoted poetry.

But not so my friend. As the spring deepened I saw a shadow over his piercing eyes, his smooth forehead darkened. He read much, many books of the New Learning, forbidden but which he somehow procured. He would speak of machines and inventions, and I begged him to be careful, eager all the same to hear about these terrifying and wonderful things.

About the crowded teahouses went the spies of the Manchus. In the open-air spaces, under the trellised honeysuckle dripping fragrance and shade, between the harmony trees and the bamboo groves, agents of the dynasty loitered, sipping tea, listening to the talk of the scholars. The Manchus were afraid of intellectuals, afraid of new ideas.

The copper kettles jetted steam, on lacquered tables the tea-cups shone their flowered porcelain, on the bamboo chairs waiters slapped embroidered cushions. Beggars dragged their sores and drowned our talk in sing-song lamentations; wizened children somersaulted and twisted their heads backwards between their feet among the tables, shooed away they returned, pertinacious as flies, hungry and mangy like the dogs about our feet with which they fought for scraps.

The brothels hung out tasselled lanterns of welcome, the singing girls went in clusters to the flower show; some of our older friends were adepts, but Tachun and I were young and only heard their stories. In each brothel was a spy, to report on the scolars frequenting it, to ask the girl what had been said. And now that the city was filling with scholars come for the matriculation examinations, the spies were very busy. An old man for forty, whose wife and daughters worked at stitching cloth and embroidering coats to support his examinatorial attempts, in Chengtu for a fourth try at the examination, came to a grim end that spring. He never spent money in the tea-houses, for he was witty, and the sons of landlord families paid for his tea and his company. He managed to visit the whorehouses, and there amuse everyone yet spend very little. He was accused of being a rebel, in league with rebels, and beheaded.

As the spring went on, the countryside rose, spasmodic out-bursts here and there, and Manchu garrisons went out to slaughter the peasants. Not only our Brothers of the Robe, but other brotherhoods, the White Lotus, the Small Knives, the Heaven and Earth, and the Triad, in other provinces, performed anti-dynastic rites, and prepared banners calling for the dynasty's overthrow. Persistent reports from the south of a rebel named Sun Yatsen, a monster who had eaten Christianity and wanted to overthrow the Empire, filtered through to us. Even some of the scholars of the Examination Board were mutinous; two of them petitioned the Throne, saying they could not go on correcting essays on antique poetry when the country was torn to pieces by foreigners, sold piecemeal in front of their eyes. They asked for a reform in the themes set for the examinations. One, well connected, was allowed to retire, the other was banished to the frontier province of Sinkiang.

The *Imperial Gazette* from Peking not only carried court news, but also printed news of rebellions being suppressed, and now there were so many suppressions, that although the rebels were always spoken of as bandits, and the ending was always the same, that the rebels had been exterminated and pacification perfected, we had begun to count these risings, and were excited and pleased in our hearts when they occurred.

At night from the streets we heard the click-clack of the bamboo clapper, and the high thin note of the three-string violin; an ambulant story-teller, singing tales of the last Ming days, scarcely disguising the names. And there were prodigious stories of cocks changing into hens, of women giving birth to monsters, of stars falling to earth; and these, with the floods and the droughts alternating every year since 1892, were all portents of disaster, of the passing of a dynasty.

And Tachun one day spoke to me of the long-haired Taip-ing, and told me that their last stronghold, Nanking, had never surrendered. Breached by dynamite, set off by the Englishman Gordon, not one of the forty thousand citizens left alive in the starving city surrendered, and all were put to the sword. "What magnificent courage," he said. His eyes were dilated, his voice choking.

"The Taiping were rebels," I replied.

And Tachun lowered his eyes, and said no more.

Another time he spoke of what some scholars were writing. Reformists, they were called, not of our province. They wanted changes to be made. "Nothing in the universe remains without change. Formerly India was a famous nation, but she preserved her traditions without change, and with a trading company of one hundred and twenty men the British subjugated her. Mencius said: 'A state first smites itself, then others will smite it.' "

He read to me from a book which he had obtained: "It will not be long before we, in China, will become as the Africans, slaves; for Westerners are very strict about race, and look upon other races as their enemies, treating the natives as cattle and horses. If we do not plan in advance, but are divided among ourselves, our fate shall be unspeakable, utterly unspeakable ..." Tachun's voice shook. "I do not know anything about Africa, except that their people have black skins." We stared at each other, full of wonder that some scholars were courageous enough to write these things.

As the spring became young summer, Tachun became bolder.

Persecution matures young rebels. At thirteen, fourteen, fifteen, some like Tachun already were rebels at heart, a word which really means patriots, in that they wanted to save our country, for it was clear that China was to be dismembered. But in Szechuan many of our elders were fearful of any change or reform, which they called the New Learning, and above all they were afraid of the moral pollution from the West. "Must we discard our institutions in order to save ourselves? Must we become barbarians in order to avoid annihilation? How can we learn strength, yet remain civilized? Learn to build machines and become powerful, yet retain our souls, our morality, our civilization, all that distinguished man from beast?"

While our elders debated this question, which they had been debating since the Taiping thirty years previously, the young were restless, saw too well what was happening, and questioned everything. Some, like Tachun, asked the scolars or merchants who travelled to Peking or Canton to smuggle books or essays of New Learning, or assembled in the teahouses to talk of reform and even of something more than reform. A few whispered the name of Sun Yatsen, the arch-rebel, who had a price on his head, and wanted to abolish the dynasty.

"Not all our art and poetry will save us. We must learn from the West everything except their wickedness. But we cannot learn unless we first become ourselves again. For three hundred years we have been under a foreign dynasty. To get rid of the foreigners, we must throw out the Manchus who are selling us to them ..."

"Doctrine or the moral concept varies according to the machinery which gives it concrete existence. A concept must be accomplished before it can be seen; the machinery for its accomplishment varies according to the means of production. When the machinery by which it is given being is changed, then the moral concept also finds itself changed ..."

These ideas in the forbidden books were so new, so staggering, that we could not apprehend them. What was a means of production? Afterwards I knew the name of the writer: a Reformist, called Tan Szetung.

When some railed against the Christian missionaries, Tachun would differ. "They are but instruments, not prime movers. Were we strong, they would not profit from our weakness. Are not our own officials in their cowardice helping them to oppress our people? Let us change ourselves, becoming strong, and they will go away."

But this was difficult for us to accept. Easier to blame the accessible, visible foreigner, the missionary, for every ill; the other concepts were too abstract for us. Tachun did not believe that missionaries gouged out the eyes and the hearts of children, a rumour much in vogue in Chengtu which led to attacks on the only missionary hospital in the city in 1899. When people shouted: "Kill the foreign sons of turtles," Tachun said: "It is like attacking the servants in a house, rather than the lord of the house." In this also he believed Tan Szetung, who ridiculed those who were blindly anti-Western, because he understood the precise way in which exploitation, with the compliance through cowardice of our own officials and the Manchu dynasty, was carried out.

Thus the currents of resentment ran strong, and the

Manchu dynasty was aware of them. They had agitators among us, skilled of tongue, smooth in argument, who spoke at the fairs, in the streets, to people gathered round them. And they deliberately focused our wrath on the foreigners. They circulated pamphlets depicting missionaries with red beards cutting the testicles of young male children. "Destroy the hospitals, refuse Western medicines, they are made with the organs of young children ..." They managed to twist the demand for change and the hatred against the Manchus into a hatred against the foreign missionaries alone.

Confucius said: "To lead a people into battle without first instructing them is a crime." The Manchus were clever: they turned the ire of the uninstructed against the foreigner, using their own subjects, whom they feared, to kill the foreigners, whom they hated.

The missionaries were now accused of monstrous crimes, which they had not committed. At that time the peasants did get rid of children born defective, sold their daughters when too many were born, because they were so poor they could not feed helpless or useless babies. It is not so now, there is no more infanticide. The missionaries picked up the babies, sometimes bought them, brought them up as converts, the results of their charity. Likewise they made converts, chiefly in times of famine and disaster, for the starving will say they believe anything to get a bowl of rice. And the missionaries had to show results for their efforts.

In times of famine to sell girl children was hard, and I have seen parents weep until they fainted as they sold their little ones; but it had to be done, and it was better to sell the child to a rich family that she might eat and be saved, than to let her perish of hunger. Likewise it was hard to put away a defective child, but why let it endure a life of suffering and die anyway?

All this was because of the poverty, the harsh, the terrible poverty of China's peasants. It can therefore be said the missionaries did "good" in rescuing a few, but this "good" was based upon our misery, and we had been reduced to this state in a great measure by the wars, and the indemnities exacted from us by the governments of those very nations which sent missionaries to us. The exercise of charity thus seemed no more than mockery of our pitiable state.

Upon this feeling the agents of the dynasty worked, nimble-worded, until the rousing slogans of the brotherhoods,

"Down with the Manchus, restore the Ming dynasty", changed and became: "Uphold the Dynasty, kill the Foreigners."

Came summer, with its long evenings, and sudden as pelting thunder the news that the Emperor, Kuanghsu, had at last received a petition of the scholar Kang Yuwei, the leader of the Reformists, accepted it, and issued an Imperial Edict to the nation:

Those who claim to be conservative patriots consider that all the old customs should be upheld and new ideas repudiated ... How can we possibly hope to hold our own among the nations with our army untrained, our resources disorganized, our scholars ignorant, our artisans without technical training ...

More edicts followed, sweeping headlong as autumn leaves in a wild wind, so fast the engravers had no time to carve them in stone. The Official Mansion was crowded, as were the teahouses, by students, scholars and the gentry, to read the *Imperial Gazette*. Some horrified, others elated, all stunned, the officials knelt to hear the edicts in the courtyard of the Official Mansion. Dreams fulfilled, without pain, without labour, for who was higher in the land than the Emperor? And if the Emperor wanted reform, who could oppose him?

Kang Yuwei was a gifted scholar, of an old family noted for its neo-Confucian scholarship. He and his friends, Liang Tsichao, and Tan Szetung, Tachun's favourite essayist, now became famous throughout the land. Even the foreigners were said to look favourably on Reform; good reports of Kang Yuwei had circulated abroad. Truly the beginning of a Golden Age, when kings listened to sages, and wisdom reigned supreme. If even the foreigners approved, then perhaps they would cease their ruthlessness, give up their exactions, and return in peace to their own lands? That was all we wanted.

Kang Yuwei's style was felicitous. His petitions were couched in deeply loyal terms. The reforms he proposed were presented as a recovery of the classical tradition, a reinterpretation of the past, rather than an innovation; and to be able to quote the past in support of changes validated them for our reluctant elders. But chiefly he and the other Reformists were of the gentry, scholars of our class. Of all the edicts, those which pleased young scholars like myself and Tachun most were the ones dealing with the building of schools of New Learning, and the reform of the examination regulations.

From now on, the themes of examinations would be current affairs, and the essays would be on modern subjects. We decided to prepare ourselves, by writing an essay on the reforms needed in Szechuan, and to set up a Young Reformist Study Club, whose aims would be National Salvation and Self-Strengthening, the aims of the association the Reformists had already set up in cities of the coast.

In July and August of 1898 more edicts came, encouraging the circulation of newspapers and magazines through the country, approving of the translation bureau for books on science and literature set up by Liang Tsichao, and exempting translated books from tax. This made us so happy that Tachun and I immediately decided to study foreign languages, and to set up as translators. But which language would we learn first? We decided it would be Japanese, because we could read it more easily, the characters being our own Chinese characters.

Some provincial governors also favoured reform and memorials came from them to petition the Emperor. Nearly every week now our elders assembled for discussion of the edicts, some in great dubiety, others in hesitant approval. In our family the edicts favouring trade and industry, the regulations concerning an abrogation of the onerous road-toll tax, lightening the duties which suffocated our commerce, won much approval; our tobacco trade would now be able to carry on without losing money.

Translated books now filtered in, brought by merchants from Canton and Hankow, and in August of 1898 a few schools for New Learning advertised their opening in Chengtu. But they did not open.

By September reaction set in. It was the abolition of sinecure appointments, the cutting down in expenditure in official posts, the doing away of certain provincial governorships, forbidding the sale of official ranks, the revision of civil and military posts, the suggestion that an examination be held to inquire into the competence of officials, which roused the gentry's hostility. Their employment as officials would be affected, should they be interrogated; there was already massive unemployment among many of the second- or third-rate scholars, the half-failures, and the lower gentry. Officials complained that Kang Yuwei was trying to break their rice bowls, military officers who held sinecures were angry and frightened. Rumours of the Emperor's illness circulated; some said he was mad, others that Kang Yuwei and Liang Tsichao were too arrogant, that they wanted power, and were giving the Emperor poison to numb his brain.

On September 21st, 1898, the Empress Dowager, Tze Hsi, mother of the Emperor, came out at the head of a group of officials and Manchu noblemen, and issued an edict that her son, Kuanghsu, was ill, that he could not manage affairs of state; thus it was necessary for her to abandon her retirement and to instruct the administration. It was Yuan Shihkai, the future strong man of China, who was to be so much liked by English politicians in the next two decades, who betrayed the Emperor and the Reformists to the Dowager Empress.

Now the most corrupt and retrograde Manchu nobles, Chinese officials and eunuchs took over the powers. September 21st was Emperor Kuanghsu's last day of freedom: for the remainder of his life he would be his mother's prisoner, until his death in 1908, which preceded that of his mother by thirty hours.

Immediately after this Palace *putsch* there were arrests and executions all over the country. Reformists were hunted down. Kang Yuwei and his friend Liang Tsichao escaped, with the help of Japanese and British diplomats, but Tan Szetung and five other scholars were slain by being cut in half at the waist. Magazines were banned, students' clubs were closed, all assemblies of students or scholars forbidden. All copies of Reformist writings were suppressed. A great bonfire of "corrupting and vile books" took place.

Within a month all reforms were rescinded. The examinations were to be held in the old manner, themes from the classics to form the topic of the essays. The special examination on economic affairs for officials was abolished. All books advocating reform were seized and destroyed; books advertised by the reform newspapers, and the printing presses which published them, were also destroyed. The translation bureau was closed. There were to be no more newspapers. Everyone, including scholars, was forbidden to submit memorials to the Throne or to discuss state affairs. Public meetings were forbidden. The editors of all newspapers were arrested. It took months before the fury of the purge began to slacken.

No one now dared to comment, or even to speak to friends, for fear of being betrayed. Some scholars who had acclaimed

Kang Yuwei's Reformist essays now condemned him, and posted denunciations on public boards that Kang was a monster who followed the Western barbarians in his inner mind, that he was trying to sell the country to the West, that he had blasphemed Confucian doctrine, should be condemned to ten thousand deaths. And yet, but a few weeks before, at least two scholars of Chengtu had circulated elegant essays on the necessity for reform, and even called a meeting to discuss a new strange word, difficult to pronounce, democracy.

From the first Reform Edict to the first head to roll, near one hundred days had passed, a middling summer, and now nothing would change, everything was as before.

The heat was going. The silkworms had done their hatching. The shimmer of heat above the fields, haze of moisture exhaled by the slack plain rising above the harvest rice, had given way to a sharpness, autumn. The moon was preparing its zenith, the cicadas had ended their summer shrieking. Soon the autumn rain would come, sinking quietly into the prepared furrows. A summer's storm bringing down a rush of leaves, the Reform Movement had come and gone bringing down heads, but all was as before.

Tachun and I still met daily, walked together, talked, but a subtle unworded change had come between us. We endured in each other's company a reticence and a fear. The future enters, transforms itself in us, is shaped and shapes us, as we are still in the present. Before the Hundred Days we believed ourselves but one spirit; when they had passed we found we were different, and daily the difference grew. One afternoon, for no reason, we quarrelled and I taunted him: "Have you burnt your books?" It was as if I bore Tachun a grudge because reform had failed. We had both been so elated, Tachun in particular, and now felt as the philosopher must have done when he rode the wind for many days aloft, borne by some invisible power, and then thinking an evil thought the weight of it bore him crashing to earth. We had crashed, lay prostrate, vaguely guilty. All our words were sickness, sourness, in our own mouths.

When I said: "Have you burnt your books?" Tachun began to sob, fists in his eyes, head upon his desk. Tears ran over his knuckles.

I walked out of his study into the garden of his house, along the winding pathways fragrant with autumn cassia, and when the black gates opened like a yawn to let me out the red sun at the end of the street was like a massacre. Here then we must sunder, going through a thousand miles of dead grass. Cold is the old well. Always the apt quotation came floating up, but it turned my belly to dark, dirty water.

Home and back to the classics, shrugging my shoulders against the importunate memory of Tachun's tears. No longer would I believe in anything; never again would I give myself to enthusiasm; it hurt too much to come tumbling down from heaven. I smelt the autumn chrysanthemums' sharp, spiky flavour, had a premonition of young manhood growing upon me, until then unknown. I emerged into knowledge of the flesh, tension of the pubertal body which makes for writing lyrics and falling in love with the idea of woman, and then with woman. But for me this first inkling of manhood was compounded with fear, with bitterness, with a world of ideas half shunned which had lasted a spring and a summer, and I was so infected by its outcome that I would for ever doubt the validity of further effort. I started then on the road of the indifferent, the timorous, the resigned, those who accept any tyranny with the excuse that they "hate hate" and "loathe violence", and believe in universal love. I wrote down, strong with ignorance, convinced after only one small failure: "I have seen men revolt, fail, and die miserably, all in vain, for all was as before. So what is the use of rebellion? Better keep quiet ..." I was to learn one day that this tacit acceptance of turanny is tyranny's strongest rampart and fortress, and that apathy, fear and indifference are the true murderers of men's liberties. But that was to come later.

I do not remember the themes of my examination; the days spent composing classical poem and rigid essay have gone from me. After the ceremonies at the Confucian Hall, two thousand of us sat in cloistered cabins, in the long examination rows, secluded for days. I do not remember a word of what I wrote, but I knew that as my hand held the writing brush poised above the paper some warning voice inside me whispered: "Be not too bold." Here and there the interjections of a word denoting some happy newness, but not too much newness: the Examiner was very much against New Learning. Some spirit other than my own guided my brush in genial sentences; my mind, clear as those mornings when the peak of Miniaganka, triangular shaft of snow piercing the sky, can be seen from the walls of Chengtu, produced sentences of pomp and rhythm which meant absolutely nothing. I have of course erased them from my heart.

The result was that I came out at the head of the list of candidates. Many failed. Tachun also failed.

A few weeks later Tachun came to see me one evening. We strolled the bamboo groves by the river garden, a steady cold wind blew the bamboo about, our talk was strained. Night deepened, our servants waited, grumbling for their food, holding the lanterns as we paced. Tachun told me he was going away. "To Canton. Then I shall leave for Japan. To join the Revive China Society of Sun Yatsen."

Again my heart beat intolerably, a renewal of this fearful, dangerous restlessness, and a dread seized me so that I felt shaken, seized and clawed at. I cried: "Sun Yatsen is a known bandit, and this is an illegal society, it advocates violence. Anyone who is a member is to be executed. Sun is a notorious rebel who has eaten Christianity, a hideous monster with green eyes and red hair."

"But he is right in what he says. Reform will not do. Nothing will succeed except a revolution."

"If even a scholar like Kang Yuwei has failed, what can Sun Yatsen do, who is not even a scholar?"

"Do you think that we, the scholars, are really all-powerful, all-knowing? Do you think that we have made Heaven and Earth? The first Ming Emperor, Chu Yuenchang, was a renegade monk and a peasant. My ancestor, Liu Pei, the Han Emperor, was a pedlar of straw sandals. Have you forgotten history? We the scholars have done little but write memorials and protest."

"But Sun has told people he is a second Hung Hsiuchuan, leader of the Taiping. He wants to do as the Taiping did. This is rebellion."

"Who says the Taiping were wrong?"

This was too much. After all, Great-Grandfather, Grandfather and Father had fought to put down such rebels as the Taiping. A true scholar stands by his steadfastness. Tachun was now becoming a traitor, a rebel. While I groped for words, he went on:

"Why don't you come with me? There are many who want to join Sun's movement. Many who want to save China."

In the autumn night I hoped Tachun would not see the fear in my face. The reticent moon did not appear. The wind blew moans into the bamboo groves. Spies might be lurking behind every one of them; the trees siding the alley we paced were like gigantic listening eunuchs.

"Tachun, I pray you, reflect. What shall we do if the dynasty is overthrown? A house without a master is open to the robbers from four directions. This is against Heaven's law."

"You know the classics," said Tachun, sarcastic. "But Heaven sees through the people's eyes, hears through the people's ears. The people have always risen to destroy dynasties when they proved incapable and tyrannous, and this too is a law of Heaven and in the classics. It is right and virtuous to rebel against a wicked rule. You know that, my so able friend."

He said this bitterly, and I felt that however much Tachun loved me it must have been hard for him to stomach failure while I had received honours as a brilliant talent.

"Sun Yatsen's reputation is very bad. Even the Reformists call him a bandit. Why rush to this fellow, who has a price on his head? When the waters are turbid with mud all fishes' eyes are pearls. Think of your family, what will happen to them if you are known as a rebel? They will suffer for you, be punished for you, as the Hung clan was put to the sword because of Hung Hsiuchuan."

I was left alone with the nostalgic colour of longing, the colour of the night, a moonless night, a scattered sky.

In 1908 while I was still in Europe a friend wrote to tell me that Liu Tachun had died. He had gone to Canton, then to Hongkong. I do not know whether he met Sun Yatsen; but after the Boxer uprising of 1900 he sailed to Japan, in 1902 or 1903. There he later became a member of the Revolutionary League founded by Sun Yatsen, and took part with other students from Szechuan in beating up an official sent by the Imperial Government to watch over students in Japan and report their revolutionary activities. Later he came back to China, and in 1906 and 1907 took part in armed uprisings (two of the many engineered by Sun Yatsen's Revolutionary League between 1904 and 1912). He was captured. Dressed as a peasant, he refused to recant, insulted the magistrate, and was beheaded.

The friend who wrote to me of his death thought it fitting to eulogize his brilliance while mourning his end: "Ambition boundless as the ocean, but a fate as thin as paper, the intrepid son of a noble house falls ..." A disaster, for he was an only son, and the branch of the great family to which he belonged became extinct with him.

But Tachun was the voice of my heart in the year 1898. Even now I feel the yearning for his presence, his mind, for the honour, the courage and the vision he had, shining in my memory as the peak of Miniaganka seen that spring morning above the plain. For an old man, there are no new emotions; remembered emotions are his treasures, and if he can still feel them as he once did, if they have not turned to dust with the years, then he is indeed lucky. I can remember that autumn night better than I can a good many years with my wife Marguerite. Yet in the matter of time, she occupied nearly the whole of my life, Liu Tachun only a few months. Perhaps I should have gone with him ... but I was not a revolutionist, I would never be a pioneer of any kind.

And now my seventieth year sees no son or daughter of my own by me, and the only person in the world to care for my comfort, to bring me tea when I work, is an ex-soldier of the Red Army, Comrade Lu, a peasant. He is nearer to me than any son, as he bends over my old blue prints, assiduously learning from me, the intellectual, the scholar, and those like me who had everything and who did so little. While his father and grandfather suffered and starved, were killed, paying with their labour and their lives, and the lives of their children dead or sold, for the sustenance of an old, stinking, dying order, while his kind was cut down, as grass is cut down, in those countless peasant uprisings that have gone on and on and on through the centuries, until the last of all, the triumphant one that changed our world for us, what did we do? We wrote verse, each rock and mountain and pavilion bore evidence of our noble sentiments, our refined taste. It is good that some of us, like Liu Tachun, went out to be with our people, to suffer and to die with them. Too few perhaps, but better than none.

Today we meet over the same blue print, Lu the peasant and I, and he is nearer to me than any son. Lu the peasant will be here, continuing my work, when I am gone; and no son of my own is worth what he is worth.

The next year, 1899, in spring I went back to the Ram Temple with my brothers and some cousins. But I could not bear the spring or the flowers, and went home swiftly, pleading sickness, and never returned to the Ram Temple again.

From 1898 when my father, Chou Yentung of Chengtu, took the old classical examination after the One Hundred Days Reform had failed, to 1964 when I read his memories, is sixty-six years; but in man's mind, untrammelled by immediacy, undeluded by clocks, it is but yesterday and today.

In the autumn of 1964 I, his daughter, went to visit the Ram Temple of Chengtu. Like all monuments in China today, it was repainted and repaired. The gardens had been enlarged and turned into a permanent park. Between the flowery bushes, under the honeysuckle in arches, by the wistaria drooping over rocky ponds, along the alleys boled by paulownia, cedars and camphor, young lovers walked, holding hands and giggling, or sat on benches and talked earnestly of the future. I walked inside the main temple building, and there were the rams, right and left of the altar with its Taoist Triad. They shone as they always had. On the left the benevolent one, a true bovine, meek, almost pretty, wore a shining copper bell round his neck; on the right the combative one-horned beast, his face worn into holes with rubbing, his ears worn with whispering, a small plaque upon his chest on which half-disappearing characters could be traced: Peking, Liulichang market. It has the pads and claws of a tiger, the tail of a lion, the slim body of a deer; in the centre of its forehead grew a single horn.

"Why, it's a unicorn," I cried.

My cousins who were with me, the sons and daughters of my father's brothers, said that it had always been called a ram.

The ram-unicorn looked strangely like the beautiful beast I had seen in a Beauvais tapestry hung in a Paris museum, where it held converse with a lady in a field of flowers.

"Let us take a picture of you with the one-horned ram," said my cousins.

In front of the main temple building the octagonal pavilion with yellow glazed tiles still sheltered the statue of Laotze, riding on his black ox in search of Verity. He was now protected by a glass case. Before him glowed an oil lamp. On the floor were the Three Dots of the Taoist Trinity. On the wooden ceiling were carved the Eight Trigrams. The Taoist flag, with its Northern Star, symbol of Tao, which had led so many peasant militias to war against oppressors, hung on the wall.

The Taoist clergy were in conference, a meeting of philosophers. In Peking, Chengtu and other cities, scholars were re-assessing the writings of Taoism. Taoism, more than

Confucianism, had contained the germ of scientific ideas. A famous English professor and Sinologist had been here very recently and had discussed Taoism with the clergy. They had no time to talk to me of rams. But my cousins told me that every year, in spring, the flower fair still takes place. It is, so my cousins say bigger and better than ever.

EIGHT

LIKE all Chinese of his generation, and mine, Third Uncle dated events in his life by historical episodes. The year my father was born was spoken of in the Family as "the year after the Sino-French War", and 1898 was always "the year of the Reform Event". Everything that happened on a large scale influenced also private life; passive or active, all participated in the history of their country. The Chinese have always been history-minded, the one people with a continuous recorded chronicle of their own for two thousand five hundred years; and the happenings of the past century have only confirmed this historicism. No peoples escape history, but they are more aware of it than some other nations.

Hence the Revolution has made no break in the loom of chronicle, there is no chasm between past and present as some Europeans imagine. The Communist Party of China claims itself heir and descendant of the Taiping; the Taiping themselves were an immense peasant uprising successive to so many others which occurred sporadically throughout the centuries. Always there is a progenitor, and the shuttle of time goes back and forth, weaving the centuries into a wholeness. The pattern changes, but it is one loom, one fabric, one uninterrupted thread: the history of a people. Like the Great River, it moves on through the landscape changes.

"In the year of the Righteous Fists, I was thirteen years old, old enough to understand what was happening." Thus Third Uncle of that watershed, 1900.

The Righteous Fists were one of many secret societies, such as the Szechuan Elder Brothers or Kelao. They already existed in the eighteenth century among the peasantry, which has a singular and immortal talent for such brotherhoods. With incredible speed, out of a placid unmoving landscape of growing rice and waving wheat, from the bent backs of stunted people moving painfully about, working, working, always working, out of creatures clothed in rags, spring generals and leaders and heroes followed by immense, many-millioned cohorts, overrunning areas as large as Europe. Indestructible as grass, all-devouring and immortal, rooted in earth as grass, they rise and fight with all the genius of a people fighting for justice. And this impulse can never die, for revolution is just as much a human right as the right to eat and to love. The Righteous Fists were but one more time, one more place, one more episode, of this ebullience, perpetual ferment, arising out of poverty and hunger, devastation and want.

As the armies of the Monkey King, who plucked a hair to conjure a host into being, so peasant armies tied a coloured cloth round their foreheads, beat the iron of their ploughs into the tips of spears and their saucepans into swords, and rolled forward like the ocean, amorphous, inchoate, irresistible.

Sometimes the gentry were also involved. Often, in the cities, they sought to control the secret societies and the brotherhoods, and through them the mass movements of the peasants, turning them into docile armies to their own profit.

The Righteous Fists rose in Shantung province, because Shantung had been hit by three disasters all at once: floods, famine, and the Germans.

Yellow Peril Wilhelm, late on the field of plunder, found that nobody took his leadership of the White Race seriously. It needed another thirty years and a Hitler to push the idea forward to its hideous maturity. For two murdered German missionaries, Wilhelm demanded and received a huge indemnity, railway and mining concessions, and Shantung province as his sphere of influence. Four years later, the Righteous Fists rose in Shantung and spread to the whole of North China.

The Catholic clergy in China also chose the years 1898 and 1899 to make more sure of its extraterritoriality, special rights and privileges. On March 15th, 1899, by Imperial Decree, further powers were given to the French Catholic clergy, confirming what had already existed in fact, a position of equality with viceroys for the bishops, and with judges and prefects for the priests. The passports issued to the bishops were ambassadorial, thus worded:

This envoy of Great France is to reside in China, generally to manage the affairs of Great France; as an envoy plenipotentiary, with all rights. This revered holy man is a renowned scholar, with virtue and knowledge excellent beyond compare. Let all officials give every facility to all his activities, his preaching and living, his purchasing of houses and lands, erections of churches and buildings, to be made according to the will of the noble envoy, to be upheld, supported and aided in all ways. Trembling obey these words.

To their credit, the Protestant Missions rejected these rights in 1899.

And so the peasants wound a bright red cloth round their heads, and went forth to fight in 1900. But they fought the wrong way, for they were misled by their leaders; missionaries were massacred, converts cruelly murdered, the carnage was fearful. But the retaliation in carnage was even worse. Peking was sacked by the armies of the West and Japan, fifty thousand people died. The wells were filled with corpses, the streets with bodies of men, women and children in pools of blood. Soldiers of France and England and Germany went about with open trousers to rape the women, and spears to impale the babies. Some young men from the legation quarters armed with shotguns practised their aim on passers-by in the streets every afternoon for sport. A few militant missionaries boasted of the number of peasants they shot after baptising them. One of them, an American, wrote: "I sent eight hundred and forty-one new souls to heaven this week." And there is that entrancing phrase of a German officer having his fun in Peking, quoted by L. D. Lyall in his book on China published in London in 1934: "When I go pheasant shooting I shoot cocks and spare hens, I kill the old birds and let the young ones go; but when hunting Chinese I kill them all, men and women, old and young."

In this horror the Manchu dynasty had its share of guilt. Knowing the rising restlessness, they knowingly diverted the violence, which threatened to be anti-dynastic, to an anti-foreign frenzy, then condemned it. The facts are well known. The Empress Dowager left Peking to take refuge herself in Sian, but returned in 1901 to an almost triumphal welcome into Peking; the ovation coming not from her subjects, but from the very foreigners whom she had done her best to murder and who now crowded to welcome her back. For now the dynasty and the Western powers knew they needed each other. What had been implicit was now explicit: they must ally, to keep the people down. All the Western diplomats understood this very well, and all corpses were buried in mind, since after all they were mainly Chinese corpses. The Dowager

Empress suddenly became a charming old lady of culture and refinement, and European ladies vied for invitations to her tea parties, while Western newspapers eulogized her breadth of vision and grasp of politics.

The year 1900 was the end of one century. But it was also the end of a state of mind. The Empress Dowager had come back, but the minds of the people had changed. Reforms were now proclaimed, but it was too late. After the rising of the Righteous Fists Kang Yuwei and his Reformist Party lost all influence in China. No one believed in reform any more, while everywhere people spoke of Sun Yatsen and of revolution.

From 1902 onwards there were again uprisings every year, sometimes twice a year. Each time defeated, Sun's star yet grew bigger and brighter on a horizon of despair; he never gave up, though the prospect looked unpromising. Sun was the gentlest and mildest of men, but he knew tyranny cannot be cured with words.

In the Boxer Protocol of 1901, imposed after the defeat, China had to pay five hundred million dollars (though Yellow Peril Wilhelm would have liked very much more), open more ports and cities, accept a permanent garrison of soldiers in Peking and other towns and along the existing railways. Among the clauses was one which affected the scholar-gentry: the powers forbade China to hold the Imperial Examinations in any of the main cities where there had been anti-foreign demonstrations. This at once put an end to the old-style examination system, and was actually a blessing in disguise.

The Imperial Court ordered reforms and asked for suggestions. The New Learning came in, and the provinces seized upon this opening with alacrity, in order to establish military academies in each province. These academies would no longer train levies in the use of the bow and arrow, a training re-instituted by the Manchus in 1898, when they tried to put time back four hundred years. Ambitious military officials, such as Yuan Shihkai, foreseeing a future in which armed might would be the arbiter of power, wanted to create a New Army, a modern army, an army equipped and trained in the latest weapons.

I was very young, fourteen in the Chinese way, thirteen if you count in the foreign manner, but I understood all this well. So did many of our gentry in Szechuan. We realised we had to build our own provincial forces, husband our own resources, develop our own strength. Everyone understood very well what the sudden affection between Manchu Court and Western powers meant. They were now allies, against the people of China.

Many lives were changed by 1900, among them that of your father. My life too was changed. Had the old Imperial Examinations not been abolished, your father was destined to go on taking examinations in the classical tradition. Who knows, he might have become a Hanling Academician.

A memorandum recorded a council of our Chou Family held in 1896.

Great calamities have come upon our country, disaster upon disaster, so that men's hearts are not at ease. Families must have a guiding rule, lest their spirits disperse, and ruin and desolation gnaw at their existence. Today, scarcely daring to breathe, we ask fearfully: what will the morrow bring? Some years ago the Japanese without declaring war attacked us, and have taken as prize of war Korea and Formosa. All of us have to contribute sums of money to pay for the indemnity they demand, and yet we have not finished paying the previous indemnities of other wars. Our ancestors worked hard to accumulate some comfort and ease for us. How can we face them now?

What is to be done? Already among us men have risen to say that only by reforming our education, by learning from our enemies the new science and the arts of industry and war, can we too become strong. But our family elders have noticed one thing: that such learning is not moral nor righteous; it depraves men's minds and makes them heedless of virtue; its corrupting influence extends to both male and female, so that some females have even changed to male, a monstrosity to make one shudder. Therefore we enjoin our descendants not to fall into the trap of the new learning, nor to forget their primal being in their acquisition of perverse knowledge.

But in 1902 the Family held another council of elders, to decide upon the education of its young.

It was decided that Eldest Brother would go to Japan, or the Eastern Ocean, to study teaching; your father, Second Brother, would be sent to the Western Ocean, to Europe, to study science; and I, the Third, obeying the commands of the Family, would enter the Military Academy for the New Army recently opened in Chengtu. This suited me very well, since my mind had seen the problem of power. In fact, I would have chosen it myself had it not been allotted to me. Around me I saw the scholars disputing and debating, writing essays and making speeches. But so many of them were without hope of employment. Whereas there is always employment for those who carry a gun.

The memorandum of the Elders thus advised:

Seeing that our eldest son obtained his degree of bachelor and is of a studious bent, and as he is the Eldest Son, let him be married that he may bring up posterity to replenish the house and fulfil the rites; and after that, let him pursue deeper studies in the Eastern Ocean schools, for a civil career in the administration of our country. And as for our second son, he is of an inquiring turn of mind. We shall seek an opportunity for him to acquire New Learning in the sciences, such as mining and the railways, since our province is to develop these resources, and he may go to the Western Ocean. And for our third son, let him enter the military academy, that he may be trained to defend our land . . .

I remember thinking at the time: where will the money come from, for all these travel expenses? I hoped I too might go abroad, preferably to Germany later, for the Germans were reputed the best soldiers in the world at that time. Fortunately each province now wanted to send some worthy young men abroad to study. The Elders were far-sighted in providing for the Family. They took counsel with each other, and as we were linked by kinship commerce and class to so many other gentry families, we already knew the provincial government would provide for the well-born, the well-connected; in fact, its own sons, the sons of the gentry.

As the boatman smells the wind in the gorges of the river and trims the boat's sail to catch the wind, so the Chou Family, loyal to its own interests, reversed their decision, accepted the New Learning, and sent your father to Europe, your Eldest Uncle to Japan.

But there was more to it than merely sending students abroad. After 1900 there was a new feeling about. Each province wanted to develop its own resources, and in Szechuan we had much mineral wealth, abundant coal and also iron; what we needed, above all, was communication, a railway, to bring our products out of the province more easily.

It was because of this railway that your father was sent to Belgium. At that time the railways concerned not only our province, but each province of China. The words "the Iron Road", which means in Chinese "railway", suddenly acquired such tremendous political as well as emotional significance that they became symbolic of national independence, and ended by being one of the main factors in bringing about the Revolution of 1911.

From the Righteous Fists of 1900 to the Revolution of 1911 only eleven years elapsed, but in these eleven years the Empire was overthrown, the Republic proclaimed, and China began her long and arduous journey forward, into the modern age.

NINE

IN my father's writings there is nothing about the Righteous Fists, except a folksong of the time. He may have heard it sung, or even sung it himself:

> The spirit soldiers will come
> With gold helmets and silver shields,
> Riding on grand white horses,
> Wielding swords of righteous deeds,
> They will kill all the invaders,
> Revenge all our wrongs ...

These lines are ensnared within a sketch of some sewage tubes, mathematical formulae, a jotting of daily expenses and the address of one of my sister's silk shops, the larger one which her husband had given her and which was confiscated when she did not claim it in 1951 as she had gone to America.

It was not the spirit soldiers that saved China, but it was something more prosaic: a railway.

Father also omitted to describe how and why he had been sent to Europe by the Szechuan provincial government. He was, as Third Uncle phrased it, a poet; he was writing to please himself, not a chronicle of his years.

The next fragment of his autobiography deals with his voyage out of the province, omitting the years between 1898, when he passed the provincial examination, and 1903, when he left Szechuan in a blaze of grand expectations. But others remembered, many others. For the iron road question occupied the minds of all the gentry of Szechuan after 1900; and not only the gentry in our province, but in Hupeh and Hunan, in Kuangtung and in every province, the gentry and the merchants now began to demand an iron road, a railway of their own, and the right to build and to operate their own railway. They demanded the right to exploit their own mines and quarries. In short, they wanted to build up their own national enterprises. But that meant also rescuing these rights from the foreigners, taking back the mines, the railways, the quarries, the facilities already sold or mortgaged to them by "treaties".

Everybody, from high to low, now understood the slogan: China to the Chinese. But because the conviction was less vocal, because it did not spend itself in defiance, some Western observers thought that China was "at last" beaten to her knees. "Things will be easier now," they reported after the Boxers. "All the same, we must be cautious not to provoke another outburst."

In Szechuan there was no longer a hurling of stones at the Western missionary hospital; on the contrary, there was talk of building a Chinese hospital. Everywhere schools of New Learning opened, and there was a great demand for translations of scientific books. But the main issue was the railway.

In 1901 the provincial government of Szechuan, and the merchants' guilds, petitioned the Court for permission to build their own railway, and in early 1903, through Hsi Liang, the governor, the merchant-gentry was granted the right to build a railway, with funds raised in the province itself. The railway was to run from Chengtu to Chungking, then to Ichang on the river, and on to the Triple City of Hankow–Hanyang– Wuchang in the province of Hupeh, the adjoining province. There it would link up with railways already in existence.

It was on this railway issue that the imperious consciousness of change began to solidify, assembling into a mental structure capable of being handled, capable of specific demands, a concrete, practical issue demanding a positive, inescapable answer. And it is this crystallization, this solidification into concepts easily handled by everyone, peasant as well as official, which precedes a revolution. And this psychological pre-revolutionary mental state is a phenomenon least understood of all.

Many books have been written on the history of Chinese railways, and the role each Great Power played in them. Many have been written by Europeans and repeat time and again that the Chinese were hostile to railway building because of their superstitious fear of disturbance of the graves. Yet the firm of Jardine Matheson found buying land (including cemeteries) for railway building in the 1870s quite easy, the peasants willingly moving their ancestors' bones elsewhere, provided there was adequate compensation in cash. But the officials, aware of the strategic implications of railroads, objected. Railways, like Christianity, loans and opium, were not primarily for the good of the Chinese, but for the good of the foreigners. Railway building was not only a matter of means of communication, it was above all a strategic and political issue of enormous importance. It was known that

Russia had built the Trans-Siberian and railways in North China to transport her troops to her new frontiers on the Pacific. The British and the French both had built railway lines in China, to move their goods tariff-free and their troops easily in and out, in their politics of dismemberment of China. Why should the Chinese agreeably give foreign powers these convenient inroads into their country? Why should they put themselves completely in their power? Each "private" foreign company, offering to build railways in China, was solidly backed by its government to the extent that at least twenty-five per cent of the money put up was government money.

The Boxer episode had proved to the Chinese how easily troops could be moved by rail to occupy Chinese cities. Railway loans were most onerous; the land on both sides for ten miles, and all mines, quarries and natural resources found within those limits, was also under concession to the foreign power which had built the railway. The railway itself, its land, its rolling stock, all its property, was held in mortgage until the building loan had been repaid, and the loans were not supposed to be repaid for forty years. Upon these railways foreign goods travelled nearly tax-free, while Chinese goods were heavily taxed. Why should China be willing to build railways under such conditions? However unreasonable it may appear to the West, the refusal to build railways was actually sound common sense.

After 1900 the demand that Chinese railways must belong to the Chinese was also a claim to real independence, an end to subjugation. For true independence is not only political but also economic.

Much has been written about England's ugly role in the railways of China. Like the Opium Wars, the story is not pleasant, and has left on the Chinese side emotional sores, raw places, where old wounds quickly rub new again. But no single Western country can be singled out more than any other for perverseness in this matter. If there is more material available, printed and published, about England's nineteenth-century exploitations, that is because she was the dominant power, in all her greatness and also in all her meanness. But had Germany's Kaiser Wilhelm been the dominant colonial exploiter of the time, things might have been even more hideous. Certainly Japan, though an Asian nation, did not behave any better towards China. As for the United States, who came in as a novice in the colonial plunder-games at the tail-end of the nineteenth century, she was at the time preoccupied with her loot in the Philippines and with Latin America; she also tried to get railways and concessions in China, but was not the great power she is today, having scarcely begun to extend her frontiers across the Pacific; so she propounded the Open Door, free-for-all policy, just as the Kaiser tried to raise the standard of White Race *über alles*. And what about France, what about the other powers? Would they have acted better, would China have fared worse? Sometimes when the subject of China in the good old days crops up, one or other European will say: "Oh, it was the British (or the French, or the Germans, or the Italians) who behaved badly, but *we* did not. We were always loved by the Chinese. We were not like the others." The truth is, they were all the same.

For exploitation and oppression is not a matter of *race*. It is the system, the apparatus of world-wide brigandage called imperialism, which made the Powers behave the way they did. I have no illusions on this score, nor do I believe that any Asian nation or African nation, in the same state of dominance, and with the same system of colonial profit-amassing and plunder, would have behaved otherwise.

Take, for instance, little Belgium. I was born, as were five other of my mother's children, on the Belgian-built railroads, slept and wakened to the hoot of engines, the clatter of wheels, the smell of smoke, the long trance of endless metal rails whiplashing across the plains, the roar and receding melody of a dashing caravan of wagons. My father worked on "Belgian railways in China" for twenty-five years. He spent days and nights, weeks and months, years, his whole youth and middle age, upon the iron road, trying to make the railways go, trying to save the rails and the sleepers from wars and pillaging soldiers.

Of all the Powers pushing China indefatigably to her ruin, Belgium appeared the most inoffensive, the most harmless, the only one with honourable intentions of commerce alone.

"The country of Belgium," wrote Viceroy Li Hungchang, "is small. Moreover, they do not desire to take anything away from us ..."

In 1896 the great Viceroy Li Hungchang had visited Belgium and been royally entertained. He had been impressed by Belgium's industrial competence, especially in the matter of railways and mining.

Belgium's behaviour over the Boxer uprising had favourably

influenced Chinese officials. The Belgians did not send many troops to the rescue of the beleaguered diplomats in Peking; their newspapers deplored the "barbaric excesses" of the armies of other Western powers who sacked Peking. When the Protocol was signed in 1901 giving the Powers the right to maintain garrisons in China's capital, Belgium sent a token twenty men.

The Belgian engineers' efficiency and reasonableness when at work also impressed the Chinese. Whatever the motives of the Belgian government, their engineers and technicians in China were hard-working, honest, and what they promised they did, in record time. They were also exacting towards themselves. The Chinese were not afraid of small, hard-working Belgium; they liked the hard but tough and efficient engineers on the railway.

The Belgians always recognized that there were well-founded political reasons for Chinese reluctance to allow foreigners to build railways. As Ullens de Schooten, a Belgian diplomat, wrote: "The prejudices and superstitions against the railway are understandable. Let us remember our own ancestors, and their horror at the first steam engines ... The Opium Wars, the sack of Peking in 1860 the war [imposed] miseries, everything has shown to the Chinese the danger of allowing foreigners into their hinterland."

It was this understanding, the prudence of Belgian policy, which won them a relative confidence from the Chinese at the turn of the century. How right, or how wrong, the Chinese were in their trust, certain books by Belgian authors, such as the Jesuit Father Frochisse, and the Count de Lambermont, will tell us.

It was after 1864 that Belgium began her own drive for markets in the Far East. Her separation from the Netherlands in 1831 had lost her the Dutch East Indies markets for her industry. She sought orders, chiefly for railway material, from China. In 1867 a project for three railways, one from Canton to Hankow, one from Canton to Calcutta, one from Hankow to Peking, had been envisaged by combined British and Belgian merchants, but it came to nothing owing to the well-founded Chinese suspicion that such an enterprise would be used to convey British troops into China.

From 1867 to 1895 stubborn refusal obstructed all plans of foreign powers for a drive into China through the railways. It led t'Kint, the Belgian delegate who was trying to promote

Belgian interests, to write an exasperated report: "There *must* be a necessary solidarity between all of us in the Far East ... We *must* use the most energetic measures and the most salutary pressure to obtain our ends ... Only under the protection of the combined bayonets of France and England shall we be able to construct railways ... linking the principal cities of China."

Unsuccessful in the Chinese commercial sphere during those thirty years, Belgium nevertheless succeeded in delimiting a spiritual sphere of influence for herself. The Flemish Scheut Missions were grafted into Inner Mongolia and the provinces of Chinghai and Kansu, the Central Asian plateau. These areas were arid and poor and sparsely populated. Few were the Europeans willing to encounter their hardships. The Flemish were hardy and willing. Commercial rivalries had their counterpart among the various orders of the Church. Should the Franciscans occupy one province, they petitioned the Holy See that it be left to them, and the Dominicans or the Jesuits directed elsewhere. No such orderly delimitation of spheres for conversion existed among the Protestant sects, they always got in each other's way, with the amusing result that their "converts" were almost professional: refugees from flood or drought in need of rice and shelter, they lapsed and found the Light again with great regularity, going from Baptist to Presbyterian to Lutheran to Adventist and back again to Baptist as often as it was necessary for their sustenance.

But the Catholic Church was more methodical; Inner Mongolia, Chinghai and Kansu were delimited as a sphere of conversion to the Scheut Missions, who acquired great tracts of land and prospected their sphere of conversion for gold, iron, coal and other metals. The Belgian Bishop at Lanchow sent regular reports not only to the Vatican but also to his King, Leopold II of the Belgians, on the results of his missionary treks throughout his territory.

Leopold II, King of the Belgians, was a formidable person. Tremendously hard working, he harboured visions of power and glory unmatched by other monarchs of his time. *The Life of Leopold II* by his admirer, Count Louis de Lichtervelde,* reveals the immense scope of his ambitions. In 1869 Leopold had thought of acquiring the Philippines from Spain. "The consular reports and the private sources of information of the King," Monsieur de Trannoy, another Leopold admirer,

*Count Louis de Lichtervelde, *Leopold II*, Cowdray Co., New York, 1927.

writes, "had revealed the richness of the Philippine Archipelago, and the considerable profits to be drawn from a more intelligent exploitation of the soil and the underground resources of the islands. The tobacco monopoly seemed of itself capable of producing a favourable return."

But this ambition could not be realized due to the "stiffnecked pride of Spain". Later Spain and the United States struggled for the Philippines; the United States won. Leopold tactfully looked elsewhere.

"We must seek," the King wrote to his ambassador, Count de Lambermont, on January 24th, 1874, "to associate ourselves with each of the English railway projects in China."

"The King was convinced that Belgium was in the best position to obtain concessions in China, by delicate treatment of the susceptibilities and distrusts of the Chinese. His ideas were so well understood by his entourage that some feared to suggest things to him which harmonized with secret tendencies almost irresistible to him." In this delicate manner the Reverend Father Frochisse, s.j., writing in 1912, introduced the tale of his King's exploits.

"Do not be alarmed," wrote one Jules Devaux, a Belgian officer, to the King's biographer, "by my bringing to the attention of you-know-who the proposition of occupying a Chinese province with a Belgian army and Belgian colonists."

In the division of Africa, the Congo had fallen to Leopold by the most prestigious and adroit diplomacy. The scramble of the Powers there was more furious, headlong, and encountered far less resistance than in China; it had rolled inexorably on to the final, total carving up. The signature of illiterate tribal chiefs, on pieces of paper, in return for bolts of cloth and glass necklaces, gave the predatory nations huge pieces of Africa for a few pounds sterling of baubles. According to the biography of Sir Henry Morton Stanley by Lady Stanley, more than five hundred such treaties were signed between African chiefs and the explorer Stanley, in such good and sufficient form as to be capable of satisfying the juridical formality of the European chancelleries.

The Anglo-Saxons in America had resorted to this method in America in dealing with the Red Indians, Count de Lichtervelde tells us. University professors were found, a Mr. Arntz of Brussels and a Sir Travers Twiss of Oxford, to recommend this method of acquiring sovereignty. Thus a pious travesty of legality was preserved.

In spite of English attempts to establish themselves in the Congo delta, and Portuguese attempts to annex parts of his colony, Leopold II triumphed and earned what he called "the lion's share of Africa". The Congo was acquired by him as his personal property, and he was later to deed it in his personal will to Belgium.

"But it was above all in Belgian enterprises in China that Leopold II showed the full measure of his ability. As China became more and more the object of the cupidity of the great powers, Leopold saw that the very weakness and smallness of Belgium might aid her in acquiring there an almost preponderant economic position."*

And now various Belgian missions went to the Far East, no less than four in 1898–1900, for Leopold wanted to push ahead in China. Through Queen Victoria, his niece, to whom he wrote assiduously (and gave advice), he was able to keep in touch with English policy, though the Foreign Office did not entirely like the Queen's uncle and his meddling ways. For his Chinese venture, the King needed specialists in exploration, men physically fit and mentally alert, and chose army officers of the Congo campaigns, who were also trained prospectors, geologists and engineers, to be his pioneers in China. They were known as "the King's men", being responsible to him alone. History does not mention whether, in addition to their officers' salaries, Leopold paid them from his own purse, but it is certain that he managed to inspire them with a sense of mission and of loyalty to himself. "Belgium's stability in the future can only be assured by her prosperity, and this means foreign markets," he told them. He was a sound judge of men, and those he chose for China erred only in displaying too much enthusiasm for their King.

To avoid diplomatic complications, Leopold gave his pioneers a mandate from the "Independent State of the Congo", whose citizens they became. Since the Congo was his personal property, no government could write stiff diplomatic notes to the Belgian government about Congolese officers on mission to China.

Leopold's choice of a Chinese Congo fell upon Kansu province, the province where my great-grandfather and grandfather had administered a border town and fought to put down revolts. It was considered the poorest and most difficult of access of all China's provinces (bar Tibet and Sinkiang),

*Memoirs of Baron van der Elst.

and hence neglected by other Powers. But the King had read the tales of travelling missionaries, knew von Richtofen's travel books, pored over maps of Central Asia, and in his mind the view of a China dismembered between the Powers contained, right in the centre of Asia, another Congo, the lion's share, Kansu. "I'll get the choice cuts of China all right," he said.

I do not invent this. It is in his biographies, written by Belgian admirers.

Kansu was prospected by Scheut Flemish missionaries. It was a land of utterly miserable and poor people, but beneath the soil it had iron and lead, silver and gold and copper, salt and saltpetre in its saltpans, ochre and coal, and of the latter enormous amounts, and also uranium and oil. Crossing Kansu, along a string of oases between the Ordos Desert and the mountains, lay the great Asian silk road, along which for fifteen hundred years had gone the commerce from China to Europe.

Much of Kansu was a long, stretched corridor, and Leopold envisaged a railway along this corridor, a railway controlled by Belgium, from the China Sea in the east to Lanchow, the capital of Kansu, and on across Asia to Turkey through Persia. Lanchow was a meeting place for Mongols and Turks, Tibetans and Chinese, Persians and Afghans, and all the peoples of the steppes. It was the start of the camel caravans across the Eurasian continent. A railway through Eurasia, built by Belgium ... think of the profits! Leopold thought of them, and also of the minerals below the Kansu soil. The other Powers might be in at the death of China, squabbling in their orgy over the bloated corpse in the familiar and easy provinces of the east, but Kansu would be forgotten, and Leopold would quietly take it, without any English, German, French, Russian or American diplomat tapping him on the shoulder and demanding a share.

However, if the Chinese learnt of this, all would be lost. These plans were to be kept a secret, and the suspicious, mistrustful Chinese lulled to confidence. Belgium was too small, only interested in building railways for commercial reasons, "the only country with no dishonourable intentions towards us". Thus wrote Li Hungchang.

The King's man who did the Kansu reconnaissance in 1898 was a Major-General Wittamer, an officer of the Congo. He was accompanied by an extraordinary man, whose name was

Paul Splingaerd. In their travels they utilized the missionary outposts of the Scheut to rest and replenish themselves in food and money. Major-General Wittamer kept meticulous notes all the way and was most faithfully aided by the Belgian bishops, only too happy to see two compatriots arrive. This mission of two men went almost unnoticed, by-passing the British and the French spheres of influence, skirting the Russians to the north, in a grand peregrination through a vast area. It could not have succeeded without Paul Splingaerd, whose life has never been recorded. Splingaerd went to China at seventeen as the valet of a Belgian consular officer, learnt to read, write and speak Chinese, married a Chinese woman, and became intelligence officer to the Belgian government. He later settled in Tientsin as a customs officer, and made a lot of money. His eldest son lived in Peking as a merchant, and married a Chinese woman, and I went to school with Paul Splingaerd's grandchildren.

The two men boated up the Yellow River, on a raft, from Lanchow to Ninghsia, and there the mountains "nine times folded" twisted the river into gorges and rapids, in a manner similar to the Great River gorges of Szechuan, the river-bed narrowed down to about sixty yards across, whereas above and below it broadened to half a mile.

They reached Mongolia and the residence of Monsignor Hamer, the apostolic vicar of south-west Mongolia, in the summer of 1900. Then came news of the Boxer uprising Monsignor Hamer asked Wittamer to go to Peking to request help from the French forces there, as he foresaw that the troubles might spread to Mongolia and the Ordos Desert; Manchuria, he had heard, was already a sea of blood. Actually Monsignor Hamer was killed in Mongolia in July 1900. Wittamer could not reach Peking at the time, but after more adventures he was able to leave China to report to the King in October 1900.

Another expedition, that of a Colonel Five, also went to Kansu. Colonel Five was also an "old Congo hand" among those affectionately named by Leopold "my faithful Africans". A third agent, George Warockque, investigated mining resources in Kansu.

However secretive these missions, the other Powers finally got wind of them, and fell into a state of agitation over Belgium's intentions. Count Charles d'Ursel, who went to Peking in order to "stimulate" commercial relations between Belgium and China, then wrote: "All the diplomats in Peking defend, inch by inch, the interests of their governments. How many occasions of conflicts between the European nations does China represent!"

The Chinese now became aware of the rivalries which the greed of the nations towards them provoked. They were to initiate, for some years, the game of playing off one nation against another, in a weak attempt to safeguard whatever could be left of their own integrity.

Count Charles d'Ursel also was a "representative" of the Independent State of the Congo in China. The German ambassador, Baron Heyking, finally made an open complaint to the accredited Belgian minister in Peking about "these Congo Belgians". The British, more diplomatic, showed no outward unease, but privately were pressuring the Chinese to "refuse any concessions" to these upstart newcomers the "Congolese".

The diplomatic correspondence of those days makes amusing reading. Father Frochisse in his book relates a story, which was also related to me by the son of Paul Splingaerd in Peking in 1932. It appears that Count d'Ursel, accompanied by the ubiquitously useful Splingaerd, visited Li Hungchang the viceroy, whom the Belgians had invited to their country and from whom they hoped to get railway and mining concessions. Li said to him: "You are supposed to represent an African state. How is it then that you are not at all black?"

After some negotiations, all the privileges, concerning persons, goods and extraterritorial rights which other nations enjoyed, were also granted to the Independent State of the Congo in 1897, and thus the Congo Free State became the financial instrument of the policy of the King of the Belgians in China. Loans issued for the Congo in Belgium were often diverted from Congo ends, and devoted to the pursuit of concessions in mines, and especially railways, in China.

But none of this was known to the Chinese; nor, for that matter, to the inhabitants of the Congo themselves. Belgium, in the eyes of the viceroys Li Hungchang and Chang Chihtung, was "the best". No voice spoke for Africa then, except those strangely light-coloured representatives of the Independent Congo State. When the construction of the Peking–Hankow railway was suggested, and intense competition between the Americans, the British and the French began for its building concession, Belgium found herself able to compete, although much smaller, with the head-start of an enormous psychological advantage . . . "no evil intentions".

The man appointed by the Manchu Court to deal with all railway matters, supervisor and negotiator-in-chief, was named Sheng Hsinsun.* He was a most corrupt and unscrupulous person, with unrivalled ability to make money from all sides in any negotiation. Sheng at first was in favour of giving the United States the concession for the Peking–Hankow railway; in fact, the United States were given first priority. The British lost the opportunity because their representative, thinking he had the upper hand, became too arrogant and the demands were excessive. The Belgian agent appointed by Leopold II to negotiate the railway contract was Emile Francqui, another "African" officer of the Belgian army. He was named consul at Hankow, where resided the viceroy Chang Chihtung (who actually favoured the British, but could not stomach the British delegate's insolence), expressly to push railway negotiations and to keep an eye on the comings and goings of other negotiators. Hankow, one of the three cities bestriding the Great River, right in China's centre, was to be the fulcrum for all railway lines, as well as river transport, in China. Francqui sat in Hankow for months, through the stifling summer and the icy winter, trying to negotiate.

Meanwhile Sheng went on negotiating with the American China Development Company, backed by American financial groups and money. Gifts were exchanged, the "golden cords that bind favour". The English again offered a loan, but again the terms proved too onerous. More gifts were exchanged. The amount of money needed for building this railway was very large, and it seemed impossible for Belgium to find so much money by her own efforts. The King wrote to Francqui to push negotiations. Belgian bankers, always timorous, demurred when they thought of "this perilous Chinese venture". They suggested a combine for a railway loan, and approaches were made to French financial circles, seeking an alliance with France on the question of a loan for railway construction. This would also strengthen Belgian resistance against England's displeasure, for little Belgium did not wish to displease the Bank of England. On the other hand, a *rapprochement* with France might defeat Belgium's advantage in China, founded on the fact that Belgium was looked on as "less rapacious and sanguinary" than others. No one had forgotten

*Also known as Sheng Hsuanhuai.

French "intelligent terrorism" practised on several score of the sea-coast villages in 1885.

Perhaps the money could be raised in France, but Belgium would build the railway, furnish all the material and rolling stock, spare parts, for decades to come, not to mention the making of enormous profits and influence ... and Kansu in the end.

The financial negotiations with France were to be kept secret as long as possible, especially from England and from Germany. Leopold II's talent at manoeuvring now revealed itself in the directives, precise, lucid and full of guile, which he sent to his faithful Africans in China.

But in Peking, in the small circle of the foreign embassies where the diplomats met each other, played with each other, and made love to each other's wives, it was extremely difficult to keep anything secret.

The French minister in Peking had a brilliant idea: why not bring in the Russo-Chinese bank as intermediary, to fox the British? His best friend was minister of the Tsar in Peking. The French-Russian alliance was a factor in European diplomacy. And, best of all, the Russo-Chinese bank was neither Russian nor Chinese, but financially French. Ostensibly a loan from the Bank would not be for the Peking–Hankow railway, but could be for some other project.

By feint, evasive action, circling, and other guerrilla tactics of finance, the British were thrown off scent, and only in the last few weeks of negotiations did they become aware that these disparate manoeuvres were all part of the same railway loan scheme. It was George Morrison, correspondent of *The Times*, who in May 1898 finally discovered what was going on and warned the English of this Belgian-French-Russian entente on the Peking–Hankow railway project; England would be cut out of anything to do with the most important railway in China, the one running from north to south; this railway actually traversed England's sphere of influence, the Great River valley, and it therefore imperilled her commercial penetration of China; the danger to British interests due to "preferential freight and differential rates [on the railway] which might be made to subserve national ends" was very great indeed.

As Archibald Little wrote in October 1898: "As things are now, Russia (who has just overrun Manchuria) has cancelled a British lien on a (northern) railway, Germany has warned us off Shantung, France puts a transit duty of ten per cent on British goods to Yunnan; at the same time she has compelled the wretched Chinese government to admit goods over her border for two-thirds of the five per cent duty collected by the Maritime Customs at the other Chinese ports. With preferential transit and other tariffs directed against us, we shall have handed over the solid work of three generations of Britons in China to our *unscrupulous* rivals, or else be driven to fight for our tradal existence..." He added: "There is no other alternative left but to take our share in the partition now going on.

Matters came to a standstill, and stayed thus for a good while, during which most delicate manoeuvring by the Americans, the British, the French and the Russians, each trying to double-cross the other, and accusing the others of unscrupulous dishonesty, went on. More and more gifts were pocketed by Sheng. Viceroy Chang, who still favoured the British, refused to receive Francqui. Father Frochisse says he "never received any European," but that is not true: Chang had given audience to an English envoy. It now appeared that the Americans had inched themselves ahead in the field of favours; not only Sheng, but also Chang, now inclined towards the Americans.

Francqui however succeeded, by "paving the way with gold", in being received by Viceroy Chang, who told him bluntly that the best offers for the Peking–Hankow railway loan had come from the American China Development Company. Would Belgium consent to the same conditions as the Americans? Yes, said Francqui, without arguing. Both Chang and Sheng, by now agreeing to receive the Belgian proposition, were reneging on the half-promise they had made to the Americans; but in Big Business of this kind the one who wins is the one who has succeeded, at the psychological moment, either with the largest bribe or with an accidental element of personal import.

In spite of this preliminary success, the wholehearted support of Belgian financiers was not forthcoming, and Leopold was furious. He could not tell them that, for him, the railway, enormous and profitable as it was, was only the beginning of a far more grandiose scheme. Chang, the most powerful viceroy, had said yes, the Americans and English were defeated, the Germans were nowhere; would the Belgians themselves destroy their advantage through niggardliness? Francqui was desperate. He obtained from the Belgian financiers, now pressured by Leopold to organize a *Société d'Etudes des Chemins de Fer en Chine,** agreement to send three delegates with full powers to China in order to deal with the matter of the Peking–Hankow railway.

Three "Belgians" arrived. The chief of mission, Rizzardi, turned out to be of Italian origin, naturalized Belgian, and totally deaf; his second, Masy, was an uncouth station-master, hurriedly bundled in as delegate, no one knows why; the third, Lieutenant, de Borchgrave d'Altena, was an exceedingly handsome young man, chiefly interested in the *ars amatoria* of Chinese women. Not one among the three delegates knew what they were there for, all three were vague about what full powers they actually had.

The delegation's proceedings read like a farce. The whole process of getting the "full-power delegation" in shape to sign a railway contract fell upon Francqui. The Chinese were puzzled, not having grasped the element of insanity which is lodged in all Big Business, whether in 1898 or in 1964. Francqui however managed to get a preliminary agreement signed by this delegation.

And now the English and the German governments were enraged. The English minister, Warren, pounded his fist on the tables of Chinese officials and threatened that the Chinese would be punished for daring to sign a railway contract behind his back. England and Germany started a press campaign against Belgium, accusing Belgium of being the mask of a "Franco-Russian alliance" and of having "broken her neutrality". The walls of London were plastered with anti-Belgian invectives. Sheng was threatened by the United States, England and Germany. But he was building up an immense personal fortune, and did not care.

In the middle of this *brouhaha* the Brussels bankers refused to ratify the preliminary agreement, insisting that the financial clauses were too lax, that "not enough security" in the form of mortgages and concessions was provided. Another delegation was sent; since the contract had already been ratified by Imperial Decree, Sheng and Chang the viceroy could not, without incurring the attacks of ultra-reactionaries (who did not want a railway under any conditions), go back on the contract. They agreed that the interest rate China was to pay would go up from four to four point four per cent,

*Society for the Construction of Railways in China.

and other industrial clauses were amended in favour of Belgium.

Even this did not satisfy the bankers of the *Société Générale:* they wanted more guarantees, and especially they did not like the Chinese insistence that the railway would be bought back within ten years.

But Leopold II was more determined than ever to get "his" railway in China. For, after the Peking–Hankow railway was built, he envisaged another one, from east to west, running from the sea to Kansu, "his" future Congo. Another mission was sent, and Dufourny, the head of this one, a public works engineer of Brussels, received a personal order from Leopold to push on. He did so in a manner splendidly literal. He betook himself to the residence of Sheng in Shanghai, where the latter had come to continue negotiations (with gifts) far from Peking, from Court spies, threatening diplomats and other annoyances. Dufourny arrived in mid-afternoon, unannounced, at Sheng's palace, and proclaimed he would not go away before he had obtained "entire satisfaction"from China, and a signed contract. Sheng was angry at this impropriety and rudeness, and made Dufourny wait several hours. But the Belgian sat in the courtyard, determined to stay, and in the evening Sheng took out his brush and wrote a few words on a piece of paper, saying: "Here it is."

Dufourny rushed out to a telegraph office and sent a cable: "The contract is signed, long live the King." That day happened to be Leopold's birthday, and Dufourny wanted to give his king a triumphal birthday gift, possibly dreaming of a barony in return.

Later that evening Dufourny went to the French consul's house, waving the "contract" in his hand. The latter called his interpreter, who examined the paper and reported that it carried no name and no date, and was not a contract.

Meanwhile Sheng Hsinsun had been given by the telegraphic office (he was also Minister of Posts and Telegraphs) a copy of Dufourny's telegram. He realized that Leopold II was personally interested in the Peking–Hankow railway line, and informed Chang. Immediately the Chinese showed themselves much more inflexible on terms, since they suspected there was more to the matter than they had thought.

In the meantime the Belgian bankers had been approached by the English, who told these insular Europeans lurid tales of woe and disaster in China. They categorically affirmed that a railway would never be accepted by the people as it "disturbed the graves" of the ancestors. The English were considered the "experts" on China, and Belgian bankers trusted the Bank of England. Again Leopold seemed baulked in his plans.

The long-suffering Francqui kept the negotiations going, however, by representing to the Chinese that a loan of over one hundred million francs was a very large sum of money to raise. The Chinese cannot have been altogether convinced, since they themselves were to repay Japan twelve times that amount for the 1894–95 war indemnity, and had contracted such a loan from the British at five per cent, which meant sixty million francs in interest per year. The total customs receipts of China were only eighty million francs in silver a year, so that three-quarters of the Customs revenue went to pay the interest of *one* loan ...

Meanwhile, anticipating that the Belgians might not succeed, the British now created a Peking Syndicate (seconded by the firm of Jardine Matheson), while another London group of financiers, Hovely and Jameson, also entered upon the scene; both were ostensibly "private" companies, both maintained agents in China, expectant of further developments in the Peking–Hankow railway affair which might finally redound to England's advantage.

Sheng, Viceroy Chang and Viceroy Li Hungchang again underwent a formidable assault, the combined cajoleries and threats of the French, the Americans, the British and the Russians. The Chinese were still hesitant over two clauses, which had been added in by the Belgian banks: (a) That all the material for construction and equipment should be Belgian, and (b) An option for the Hankow–Canton railway line, when the Peking–Hankow line should be terminated. Sheng asked that the Peking–Hankow line be terminated in three years, the work to start at both ends, Peking and Hankow, at the same time. Finally Francqui, or rather Leopold II, carried the day. The bankers agreed, the loan was provided, and a contract was signed on June 26th, 1898.

The displeasure of England now manifested itself. It was not Belgium that England was worried about, but a disguised intrusion of the Russians through the railway loan into the Yangtse River basin, the English preserve. Once again there was a pounding of fists and much shouting in the residences of Chinese dignitaries. "The Chinese had BROKEN THEIR

WORD," shouted and fist-pounded Sir Claude MacDonald (also known as Gunboat MacDonald, from his favourite threat). "China must be *punished* for this ..." wrote another British diplomat. A threat of gunboats, of soldiers descending once again to loot and to kill, and the wretched Chinese government promised "compensation" to the English, thus putting themselves in the wrong.

Today, although England is reduced to a minor power, while the young bristlingly armed United States of America has taken her place, gunboat diplomacy still tries to crush the spirit of man by a show of force. And though for the last eighty years these methods have proved self-defeating, they will continue until a new generation, crippled by their own ferocity, come to a new awareness of our one world and one humanity.

The Press campaign in England against Belgium heightened. As the American newspapers of the time report: "The walls of London are covered with manifestoes urging the government to act." Sir Claude MacDonald obtained from the terrorized Manchu Court the concession of no less than five more Chinese railway lines, and other privileges, before British ire abated. Li Hungchang, considered as having been "corrupted" by the troubles of the Tsar, was at the pressing instances of Sir Robert Hart (that English customs supervisor more powerful than any viceroy) removed from his post.

Leopold II had won what he wanted: the "Grand Central" road, the railway from Peking to Hankow, the beginning of his choice cut of China.

At its first appearance on the market the Loan for Chinese Railways at five per cent, 1898, was overbought twice, the French banks taking three-fifths and the Belgian banks two-fifths of the shares. How many of these went on to Russian shareholders is a mystery. The loan was 112,500,000 francs, at five per cent per annum. The security was the imperial revenue and the net profits of the railway. The working agreement was to run for forty years, wide powers of management being given to the Belgian Syndicate: control of the line, right to organize all service, recruit all personnel, fix tariffs, plus a remuneration of twenty per cent of the net profits of the railway after paying all working expenses and providing for the servicing of the interest etc. on the loan.

The survey of the Peking–Hankow railway was done in 1899 by Belgian engineers. In spring 1900 work began. In

1904 came completion of the road. On November 15th, 1905, the bridge over the Yellow River was finished; the selection of an appropriate spot for the bridge was made with great care by Jean Jadot, the untiring Belgian engineer-in-chief; the bridge was 3.03 kilometres long, and had 102 spans. Altogether the Peking–Hankow line was 1,214 kilometres long.

It was the first great triumph of Belgium in China, and one which Belgians refer to with enormous pride. The profits were also enormous. After that the Belgians were to build other railways, the chief being the Lunghai, the great railway from east to west, from the coast to Kansu; but this was not started before 1913.

In 1908, exactly ten years after the signature of the Peking–Hankow contract in 1898, the enduring Sheng Hsinsun signed a loan with the British Hongkong and Shanghai Bank, and the French Bank of Indo-China, for five million pounds sterling, at five per cent interest, to run till October 1923, and then at four and a half per cent till final reimbursement in 1939. This enormous and onerous loan was contracted in order to *buy back* the Peking–Hankow railway from the Belgians. Leopold strenuously objected; he begged the English and French bankers not to lend the money to China. But France, abandoning Belgian interests, was now moving to ally herself with England; the Anglo-French financial alliance then in the making was a reflection of the *Entente Cordiale,* which was to be maintained through the First World War of 1914–18. It was also the prelude of a new consortium of banks, which in order to tighten their financial stranglehold on China now acted together against her.

Immediately after the Peking–Hankow railway contract was signed, Leopold II tried his best to acquire the Hankow–Canton railway concession. "I want the backbone of China," the grim old King said. One long railway from Peking through Hankow to Canton, in one continuous, unbroken line, would allow him to dominate over all the other Powers; it would convert Belgium into a Great Power in China. After that would come the horizontal railway, from east to west, linking the sea to Central Asia ... Leopold must have stood looking at a map of China, and drawn a large cross over its expanse, an immense cross of iron, the iron road, taking in all China; a vertical arm, a horizontal arm ... and at the end of the horizontal arm the province of Kansu, his heart's desire, another Congo in China.

But the Hankow–Canton railway could not be handled without the intervention of American financiers, for the concession belonged to J. Pierpont Morgan. He had to be satisfied with sharing control of the Hankow–Canton line with the Morgan group.

Count de Lichtervelde, in his biography of the King, writes:

After 1905 the Chinese also wanted to buy back the Hankow–Canton railway concession, which the Americans had obtained, and offered a very remunerative price. The King, who had in view the conquest of the native market, did his best to induce the American financiers involved in the scheme not to sell their shares; he even begged the assistance of President Theodore Roosevelt to make the interests of white penetration prevail over purely financial considerations.

But in 1905 a boycott of American goods by the Chinese occurred, and it staggered the Western Powers. It was the first time that the Chinese used, and proved immensely successful at using, modern methods of economic sanctions. The boycott was in protest against immigration laws imposed by America on coloured and "Asiatic" labour. The Americans became afraid, and let the Hankow–Canton railway go, although at an enormous monetary profit. Leopold, who had shares in it, made a great deal of money, but was dismayed. "It is a national defeat," he declared bitterly, seeing his chance to consolidate Belgian influence in the Far East escape.

However, the Belgians did not give in. They had now obtained agreements for two more railways, one of them being the Lunghai, the horizontal arm of the cross. But they did not finalize the contract till after 1912, and by that time Leopold II was dead. And then there was the First World War, and though China was to remain in chaos for nearly another forty years, Kansu never became another Belgian Congo.

TEN

NONE of these kingly colonial ambitions, appropriate to the times, were known to the Chinese. Although a few of the more observant scholars had been disquieted by the fate of Africa, they did not know Leopold's plans for another Belgian Congo in China. Belgium was therefore considered a most friendly nation, as also the most efficient technically, and this excellent repute led the provincial governments, even in far-off Szechuan, to send from 1903 onwards students to learn engineering in Belgium. All over China, students who wanted to study mining and railway building were recommended to go to Belgium, "a small country, and harmless".

In order to build the railway in Szechuan, the private Szechuan Provincial Railway Company was set up in 1903; it took four years, however, till 1907, to obtain its full recognition by the state. Officials appointed by the government were to supervise its administration, but the line would be financed, built and run by Szechuan merchants. This system of mixed enterprise, with private capital and technique, but with official supervision, was similar to that under which the salt and iron monopolies of the state had been run for some centuries; in altered form, it can still be found in the small-scale mixed enterprises which exist in China even after the 1949 Revolution: the Communist government, when it takes over private business, allows the investor a share in the running, a fixed remuneration for services, and pays an interest on invested capital.

The merchants and landed-gentry class of Chengtu were the main movers in forming this private limited company. The gentry of Szechuan were now eager to buy shares in this new railway company. There were many meetings, much oratory, a great enthusiasm. The Szechuanese have always been famous for their eloquence, they are said to be able to talk their way up the highest mountain and down the longest river; and the only exception to this rule seems to be my own father. Not only did they talk of the iron road, but scholars wrote essays and poems, which were published in the newspapers, on the exalting themes of communication and transport. A wag even composed an essay in the name of the drowned ghosts, broken upon the rocks of the Great River – souls numerous as the pebbles shored on its narrow strand at the foot of the cliffs – petitioning those not yet water-ghosts to hurry up with the iron road building, so that the perilous play with death which travelling from Szechuan to other regions entailed might come to an end.

To set at ease those conservative elders who worried that a railway might disturb the spirits of auspicious places, produce abortion in women, or a plague, my grandfather in his capacity as a doctor also wrote some lines on the matter:

Today our country is fighting a life-and-death battle. At first only nibbling at its shores, the invaders have now ascended the Great River into the heart of our Szechuan. The gathered blood of our brothers in the north, south and east would outflow the waters of the Yangtse. In the west once again we hear the iron hooves of the Russian hordes. From all sides do they come against us, and our people can no longer endure the misery.

In the last decades wise men have taken counsel together, and today we know that, to survive, morality is not enough, ancient wisdom not enough; we must also have Science. Science has many wonderful inventions, and some were known to us many centuries ago but we did not wish to destroy the harmony of nature by inventing dreadful and terrible instruments. However, today we must bestir our spirits, learn to defend ourselves. To this end we must look to ways and means, and one of these is the iron road.

The iron road will enable our good people of Szechuan to transport themselves easily in and out of the province, thus benefiting commerce; it will strengthen the bonds between our many regions, and enable others to visit us in peace. In case of war, we shall move our troops swiftly to vanquish the enemy, instead of allowing him to march in to defeat us. No longer will the Great River take its toll of lives, and hungry ghosts will cease to afflict its banks. The iron road can do no harm, either to men alive or to spirits of ancestors.

Easing the avenues of commerce, to bring prosperity; the ways of scholars, for mutual exchange of learning; the steps of friends, for deepening the bonds of civility ... once the iron road is built, a ten-thousand-mile horizon will be like ascending one step. There will be no more robbers, since they cannot waylay the fiery engine; safely our wives and children will sleep and wake to find themselves greeted by the smiles of relatives; distance shall vanish, space will be conquered ...

Thus, lyrical about the railway, my grandfather, and in his enthusiasm no different from Erasmus Darwin's poeticizing of steam power in 1792:

> Soon shall thy arm, unconquered steam! afar
> Drag the slow barge or drive the rapid car
> Or on wide-waving wings expanded bear
> The flying-chariot through the fields of air.
> Fair crews triumphant, leaning from above,
> Shall wave their fluttering kerchiefs as they move ...

And if today in China writers laud electric pylons, aeroplanes and dams, so did conscientious English poets even as late as the 1930s. For these are still wonders to many of us in Asia, and especially wonderful that we can build these things ourselves. Thus my father and other old engineers, seeing in 1952 the railroad built in Szechuan at last, that very same railroad which had been planned fifty years before, the iron road for the building of which they had been sent to Belgium to learn engineering in 1903, felt at last fulfilled, after a lifetime of frustration and despair; one of them, blind with age, bent down to stroke and kiss the rails, not only because it was a railway, but because it was built by the Chinese, for the Chinese. Such deep, fierce feeling may sound otiose, naive, woefully childish, to Europeans of today, but it happens to be the truth not only about China, but about Asia and Africa, and tomorrow Latin America as well. And men like my father were reconciled to a government which was making their dreams of fifty years ago come true at last.

For even in China today the iron road is more than a link between places, more than transport, communication; it is the arteries of our unitary body, the image of our desires, the binding meshes of our continent; and the romance of pioneering still travels with the railway, as the young students of today chug along in railway carriages, rolling on steel from China's own steel works, kilometre by kilometre, into their own heartland, opening new places, conquering the mountains and rivers of their own country. This is the Industrial Revolution of China, fifty years late. But it has come, and no one can put time back.

The shares issued by the Szechuan Railway Company were of two kinds: big shares at one hundred silver ounces each, small shares of ten silver ounces each. Some families, such as ours, bought many shares. Third Uncle showed them to me in 1940, a small trunk full of useless printed paper. He kept them as a souvenir. He also took me walking to the site where the roadbed ought to have been built, and there, where nothing was, spoke of the railway planned in 1903.

Because the Szechuanese wanted to be sure of controlling their own railway, no foreigner was allowed to buy shares, and the term foreigner also covered inhabitants of other provinces; this was to prevent European firms taking over by buying blocks of shares through middlemen or through Christian converts. It was quite evident that the Powers did not care for this new spirit of Chinese railways to the Chinese. They made fun of it, predicted utter failure, pointed out that China lacked the capital, the know-how, the ability, persistence, discipline, to build anything or to run anything with efficiency. But the feeling against foreign interference was so strong between 1901 and 1905 that the Court gave in to the provinces' demand, and resisted the verbal, financial and physical bullying inflicted upon the officials by foreign diplomats in Peking.

The Szechuan Railway Company also made sure that no missionary would acquire shares. It was known that the British government had tried in 1898 to acquire land in Chengtu for a future consulate. An English missionary of the China Inland Mission had been approached by his government, and a large piece of ground of about twenty acres marked down for sixteen hundred silver ounces, ostensibly for building a school. A certain Dr. Kilborn, and a Dr. Endicott, two Canadians attached to the hospital in Chengtu, heard of this, and organized an indignation meeting to protest against this illegality. It was in order to forestall any such attempt to buy shares that the Szechuan Railway Company scrutinized the bona fides of all shareholders, reserving them solely for the gentry of Szechuan.

But the Manchus needed money, and the customs revenues were under control of the Powers, who knew how to bide their time; they would let inefficiency and venality do their work. Meanwhile, they garrisoned the chief cities and the most important railway stations along "their" railways.

The money collected by the Szechuan Company, and the railway companies of other provinces, was to be placed for safe-keeping in a newly created bank, called the Bank of Communications. And there was the rub, for Minister Sheng Hsinsun, so apt at deals, now became Director of the new railway enterprise, as well as Minister of Posts, Telegraphs and Communications, was also a director on the board of the new bank.

A Railway School was set up by the Company in Chengtu, to train foremen, technicians and expert workmen for the railway. It opened in 1904, and French and Japanese instructors were hired out of the money collected in the province. The provincial government also selected "the most promising young men of the province" to study railway engineering and mining in Belgium. It was with this money that my father, "from a scholarly family of high virtue," and three other young men in the summer of 1903 left Szechuan to go to Belgium, there to study how to build an iron road for their land.

By going abroad to study my father became what was later to be called a "returned student". This phrase, which was to be used in China for the next five decades, meant a student returning to China after having studied in Europe, America or Japan. Privileged among the privileged, scholar of the New Learning, the returned student was looked up to, revered, sought after, exalted, as a combination of knowledge of both

East and West, destined to save his country from destruction. This was his destiny, his responsibility, his historical task, in a land where the recording of history was one of the fundamentals of culture, and where an apprehension of disappearance from the world as an entity and a culture, and the most stubborn and tenacious reaction against such a fate, have been for a century the most pronounced emotional tone of an entire people.

It was from the Chinese gentry, which produced the mandarin class, that the bulk of the returned students, those Mandarins of the New Learning, were to come. The Manchus profited little from the rush to learn abroad; at first they were not keen, and later no longer in power. A good many sons of the new rising merchants' and traders' class benefited; even if not endowed with scholarships, they were usually able to manage the funds to go at least as far as Japan. Many poorer scholars managed later, by a work and study scheme, to do the same, among them some of China's most outstanding men of today.

The total number of gentry in China at the turn of the century was 1,443,000, out of nearly 400 million people, an average of less than two per cent, of which no more than one-third were employed in administration, leaving a large residue of semi-employed and frustrated intelligentsia. A privileged class, they were by virtue of the examination conferring upon them the status of scholar, which was China's only aristocracy, exempt from manual labour as well as from corporal punishment. The upper gentry had less land tax to pay, the land tax being so badly arranged that the smaller the land property, the heavier the tax. They had, in the nineteenth century, begun to acquire military power as well. And now, in a provincial government which itself was made up of official-gentry, the selection of candidates for going abroad would obviously be largely within its own privileged class; the peasant would have no say in this. In 1904 and 1905 hundreds of young men managed to get away, and there were four thousand students from Szechuan in Japan by the year 1906.

The consciousness of privilege, of rank as well as of merit, remained attached to the students thus selected or selecting themselves to go abroad. Hence the prestige attached to returned students, a prestige which continued to operate, even when it was quite obvious that no matter how many returned students went abroad and returned, China could not be "saved" by them alone. And yet, it is also true that among these returned students from Japan many leaders of the Revolution of 1911 were found.

There had been a few returned students before 1900, when the idea of sending young men abroad to study was first put in the head of Tseng Kuofan, the general who fought the Taiping, by Jung Hung, a Cantonese, whose father was a middleman trader dealing with British firms in Hongkong. Jung Hung was the first returned student from Yale University, where he went in 1846 on private funds. On his return he was employed by Tseng Kuofan to set up an arsenal, since Tseng had become convinced after the Taiping of the necessity of modernizing the Chinese army, "but without abandoning Chinese recitude and civility". Jung Hung was commissioned to purchase plant and equipment for this arsenal; in 1865 the Kian Nan Manufactory in Shanghai, China's first modern arsenal, was set up.

But Jung Hung's heart was not in creating arsenals, it was in sending more young men to study abroad. He suggested to Tseng that one hundred and twenty should be sent. Tseng passed on the petition to the Imperial Court in 1867; four years later the petition was granted, in 1871. Intelligent boys of twelve to sixteen were to be selected to go abroad; however, not more than thirty a year, for four years only. They were to study abroad for fifteen years: two years were set aside for the voyages back and forth, and thirteen years were to be devoted to study. And one condition of their being granted scholarships was that they should not marry European women.

The most outstanding student of the first lot sent abroad was Chan Tienyu, a railway engineer, who in 1909 built the Peking–Kalgan railway, the first railway built and run entirely by Chinese during the first decade of the twentieth century.

Between 1872 and 1876 one hundred and twenty students duly went abroad; a further seven were sent to study military matters in Germany in 1875. The young men all received six months of foreign language training in China, and were allowed four months to perfect the language in the country where they studied. They were to keep a diary, recording their thoughts, deeds and events every day. Every three months they were visited by a supervisor of studies; the latter inquired after the student's welfare, read his diary, admonished the young man, giving advice or reprimand as circumstance demanded. They were enjoined not to eat Christianity, nor to marry foreign women. Far from being resented, this tender care of the state for its most precious assets, the students abroad, satisfied the families. The Japanese students abroad, incidentally, received the same admonitions, were under the same kind of tutelage, and their discipline was actually far more efficiently strict than that enjoined on the Chinese. For, in spite of this, some of the Chinese students, even very early on, did marry European women, and return with their brides; they fared neither better nor worse than the others in the matter of work, though their private lives, influenced by the marriage they had contracted, ran a somewhat different course.

But the Manchu dynasty, as it became weaker towards the 1880s, became more intolerant. The demand for reform was growing, the students were obviously infected with new ideas, and the supervision of studies became a frankly political surveillance. And this was to continue, for even in 1935, in the time of Chiang Kaishek, when I was a student in Brussels at the same university which my father had attended thirty years previously, the political control exercised upon the student body by the Kuomintang Embassy was quite extensive; it led to the beating up of "subversives", and even to the murder of one student, said to be a Communist, in 1936 in Berlin.

In 1881 the Dynasty refused to send any more students abroad, and tried to withdraw the supervisory bureau of which Jung Hung was commissioner. In America the writer Mark Twain, always profoundly interested in China, organised a petition, signed by several chancellors of American universities, asking that the students already there be allowed to continue, and that more students be sent. But the students were also recalled.

However, in 1882 a group of ten students, and in 1892 twenty more, were sent to Germany and England, to study army and navy matters. This was done at the instance of Viceroy Li Hungchang, who wanted officers for a modern army and navy. But between 1882 and 1892 students in other branches were not sent by the Manchu government. After the Righteous Fists in 1900, the gates were widely opened at last, and this also was a reflection of the growing power of the provinces at the expense of the weakening central authority. Provincial railways, provincial militia, provincial scholarships, were all aspects of this same trend, which had started with the passing of military control to the Chinese gentry in the provinces, after the Taiping.

By 1949 there were a bare fifty thousand returned students in a country of near six hundred millions. Many, like my father, and later myself, had gone on scholarships. The sources of these scholarships were various. It began with provincial government scholarships, but after the Revolution of 1911 there was chaos for a long while, and few students went abroad on government funds till 1928, when with the advent of the Kuomintang government of Chiang Kaishek scholarships emanated from the central authority again. Many of the scholarships came from other sources, chiefly American and British. After the First World War and the return to China of the Powers, a movement to finance a new westernized Chinese élite began among the Powers. Each country hoped that the Chinese educated by them would naturally favour their country of education; gratitude, ties of friendship, as well as cultural and emotional orientations, would see to that. This also Leopold, the astute King of the Belgians, had foreseen. He had spoken of it, urging that young men be sent to Belgium for training. *"Ils seront des nôtres,"* they will be ours. A few years after the Boxer uprising, both Belgium and America negotiated to return their share of the Boxer indemnity to China, with the proviso that the money should be used for educational purposes, and this gesture elicited gratitude on the part of the Chinese. On this money America financed a university in China (Tsinghua University in Peking), and one hundred students were sent to the United States in the years 1909 and 1910.

Thus the policy of the client-state was inaugurated in China, whereby an educated Asian élite is trained, whose minds, desires, emotions, are oriented towards the land of education rather than the land of birth, and who often feel disinclined to return to the land of their birth, because they feel their talents, matured abroad, are wasted in their motherland. This is still, in 1964, a problem of the returned student in Africa, in India, in Indonesia, as it was in China before 1949.

Many Europeans feel that their willingness to give Asians training in their universities, to give money for scholarships, is proof of their altruistic motives, of their intention to do good to Asian countries. And they become quite rightly indignant when their motives are impugned, as they are today, and they accuse the Asians of biting the hand that feeds them.

Unfortunately many Asians today, even such as the Filipinos, have become embittered by the past, and feel that education is only another means the Western powers are using to maintain their influence and to form sympathizers for themselves.

Where does the truth lie? The West did not act entirely through philanthropy, although there are enormous numbers of kind, charitable people in the West, who give money to good causes. Out of evil good comes, and whatever the motives, some good was done, and one day it will be possible to study anywhere, and not be influenced or subject to influence. I myself was, in 1935, a recipient of a scholarship derived from the Belgian Boxer indemnity fund; I went to study in Belgium, following in my father's footsteps. But it was, in the end, China's money which was being spent to educate me, it was the Chinese people paying the Boxer Indemnity of 1900 who paid for my years in Belgium. And so my gratitude must go to them, for making me in turn, as they made my father, a privileged person, a returned student from abroad. Later I was to study in England, on a British Council scholarship, and also be grateful to England. But this has not influenced me in the end. For truth is truth, and cannot be bought at any price.

On an auspicious day in the late summer of 1903, when the Great River was in spate, in the benumbing din of firecrackers, after being feasted by the governor and the notables of Chengtu, having wept at taking leave of the ancestors, wept and kotowed to the graves of the dead, wept and saluted the living, in his ears still the last motto: "Never eat Christianity, for that is to be cast out of the family", Yentung and his companions left Chengtu, travelling on a large passenger junk. They started the voyage from the city at the Nine-Eyed Bridge, which still stands today and where the last goods junks are still moored. Amid bales of silk, casks of opium, bundles of tobacco, their boxes of lacquered hide with the copper edges, their chests of camphor containing their furs and winter garments, were bound with ropes to the floorboard iron rings. Thus they began the perilous voyage in the blunt-nosed craft down the Mien River on to the Great River, and to Chungking, thence through the gorges to Ichang, to Hankow, and from there to Shanghai. Before boarding the foreign steamer which would take him to the West to learn Science

Yentung, with his companions, was to study French for six months at the Language School in Shanghai.

In October 1964 Third Uncle gave me the photograph of my father, taken in 1903 in Chengtu, a few days before he left on his voyage. It shows a thin young man with a pointed face, wearing silk boots, silk jacket and trousers, all of best black silk. The jacket has the typical Manchu horseshoe cuffs, and the hair is dressed in a queue. He looks remarkably like his own father; a scholar, not an official, not avid for authority.

I have a feeling that in leaving his family my father was conventionally sorrowful, yet in his heart happy and excited; and that for all his outward docility, he felt like a bird released. "As I leave for the Western Ocean, my sorrow is great and tearing," he wrote, conventionally. He must have wept, conventionally. But he was young, and sorrow slipped off him soon, for he had already made his own private inquiry into the New Learning, into Science, and had developed a passion for it.

Before his journey he was part of a Family, part of a living organism made of multiple personalities, all subdued to an organic, amiable wholeness; he really had no visage of his own. He had to be prised free from this structure, and it must have been difficult, mortared into it as he was by his classical education. But after he had left the Family he gradually became himself, in charge of himself, responsible for his decisions to none but himself, and knowing the anxiety of being alone. He was to use this freedom, and to pay for the exercise of it, all his life.

ELEVEN

He who has not travelled the ways of Szechuan
Does not know what travel is.
Look at the boat inching its way up the River.
Bent on the ground, earth-crawling
Pullers strain, pant, pull as the ropes creak,
Cutting their backs,
And the stone cliffs that wall them in
Echo their groaning.
Narrow and high the sky above the gorges,
And at White Emperor's City
It is still, as frostbite upon wood.
Only the breath of spring,
Can carry you out of the strangling gorges . . .

Their large passenger junk, heavy-laden, hoisting all three sails, followed the Mien tributary to its junction with the River of Golden Sands, and was then upon the Great River proper, Son of the Ocean, going towards Chungking, a journey of ten days or more, depending on the wind's will. The junk was the usual forty-seven foot long, low-decked, with eighteen rowers and the rudder-man, or skipper. It would pick up a pilot at the guild in Chungking to cross the gorges on its way to·Ichang.

At dawn the mooring taxes were paid, the river deities propitiated with firecrackers, roast pork and oranges; in the evening the boatmen would be given their daily string of cash so that they could smoke their opium and eat their rice. Some of the passengers smoked too; the wealthier merchants smoked "Yunnan earth", reputed of better flavour than the Szechuan product.

At Neichiang, the sugar and ramie-cloth town midway between Chengtu and Chungking, the scholars were greeted by a delegation of the local merchant-gentry, who were collecting funds for the railway company and urging the gentry to take shares. When built the railway would pass through the town, so that the sugar and preserved fruit for which it was famous might be exported at a lower price. The scholars were feasted, each given fifty catties of Neichiang comfits, nuts ground with honey, fresh oranges and sugared fruit. The city magistrate and officials were at the banquet, and the following day gave them a send-off with firecrackers. The local newspaper, established by an enterprising New Learning schoolmaster, compared the departing young men to the intrepid monk Hsuen Tsang of the Tang dynasty, when he journeyed to India in the seventh century to collect Buddhist scriptures: "Ten thousand hardships leave them unruffled." These brilliant youths, wrote the newspaper, would bring back Science, the new saviour, to make China strong and able to lift her head again. "We have been insulted enough. We have been treated with contempt enough. Now we shall stand on our own, equal to other nations, and those that have come to despoil us will return where they properly belong, to their own lands, and leave us in peace." This was the tone of their high hopes, like the boom of an ample wind, wafting them on, out of Szechuan.

Chungking, the river port, loomed grey in the haze, a mountain city, grey like thicker smoke squatting upon the grey limestone cliff which it bestrode, a phantom horseman riding into the river. Here Son of the Ocean was nearly a mile from bank to bank, its current swift as a steed at the gallop. Here yet another tributary, the beautiful Kialing, flowed into the already monstrous stream. Startling their meeting, for the Kialing waters were bright blue, but Son of the Ocean, pelting its millions of tons of red earth, was the colour of red gold. Side by side they flowed, main stream and tributary, gorged with the melted snows of all the mountains, pushing that swift flux onwards towards the mountain ramparts it would breach to escape to the plains and the sea.

Girdled by its walls, crumbling verminous huts gripping the flanks of its supporting rock, Chungking riding its jutting rock was tumultuous, cholera-ridden, and full of starving peasants selling their children, for there was a famine in the north and girls were to be bought for twenty strings of cash. The wealthy had got themselves to the sulphur springs to pass the fetor-infested late summer and autumn away from the squalid death that strewed corpses up and down the staircase streets of the city. The city was a hive of flies, buzzing over the excrement and the corpses. The rats were cat-big, ate the cats and the corpses, and sated fought in great bands; mothers suspended their babies in wire-net cages and baskets from hooks hanging from ceiling beams, but the rats were too clever, they climbed upon the beams, then let themselves drop upon the babies and ate them.

The scholars were taken to the mansion of the local president of the merchants' guild, on an eminence overlooking the Kialing, cool in the clamped moist heat. Here again was much talk of the railway. The Chungking officials already had lists of shareholders; they hoped that the railway would start from their city and be built in both directions, from Chungking towards Hankow, and from Chungking towards Chengtu, since Chungking was the most important river port of the province.

Chou Yentung had relatives in Chungking, and called upon them. They complained of the road-toll taxes on their tobacco; small industries were already bankrupt, and only foreign commerce prospered. If the new taxes on junks and native craft operated, the boatmen would suffer more. There was no tax on the British paddle-boat which now plied the river to Chungking, and this also was breaking the rice-bowl of many.

Yentung dutifully wrote this complaint back in a letter to

his family; but he chiefly wrote some poems about the city of Chungking. He mentioned the cholera, and also beriberi, calling it by its Chinese name, foot-swelling breath disease, thinking his father would be interested. Beriberi was attributed to a poisonous wind, most common in wet areas, whose evil breath rose from foot to chest, producing disturbance in heart and in the pulses, and when it affected the breathing it became mortal. This was 1903, and at the time western medicine also thought beriberi an infection.

Leaving Chungking Yentung now played mahjong, that sailor game brought back by the navigator Cheng Ho, with friends on their boat. Before setting sail the offerings of the boatmen to the river spirits were solemn, for the dangerous part of the journey was about to begin. The waters were high, the marks along the shore rocks, grooved by their flow, like the horizontal strokes of a brush; the boat went swiftly, borne by the strong current. Going down river when the faceted sails hung slack and folded might take less than two weeks; up river took two months or more; but both ways it was easy to get broken in the rapids, each of which had its own name, legend, song, propitiation, peculiarities, whirlpool and deceptive seasons. Only the pilot knew them. He stood at the boat's helm, his eyes upon the waters; his fingers moved, giving the signals to the oarsmen plying their assiduous strokes.

Oh hasten, boatman, for like a humped tortoise up wells the giant water, its scaly skin like the polished shields of ten thousand swordsmen, it seethes with life yet looks so sleek almost you can handle it, like silk cloth – but beware its treachery. Hasten, for now they pursue us, the monsters, coming up swiftly on either side of our planks; and look at the monster eyes watching us, look at the bubbles of their breathing, as the water hisses and boils and sags back, sucked back into its own depths. See this wondrous thick water, colour of gold, colour of our red earth, as it hurries past like a hundred thousand horses galloping together. Fear is upon me, boatman, so hurry and light more incense sticks for the altar to the hungry ghosts of the drowned, so eager for another human to pay fee to the River Dragon. Lay out the dishes of roast pork and chicken, and fragrant oranges, and call the spirits of the drowned to have mercy and let us cross safely the rapids.

The songs of the boatmen floated round the forward cabin where under matting lay the passengers, shielded from the sky-scattered sun, for summer on the River is a canopy of cloud which twists the sun's orb to a shapeless white sprawl.

The helmsman, leader of the boat, started the chanting when he perceived the first rapid:

Haiyaya Haiyaya Heiheihei
A small wind blows, my body's cold,
Hei Hei Hei
Together push this boat to Peichow,
Chained together.

Hei Hei Hei Haiyaya Hei
Those who have money are seated at home,
Hei yaya Hei
But who knows the empty ones,
The dry ones, their worry and their woe,
Heihei.

Nearing the Kuanyin rapids, the helmsman's song changed its rhythm. It became more urgent, the rowers' "hei hei" swift.

Hei yaya Hei
In front of us the Kuanyin rapids,
Hei Hei Hei
Kuanyin the goddess merciful does not hear prayers,
Hei yaya Hei
She has no eyes, no ears – hei hei
Without our own strength, our own arms,
We cannot pass her rocks.

Hei yaya Hei Hei ya ya Hei
You and I, chained together, each one of us a hero,
Hei Hei Hei yaya Hei
This one is to pass . . . oh pass . . . oh pass . . . to smooth river,
Fight up a strength oh, move oh, move oh, forwards . . . aaaaaah!

The young men heard the final yodel of relief as the boat shot over the Kuanyin rapids and the boatmen relaxed, laughed, made jokes, and then, rapidly, silent, one by one went to the stern, each to lie down for a few minutes and to smoke a ration of opium.

Coming up Demon's Pass, the most dangerous rapid of all, the head boatman would warn the passengers. The pilot stood scanning the reflection of light upon the water, and the rowers would say to each other: "Look at him, taking the pulse of the Grand Old Gentleman, Son of the Ocean, for he knows the pulses, the arteries and veins of the Old Gentleman, and of the River Dragons". Their eyes upon his hands, they sat gently, gently, feeling the octopus water, divining its temper, testing their muscle against that muscled monster. With minute finger nods and his head bent slightly, the pilot directed their strength.

And now their song was precipitate, hurried, like a quick drum its tempo: and the rapid loomed upon them the black-green mass of Devil's Rock, with the water screaming a large hole at its foot, the whole river circling round this yawn. Already the boat felt a soft vibration through its wood as it heaved, soaring into a beginning circular motion, a swivel, narrow and more narrow.

> Helihaha ha he, Ah the sky has changed
> > He he
>
> The wind lifts storm
> > He he
>
> The big waves rises
> > He he
>
> Helihe he Helihe he
> Don't fear the wind he he
> Don't fear the wave he he
> > Add a gaff of strength
> > > Hei hei
>
> Stand a firmness
> > Heilihei
>
> Rush it through,
> > He he
> Helihehe he ... he hetsohetsohetsohetso ... aaaaaah!

They were through, and in sheer gratitude the head boatman sang with the boatmen:

> Walked aiyah, one pass loah
> > another pass naole
> One stone ... is over ... h e e i ...

The boatmen dragged their song, relief ended their panting breath with a long, meditative yodel which came back at them from the cliffs, until they seemed to float in their echo.

> The sun in the east
> > throws a clearness looo ...
> The sun shines clear on the Chialing water
> > lei he he
> That sun shines clear on the heart of
> > brother and sister
> > > loo he he
> Row her to bite the water-side, and make her fast,
> > he he
> Buy a bit of flowery cloth for my sister to wear
> > loo ah hei
> > > he he
> Get up, wei
> > All we dry ones, waa ... y!

And then only they would complain of their lives, in the way all the world over the toilers have put their work into song:

Oh push boat people are bitterness on bitterness heaped hei hei
In rain and wind must always find the anchorage hei hei
Say a few words and the wind blows them away hei hei
The wind blows our lives away.

In 1962 late summer I made the same trip as my father had
done sixty years before, but there were no more small junks
for passengers. There were still barges loaded with goods, but
only for short hauls. They were still pulled up river by men,
as my father had seen them, as my mother had seen them.
And though they were few where they had been many, they
were still there, naked men, bent horizontal like sun-tarred
maggots, naked naked, pulling the twisted bamboo cable that
deformed most hideously their backs, walking step by step
the giant worm's grooves of the cliffs' base. But there
was hope for them now. They were the last generation who
would have to pull the boats. Another five, ten years, and
there would be no more pulling. The pullers also knew that
this was the end, their sons would be in factories, in schools.
There were now three steamboats going up and down the
gorges, and soon another three would come. And now the
loudspeaker on the small steamboat I travelled on sang a new
song of the boatmen:

> On the boat, stand up straight,
> Come on, come on, move your oar,
> Move your oar, more strength rises,
> Boat flies forward, forward, he – he – he.
> If this boat had an engine,
> It would be a machine boat,
> Then would be quick and easy,
> Then would be quick and safe.
> If we want to get to that,
> Still must add some strength today.
> Talk of it and it will come,
> Talk of it and it is here.
> You and I, all chained together,
> Let our eyes fly forward, oh,
Steady, hearts, steady hands, steady ... wait ... steady ... aaaaaah!

But if the songs had changed, there were still the rapids,
though the more dangerous rocks had now been blasted. The
dreadful sucking water, with its visible, audible sucks and
hisses, was still the most fearfully alive water I have seen.
From what seemed most hideous depths came another skin
of water, welling up and swishing itself upon the surface into
a carapace design, like a turtle's back, an outline of diamond

shapes, and at each angle a hole formed and sucked back into itself, sucking back the dissolving diamond; a little farther bubbles pouted, pouting spurting then breaking open; and up welled and surfaced out another hexagonal animal skin. It took little time to be persuaded that one was riding the back of a prehistoric monster, whose skin wrinkled and relaxed while the monster shuffled about. A faint froth, a scarcely perceived rock just breaking the surface; and there were the whirlpools and the sudden notion that water and sky were swivelling round an almost unperceived centre of light delicate froth, which softly, softly, began its inward funnel, sucking one back into the depths from where all this came up; and this went on all the time, for two hundred kilometres of the gorges.

Thus in 1903 the junk rode through the gorges where sky and water are the two sides of a crevice in the rock, where the creak of boat and the voice of men wheel and toss and are never ended in the reverberation of the wind; driven by current they swooped past the junks going upstream, hauled by twenty or thirty totally naked men, pulling in a long line, pulling the boat, up the grooves in the cliffs hewn for that purpose, a giant worm's track gouged where no foothold was possible; for here the River, a mile across at Chungking, bore through a tunnel with scarce two hundred yards from side to side, yet the whole of it had to go through. One was never sure when to turn the boat's head, for all the time the direction changed, as the tunnelled water bored its zigzag. The rocks on either side pawed at the River, which lashed back at them; in the middle rose a spine of crested rocks where mountains lay submerged, and there very often the junks had been dashed to pieces.

The scholars lashed themselves to boards and casks in case of shipwreck; they might then float awhile, though they could also be broken against the rocks by the whirlpools. In between worrying over their lives, they recited poems; for here again all was named, described, legended, component of their selves. Here were the battlefields of the Three Kingdoms; Liu Pei, ancestor of Liu Tachun, friend of Chou Yentung, had fought here for empire; on this hillbrow was the temple of Chang Fei, Liu Pei's great friend, fallen in battle, his head buried here. On that slope lay the maze, drawn by the wizard wise man, Chuko Liang, to confuse his enemies.

In the morning the sun came out to interrogate the trees

in their serried ranks up the cliffs. There were caves like pock-marks in the rock face, in which lived runaway peasants, said to be half-monkeys, said to be remnants of the original in-habitants escaping the slaughter of Chang Hsienchung, so poor even their women went naked; troglodytes to be pelted with stones.

The White Emperor City reared its temple roofs and pillars, like a mirage, between sun and gleaming water. Clouds hung about its eaves, as the poet had described them, coming out from under the city as out of a door. The roofs picked out in white of Hsianghsi village looked as they looked when Chu Yuan, the poet and statesman, was born there three hundred years before Christ; and though he had been drowned eight hundred miles away, the fish of the small Hsi Ling stream, which rippled into the Great River just where the village started, swam all the way to find him and bring his body back to his native place and to his sister, who had continued to live in Hsianghsi. From that time the fish were named rain-bow fish, or the peach-blossom fish, because they acquired lovely colours through their love service to the dead poet; and no one ever netted or killed them.

The young scholars were overawed by the greatness and the difficulty of the River. One wrote: "I was overwhelmed." An-other, quoting the poet Su Tungpo: "Man is always mortal, yet how uneasily does he meet death." But not a word of pity for the boatmen, not a word, not a look at the crawling worm-men, crawling their way, chained together, pulling the junks upstream ...

Twice again Yentung was to make this voyage, in different circumstances. He left this verse, written with hindsight, un-dated:

Too young to know greatness then;
Only contemplating the landscape and quoting poems;
How callous youth shields us from pain!
Often now I dream of the city, like a cloud on the cliff,
And the songs of the boatmen make me weep at waking ...

They sped through the gorges and were safe, as in 1962 I went safe, through that maze of wind and rock and water, and strange sky like a grey dead eye peeping between the cliff-tops a thousand feet above the canyoned water. The voyage was to remain with them all their lives, the relentless vibration of boat and oar and rock and voice and sucking wave, a wild-ness of sound imprisoned without escape. And in the same way the sound, and the wolfish shadow of our own steamboat at sunset hunting the gorges, would remain with me. Two hundred kilometres later they were out of the gorges at Ichang, where British gunboats were moored, a high white Christian church reared on the cliff, and another province began.

The River now broadened, mile by mile it became broader and smoother, until again it was a mile across, then more than a mile, flowing through land like a sponge replete with water, land water-logged and heavy with lakes and ponds and wet sweltering fields. And the River went on widening, widening, until it became wide as the sea, no banks visible. Finally they reached the city of Shanghai. But Son of the Ocean went on, pouring itself into the ocean; driven by the snows of a hundred mountains in Tibet, it poured its rich red gold into the ocean, and the ocean was gold for many miles around.

TWELVE

SHANGHAI was already not-China to Yentung, though it was nearly all-China for Western enterprise. Here was gathering, and would remain for the next fifty years, the greatest concentration of wealth and misery that any city of China would know. Here rose the middling – but then so massively powerful – brick and stone and marble banks and business edifices of foreign enterprise, their solidity another great wall, fencing out the vast and hungry continent with its four hundred million, which seemed to the inhabitants of these imposing fortresses a kind of adjunct, a wilderness for the recruitment of servants, cheap labour for the cigarette factories, flour mills and textile mills. Every foreigner that came to China mistook Shanghai for China: Shanghai was China to him.

At first Yentung was overawed, dazed, impressed. "What great might do these foreigners have!" He admired, though he also resented. The firm of Jardine Matheson was spoken of with bated breath as the Princely House. There were whole streets where Chinese, unless they were servants of foreigners, could not walk because at any moment a Sikh policeman might kick them if they loitered, or beat them with his stick. On the River the gunboats of five Powers plied, on the broad streets the soldiers of seven nations paraded; but the Chinese only had wooden sailing junks, and a whole population of former boatmen lived on them, reduced to stark beggary now

that the foreign steamboats had taken much of their liveli-
hood away from them.

Beyond this Settlement of foreigners was misery such as
Yentung had seen, but not so concentrated, plangent, ruthless. Just where the high walls, with their broken-glass top-
pings, sheltering English lawns planted with English grass,
where weeds were hand-picked by teams of coolies every day,
ended their forbidding blankness, began the sale of little girls
of six or eight for the brothels; a little beyond spread the foul-
est slum of the world, where two hundred thousand people
rotted alive; scavengers, pullers of rickshaws, prostitutes too
old and too diseased for anywhere else, and all the thieves,
murderers and small-time hooligans to be hired for the dirty
jobs of finance politics. The recruiters of cheap labour for
the South Seas and the Americas found this place a good
hunting ground, so that the term "shanghaied" came into the
Oxford English Dictionary, meaning to kidnap for work on
board a vessel wanting hands.

The people of Shanghai wore clothes like Yentung's clothes,
but were of lighter build, spoke an atonal dialect all hisses and
sibilants, shoved and pushed, swift of foot, and scarcely
smiled. They rushed, they pushed, they muttered obscenities,
their faces sharp as knives, wary and ready to stab. To him
they appeared at times as foreign as the Europeans out of
whose way he kept, for here in Shanghai to approach a European was to court trouble: one never knew whether he would
hit, or merely curse, and there could be no redress.

Chou Yentung at first stayed near the Language School,
which was later to become part of the French Aurora University. But after a while the Szechuan students complained
of the insipid food, and moved out to board with a Szechuanese merchant from Kiating named Wu Ling, who acted as an
agent in the commerce of timber, and also some opium, to a
British firm in Shanghai. Wu Ling lived in the Chinese city;
in a narrow house of brick, very ugly, with stairs; he was saving money, and sending it back to buy land in Szechuan.
Two of his sons were clerks in a British company. They were
small, thin and supercilious, and smoked "Three Castles"
cigarettes, which were English though the tobacco was from
China and the factory on Chinese soil. They took the Szechuan
scholars to Shanghai brothels where two of them promptly became infected. Yentung wrote to his brother: "I did not go,
mindful of our family's principles. But the water and the earth

here are strange to me, hence my bowels are disturbed. However, do not let Mother know, lest she grieve." He was sent hampers of beancurd, pickles and ham, and survived.

Never had he seen so many foreigners about as when on his way to the Language School. And he always felt a hand of disquiet about his throat when he met them. The most terrifying of all were the giant bearded Sikh policemen, wielding batons, pistols in their belts. Beards are very rare in China; their occurrence, as an occasional white prolongation to the chin of a scholar, is a complement to mildness, token of wisdom rather than a physical attribute. For Yentung beards now became linked to the Great Perplexity which bedevilled him when he tried to understand the incomprehensible Europeans. He wrote to his brother: "They always bewilder me. I can never be sure of what they will do next. At once most ruthless in the pursuit of their interests, caring nothing for the wholesale misery they bring, at the same time their papers are full of verbiage of their nobility, rightness and the good they do. They become indignant at our public executions, and our cruelty to dogs. Yet the record of their lootings and killings in our country shows no such correct compassion."

How could the West rob China every day and in so many ways, support the Manchu dynasty because the dynasty was guarantor of their interests; and on the other hand, in the International Settlement of Shanghai, and in the Concessions, give asylum to revolutionaries and rebels, such as Kang Yuwei and his friend Liang, and thus prevent the Dowager Empress from executing them? How could they allow the printing of articles which demanded reform, and at the same time continue the exploitation which was making reform impossible?

"They are illogical and incomprehensible, my brother."

This ambiguity, gap between word and deed, between pious moralities and self-interested realities, produced a confusion in Yentung's spirit.

"They never know what they want, except that they always want more. Unbelievably rapacious, they yet weep tears when they give money to beggars. But they will let thousands die of hunger, for the pleasure of doing good by giving alms to a few." Thus he mused and in this was like thousands of his kind faced with the world of the West. "I admire their inventiveness with machines, but I cannot admire anything else in them. How shall it fare with me in their country?"

And this perplexity became somehow attached to the

presence of beards. Of beards Yentung was plainly terrified all his life. Not the theatrical Chinese beards, which are stuck on wire and hooked over the actors' mouths and cheeks, but of real beards, Sikh beards, and bishops' beards. For the beards of the Sikhs became linked with another episode.

Once in the Silversmiths' Street of Chengtu, in 1899, he had seen the French bishop pass in his great sedan chair hoisted upon the shoulders of eight men. The whole street fell quiet, and the men took off the white cloth round their heads as for a viceroy, for such was the new law; in front went the lictors in brown with staves which they twirled about as if to clear the air of breaths, and a drummer with a gong shouted: "Make way for the Illustrious Great Man, make way!" After the procession, at a distance, came the usual crowd, beggars and the ragged children with laughing curses. Upon the bishop's belly was a great shining cross; and a beard, a formidable beard, swept down to it. The Sikh policemen had the same beards, and also large, hard bellies. They also swept their clubs about, and they kicked the rickshaw pullers and sometimes broke the handles of their carriages; and nothing could be done, nothing at all.

Mr. Bonami, his French teacher at the Language School, also had a beard, though smaller than that of the bishop. Yentung was almost persuaded that all eminent Europeans had beards; and perhaps he was right, in 1903.

He therefore always became agitated in the presence of teacher Bonami, whose lip movements he could not see because of the beard, and this made it difficult for Yentung to visualize the sounds of French. Within three months he had mastered many written words, and could produce a tolerable letter; in four months he could write simple compositions. But he could not speak well, he never heard the words properly because of the beard.

And then something else happened to increase his confusion. He wrote about it in his memoirs.

After the Righteous Fists I was able to study the New Learning at last. A student returned from Japan opened a New Learning school, and I attended it. But most of my study I did at home, teaching myself. I began mathematics; borrowed what I could find to read on world history, acquired two books on physics and on biology. I became enchanted with Western Science, the sublimity of its logic. I do not think it

extravagant to call it enchantment. My adolescence was somewhat retarded by much studying, but Science made me suddenly feel mature, in possession of all knowledge. Unlike
others of my generation, with friends to acquaint them with
the delights of courtesans, I was disinclined to such pastimes.
Books gave me almost physical pleasure. The discovery that
the Universe was regimented by laws mathematically proven,
that all phenomena, regarded as mysterious and transcenden-
tal, were predictable, within range of man's reason, exhilarated
me. Here was, at last, what I was looking for. What tremendous power lay in Man! Verily Man could be Master of his
earth, would he but recreate his earth in wisdom and nobility.

I read of Europe's scientific and industrial revolution, and
felt that my generation must also accomplish this for China,
lifting her from her backwardness to the modern age.

This consecration now acquired a new meaning. I felt the
discoverer of a new universe. As when a star explodes, comets
swing into the sky and set it afire, innumerable questions now
came to me, to be answered by the New Learning. I discovered
a virtue which our classics had not emphasized, the spirit of
curiosity, of independent inquiry. So that was what the West
meant by freedom! For it was in Europe that the spirit of
speculation had found itself most free. There man had boldly
questioned all things, even his own body, and his own con-
victions, even at the risk of disrupting the universe and killing
himself. No moral code, no ethics, stood in the way of this
outrageous passion to know. Perhaps that was why European
man had remained so barbaric, and was so impatient, his un-
couthness only part of a total lack of reverence for all things,
a churlish youth hurling him forward without heed of consequences; and although this was evil, perhaps one day, all
answers found, Western man would become good and noble,
would learn from us a sense of wisdom, forbearance and respect for the life of his fellow being.

In euphoric mood I read the first Chinese translation of
Huxley's *Ethics and Evolution*, a translation done in 1896; it
was brought by a Hakka merchant from Canton. After reading
that, I could not sleep for some nights. It was the most wonderful book I had ever read, questioning Man himself. I was
overwhelmed.

When Mr. Bonami asked us to write an essay on "The best
book I have ever read", I wrote on *Ethics and Evolution*. I
bared my emotions, recounted how this book had been for

me a revelation. I wrote as in a fever. I was pleased to think that this would show Mr. Bonami that even in Szechuan we had read such a great book. For Bonami often treated us as if we were ignorant children, and though I said nothing I did not like it.

The next day Mr. Bonami called me to his office, which was a large room with a large brown desk and a rug on the floor. He sat behind the desk. Suddenly his beard quivered, and he started shouting. I was so frightened that I could not understand him at first. Then his mouth opened wider, and he came nearer, shouting in my face, so that I saw his teeth and palate.

"Such sacrilegious ideas, such trash, men from monkeys, by that infamous Darwin and his gang of bandits," he cried, with great passion if without any accuracy. "Where did you get such stuff? If that is the kind of thing you read, when you go to acquire civilization in my country I shall ask my people to watch out for you!"

There was more of the kind. He paced, shouted, beard wagging in profile. At any moment his flaying arms (for he moved them about as he paced) would hit me, and then what would I do? I would lose dignity. I could not submit to being struck by anyone, and therefore would possibly have to kill him, or to kill myself, that my spirit might exact revenge upon him after death. He towered above me by a head, and must have weighed twice what I did. I wanted to run away, but pride kept me nailed, standing in front of him. I sweated with fear. Physical violence always nauseated me.

I walked out, my essay in hand, torn across. It took years before I began to comprehend. Were not Huxley, Darwin, part of European Science? Did not the European world mean Science? Was I not to learn from them what they knew? I felt I could never face Bonami again, and thought of returning to Szechuan. I tried to procure another teacher on private tuition; I explained to the supervisor that I was unwell and could not attend classes. But after a while the supervisor persuaded me to return to Bonami's class, otherwise I might not be able to proceed to Europe. After three weeks I went back. Bonami sprang from his chair, greeted me warmly, and asked if I was better. He had forgotten everything, everything. But I would never forget.

*

Mr. Bonami was probably a staunch Catholic, and therefore took exception to Huxley and Darwin, both condemned by the Church. But Yentung did not know this. He did not know that Europe had persecuted her own scientists and inventors and discoverers; and this is not ended. In 1964 in Mississippi, U.S.A., a schoolteacher lost her job because she tried to teach Darwin's Evolution to her pupils. In the context of prejudice, Mr. Bonami's wrath in 1903 becomes understandable.

But to Yentung this was a crisis of conscience, of confidence, a time of duress; for if he was not to believe in Science, what *could* he believe in? The whole subject of foreigners and of Christianity was already for him (as it still is for so many Asians) supercharged with emotional overtones. The scars it left upon his make-up went much deeper than he himself realized. That he overcame his fear, returned to Bonami, required much logic and effort. After some years in Europe he began to understand the diversity, the violently contradictory flux and reflux of ideas and actions which was Europe in those years. But he never lost his fear altogether, in spite of what happened later. He was uneasy and restless in the houses of Europeans, never natural, anxious not to draw their so ready violence, verbal or physical, so that he became almost obsequious with them, and when they spoke of China he fell silent, turning himself into a sealed hermetic box, lid on. Like many of his generation, he always had the feeling that they tried to pry into him, to "open a hole into his soul", because of their avidity for "understanding the Oriental", which he considered an insolence. For Chinese courtesy taught that relations between gentlemen and friends must be smooth, uncompelling, easy as the flow of water, and affection cannot be laid on anyone by compulsion, even of love.

This experience with Bonami was not isolated. It was that of many Chinese, put off from Western learning by the missionaries who came to "teach" them, and taught them badly for they insisted on teaching religion as a prerequisite to any other learning. Had they given of their secular knowledge, given the best that the West had to offer, science, philosophy, humanism, literature, to the scholars of China, perhaps history would have been different. Instead, they offered these often erudite men naive and childish tales of God and Devil, promise of heaven and threat of hell, all things regarded as despicable and unworthy of the civilized. For a century they mostly contented themselves with translating the

Bible; education without Christian conversion was not their aim.

And so Christ became identified not with learning, but with opium; not with saving mankind, but with robbing China. And the scars of this outrage are there today, even unto my own generation, and not only in China.

It was the Chinese scholars themselves, the reformists and later the revolutionaries, who began translating books from the West, in the teeth of opposition from the Manchu dynasty and with little help from the mission educationists, apart from a few single individuals more often disapproved of for teaching "what was not necessary" to the Chinese and thus "encouraging the growth of rebellious ideas".

After the episode with Bonami, Yentung confided to his brother: "I feel more frightened than when I was crossing the rapids. Then, I knew my life in danger; now, it is my mind which seems to hover above a dizzying precipice. I no longer know what to believe, and I even doubt the categories: hard and soft, liquid and solid, everything is topsy-turvy; when I walk I know my body is propelled from one point to another, but can no longer remember how I got there. Where is the essence of the West, and how shall I ever understand it?"

Thus his despairing soliloquy, as he was confronted by what appeared to him the inscrutable, double-faced, schizophrenic West. The fear remained, even if the confusion resolved, but it did not prevent Yentung from boarding the boat which left Shanghai for Marseille in late 1903. He had kept his queue, despite the fact that some merchants and scholars going to Japan cut theirs at their peril; as late as 1907 one man was beaten to death at the railway station in Peking because he wore a false queue and inadvertently lifted his hat, exposing his queueless condition. Yentung was to cut his queue off, though his mother did not know he had done so until he returned to China ten years later, in 1913. And by then nearly all queues were cut.

THIRTEEN

THE Szechuan students who climbed on board the French Messageries Maritimes boat *Porthos*, leaving Shanghai for Marseille in the winter of 1903, carried much luggage in edible, aromatic form,

Chou Yentung had five large preserved fish, in osier-bound baskets; five wicker hampers, each weighing eight catties,* lined with lacquered and oiled cloth, loaded with fermented beancurd in chilli sauce; ten two-foot-high porcelain jars, filled with diverse sweetmeats, lids airtight; cakes with rinds of fruit, honey, lotus seeds and almonds, their flaky envelopes speckled with black sesame and pepper; preserved fruit in crystallized sugar, quinces, lemons, sour plums; olives against nausea, packets of birds' nests for strengthening soups; parcels of Chinese medicine for various diseases, prescribed and prepared by his father, for weakness, for cold, bone ague, fever of all kinds, all in dark-red waterproof oilcloth; preserved lacquered ducks, dehydrated and flat, slipped in flat rattan chemises with red and gold foil, their outstretched beaks pierced with a hole threaded with plantain fibre for hanging. He also had two hams from Yunnan, hog's foot attached, also convenient to string up. He had four baskets of oranges, bamboo boxes of preserved cumquats, lacquer boxes of tea, twelve jars of pickles made by his mother, and various condiments and preserved vegetables in salt and cloves.

No doubt the others had a similar amount of victuals to keep them from famishing in Europe; for their great complaint was discomfort in the stomach, a craving for the warm satisfaction of rice, a palate yearning for savours and textures unreachable; for tongue and finger, as well as eye and ear and nose, all suffer from nostalgia, all need familiar touch, savour, shape, sound, aroma, to relay to the mind a soothing. And the Szechuanese, by their strong addiction to chilli, the tear- and sweat-making red pepper in which food is cooked, complain of stomach unease abroad, which means anywhere else but in Szechuan.

When all this store of essentials against the hollowness within had entered the cabin which the four students shared, there was a quarrel with the under-steward. Wu Ling and one of his sons, who had accompanied the party, now intervened, Wu Ling handing out his card, which was printed in English on one side, Chinese on the other, in a lordly way to the under-steward.

Surly, Wu Ling's son said to Yentung: "Your family must be very wealthy." He was looking at the camphor-wood chests with their elaborate engraved copper bands, the brown lacquered pigskin chests containing the furs, lined long silk gowns

* 1 cattie=1·1023 lb.

and satin doublets; the smaller leather chests, lacquered black, with cloth socks, waistbands, silk underwear; the various chests with scrolls and books; a procession of boxes on the heaving shoulders of coolies being carried up the gangplank. "This vulgar way of alluding to wealth is prevalent in Shanghai," Yentung wrote. "I took no notice."

The under-steward, an Annamite Eurasian, behaved arrogantly. Yentung wrote of the half-breed with contempt: "He tries to curry favour with his white master."

When the French head steward came, Wu Ling did not utter a word, but submitted to being told, with the rudeness which was the usual accompaniment of the White way of speech and action in those days, that all this stink could not be taken on board a French ship; some of it must be left behind. Yentung sacrificed the fish, some of the vegetables, and one ham. He judiciously remembered there was some silver in his pocket, and a gleam of coin produced sympathy. "I refused to let all the food be taken away, as I knew we would need it on the voyage."

The French steward gone, the Eurasian also went, and suddenly the cabin-boy, a Chinese from Annam, a Hakka, found ample space for storage. The fish, the ham, the vegetables returned. Special arrangements with the Chinese chef procured food cooked for them, for very little extra money, and served in their cabin. They avoided the French-style restaurant, eschewed sitting in the second-class dining-hall, although enjoined to practise using knife and fork during the voyage. "Let us not forestall the grim day when, along with Science, we shall have to wear European dress and learn how to eat their food."

In the hour of parting, poems were composed with allusions to former travellers who "carried the wind in their sleeves". Friends seeing them off vowed to stand on the lonely strand with eyes scanning the horizon, watching for their return without daring to shut their lids.

Wu Ling was to die during the 1911 Revolution, suspected of having betrayed some revolutionaries to the Manchus: the British had seized smuggled ammunition, the Manchus executed young students. Suspicion fell on Wu Ling, who was privately murdered.

A tremor shook the *Porthos*, sirens hooted, Yentung felt imprisoned by a headache. He watched the coast recede, the yellow-gold water turn to blue. His hand went to his cap, wind-buffeted, touched his queue.

The *Porthos* stopped at Saigon, now a French-occupied city. The students were welcomed by the Chinese merchants' guilds of Cholon, the Chinese commercial sector of the city, and immediately engulfed in another China, the China Overseas, a trading, bluff, prompt, money-minded, raucous, jostling China, quite unlettered, but intensely concerned with what happened in the Old Mountain of the Ancestors, and fiercely anti-Manchu.

They had friends and relatives of the "bamboo-shoot" variety, by adoption and affection, there as in Singapore, for Hakkas in whatever part of the world call each other "cousin" and "brother", help and lend money to each other, and are reputed not to cheat each other (which is incorrect, they do).

Again Yentung confided to his brother: "How lively, how quick witted, but also how concerned with making money they are, compared to us in Szechuan! We are lethargic, here they bustle. The weather is for ever like our steamiest summer, but nothing alters their energy. And how they hate the Manchus!"

To the Overseas Chinese the name of Sun Yatsen was becoming magic. They spoke of him at all times, not frightened of reprisals. But the most wealthy of them still spoke of Kang Yuwei, the Reformist, as being "more reliable than Sun".

"We met Nguen Wenhsin, an important man here, whose elder son is studying in France. He is a follower of Sun Yatsen. Sun himself is said to be in the north, in Hanoi. It is said that he thinks of an uprising which he will lead from Hanoi into Kwangsi province. Others say Sun is not here, but in America. Sun is here, Sun is there, Sun is everywhere at once. But no one has actually seen his face."

Nguen Wenhsin's father had been a Taiping, small leader of some peasant battalions, and had fled after the failure in 1864. Wenhsin's brother had been press-ganged and sold for labour in Malaya, where along with hundreds of other coolies he felled the jungle and built the roads for five years, and finally redeemed himself, walked to Siam, worked in a small sawmill, learnt to drive elephants used in felling lumber in the jungles, and by extraordinary exertion in thirty years made money and became wealthy. The brothers, one in Bangkok, the other in Saigon, ran a timber business. The old father hobbled about, and told the story of his Taiping days:

"It was the autumn. A number of us Red Turbans were manning the river fleet from Canton, and when the Manchu dogs tried to cross the river they ambushed and killed about five hundred of us. There were some British and Americans helping them, but we let them go, for that was the order of the Heavenly King, although they sank fourteen of our junks. But more dog-soldiers came, and we had to run away, in a junk, two hundred of us. We only had room to sit, and nothing to eat or to drink, and half died on the way, of wounds and thirst; and we were lucky, we struck a shore, and then it was Annam and French soldiers came and put chains on us. After a few days they marched us off into the jungle, and there we built a road, and after four years, out of eighty of us, there were only fifteen left."

They let him go and he lived, incredibly, becoming a small pedlar, selling paper toys and blow-glass bubbles for children; he saved enough to buy a hawker's stand and to pay the poll tax which the French imposed on all the Chinese. "And now I wait for the Revolution to come, that I may return to my ancestors' land. I do not want to die before I see the Revolution."

The old man gave much money to Sun's cause.

Both Wenhsin, and Wenhsin's son, only sixteen years old, were to die in an insurrection organized by Sun Yatsen from Indo-China in 1907 or 1908; they were hacked to pieces, along with a hundred other revolutionaries, in a pitched battle.

In Saigon China suddenly became more real, a sharp, vivid entity, to Yentung. It was not only Szechuan, his province, it was all China that he suddenly became aware of. Did he then think of Liu Tachun, his friend? Did he inquire? Yentung does not mention this. But he writes: "Suddenly I realize far better the need for change, and the sufferings of my people."

From Saigon the boat, now full, with many Frenchmen in first class, Annamites and Tonkinese merchants and Chinese students in second class, developed some engine defect so that it went limping into Singapore harbour, which Yentung found to his surprise was yet another Chinese city, though run by the English. "We are being entertained by the local merchants' guilds. Some of the merchants here are extremely prosperous." Here Sun Yatsen's influence was not as great as in Indo-China, though later Singapore was to become one of his financial mainstays for the Revolution in China, and by 1910 he was reckoned to have ten thousand supporters there.

The feelings of resentment against the Manchu dynasty were also outspoken in Singapore. Already in 1898, Yentung learned, there had been much agitation to cut the queue, and this had not abated. Most of the Chinese here had arrived as "pigs", or indentured labour. There was also a minority of political exiles. In Singapore the British ruled and the Chinese worked. The British Empire needed more industrious, hard-working "human pigs" to go into Malaya and work there as well, for the Federated States of Malaya had now been opened to British conquest.

The first nation kidnapping Chinese for use on their vessels were the Portuguese, who made raids upon the coasts all through the seas from India to China. The Dutch, needing labour for the East Indies, first organized the Chinese "pig" system of contract labour. The Manchu dynasty did not allow anyone to leave the country on pain of death; however, the poverty, the constant revolts and their suppression, led to a fund of human pigs, men ready and willing to leave, especially after the Taiping. In 1860, by treaty, the Powers forced the dynasty to allow Chinese to leave their own land, which enormously facilitated the trade in "pigs". The price paid to the recruiter was forty silver dollars: ten dollars was given to the labourer recruited, thirty paid for his transport. His sale for labour in the Dutch East Indies brought the contractor there one hundred dollars. The man signed a "contract" (which he often could not read) with his thumb mark, stating that he would work for three years for the sum of one hundred and eighty dollars, or sixty dollars per year. To redeem himself at the end of three years he would have to repay one hundred dollars to the plantation master. He was dependent for food on a canteen run by his employers, where prices were high. He could not leave the plantations. Opium dens were kept on the plantations, and there he spent more money. As a result he soon owed much more than a hundred dollars, and at the end of three years would sign another three years' contract. The system followed in Malaya by the British was along the same lines, and by the 1900s the pig-runners were British and Portuguese merchants, but the people who did the press-ganging for them were Chinese gangsters in Shanghai, Canton, and other ports.

Yentung found that Kang Yuwei had staunch supporters in

Singapore, chiefly among the more respectable and prosperous. But Sun Yatsen, though controversial, held the imagination of the many. The fortune-tellers of the Monkey shrines in Singapore and Penang predicted victory for Sun Yatsen; they told how in 1894 Sun, with eighteen other men, had formed an Association, swearing to "make a Revolution", and of the eighteen, seventeen had been captured and beheaded, leaving only Sun to carry on, to make the Revolution ... This showed that Heaven was on his side. He had been captured in London, but again Heaven had intervened to save him, in the person of an Englishman, Dr. Cantlie. Sun travelled all over the world talking of revolution, and though many were the traps to waylay him, always miraculously he eluded them. He was also a member of the Triad Secret Society, so called because their emblem was three circles representing Heaven, Earth and Man, usually found engraved in the floors of Taoist Temples in Szechuan; this secret society was very powerful among the poor "pigs" in Singapore.

Kang or Sun? Who was the one to save China? Kang was collecting money for risings in China, but they were risings to release the Emperor and to maintain the Empire. In June 1900 two Japanese, Miyasaki and Kiyafugi, friends of Sun Yatsen, had come to Singapore on Sun's behalf to offer Kang an alliance. But Kang said the Japanese were sent to assassinate him, for on them had been found money, and both carried for self-defence the usual knives that Japanese (and also Malays) carry in their belts, a symbol of manhood. Kang reported the Japanese to the British authorities, and they were imprisoned. Sun went to Singapore himself, in July 1900, to obtain their release; which was extremely brave of him, since the Manchus would have done anything to kill him. The British did not want him in Singapore, and told him to go. Once again he offered Kang an alliance, but Kang refused, saying he did not believe in violent revolution, only in orderly reform. They parted, never to meet again.

To the wealthy merchants of Singapore, Kang was the Emperor's tutor, a scholar of renown, although in temporary disgrace. The abject and vicious Dowager would not live for ever; at her death the imprisoned Emperor would be released, he would recall Kang, the Reformists would rule the Empire. Therefore, to give Kang money seemed to these calculating businessmen a good investment in future influence. Sun was poor, unknown, proscribed, not a scholar, certainly not a

gentleman with a good name. When Sun's partisans went collecting money for the Revolution, the rich merchants said:
"If you can guarantee that the Revolution will be successful,
then we shall give money, but not otherwise." Sun's influence
was among the small shopkeepers, the labourers, the coolies,
and the younger merchants, and they were ready to die for
him.

All this Yentung learned from Chia, a Hakka merchant,
who received and feasted the students in his residence in
Kling Street, Singapore. Chia was a public-spirited man, the
owner of some wealth in pineapples. His father had fled at
the end of the Taiping; his mother had fought in the Taiping
women regiments, and been killed; an uncle of his owned
pepper plantations in Borneo. Chia gave money to Sun Yatsen's cause, and was a member of the Triad secret society in
Singapore.

Once again Yentung was perplexed. The British, whom he
had learnt to hate in Szechuan because they openly wanted
the whole of the Great River basin, were here the protectors
of the Chinese; under their rule the Chinese in Singapore prospered and made money, and many praised the British. Here
was Kang Yuwei, a refugee from China, smuggled aboard an
English gunboat in that fateful September 1898 when Reform
had failed, hiding under the protection of a Sikh police guard
(one of those so loathsome bearded giants). The Manchus had
sent gangsters to kill him, but with the connivance of the British he had stayed in Singapore. And yet the British also
openly supported the Manchu dynasty . . .

On the other hand, Sun Yatsen had been saved in London –
where the Manchu Embassy had kidnapped him with the passive connivance of some English Foreign Office diplomat – by
another Englishman, Cantlie, a doctor who had been his
teacher and friend when Sun was studying medicine in Hongkong.

During the forty-eight hours the ship stayed in Singapore
harbour, Yentung experienced the patriotic fervour of the
Overseas Chinese. It seemed to him he was in a maze of quid-
dities, contradictions, which annulled each other and produced in him stupor. The British brought into Singapore
opium from India and China at cut rates, farmed out the
opium establishments to Chinese merchants to run for them;
the Chinese merchants sold the opium to the poor Chinese
coolies, those who were themselves sold by the boatload to

work in the jungles, and had no home, no wife or child, nothing except opium to ease their pain away. In this evil system the British contrived to get most of the cash and yet to let the Chinese do the dirty work; and the rich Chinese also made money out of the opium sold to their poorer fellow Chinese. Fifty-nine per cent of the total revenue of the British government in Singapore and Malaya in 1903 and in 1904 was due to opium. Yet in England was great agitation to ban the curse of opium, as there was agitation to put an end to the slave traffic, including the traffic in human pigs.

On the morning of his second day in Singapore, a few hours before returning on board, Yentung went to a Chinese barber in Cross Street, and had his queue cut off. Perhaps this act was due to the feverish, almost tranced patriotic consciousness awakened in him. Much queue-cutting had already taken place in Singapore, and here the snip of scissors was not as dangerous as in China. Accompanying him to this momentous first disobedience and explicit rebellion (and revolt against the Family too, for his mother had warned him that to cut off his queue was to cut off his life, which was true since heads were lost when queues were cut) was a young Cantonese man named Tan Hsiakkim, a nephew of Chia, and a prodigiously versatile young man: he could sing opera, wrestle, play several musical instruments including the western piano, and was to die in 1909, when he smuggled himself back to China, in yet another failed uprising. "He most closely resembled my friend Tachun, stood by me while the barber's scissors snipped; he afterwards joked that now my neck was naked and it would be easier to cut off my head. He had no fear of taboo words, unlike most Cantonese, who never mention 'knife', 'cut' or 'death'."

During the rest of the voyage Yentung let the hair grow on his forehead. When he became a young dandy in Brussels he learnt to part it and to use pomade. After his return to China he was to wear a crew cut.

The queue was placed in a sandalwood box with a tight-fitting lid. It stayed among Yentung's belongings till his wife Marguerite found it. She described it to me, her child, in her usual vivid present tense, her hands motioning the rummaging she had wrought.

I am turning over everything, in the new house. What am I to do with all these coffers?

So I find this box, and what do I see? I think at first it is a snake, your father has all sorts of Chinese medicines with him which I throw away. I want to throw this out, but the box is so pretty, and the object is wrapped in paper, so I ask him first:

"What is this?"

And your father says: "My queue."

"What on earth do you keep it for?"

He says: "For my mother."

Otherwise his mother would have worried, because anyone who could find his hair might throw a spell to harm him. So he gives me the box, and I put my handkerchiefs in it, and I put the queue in an envelope. We took the thing back, and he gave it to his mother. Oh, I had to laugh.

*

On board the *Porthos* Yentung thought he had discovered the European woman. And to him, until he met Marguerite, they were "the ugliest things on earth", as he wrote to his younger brother. Particularly repulsive to him were their voices and their feet, bigger than his, in heeled leather. Their hands, their noses, the way they laughed showing the whole of their mouths, everything about them shocked him. How *could* anyone even think of such creatures as women? And yet, in his very insistence upon their ugliness, is there not already some hint of fascination?

He and the other students discussed Woman freely, and wondered that a few of the Chinese students who had gone abroad had married European women. "In fact, I am told that they really have long, hairy tails, which is why they put on those many skirts, to conceal their rumps." Thus he wrote at seventeen, knowing nothing of Woman.

(Incredibly, fifty-two years later, I was to find the same hoary myth, that European women have tails, still current among some of the Overseas Chinese in Malaya.)

After Suez the sun grew paler, replaced by the diffuse grey light, compound of grey water and leaden sky, and in this light the women on the boat looked different, their skins finer and lighter, more delicate, their non-black hair pleasant now, as they laughed gaily at the tossing spray, and the wind blew their skirts about.

And now the torn seas of Europe, the Mediterranean

shrouded in stiff grey, which Yentung hated until he discovered its energizing quality. The wind cut his face as, clad in fur-lined gowns, he and the other students landed at Marseille, the objects of immediate and congregating curiosity. "People came up to touch me, my robe, my hat. I had never seen so many of them."

He had survived the separating oceans. The year was 1904, a cold February.

A representative of the Chinese consul met them. The students donned their caps (false queues attached); luckily Chinese etiquette forbade the doffing of headgear. They saluted the vice-consul, and a foreigner with him, enormously tall, once again bearded. Yentung noted: "The foreigners in their own country are much more polite to us than they are in China." In China the foreigners of Shanghai had looked at him with contempt, he had been pushed and kicked by a Sikh policeman. Here he was received with smiles and courtesy, though the tall man gripped his hand too hard, and the beard frightened him as usual.

Around him crowds gathered, curious but kind. "A Chinese, a Chinese," they whispered. And some came up to him to say: "Welcome to my country."

The first sight of Europe was for him, as it was to be later for his daughter, a gloomy, sad-making impact. People seemed to hurry so much; they looked worried, and all was grey: faces, streets, houses, sky. "It induced in me an almost intolerable heaviness, my brother. Here people live ensconced in stone houses, behind the malevolent glint of their windows, and the street is brusque and not for the loitering of friends, as with us." His eyes in their first European winter were unable to pick out the subdued colours and tints of European cities, to distinguish verdigris from silver grey, to make out the subtleties of the blacks and browns. The blue eyes, the beards, the jerky movements, a kind of overall clumsiness and violence; not the swift venomous violence of Shanghai, but another kind, as of children maladjusted, tense muscled, who break things because they have not been taught how to poise their own effort with gentleness, gave him that almost constant queasiness in the stomach from which he suffered all his life. And yet, again, he was to marvel at their deftness with machines, though they appeared to him so clumsy in the everyday acts of living. He was to learn to love and to hate, all at once; but all his life he could not really get away from Europe, except by shutting himself into himself.

The tall bearded man took them in a carriage with a horse to a hotel, where he thought the room very small (his luggage had partly entered it). The Beard laughed at the luggage, slapped him on the back. He winced, was ready to be insulted, and took some time to persuade himself that this gesture expressed friendliness. The Beard indicated that the students should now sleep. He then showed his watch, which was upon a chain, pointed to his mouth, and started counting on his fingers, which Yentung understood was to tell him the time of the next meal. "Je comprends," he said, and the Beard was delighted. "What excellent French you speak. A tantôt, monsieur."

The following day they took a train. Yentung had not been in a train before, though he had seen the railway station in Shanghai. People stared and whispered: "Ils sont Chinois, des Chinois." He was prepared again to resent them and their smell, which "still makes me retch", but they were so friendly he relented.

They reached their destination, and the Beard, whose name Yentung found to be Monsieur Navarre, conducted Yentung to a narrow grey house, where they were received by a white-haired lady, very fat, and a younger woman, also plump, and another man with a beard. Yentung found that it had been arranged that he should stay with this family and he was shown his room, which was large, warm, with two windows, curtains, carpets. He found it delightful, but too enclosed; he was accustomed to open windows. When his luggage arrived, the plump white-haired lady raised her arms high, a gesture which Yentung did not understand until, as the chests came under her small blue gaze, her face assumed an expression which he recognized for having seen a similar one on Wu Ling's face. The unconsumed preserves produced a violent recoil from her, another expression and a flow of words. She shook her head violently from side to side. Luckily not much was left, though he expected another shipment soon. The other students were to be lodged in other houses, also with Belgian families.

That night he ate with the family, whose name was Berckmans, and they watched him eat. He now began to talk with them, and gradually found it pleasant. The women laughed all the time, especially the plump girl, who had an enormous amount of yellow hair flying in all directions. Afterwards he went back to his room. The bed was large, and he felt partly suffocated with the hot softness of the eiderdown. But he liked the sheets, and the smell of lavender. It took him a long time to fall asleep.

The next afternoon the Beard came again, and took him and the three other students for a walk. They walked into a large shop and bought clothes and shoes, a hat, a coat, an umbrella. Everywhere people gathered to stare at them, and whispered: "Chinese or Japanese?" When he returned to the house Yentung put away his Chinese clothes in his chests, and locked them. It was like putting away another person, becoming someone new. He had come to learn how to be strong, as the West was strong. For this he would wear their clothes, eat their food, keep his Chinese self locked away and safe, away from them and their curiosity. This is what he thought, but things did not happen that way.

Whenever Chou Yentung was asked: "Did you enjoy your student years in Europe?" he looked puzzled, then he smiled, and usually glanced towards his wife, Marguerite, before answering: "In those days I was studying very hard. We had not much time to enjoy ourselves."

Enjoy. The word to him meant something other than the process of experimentation, tasting, guzzling, pondering, jostling, laughing, getting angry, being insulted, loving with a rapacious quality unknown before, being bored, not being bored, being homesick, drinking, drowning into self and into actions, gestures, moods, emotions, that were to come off him later like the skins off a lizard. Yentung in Europe was another Yentung, a not-he, as later his daughter in Europe was a not-she. Yet neither father nor daughter ever forewent completely that other self, that identity kept tucked away, folded up, preserved from contact, watchful and reticent, the Other One within crying its loneliness out into laughter, crying its puzzlement in jeers, boisterously imitating the whole incoherence of gestures and talk and pretence which was necessary in order not to appear different. In order not to be alone, in the loneliness of Europe, Yentung did things in Europe which he would not have done in his own country. Very quickly he adapted. Within three months he sauntered at ease in his clothes. He found studying easy, and enjoyment plentiful.

A servility of smiles crept over him because he wanted to be liked, or rather not interfered with, accepted without altercation. And he soon found out that smiling kept others happy about his being happy, strictly proving the myth at that time current in France, due to a popular operetta, that Annamese and Chinese were very happy now and always smiling.

Yentung wrote to his brother: "They are extraordinarily full of energy, their cities clean, their houses neat. They work very hard. Ah, if they only wanted to do so, they could help us so much!"

He studied fiercely, in a fury of wanting to know. Less and less did he try to explain China to his fellow students. He let them talk.

"Are you a prince in China?"

"Is it true you eat mice?"

"Is it true you cut off the feet of little girls?"

"How many pipes of opium do you smoke a day?"

This was mixed with:

"The Chinese have the oldest civilization in the world."

"You are a highly cultured nation."

Immediately followed by:

"Our priests are bringing you civilization at last."

"It is our duty, as white men, to bring justice and civilization to the coloured races."

For in Yentung's days as a student in Europe the Whites spoke freely of their duty as "white men", they acknowledged their own superior status without shame or guilt. It was heaven-ordained to them. The newspapers said it, and the books taught that the white man's brain was the biggest, and weighed more than the brains of other races. In the churches there were posters:

"Give, for the poor little negroes of our missions."

"Charity, for the pagan Chinese, sunk in their superstitions."

"Your money will save Chinese souls for Heaven."

There were pictures of Jesus Christ, in Heaven, rays issuing from his chest where a big fire roared its red flames, and these rays went down on earth to two people, a priest in brown and a nun in white; from their hands again issued rays, in lesser quantity, which now dispersed upon the heads of black curly negroes, on their knees, Chinese with pigtails, on their knees, and Red Indians with feathered headbands, hands folded, eyes upturned, on their knees. The background was fumous grey clouds from whence multitudes issued, going towards the Light.

"Ten francs will buy a little Chinaman."

His landlady, Madame Berckmans, brought back one of these pictures from a mission sermon on China she attended. She told Yentung at dinner about it.

"Such a nice missionary, Mr. Chou. He has been five years in your country. He told us all about the tortures that you Chinamen practise. It was horrible." She shivered deliciously, shaking the firm, over-rippling folds of her neck. The rest of her was encased in stiff garments that crackled and made various noises similar to small explosions. It was only after Yentung met Marguerite that he understood the various noises Madame Berckmans emitted. She was laced into her stays by her maid, as Marguerite got her maid, Josephine, to lace her in, pulling hard as she held on to the door knob, while the maid braced her feet against the floor.

Monsieur Berckmans always stared at Yentung with a stuporous surprise as he went upstairs and downstairs. It was as if he saw him for the first time every time they met. Dressed in the evening in a velvet coat in the winter, in the summer in shirt sleeves, he had a moustache hanging down both sides of his face, very black because he dyed it. He had a beard also, unremarkable below this moustache, which he forgot to dye. The arrangement, with the full blueish lips in the middle, looked nearly obscene to Yentung, who compared him to some of the more evil masks of the Chinese theatre. Later when he had had some modest experience of European women, he began to ponder the conjugal life of Monsieur and Madame Berckmans.

Then one of the Chinese students went mad. He had arrived in Brussels at the same time as Yentung. There were now about fifteen students from China in Belgium. They had formed an association and held correspondence with other associations of Chinese students in Paris, in London and elsewhere. Once a month, on a Sunday, they met in the room of one or other student to speak of China, and of the Revolution and of Sun Yatsen. Soon, pooling some money, they rented a room above a café, which they turned into their club. There they could even cook, and once a week they did cook a Chinese dinner. It alleviated their nostalgia.

And of course they talked of white men, and their assumption that they were born superior, their conviction that they knew everything.

"Ah," Monsieur Navarre said, when he met the students, which he did once every quarter, "what need do you have of our machines, our wealth (actually we are very poor, we have to spend so much on our colonies), our science? You have your Wisdom, the Wisdom of the Ages, Confucius."

The boy who went mad had been shy and withdrawn from the beginning, and very homesick. When the Chinese students formed their association he came, and spoke of the spiritual superiority of the East versus the material advance of the West.

This spiritual elevation, being the only thing freely left to China, gradually implanted itself in the minds of the Chinese students as evident, true and admirable. They had anyway been conditioned to regard themselves as owners of some higher wisdom, some morality not amenable to the sordid materialism of Western life. And this conviction, founded on nothing, became once again their refuge, their escape valve; they reverted to the attitude of their elders, who spoke of preserving Confucian morality and virtue while learning the practical achievements of the industrial revolution in Europe. The materialistic West, the spiritual East, became a satisfactory antithesis for the young homesick men. It made their love-hate relations much easier to bear. They might be a beaten, humiliated, inferior nation, inferior in everything but in this, this incredible wisdom, a veiled splendour which somehow made them the acknowledged masters of hidden mysteries and which the West envied them ...

The student who went mad wanted to study literature, because he wanted to write poetry, a blend of East and West, but gradually he began to say that he had nothing to learn from Europe; that all was infinitely better in China.

He lived, as they all did, in a spare room in a Belgian house. He had now started to cook for himself, and there was a feeling among the other students that he could not feed himself properly because he became thinner as the weeks went by. Most of them received food from China, which took three months to come, and quite a few of them became clever buyers, doing their own marketing at the butchers and fishmongers. They tried to make him eat, cooking dishes for him, but he smiled and shook his head and said he had already eaten, he was not hungry. He brought his flute with him and played old airs, and the students sang opera arias. They recited poems, and for some hours felt happy, nearer to China.

The mad boy sat smiling, apparently enjoying it all, and then one day he did not turn up. They heard he was ill. Yentung and two other students went to see him.

They found him in his room playing the flute. He was very thin. All the windows were shut, though it was summer and quite hot. They opened the windows, and tried to take him out for a walk and a meal. He said, smiling, that he had already eaten. When they left they saw the landlady in the corridor. She had opened the door to them, and they had, as taught, doffed their hats and said: "Bonjour, Madame," smiling strenuously. Now Yentung looked at her. She was fat, like his Madame Berckmans, but her fat was a different texture, not a fatness replete with the juices of the last meal, but an impervious, opaque, white-wax, dead fatness. She moved silently. There was a musty smell in the corridor, which seemed to emanate from the walls and the furniture and even rise from the floor.

Two days later the boy was in an asylum. It was Monsieur Navarre who told the students. Monsieur Navarre used to drop in on their "club", jovially impromptu, so that the students invited him to dinner once a month, knowing that he expected it. He did not stay for dinner, but sat for a while, asking questions of each of them. Gradually they had begun to feel that he wanted to "bore a hole in their souls". They never contradicted him while he lectured them on their own country, and the more he asked, the more they smiled heartily, and told him only what they thought would please him.

"Ah," said Monsieur Navarre, "how fortunate you are, my friends! You will ally in yourselves the wisdom of the ages and our modern civilization, which will benefit your people immensely. Never forget, never forget however, that you Orientals have a different tradition from ours. Your peoples are happy peoples, do not try to change them too quickly. Do not listen to these monsters who speak of revolution! Reform, orderly change, tradition! That is the future for your country."

The students nodded. Always they gave him their smiles, always an impressed attention. When they went out in a group, or were taken out by Monsieur Navarre, they smiled until their faces were sore.

After the student went mad, Monsieur Navarre came to the club to tell the students, although they already knew it. "Your friend, alas, is now in an institution. His mind is deranged." He paused here, impressively. "We found that he had many books" – pause – "many EVIL revolutionary books among his belongings." His face went purple, his features frozen in stony anger, his hand went up, index finger wagging, his beard twice its usual volume. "My children (for I can call you so, since you are under my care), let this be a lesson to you. Never read this ... this filth. Yours is a grave, a serious responsibility. You must maintain the noble, the sacred, the admirable virtues of your great country. Read your classics, your sages, do not become poisoned, I beg you, with such propaganda from the mills of Hell, offensive both to religion and to the natural order." He went on for a long time about "these abominable nihilists, who are against every sacred institution, who would spread bloodshed and immorality all over the world", and finally adjured them: "Be loyal to your Emperor, worthy of your noble families."

The students smiled, and nodded repeatedly.

Monsieur Navarre's discourse, instead of frightening Yentung, had the effect of making him remember Liu Tachun and the talk of Sun Yatsen, remember the cutting of his queue in Singapore. Here in Europe there was only talk of progress in China, but the Chinese newspapers the students received also carried news of risings and bloodshed. He could not get the mad boy out of his mind, and on the third day took hat and cane and went to the madman's lodgings.

The same pale, heavy woman opened the door. He stood stammering.

"Your friend is not here, he is ill," said the woman, "but enter, do, sit down for a moment, rest yourself." He was in a room with embroidered cross-stitch upon the chairs, a lamp with a lampshade of purple velvet, a marble mantelpiece on which a clock, gilded, with cherubs under glass, showed the time. There were wax flowers under glass, and rushes and peacock feathers in a large jar in a corner. The woman sat facing him. She looked at him fixedly.

"Your friend will be ill for a long time, he is delicate and nervous," she said. "His room will be vacant. It is a pity."

Her blue eyes, which he noticed were lashless, held him.

"Why do you not come here, where you can have a small kitchen and cook your meals? The food is not good at Madame Berckmans' house, I know her. She economizes on everything, she is cheating you. Now, here you would be much better off. And it is cheaper."

She edged nearer, he now caught her smell, musty, like everything else in her house.

"I always look after my friends well. There are never any complaints. And I like Chinamen. I like you. Your skins are so wonderful." She raised her hand, and stroked his face. "Like a baby's," she said, "you have no hair on your face."

Yentung sat paralysed, skin crawling with horror and with a fascination which kept him immobile while she went on stroking. She started at the temple and down, and did one side, then the other, softly, regularly. The texture of the skin on her hand was a little moist, as if she had rubbed it with an emollient. But when she started fumbling with his tie, and putting her finger insinuatingly between his neck and collar, he got up, saying: "I must go," and went to the door, opened it, and was out, fumbling at the front door, terrified that she would come from behind and put those fingers down his collar from the back. He was in the street, and wondered why his legs felt strange, the whole of him so strange.

When he got back to the Berckmans', quivering with disgust and fascination, there was a letter from his friend Poh Hungwen. The students in France were organized into an Association. Would he come for a few days to Paris?

Yentung told Monsieur Navarre that he was going to Paris for a few days to see a friend, and Monsieur Navarre said that was a good thing. "You have worked very hard, kept away from these monsters who have corrupted so many young minds," he said. Suddenly he put a hand upon Yentung's shoulder, looked at him deeply, fully, turning the full power of his beard upon him. "When you return," he said, "we shall arrange for your summer holidays, but also for something else. Tell me, have you never felt the need for a God, for a kind Father to whom you could run for protection, whose Love would always be ready to help you in your need? Have you never wanted to understand the consolations of our religion? Ah, Monsieur Yentung, we have watched you, and of all the students I have known, I have found you one of the worthiest."

Yentung remembered that Monsieur Navarre had said the same thing to another student, who had repeated it, with much laughter, at the club some weeks previously.

"When you return, would you not like to receive the divine message from one of God's own servants?"

"My mother," said Yentung, "my mother would have to be consulted."

Monsieur Navarre did not give up. "By all means," he said, "we never force anyone to believe against their will. But you should keep your mind open. You have come to learn our science, our knowledge, our civilization. Why not at the same time learn that most precious of all the benefits we can confer on other peoples, our religion?"

But on this Yentung remained adamant. He would not nod, smile, nor agree to this; for this, he knew, was the one thing which was impossible.

"I venerate my ancestors, and I would have to consult them before I could take up your noble religion."

Monsieur Navarre dropped his hand. Yentung felt harried and exhausted. He was glad when he got on the train for Paris. Madame Berckmans and her plump daughter took him to the station and put him on the train, finding a corner for him, waving goodbye, Madame kissing him on both cheeks as if he were her own son.

"And don't fall for a French girl, they're no good," cried Madame Berckmans, agitating her handkerchief, and Yentung nodded, not quite understanding what she meant.

When the train had pulled out, he rubbed his cheeks where her moist lips had touched them. All this kissing made him feel very nervous. And yet he was attracted. He did not know whether he hated it or liked it. He no longer knew, for he was beginning to live, and living means to forget one's own changefulness, as the live serpent forgets its unkind sloughings and renewals.

Yentung was met at the station by Poh Hungwen, a student whom he had met on board ship. Poh was tall, good-looking, dressed very well, with a pearl in his tie. His father was a banker in Shansi province. Yentung liked the laughter on the streets of Paris. People here seemed less constrained. They sauntered freely, talked and joked loudly. Yentung liked Paris immediately.

"But the best thing here," said Poh to him, "is our Revolutionary Party. I will take you to a meeting tonight. You should really come to Paris to study, it is wonderful here, it is truly democratic, you can say and think anything you want."

Yentung noticed also that his French was different from the French that Poh spoke, and Poh laughed at him and at the way he pronounced words, saying: "You are speaking typical Belgian French. People in France will laugh at you."

The meeting was held in the upstairs room of a very small Chinese restaurant which they rented for such meetings. There were about forty students; some were actually Annamese, and some French girls. These latter were the students' friends, easy-mannered, and he found they were pretty, with soft faces and hair.

They had Chinese and Annamese dishes, and Yentung drank some wine. Everyone around him seemed intelligent, knowledgeable, talking so freely of revolution, also of the French Revolution. "This is what we need for our own country," they said, "a revolution, like France. Only of course on a bigger scale." They drank a toast to freedom. "It truly means something," Poh Hungwen said to Yentung. "We know what freedom is now. We have a task in front of us, to go back and make a revolution, and then our country will have freedom, equality, brotherhood, as in France, as in European countries." He added, in a low voice: "Do you know, Sun Yatsen will be in Europe soon? We are going to prepare a most important meeting. We must get all the students in Europe to send representatives so that we can listen to him carefully and unite for the Revolution."

Yentung went home with Poh, whose room he shared that night, and they spoke till late at night, feeling a brotherhood which abolished at once all their doubts and fears. They really did feel strong and united at that moment, though nothing yet had been done.

"We must be practical," said Poh. "We must think scientifically. We must organize the Revolution scientifically."

He himself was studying architecture, and had great plans for turning all the cities of China into incomparable metropolises. "They will look even better than Paris."

Yentung felt overawed by such vast schemes. He had not thought along such grandiose lines. Only of one railway, in his province of Szechuan. "Of course we need railways," said Poh. "My father says we need them, but we also need beautiful cities."

They went on to elaborate the future government of China, and already Yentung saw himself directing the building of many thousands of kilometres of railways; at his bidding trains came and went obediently, carrying coal and iron to big factories smoking against the sky. Long smooth lines of steel spanned the land from east to west, north to south. No more poverty and famine, floods and misery, and especially no more humiliation and insult. "We are just as good as anybody else. We have survived five thousand years. What is their civilization compared to ours?"

Thus went their thoughts and their talk.

On the second day as they returned from a stroll along the Seine, two police agents, not so polite, were at Poh's lodgings asking them to follow them to the police station.

Yentung was terrified. What was this, what was this? Was not France the Mother of Revolutions? Had she not had her own Revolution, cut off the head of her own king (admittedly a hundred or so years ago, but what was a hundred years in the history of a country)? And now these policemen were asking them the names of all those at the dinner, what were they talking about, and particularly about the Annamites attending – what had they said? They turned on Yentung, and asked him minute questions. Why had he come? Did he know a Dr. Sun? Had he ever met him? When was he returning to Brussels?

Yentung answered so badly that the policemen became very impatient with him. But Poh, much more self-assured, replied boldly. Yes, they were students, yes, they were forming an association of students, a democratic association. No, they were not going against any laws, they were putting down their names for contributions for social welfare, they were forming an organization of students to help each other, that was all. Dr. Sun? They did not know Dr. Sun, they only heard that he was a great man and a great patriot, they had no dealings with him.

Finally, the policemen said: "Now, you have come to study, not to make trouble, remember," and let them go, like naughty children admonished.

Returning home, Yentung said to Poh: "I thought you said that France is a free country?"

"Yes," said Poh. "But not always the police, and of course you must understand that the French are really oppressors of the Annamites. They are afraid that if there is a revolution in China, there will also be one in Indo-China."

But Yentung found this difficult to understand. Why did they not welcome a revolution in another country, a revolution similar to theirs? "Why should they do this to us? We have just as much right to a revolution as they have."

Poh sighed. "My friend, what is good for them is not

necessarily good for us, they say. When we have our revolution we may kick them out, that is what they are afraid of."

Yentung returned to Brussels. And it was in Brussels, in May 1905, that Sun Yatsen held a meeting, attended by many students, who came from all over Europe. Thirty students joined the Association he created then, which was to become the Revolutionary League. But not a word about this meeting did Yentung write to his brother, or leave extant anywhere. Yet he does seem to have attended the meeting and to have seen Sun Yatsen, because he told me so many years later.

It was a cold March day in 1925, in Peking, with swirls of sand from the desert wind whipping our faces. Father and I, I with my heavy coat and boots, and the long scarf I liked wound round my neck with the two pompoms beating my back, stood on the street among a million mourners, stood for what seemed hours, and Father was looking, standing straight, head raised; and I could not see anything, until Mr. Hua Namkwei, his friend who was with us, hoisted me on to his shoulders to catch a glimpse of the wreaths and the flags and the criss-cross of banners in white covering the box which enclosed the body of the man who had made the Revolution of 1911, and changed all our lives, and died insisting: "The Revolution is not ended. You must go on."

Mr. Hua's spectacles glinted, and he breathed in a funny manner. Father just looked, and I followed his stare. But there was nothing my eyes could grip in the enormous flux of people going, going, going, faces huddled black bands, banners, an enormous compact tide of sadness and silence, and though I wanted to cry, there was no core to the sorrow I was ready to wring out of myself, only weariness and irritation.

"Father, Father, who is he?"

"I will tell you, not now."

"Is he a friend of yours?"

"I met him only once, in Belgium."

"Father, why did he die? Why are the flowers all white?"

"Not now. Later."

But later never came. We went home, I was not told. But I found out. It was Sun Yatsen.

FOURTEEN

LET me spread out the photographs.

Groping for the solid past, I wonder now that what was so alive has become so muted, stabbing incoherence resigned to ethereal order. Perhaps it is true that the most enduring thing about a man's life is the epitaph upon his tombstone. In my case, a classical education drained my reality of its marrow juices, all events strained through the brain sieve, vocabulary, before I could accept them. And yet I too became capable of passion, the world a glory of desire; I too owned a rainbow in my sky, even if it became a carcan welded round my neck.

I sift the dust in my possession, stare into it the warmth, the violence, the time-sunk splendour once lived. I spread the photographs.

Screaming like a kite our servant, Hsueh Mah, who remained with me when Marguerite left me, shouts again: "Ah, Old Master, again you are looking at the photographs." Always, politely, she states what I do: "Ah, Old Master is looking at the vine; Old Master is eating . . ."

I spread them out on the counterpane, those likenesses laid flat, and Hsueh Mah hovers, looking over my shoulder, although she has seen them as I have, one hundred, two hundred times, perhaps more; I cannot recollect how many times I have taken the photographs out of the top layer of the trunk, that black trunk which came with us from Belgium in 1913, which was left behind in 1948, left with me, because it was useless, as I was.

For the hundredth, or two-hundredth time, Hsueh Mah prepares the proper little sounds of interest, of pleasure; exclamations, sighs, for she is dutiful and courteous in her peasant way, and she knows she must say these things, show that she gives me her attentiveness.

"Ah, that is the Old Mistress when young . . . how beautiful . . . what nobility . . . but was she not cold with those bare shoulders?"

The evening walks softly inside the house, the garden loses its sparrows, a single magpie swishes its wings as it returns to nest.

Marguerite looks out of the large photograph mauved by time. Oval face, large amber eyes, red hair coiled, shoulders bared, swathed just below the shoulder blades in the fine muslin that was worn in those days, 1905, 1906, a chain with a cameo round her neck. The photograph stops there, but I remember her skirts were long, and she wore boots with little buttons on the side. Her umbrella with its ruffles always matched her dress.

Until I met her, the raw material of distress and joy were held at bay by my education. As a clever fencer creates a distance with his opponent, even so skilful phrases, rhyming verse, converts into a passage of ghosts those figures whose weight and substance, like pelting stones, would assault my being. Civilization is after all verbalization, extracting from all things a relationship to ourselves, but at the same time metamorphosing it into images upon a screen. But this magic film interposed between life and myself was put to an end when I met Marguerite. Then was happiness – that premature profit of imminent loss.

I come then to my pain and joy, the love of my living days. Like swallows of a May rain, the flutter of this marvel tugs at my heart, at my temples which throb as my turgid, slow, old man's blood courses through my too brittle arteries. Tugs for a resurrection, which is not to be.

I met her at the cheese market at Ixelles on a morning so early that no respectable girl could be abroad ... but she was there.

The cheese market was a gargantuan sprawl of edible smells on flat round boards, washed and scrubbed as were scrubbed the cobbles of the square where the market spread. I have never been able to recall that scene without achieving at the same time, not the flavour of cheese, but the nostril-dilating shock of a battlefield, as if between the tables, with their red, buxom Flemish women in shawls and sprawling skirts and bouncing breasts, out of sudden trenches armed hosts had sprung into battle with great cries.

There stood Marguerite, looking at the holes in a Gruyère. I looked at her, and I was in love.

I am sure that the moment was love, because after that I could eat and like cheese, which until then I had refused to look at. Every morning I went through the market to reach the Natural Science College of the University where I studied; always I carried a handkerchief with me, muffling my nose as I edged along the southern corner of the odorous encampment, and drew breath again where a beer hall flung its morning chairs atop each other on the pavement.

There she was, standing on the cobbles, the sun just bouncing off her red-gold hair, a torrent of hair like the muscled water of the Great River. My nose-held handkerchief came down. I did not go to classes that day. Instead I followed her. As I followed her, uncalendared love became more real, more solid, at each step.

Now that I am old I ponder upon this baffling mystery of body and spirit. How one they are, how they mould each other in oneness. I think of smell, of all our senses a mainspring to knowledge. Before that day I knew smells as good or bad, likeable or detested. But I did not know that they could change places so swiftly, in one distraught moment; even smell, that most enduring premise of knowledge, suffer metamorphosis. And now that all goes thin with me, as savour flies from salt, and my memories are permeable ghosts, wind-effaced, I am left with the knowledge of this transformation, knowledge dry as dust, since I am as far away from comprehending it now as I was then; but love's miracle has gone from me.

Marguerite broke the fences within which my emotions paced staidly the run of conventional poetry, of expected sensation. From that time I was to learn the whole world anew, beginning that morning with smell.

From that day the smell of Europe and the smell of Europeans was good to me. Until then, all other peoples, other than Chinese, stank: milk smelt bad, Europeans smelt of milk and mutton; at Marseille on the cold, stoneflat winter day we landed, the smell of the horse carriages, the horses and the grit, made me long to return to Chengtu, which by contrast, in memory, smelt to me of spring plum, nasturtium and magnolia. I had forgotten the public cloacae. And now I know our senses are also conditioned by words, pre-moulded for us by education, and that they cheat us too.

It was a late spring, May in the Europe of 1905, bestarred with May blossom, riotous with roses, when I met Marguerite. I had already become aware of a new vitality, of a longing to pace for hours in the never-ending dusk. Now I saw colours emerge out of the uniform greyness which until then was Europe to me, a range of nuances for which there were no names. That day I walked and walked for hours, and the sun, stretching its finger-point delineation of each stone, produced green mirages as moving as the variegations of jade. The harshness, the coarseness, the over-stout floridness of the people, became an amiable, exhilarating overflow of robust gaiety. People were kind to me in my street, saying good day after watching me curiously. How good and kind they were to me. I liked them, I thought Brussels the most lovely city I knew.

Everything about Marguerite was wayward and headstrong, everything that I was not, could never become. She had gone to Ireland as a governess, hating the constricting life of a well-behaved young lady of her class at home, and there had caught typhoid; returning to Brussels she watched a handsome officer who rode every morning the alleys of the Bois (and that is why she was up so early), to whom she never spoke though she came out hoping to see him on his bay horse. She walked in the fresh, exultant, early morning, walked her violent, magnificent youth, walked the wealth of her red hair about the cobbled streets of Brussels, the narrow narrow town with the narrow houses looking down; and behind each lace-curtained window was a spy-mirror, to watch the street without being seen. How they must have whispered later, the people peering in these mirrors, watching us walk together. She fretted, read romances, in dreams planned impossible escapes, took singing lessons; went to church with her maid behind her to carry gloves and prayer book; ran out without a hat to buy flowers; was unhappy, and wrote and wrote her unhappiness.

That morning I followed her home, at a distance, noted the street and the house. In the afternoon I was again in her street, pacing, looking up at the tall house, with its cream façade and the ornamental ironwork, the windows pinched as the faces of women in Belgium pinch when they purse their lips as they cross the street; gazed at the street mirror, placed outside and aslant the window, hoped she would glance in it, perhaps see me ...

But the look that decided our fates (how absurd the phrase, now that the cold, premeditated look of history is upon me, and all that was so important has become dust collecting in an odd, overlooked corner) was thrown into the spy-mirror by her mother. The next day, having missed her at the cheese market, I returned to pace slowly in front of the house, back, forth, to the end of the street, and back again, as slowly as I dared.

"Who is this little Chinaman standing outside our house?"

And then, O wonder, the door opened, and Marguerite came out, and walked across the street, to me. I was standing on the opposite pavement, gazing up, and so taken aback, so troubled as she advanced, that I forgot to take off my hat.

Marguerite was to exorcize the ecstatic passion of this first moment with mockery, to turn the magic glance of her mother in the mirror into a trivial horror. She always had much power to destroy happiness, as she had power to make life ten times more alive, an abundant tropic; everything that went through her was magnified. Even when I thought I had ceased to care, she still achieved this mirror distortion, and it exhausted me. But that was much later, years later, when she became a bitter woman, old before her age, and with good reason. For years the beautiful happiness of this moment when she came towards me was to stay, and comfort me when our world of love was laid waste.

*

Oh, do not tell me there is no heaven, no paradise for me, for surely I have deserved one, I have had my hell on earth I tell you. If only I had known – but we were so happy in those first years. My son was born and I suffered so much, but he said: "My dear, dearest wife, I shall never leave you," and my mother helped me to look after him.

Oh, do not tell me that I have sinned, for I can tell you things that make hell paradise, and that also happened to me. I always wanted so many things to be. It was all those books, and having nothing to do. But if I do go to paradise, I shall want to see them, those lovely green monkeys, as I saw them on that trip when Yentung and I and my son went to China for the first time; up on all those cliffs, among the trees, loping up and down and hooting at us, and our boat shooting the rapids and we were tied to barrels; but I am sure they hooted, and I waved at them, and laughed. And I would like to see them in paradise surely, for looking at them I knew how beautiful the land was, beautiful and terrible, and it was hell, and paradise, so that I was no longer afraid.

For I have always wanted a place where I might leave my heart. But here you had to leave everything, everything. Sometimes people say I paint my memories big, but nothing was so big as that great stir, that eternity, that torment and disease and a face that answered all the loves of the world.

For love laid upon me her great load, and now to think of it makes me weep, oh the folly! – and only the green monkeys redeem the vision that once thronged with glory and now shatters with derision.

And first I must breathe hard, rub clean the mirror of memory, take off the cobwebs of silence and dreams, dust off my prisoner head the cobwebs of my dreams, open the seeing eye that shall not pity upon myself in the mirror.

I thought he was an Asiatic prince, you see, and that is how it all began, in glory and splendour, a thunder that out-thundered my family. The Denis anyway have always been so smug, I was glad I could do this to them. And never will I go back to beg from them, to have them tell me: "I told you so."

I thought he was an Asiatic prince, although now I do not know why I should have thought so. Perhaps reading all those novels. There were many of them, and I read them all. I had nothing else to do.

I looked at him, and I wanted to go away, to go away with him. I wanted to go up to him and to say: "Please, Your Highness, can I come to your country because I want to get away from this life, because I have nothing to my life and I cannot stand it. Going to Mass with a maid to carry my gloves and prayer book, and visiting relatives, and otherwise wait-ing, waiting, waiting. I have nothing to do, and I'm twenty years old."

I smiled at him, and then he took off his hat, and I was trembling from head to foot, and I said: "Will you come in and have a cup of coffee with us?" I went straight into my room and lay upon my bed.

My mother came into the room, and said: "What is the matter?"

And I said: "I have a terrible headache, that is all."

He sat with my mother in the parlour, drinking coffee. Mother said he was a nice young man, and sure to be a prince, his hands so small and white.

The next morning I got up very early. I had not slept and I wanted to go again to the market place, perhaps he would be there. But Josephine was washing the hall down and the front steps, so it must have been very early. Too early perhaps. I put my hat on and I looked at myself in the mirror, and I didn't like the hat so I changed it and I put on my Sunday hat, the one with the big roses, and slapped my cheeks to bring out the colour.

I took it off again, and started crying. Now of course I couldn't go out at all, with a swollen face, red eyes. I sat by the window and looked down in the street and saw the houses, grey, grey, sad, sad. I could see now so clearly how terrible it was, so narrow, framed in: my life, which I could not leap away from.

I must have walked up and down for hours, and my mother was worried. She wanted Josephine to call the doctor, but I said: "No, no. Let us go for a walk in the Bois."

"But you know I cannot. The doctor says I must have rest for my varicose veins."

I could not eat much lunch and this made my mother really worried, and she called the doctor, but he said: "It is only the vapours, as usual with young women. Get your daughter married, madame, and all this will pass."

"Married! One must find a good man, doctor. It is not so easy these days," said my mother.

I had heard this so many times.

When the doctor had left I sat again by the window, looking, looking. I thought I would do some embroidery, or sing. I must keep my voice in training. I started singing, practising scales, then I looked at the mirror again. And I saw him. I said to myself: You are having hallucinations.

But it was not a hallucination. I could see him planted in the street, standing on the opposite pavement and looking at our house.

I went downstairs, but when my hand was on the street door I stopped. I could not open the door to find out. I could not do what I had done the afternoon before. Upstairs again, and I called Josephine. I said: "Josephine, go to the mercer on the corner of the street, I have no more red thread for my embroidery."

Josephine was cleaning the silver. "I cannot leave off now, mademoiselle, I must finish the silver first."

I said: "I'll finish it for you – go! go!"

Oh, what a time she took putting on her hat and her coat and looking in the back garden to the sky to make sure it would not rain, just for a hundred-yard walk down to the mercer. And then she said to me: "I have forgotten to put on my shoes." She had on her house slippers, so back she went to the attic to get her shoes.

I said: "It doesn't matter, you can run down to the corner like that."

"How can I go down in the street without my shoes?" She was in a bad temper.

I pushed her. "Never mind, go on!" And she stopped again to say: "What kind of red? There are many kinds of red silk thread. What shade do you want?"

So I had to go upstairs and pick up some of the red silk and show her, and she stood there looking at it, turning it in her hands until I could have screamed.

So slowly, so slowly, she crossed the hall – and I behind her – and fumbled with the street door which was locked, picking the key – and I was behind her – and when she opened the street door there was light, and it was he standing on the opposite pavement. And then Josephine shut the door.

But I had seen him again, and I knew he had seen me again. And after that, well, what else? When your children grow up, you'll know what it is. But I hope your luck is better than mine.

I know many people won't understand. And sometimes I don't know myself why this happened. I know that I have wasted my life, my whole life. I never thought it would be like this, hell and paradise, all together . . .

And my children, they always want to know everything. Especially that one, she is always asking: How did you meet my father? I met him, I told you, when he was a student. I thought he was a prince. A Chinese prince.

You want to see the photographs? Not again. Well . . . if you must. Begin from the beginning? All right. This one was taken when I was six years old, as you are now. This picture of me, with goldilock curls, we called them English curls at the time. My clothes were sent from England, they always make nice clothes for children in England. And the hat with the blue velvet brim, and the Scottish plaid coat. We were not wealthy, because my father had disobeyed his father by marrying my mother, who was poor, and she was a Hollander and they married young. And instead of going on to study and to become a rich man like Uncle Eugene, who lives in Antwerp and has a lot of money, he had to go into the railways and earn his living and become a government servant. He disobeyed his father, and I disobeyed my father by marrying your father. It's in the blood, disobedience.

On this photo, as you see, I am six, with my small ermine muff, and the English hat and coat. We were respectable and we had a nice house in a good quarter, because Grandfather had died and left us some money; he did not cut us out of his will, as all the family thought he would. So I went to the Convent of the Ladies of the Sacred Heart, where they only admit the nobility and the upper bourgeoisie. They took me, in spite of my mother being a commoner.

But I could never be like the others, with milk in their veins. To begin with, the food was terrible, and I had a good appetite. My mother used to bring me hampers of food to eat. I ate at night, and that is why my teeth are bad: too many sweet things under the blankets in bed in the convent dormitory.

I did not like the discipline. I did not want to swallow the awful stuff they gave us, as a pious sacrifice to God. I could not kneel in the cold chapel on the stones for hours. I did not want to be a nun. I wanted to run away all the time. And I was too healthy, not anaemic. And with my red hair, the nuns tried to make me pull it down in plaits, but it did not stay down. But I learnt singing and the piano, and I ran away to Ireland when I was eighteen. I could not stand it any more, staying at home, waiting to get married. I wanted to travel, to meet people. I got typhoid in Ireland, my hair dropped off, and after that I never had as much hair as before. Before the typhoid I had hair right down to my knees. This is a photograph of me in Ireland. I am standing, as you see, behind the little girl; I was supposed to teach her French. Actually they were English people, very rich, Lord and Lady Somebody, I forget ... I ate bananas, because of the typhoid. I liked bananas. I learnt a little English too, then I returned home.

Sometimes, once a year, we would go to Antwerp to pay a visit to the family. It was terrible. My mother always came back weeping and humiliated by the family. Everybody in the Denis family was so snobbish. If you were Dutch, and not an aristocrat, they looked down on you.

In the mornings, especially in spring, I could not sleep, I had to get up and walk. My mother said it was the spring and I had vapours, but she said they would pass when I got married. But whom would I marry? "You have a dowry," said my mother, "you will marry a good man, with a good job. Someone like your father, with a pension at the end."

My mother only had me, the one daughter. My father would not let her have any more children, she told me so. He made her use cotton wool with a little vinegar, that's what the aristocrats used. It was forbidden by the priest, but they went to confession, so it was all right. Anyway, Mother was Dutch, and a Protestant, so she did not have to confess. That was something else the family did not like her being a Protestant. She was very clean, a real Dutch woman. She washed herself every time she went to the toilet.

All my mother did was because she loved me. So often she did not tell my father. But the neighbours were jealous. "There is no one as beautiful or as high-spirited as my daughter," Mother said. And one spring morning I was out, and walking, and I saw your father, standing in the cheese market, waiting to cross perhaps, with a great horse-cart full of beer barrels in front of him, and the long-fetlocked horses breathing white smoke. He stood there and I thought he was an Asiatic prince. He followed me home, but he never knew that I had seen him first.

*

Two witnessing the same event do not give the same account if it; one will have noticed details which have been overlooked by the other. Marguerite's account and Yentung's account of their first meeting differed in some respects, but the difference had to be maintained since they were two separate people. Both, resuscitating the same encounter, fell back into the breathless, shining glory of that morning. Time, which changed them both so much, scarcely modified the picture they had kept of that radiant beginning. And though nothing can have been sharper pain than this very opposition between what they had become and the unchanging memory of what they had been, yet still that morning remained unaltered for Marguerite, though Yentung complained that she tried to destroy that memory for him. From this fixed star they could measure the movement which had dragged them forwards, the suffering which shaped them and finally tore them apart. But at least they were blessed in having that unmoving luminous point to return to, inaccessible to all but themselves; and their hearts' marvel was that for so long, all through their own alterations, this brief moment endured untiring, all-conquering in the end.

But this was mere prologue. For the next three years, from 1905 to 1908, the encounter developed into a situation, and then became a scandal. How much relish it must have procured to the purse-lipped, stiff-in-their-corsets ladies behind their spy-mirrors, watching the street as they embroidered, ate cakes and drank coffee in the lengthy afternoons of those days, so inexorably soaked up in momentous trivia (whose paramountcy made up the colour and tone and very stuff of the social class to which they belonged) . . .

And since at this point my mother enters the pattern, wedges herself into her future, which was in China, I should here give some details of her own family and background.

But I was unable to delineate a profile of the Denis family until 1963, when Armand Denis, my mother's cousin – always described as "a well-known TV personality" on the B.B.C., where his films on African animals have been tremendously popular – spent three days in Singapore with me, and while we were eating roast duck and sharks' fins with sweet corn at the Chinese Capitol Restaurant, began to talk of the Denis family and what they had done, and of cousins and what they were doing.

Until then I had only my mother's reminiscences about the family, and they were not kind. I had not asked my Belgian grandfather about my relatives, preferring not to trouble him. When I went to study in Brussels in 1935 I was inhibited. Talking about family or about my mother was painful, both to myself and I felt to her father. Epistolary relations between the Denis were always very uncordial, and I copied my father's reticence; my own status as "our cousin from China" was ambiguous, to say the least. The whole subject of my parents' marriage, which had cost my Belgian family, as well as my Chinese Family, much disruption and grief, had produced an aura of disapproval which clung to me, exuding from my mother's relatives to ooze over my nineteen-year-old abashed and timid self, and like hardening jelly firmly imprisoned all conversation during my visits to them in Belgium within the safe topics of my studies, the weather and their health.

I was not to elicit more information from Aunt Lucy, the wife of Henri Denis, the Minister of Defence, another "cousin", talkative though she was, and kind enough though she was; in fact, kinder than the rest. And later, when I saw her again in 1947, her husband was too old, and she pushed him about in a wheel-chair; she had forgotten much, except the Second World War, and the terrible years which had been most unkind to both of them.

It was Armand Denis then, who in Singapore at last gave me a jumbled genealogy of sorts. His book, *On Safari,* had just come out, was a best-seller, and he had mentioned me in it, and now, under the influence of Chinese wine, he waxed genial and confiding on the subject of the Denis family.

There had been several generals of the name. At one time, he averred, fully half the Belgian higher army staff must have inter-married with the Denis. The original name was Dennys, he thought, of Flemish extraction, but later was Frenchified to Denis, and the story began with a wealthy contractor in Malines, whose brother was burgomaster of the city. This contractor was Armand's and my mother's grandfather; he had sons, but did not appear to have had any daughters, or if he had no one remembered them. Of his sons, the eldest died of meningitis at nineteen; Armand Denis was subsequently named after him. Another son of the contractor, Jean Denis, was known as the "bicycle man". My mother often mentioned Uncle Jean to me because she said I resembled him; I had, as she told me, the same "nostalgia for those of low degree" which he suffered from and which brought him low. She said it often, especially when we were playing cards, because she knew it annoyed me, since Jean was reputed the family rake; and I too was destined to be the black sheep.

Armand confirmed to me that Uncle Jean was a person of low tastes. The sole satisfying profession of his life, while a young man in Belgium, had been the organizing of bicycle races among his friends, persons of low degree such as butchers' boys, frequenters of taverns and coffee shops. And this certainly was no fitting occupation for the son of a prosperous bourgeois, nephew to the burgomaster of the city of Malines. His friends the bicycle-addicts, a half-cut lemon or an onion between their teeth to stay the wind, raced under Jean Denis's direction, and afterwards consumed much beer at his expense, and the whole effort was considered a shocking scandal in those days. Jean went further. He contracted a marriage with (according to Armand) a barmaid, according to my mother a "person of low degree", and had many children by her, among whom a son called Eugene set himself on fire with a Bunsen burner while doing chemical experiments, but came to no harm. Jean and his large crew of children emigrated to Latin America, either Argentina or Brazil, no one remembers which, and the Denis family lost sight of them, no doubt with relief. I long to meet my cousins in Latin America, though I am sure, being Europeans and not Chinese, they will not be in the least overjoyed at seeing a "relative" like myself. The notion of kinship is not carefully nurtured among them, as it was in China.

Another son of this grandfather Denis, the contractor, was

named George, nicknamed Railroad George. He became my mother's father. George also married, if not below him, at least not well by Denis standards. He took to bride a girl without a dowry, a Dutch girl, Matilda Rosalie Leenders. She was the daughter of an engineer who died at ninety-four sitting upright in his chair, and who had something to do with building the Zuider Zee dam, and was very poor. Marguerite Denis, my mother, was their only child.

A third son, Eugene, became Armand's father. He married well, a lady called Anne Van De Bogaerde, from the upper bourgeoisie, with a large dowry. She was from a family brilliant, wealthy and vital, from whom, Armand tells me, the actor Dirk Bogarde is also descended. Besides Armand, there was a daughter, Angèle, who produced seven children. I met her twice in my life and liked her greatly, for she is a nice quiet woman of great character, resembling my mother in looks but utterly different in temperament. My mother did not get on with her. In fact, she made a point of disliking all her relatives, and why it was so was not clear to me until I arrived in Belgium in 1935, twenty-two years after my mother had left it for ever, and encountered the hermetic faces, the pursed lips, the watchful eyes, of my relatives. And then I thought that whereas in China one *must* love one's relatives, in Belgium one *must* quarrel with them.

Besides these Denis, there were other Denis, less directly related. One, called Louis, was a general, and the son of the burgomaster aforesaid. He produced Henri, also a general, later the Minister of Defence, who married the kind Aunt Lucy who so often asked me to tea and gave me cakes to eat because I was so thin. He was a great lover of cars, and a very brilliant man. Unfortunately he was Minister of Defence in 1940, had to surrender to the Germans at the beginning of the Second World War, although Belgium did hold out against them for eighteen days (which was much longer than some bigger countries did). Henri Denis was, for this, vilified, and went to Switzerland, where he developed sclerosis, and his brain became affected.

Henri Denis had two sisters, Jeanne called "Floating Kidney" Jeanne, and Marthe, who married a man with a long lugubrious beard, a long face, who ate only raw eggs (nothing else is known of him). Aunt Lucy and Uncle Henri Denis had a son called Robert, who married a divorcee in 1933. This was reputed a great scandal, even in 1937, because Belgium was agog with the case of Wallis Warfield and the then King of England. Robert, after emulating Edward the Eighth, became a notary in Leopoldville in the Congo. Armand's only recollection of Robert Denis was a big dinner in Leopoldville, to which the divorcee's mother came, and lost part of her hair while bending over a goulash being passed around by the African butler, her front toupee falling into the dish. Armand tells this story with great roars of laughter and Flemish gusto, and relates how the servant went on presenting the dish in turn to the other guests, who went on helping themselves to whatever goulash could be detected uncovered by hair.

There was another branch of the family, started by a certain Léon Denis, another cousin, who appears to have been a violently anti-clerical and choleric person. He married a woman called Eugénie, nicknamed "Purgatory Eugénie". Eugénie suffered from talkativeness; she talked all the time; she talked so much that finally her husband, Léon, had her certified. For seven years she was incarcerated in a genteel and respectable home for ladies suffering from nerves. During that time she became convinced that she had died and was enduring the sufferings of purgatory; and when, after seven years, she was restored to her family, she talked as much as before, and mainly of her experiences while in purgatory.

Léon Denis had two sons, also named George and Henri, both cavalry officers. Léon's violent anti-clericalism had passed on to George, the elder, who rode his horse through a religious procession of the Children of Mary on Pentecost Day. This led to one less Denis in the Belgian Army.

Another cousin, whose name Armand had forgotten, was nicknamed The Talker. He had a chair in the coffee and beer shop near his house in Antwerp, and there perorated daily from noon to midnight; at four o'clock every afternoon he left it for twenty minutes, saying to the waiter: "Keep me my chair, I'm going to the house for a cup of coffee." Then he would return and go on talking. No one remembers what he said.

The women were neither flamboyant nor cranky, as the men appear to be. Nearly everyone of them is swallowed in oblivion, except my mother. Out of a pallid lot she stood out, violent, vivid, fascinating, tremendously alive. The impact she made must have been quite extraordinary. She was nicknamed the Romantic One; nourished her unexciting life with novels she devoured, ran away twice from her home, and was disapproved of. Her headlong pursuit of my father, her breaking down of all decorum to marry him, was still the live sore from which the Denis family had not recovered when twenty-six years later I, their daughter, arrived in Belgium. I was met by my grandfather at the station in Brussels. He took one look at me, and said: "Now I hope you won't run off with a Chinese, as your mother did." But I did run off, only it was not with a Chinese, but back to China. He never understood this, never forgave me, and cut me out of his will.

My grandmother, Matilda Rosalie Leenders, I never met. She died before I arrived in Belgium in 1935, but I was named after her by my mother, an imposition from which I escaped only after many years of wretched wincing whenever my name was called. Never were names more inappropriately conferred. Fortunately, I was christened with two other names to fall back on. A photograph of my grandmother rested on a table in my parents' bedroom at home in Peking: a typical Dutch girl, body rather plump, in long skirts, mild blue eyes, fair skin, russet-gold hair, very soft and naturally curly. The Denis have grey eyes, brown-flecked, brown straight hair, and are tall, the men averaging five foot eleven to six foot two. My mother was five foot seven or eight, fully two inches taller than my father.

If, on the Chinese side, the family seems to lack cranks, whereas on the Flemish side they abound, it is not that they did not exist; certainly Great-Grandfather had much character and enterprise. But their quirks were not recorded, their foibles were withdrawn from discussion, no nicknames were bestowed upon them in family annals. No such reverently effacing sponge, turning characters into decorous ancestors, occurred to the Belgian side. On the contrary, the Denis revelled in picking on each other, and especially in giving each other nicknames. My mother excelled at it.

When I returned to the Chou Family in Szechuan, I could never get some irreverent illumination on any of the Elders from my cousins – filial respect was too ingrained in them. I could only proceed by patient watching, awaiting some slight hint of redeeming misdemeanour. Only once did I witness an open quarrel, that being when intoxicated by new ideas, my First Aunt shook her water-pipe at her husband, First Uncle, my father's elder brother. I can still hear the water inside the pewter canister of her water-pipe slap and gurgle as she brandished it at her philandering husband. "We are in modern times, I demand a divorce. *And* alimony!" I left discreetly, decorum depriving me of inquisitiveness, exercising the three-monkeyed ability of not seeing, not hearing, not talking, fostered in me by five war years in China with the Family.

The Denis lived and certainly died in a blissful state of battle, openly aired, pursued for decades by letter, unredeemed by decease. They were adepts at trenchant gestures of dismissal, slammed doors, curl of lip, abrupt walkaways. They competed at hurling epithets and concocting adhesive nicknames. They thrived on a perpetual crusade against each other. Cutting people out of their wills was their favourite pastime.

And since my father, with his ideal of harmony and forbearance, was ill equipped to compete with all this, with my mother's heritage of verbal violence and slashing remarks, devouring passion and large craving for the larger-than-life, silence became his stronghold, and the best remembered thing about him to his children.

But I carry something of my mother in me. All my childhood I battled against her, in typical Denis fashion, and finally we forswore each other, again in Denis fashion. I am sure Mother is happier, at war with me, than if reconciliation, so diminishing, had occurred. I admire her. She created a situation, and a scandal. To any child, the particular alliance which creates his parents becomes an unquestioned, established solidity, ground underfoot; if my parents' alliance was a quirk of history, so was I. In the acceptance of abnormalcy I was chary of prodding an all-too-painful cumulus of past storm. My grandfather's first words at the Brussels station in 1935, hoping I would not run away with a Chinese as my mother had done, ended any questioning I might have begun there. The shock was still with the Denis, they pursed their lips, stared at me, and I tried to look reassuringly stupid.

It was Armand Denis again who told me that they had consulted with each other as to whether to "receive" me in their houses or not. This included his own father and mother. "A mixed-blood, Marguerite's offspring." The way they said it, I must have sounded like excreta. The receiving was done, however; somehow everyone survived.

Marguerite Denis was born in 1885. She met Chou Yentung in the spring of 1905. Soon they were meeting and walking in the Bois de la Cambre, perhaps even driving in the beautiful forest of Soignes. The Denis family could not tolerate this. One uncle came down from Malines, another from Antwerp; a cousin arrived in a postchaise from the water cure at Spa; someone else sped, also by horse carriage, all the way from a retreat in an abbey, a canon of the church. The aunts took to smelling salts, called on each other (what appetizingly interminable afternoons of talk), and rushed off to their surplus female relatives cloistered in convents to seek advice. On no account could a Denis possibly marry a Chinese (a Chinese!), and a heathen (a pagan!). It was suggested that Marguerite be sent for a religious retreat with a great-aunt who was the Abbess of a convent of Carmelites, or incarcerated in a Ladies' Rest Home for Nerves, or quickly married off to someone more eligible. One suggestion, that she might be possessed by a demon, led to a ceremony where prayers were said over her and holy water thrown about. Her own mother wept indefatigably, but connived at secret meetings; Yentung, thrown out of the front door by an irate father, returned through the back door, opened by a tearful mother, and was served coffee in the kitchen by Josephine, the maid, entranced by this romance. The ladies of the Denis family called to scold Matilda Leenders. She was Dutch, they said, her own grandmother born in the Dutch East Indies, what else could you expect? "Tainted blood will show."

They did manage to shut up Marguerite. Her father locked her in her room and kept the key. Meals were taken in to her by Josephine. One morning, when her father was at his office, Marguerite kicked a hole in the door, and got out through the hole. They were still showing the door (repaired) to Marguerite's son in 1919. She was declared insane by the Denis relatives. "We wash our hands of her."

Having broken down the door, Marguerite Denis simply went to stay with Chou Yentung. The family chronicle does not relate whether she took time off to put on her hat (the Sunday one with the roses). They ran away together for a few days, where and how I do not know, but perhaps they went to Paris where Yentung had friends. After a week Yentung returned to face the Chinese Consul, and the Supervisor of Studies. The Consul threatened to have the young man sent back to China. Marguerite was forcibly taken back home by her father. "She is now dishonoured, and will have to enter a convent," said the aunts.

But in that short interlude Marguerite had managed to become pregnant, and a month later triumphantly announced it to the family. "*Now* will you let us marry?"

It was 1908, spring again. This is when the Bishop was called in. I tried to trace this bishop, but was never able to find his name. From what Marguerite one day, in a plethora of talk, let drop into her child's retentive ears, the Bishop was called in by Grandmother Denis, a redoubtable matriarch, extremely pious, who wore jet beads in rows round her neck, and ostrich feathers dyed black in her hats, and whose sister was the Superior General of the Ladies of the Sacred Heart. The Bishop may have been a relative of hers. She was a widow, Grandfather Denis having died, without cutting off his son George, Marguerite's father, from his will; indulgence which everyone deplored.

The Bishop had a conversation with the Chinese Consul, and then with Chou Yentung at the Consulate.

I shall never know what Father said to the Bishop, nor the Bishop to him. But I did learn some decades later that the Bishop gave his approval to the marriage, in spite of Chou Yentung's categorical refusal to become converted to Catholicism.

Perhaps the Bishop was an astute politician, along the lines of King Leopold II. Perhaps he thought of the grand design, to draw a huge cross of railways on the map of China. And in order to build railways in China, to assure the prosperity of Belgium's industries in that epoch of beginning crisis just before World War I, missionaries must do their holy work among the heathen. The Bishop may have dreamt of Catholic villages, dotted all along the "Belgian railway" lines, Catholic churches, from the sea to the interior; flocks of the faithful, north and south, east and west, travelling by Belgian-made railways along the length and breadth of China . . .

"After all, due to the influence of our daughter, Marguerite, this will lead to the establishment of a Catholic hearth, a flame of Christ among the heathen. Their children will be Catholics." Never a word about the pregnancy looming so large on the minds of sundry aunts. "Let us see in this the hand of God, the designs of the Lord which are unfathomable."

"Your father could talk, when he was young. He could talk anyone round. When Papa pushed him out of the front door, Josephine opened the back door and he came in and

Mama told Josephine to give him coffee." Marguerite would say this, looking towards Yentung with that mixture of passion and hatred which characterized all her family relationships, and their daughter saw it, heard and remembered it. "He talked the Bishop round."

At this juncture Father would always get up and walk out to look at his peonies, or his dahlias, or whatever other bloom was in season.

"This young man is of good family, intelligent, not addicted to the vices common to pagans. He assures me that there is no previous attachment. So does the representative of the Chinese Empire, His Excellency Wang, the Ambassador for China. I understand the family estates are somewhere near Tibet." Monsignor waxed lyrical. "Ah, Tibet, the golden centre of Asia, heart of this inscrutable, hermetic continent, will one day belong *absolutely* to the Holy Mother Church, in the name of Jesus Christ our Lord. I believe that the Protestants are making some efforts in the young man's city, and have a hospital and a mission there; but so do we, so do we. It is time that more Catholic homes should be established in this utter darkness to bring the light of the Saviour to this province of many millions."

Since Father obstinately refused conversion, there could be no big church ceremony. And there must have been many tears, implorings, and more scandal, as the Denis family cut Marguerite dead and the hope chests were assembled in haste. Twelve of everything, corsets and pantaloons, under-skirts and camisoles and bed sheets and nightgowns; twenty-five years later Marguerite was still using the last flannel nightgowns of 1908. It had taken her altogether, from that spring morning among the cheeses in 1905, to the first of July in 1908, when they were married in a civil ceremony, three years to get her way; and now, with all haste, the marriage was hurried through.

Of course that is not the way Marguerite told of the wedding, when in Peking other women, Belgian, French or Dutch, married to Chinese, came to our house to drink coffee and to weep their woes. Then the wedding became such a grand affair, with Chinese diplomats in top hats, church ceremony at the Cathedral, the Bishop's benediction, and a veil of old Malines lace; a seaside honeymoon, "and the day after I was already vomiting and pregnant". That sentence of hers, whispered and not for my ears, I remember because I wondered at the connection between vomiting and a baby sent from Paradise in the doctor's bag.

Four months later, in October 1908, my brother Son of Spring was born.

I think Son of Spring must have found out about his birth. Possibly he was told; not straight, not well, but in waspish stabs, in sneering innuendoes that crippled him for life. I somehow cannot see some of the Belgian aunts refraining from making someone unhappy, if they could do so. My brother spent most of his childhood in Europe. Although he went back to China with his parents in 1913, he was returned by them to Belgium in 1914, just in time for the First World War. He did not return to China till 1925, and then it was too late for him. Perhaps that is why he was always so bitter, apart from being a Eurasian, towards his mother. Of course, being Eurasian was a calamity in those days, and still is today for certain people. But more than being a Eurasian, I think he allowed the fact of a legitimatized near-illegitimacy, which after all is neither uncommon nor ruinous, to ruin him, which was a great pity, for he was gifted, and could have done so much had he been able, like myself, to shake off the nonsense people accumulate to keep themselves cosily miserable, had he been devoid of a sense of sin, had he been ready to wash himself clean and light in the sun by shouting the truth cheerfully to sky and earth, defying them to do their worst, clear about what was important and what was trivial; and what is important is to live with joy.

Carefully rolled up with the parchment diploma of Chou Yentung, a diploma from the Faculty of Engineering of the University of Brussels attesting that he had gained his engineer's degree in October 1910, was also another paper, a telegram form dated June 13th, 1908, which bore the stamp of the Chinese Embassy in Brussels, where it had been received. The hour was thirteen-ten, or ten minutes past one in the afternoon. The telegram originated from Chengtu. On it were four words in Chinese, translated from the code used at the time for cabling from China: "Inform Yentung marriage permitted."

The correspondence between Yentung and the Chou Family in Chengtu, which finally led to this permission for marriage with a foreign woman, has totally disappeared. Unrecorded the grief, the havoc this must have caused on that side of the world. And no sifting of dust, no staring at photographs to stare life back into them, will bring back that deep hurt. The cable from China records the hour of permission. But how was this permission obtained?

There must have been intense and bitter sorrow in Chengtu. An upheaval equal to that which occurred in the Denis family of Brussels must have taken place in the Chou family of Chengtu. But apart from these four brief words, there is no clue to what they thought, except perhaps their very brevity.

"Your father told us that your mother came from an excellent family," was the only remark that Third Uncle once made about his brother's marriage. Otherwise I had to wait till 1964 for some word on this event, which actually shattered for the Chou family the whole pattern of the future they had planned for Second Son.

In 1964 Third Uncle, knowing the days were now shortening for him, said to me: "Yes, it must have been hard for your mother when she came to us. She did not understand us, and we did not understand her. Perhaps we were backward." He said this because of his great heart's courtesy.

And my cousin Kuangyung, whom I call Sixth Brother, now a man of forty, said to me, shyly because it was great daring even to allude to these matters: "I have always thought it very courageous of your mother to have come from so far to us in Szechuan. It must have been very difficult for her. If you write to her, tell her, tell her we the younger generation admire and appreciate her courage."

"It was. Very difficult. But it must have been very difficult for the family in Szechuan also. They had given permission for the marriage." I related how I had found the cable sent in June 1908, permitting my father to marry.

"Really," said Sixth Brother, "I would not have thought our family so broadminded in 1908. I did not know they had cabled. I was not born then, of course, but I heard later that many of the elder generation had been greatly upset and refused permission. I wonder how it was obtained?" He paused, then added: "Tell my revered Second Aunt, your mother, that if at any time she wishes to return, we shall look after her." He was offering his home, himself, to look after my mother in her old age. "It is different now, in China."

"I will tell her," I said. "Not directly, for she would not listen. But I will let her know."

In July 1908 then, love triumphed, **Chou Yentung and**

Marguerite Denis married. Victorious Marguerite had out-thundered the Denis. But these things must be paid for.

Perhaps the tragedy of my brother's life was payment for his mother's courage. There is no doubt that he was the one who suffered most for this breaking of doors, this breaking-down of conventions, outdoing Romeo and Juliet. For not only was he shown, when young, the door his mother had broken to go away with his father. The indignation at this infringement, not only of moral code, but also of property, of sacred, beloved *property*, in the shape of a door – and in the Belgian bourgeoisie doors are solid things, made of good wood, built to last for ever, and to break a door is an attaint to *property*, is to be an incipient jailbird, for who knows what door-breaking will lead to? – was made very clear to him. His own voice broke with indignant surprise when he related the matter to me fifty years later, in 1958. The collective reprobation under which he lived till he was sixteen and came to China had already done him in, de-gutted him, but I did not know it, so stalwart did he look.

Then there was Josephine, the servant. She also paid for it. When Yentung was courting Marguerite, Josephine was mes-senger, coffee-cup giver, trudging back and forth with letters, opening back doors, a very Juliet's nurse. Josephine earned five francs a month and her food, she slept in the attic, had varicose veins like coils of snakes on her legs, in the classic fashion of the lower orders of those days. Twice a day she carried the coal from basement up to second floor in winter. She was a "found child", unwanted, guilty of birth, for ever to be humbly thankful to God and society for providing her with good employers like the Denis, only three of them, a good mistress, with occasional crises of the liver, a Dutch woman, but kind to her.

To the three women, Marguerite, Matilda Leenders, and Josephine, yearning for the romantic and the fabulous, Chou Yentung was the Chinese prince. Whenever Marguerite, dur-ing the weeks when she was not allowed to meet her Chinese prince, smashed anything in the house, Josephine swept up the bits, then carried another torrential secret missive to Chou Yentung.

Josephine was sacked, with wages to the end of the month, after twenty-four years of service. She was sacked because an aunt married to a Denis, who lived in the very fashionable Avenue Louise in Brussels, came to tell Marguerite and her mother that they need no longer expect invitations to her once-a-month, and to inform them that if the young couple dared to call the door would remain shut in their faces (which with the arrangement of spy-mirrors prevalent then was easy). At this final blow Marguerite's father, George Denis, sacked Josephine. Marguerite cried, gave Josephine two francs tied up in a handkerchief, and waved goodbye to her through the window.

The door and Josephine were the two events my brother told me about when he was desolate, and I his only friend. Together we had wandered about the Western Hills of Peking, in mutual loneliness. He, a young man already lost, no place on earth for him, a Eurasian, belonging nowhere. I, much younger, watched, listened, learnt; and thus was saved.

Josephine died at the Hospital of the Poor in Brussels. She wrote a letter imploring forgiveness from her former employers. It was my brother who received the letter, and read it.

Had I known a long time ago about all this, instead of only now, perhaps things might have been different. But I only found out everything when it was too late. I was enchanted, almost ecstatic with pride, to think what spirit, what courage, my mother must have had to break all obstacles, to go forward, so boldly, go forward and take Love by the hand and pay for it all her life. Perhaps she was spitting in the wind's face, but she had bravery, and if her days to come were full of sorrow, they were not smug, except that perhaps a surfeit of suffering is also, somehow, silly? And if it was hell on earth, it must also at times have been paradise, watching the green monkeys on the cliffs when she went up to Szechuan by boat, up the River. In 1962 when I did the same trip I looked for Green monkeys, but did not see any. Neither did anyone remember green monkeys. And if she was defeated, it was only because history was too massive a flood for her to stem, because the times, not her intrepid heart, were misordered.

Sixth Brother was now making atonement, propitiating a past he had not known. "Tell her we, the younger generation in China, admire her courage. Tell her we shall look after her . . ." It was too late.

Here am I, left after my father, with the photographs on the bed, a line of Chinese poetry which says: "And still an inch of passion becomes an inch of dust . . . ", and no sense of guilt at all, only a sense of a cycle closed, a completeness.

FIFTEEN

FROM 1904 to 1913 Chou Yentung was in Belgium, as a student, as a married man, as an engineer, doing practical work in factories, mines, and on railways in Belgium for eighteen months' apprenticeship. He was happy, successful in his studies, approved of by the technical staff he worked with. Whatever slur was cast upon his marriage by the Denis disapproval does not seem to have weighed much with the young couple; the oystered pearl of their private felicity was immune to distant aunts. They lived in Woluwe St. Lambert, one of the better suburbs of Brussels; number 55 rue Albertyn was their residence during the years 1911 and 1912. After the birth of their son, Son of Spring, and at his baptism (clad in real Malines lace, and in a church ceremony), George Denis, Marguerite's father, relented so far as to hold his first grandchild over the font; it was his grandchild, and besides his Chinese name he also was given a Christian name, the same as his grandfather, George.

Thus doubly equipped, provided with two identities through his two names, rich heir to two cultures, two races, two of everything except his own torn self, George Son of Spring, also known as Chou Tzechun, became at the same time in the Chou family of Chengtu their first male grandchild, and the first male of his generation, the twenty-fourth. This promoted him to the head of the list of descendants. The Lady Hung was reported well pleased, the ancestor Chou Tao-hung, now eighty-eight, also designed to express pleasure at his foreign daughter-in-law. Son of Spring would perform the rites of oiling the lamp in front of the soul tablets, and it would also be from his index finger that would come the essential drop of blood to paint the red dot at the top of the soul tablet for his grandfather at the latter's burial. He would take precedence over the sons of all his uncles, older or younger than his father. He was First Grandson, First Great-Grandson.

Gifts were exchanged between the Chinese and Belgian families. Marguerite wrote a letter to her mother-in-law, which Yentung translated into the ritual phrases of respect and filial duty. Marguerite now began to learn Chinese. "I want to be a Chinese," she told everyone. She gave up her Belgian passport, and adopted Chinese nationality; this was to make life more difficult for her later, but she never did things by halves.

Photographs of my brother, Son of Spring, taken at that time, show a handsome little boy standing very straight, arms folded, a fine bright face, with a small silk cap upon his head and a silk brocade tunic cut in Chinese fashion. No English clothes for him. Marguerite made her son's clothes according to what she fancied was a Chinese pattern, and silks and brocades came from Szechuan, presents from the Chou family, confirming her belief that she had married an aristocrat. Now it was Son of Spring who was known as "the little Chinese prince" when he went running in the park, with Marguerite on one side of him and his Dutch grandmother on the other.

"I have a son, I am a true Chinese daughter-in-law," said Marguerite.

When Yentung and Marguerite returned to China in 1913, they took their son with them. "My son is Chinese." In the record of the registration of residents in Woluwe all three are registered as Chinese citizens.

But if time had stopped for Yentung ensconced in his happiness, it had not stopped for his country; like the Great River, carrying all before it, it had lurched on, to the inevitable break-up. Yentung was to learn that no traveller returns to the place he came from, for meantime all has changed. Not only was Marguerite going to a new country; Yentung would never go back to what he had known.

Of these ten years, 1903 to 1913, Third Uncle, who stayed in Szechuan, kept a meticulous account.

I was fifteen years old in 1903, at the departure of my Second Brother Yentung for Shanghai. Our Eldest Brother left for Japan in 1905, after his marriage; although he had been wed a year his wife was sickly and the child she had conceived was not born. She died a few years later, which made our Eldest Brother return from his studies in Japan to marry again. But it was due to this accident that the first of us to produce a grandson for our revered parents was my Second Brother, Yentung, in Belgium, an event which caused all our family to rejoice.

I myself, being the Third Son, and destined by the Council of the Elders of our Clan for a military career, never left Szechuan during those years, becoming first a student at a New Learning school opened in Chengtu in 1902, and then at the Military Academy in Chengtu which I entered in 1905. Our father had returned from Kansu an ailing man, but he understood that times had changed. Our revered mother looked after all of us. There was still our younger, Sixth Brother (two having died while in Kansu), and three sisters at home.

The finances of the family were not in good condition, and we had many troubles, but we kept these troubles secret from my Second Brother in the Western Ocean. We did not wish his heart narrowed with disquiet; while studying assiduously his health might have suffered, and our hopes for the future were on him, when he would return to direct the building of railways in Szechuan. In fact, the whole city of Chengtu, all our kith and kin, our relatives by blood and those by affection, the many friends which the virtues of our ancestors had attracted to our family, inquired most faithfully after him, and all looked forward to the day of his return.

There was indeed much change, and though young cadets such as myself at the Military Academy wore queues over our European-style uniforms, we carried swords like the Japanese officers did, and our storm-tossed hearts were no longer with the Dynasty. At night we would argue and discuss about current affairs, and now we called it openly "politics", a word recently come in, though cautious lest we be overheard. And of course the question uppermost in our minds, foremost in our talk, was how to be masters of our own land.

The wind of New Learning was blowing. We thought it mighty, for it shook some leaves down from our feudal tree, but it did not bring down the tree, though it stirred us to question more, to demand more, to new audacities. Because it had two sons abroad, our family enjoyed the reputation of being progressive. But revered Grandfather Taohung was becoming old, though still full of energy. Our father was always ill, and thus I, at seventeen, had to assume responsibilities beyond my age. Besides attending the Military Academy, I did the accounts for our tobacco company, and also helped my mother with the land rent and the taxes. All this gave me a good deal of practical experience, and was to lead to my future success in the business and financial world.

Thus I began to understand the manipulations of money. I saw a financial crisis looming for ourselves, but we were not the only ones affected. China was financially exhausted, eighty-two per cent of her revenue earmarked for repayment of war indemnities to the Powers. How was the foundering land to escape this morass of debt and misery?

At that time, besides the commerce in tobacco, some of our relatives had started in timber, but due to the disastrous *likin* tax on all transport, this went bankrupt. The tax per bale of goods from Ichang to Chungking, four hundred miles by barge, was forty ounces of silver, and it was double that to Chengtu. The land-tax was also increasingly heavy; for the same acreage it varied, according to district, from ninety-six to three hundred and eighty-seven silver ounces, the smaller the holding the higher the tax. We had to sell land to pay our debts in the tobacco commerce, and the sales tax amounted to one-third of the value of the land.

I sought the cause of this cruel ruin, paid heed and worked hard at accounts while other young men played. I found out about cotton, for I saw the foreign textiles coming in. We had had cotton in China since the eleventh century; it had come from Khotan, the short staple kind, and we had made cotton clothes and cotton shoes for ourselves for centuries. But now foreign cotton goods were coming in enormous quantities. I read about India, how their handicraftsmen who spun and wove their own handloom cottons had been thrown out of work, many millions of them, by the spinning mills of Lancashire. Now the same was happening to us, and we were swamped with foreign-made cotton, except that the textile mills owned by foreigners were established in our own country, on concessions of land granted them as their property, and they were able to use our cheap labour, cheaper than their own workers, producing cotton goods sold to us; and, since they were foreign goods, not subject to our taxes.

I learnt about opium, and how it had drained us of silver; and how after 1850 we grew our own, for the curse of opium was upon us, and now sixty out of a hundred men in Chengtu smoked opium. I learnt also about the tea market; we had sold much tea to the world before 1850, but we had lost the tea market to India where the British had made large tea plantations. And now they wanted to take away from us our tea trade with Tibet.

I read about Africa, and my heart burned within me with anger and also with horror. O Heaven, I thought, shall this happen to us?

And so I became a nationalist, and though I wore a queue

it was only to keep my head and body safely together. And many another young officer in the Academy also became, like me, a nationalist.

By 1907 not all the revenue of China was enough to pay the interests on all the indemnities we owed, let alone to give back the capital; and because silver had depreciated we had already, in 1896, agreed that the interest on the loans we contracted was to be paid in gold. To guarantee repayment our lands and mines and existing railways and natural resources were mortgaged, our customs revenue was in the foreigners' hands, and now the *likin* or mileage tax, both by land and water, was also mortgaged to them.

One thing alone was left for us to fasten on, to make secure our determination not to give in any more: the Szechuan–Hankow Railway, our own Railway, to be built by ourselves. This was our last stand, the single concrete thing upon which we would not give way, ever. There were so many other problems, but they were more vague, diffuse; we had no control over them. The railway was to be our very own. And I was proud because my brother would be an engineer, and build railways, and the Chou Family thus would find new avenues for its energies.

But meanwhile, in spite of our determination to resist foreigners, at the same time we had to learn from them; and along with the New Learning came many quaint and curious foreign things, which made us bear new desires. Foreigners were selling many of their goods, and since theirs were cheaper, we bought them. Some came up river to Chengtu, and among them were watches; and knowing that we were now so fascinated by railways, they sold us watches with a locomotive painted on the dial. They cost thirty dollars, were made of nickel, and were called "railway watches". There was another, more expensive, kind of watch, with a case of silver or of gold, which made a sound at the quarter, the half, and the hour, like a clock. The foreigners sold us lamps, table lamps with white porcelain shades. Every woman wanted one in her bedroom. To light them one had to buy foreign oil, kerosene, and the oil was very expensive. In the foreign goods shop oil for the lamps cost one ounce of silver for four catties, three hundred copper coins per cattie, twelve to thirteen times dearer than the vegetable rape seed oil we used. However, all the gentry now wanted bright lights, and the agency selling the oil was very clever. They gave the lamps free, and when one had a lamp of course one wanted to use it, and bought the kerosene for it. To make us buy more oil, at first for every cattie of oil bought one received a present, a picture of a beautiful lady to hang on the wall. And the name of the company selling us the kerosene was the Standard Oil Company of New York. And in one year they sold one hundred million gallons of kerosene for the lamps. But for the lamp in front of the ancestors' hall we never used anything but our own rape seed oil.

Later, when cigarettes came in, the same thing was done. Together with each packet of cigarettes an ashtray was given, and people thought they were getting something for nothing.

These ways to make people buy were strange and new to us, and many bought for the sheer pleasure at first of holding in the hand and talking of something new. And once this was done, it was like opium, we could no longer do without this new bauble, and thus, though we hated the foreigners and though we knew they were ruining us, we bought their goods.

Thus I learnt the art of the foreigners, the art of creating in the human heart restlessness, disquiet, hunger for new things, and these new desires became their best helpers. Later it was to be gramophones, and perfumed soap, and many other things. And all this I eschewed, wanting to preserve my spirit; all except photography, for this I have ever considered most useful.

Before 1900 our people in Szechuan did not know photography. We sought an artist to paint a picture, and the best artists came from Canton; they did likenesses on porcelain, or on glass, they fired the porcelain so that the likeness was preserved for ever. The Hakkas, who travel back and forth as merchants between Szechuan and South China, brought pictures sketched in Chengtu to celebrated artists in Canton, who would improve the features before the painting on porcelain.

Photography came in, and the old art disappeared, and there was no more painting on glass. By 1902 one photographic shop had opened in Chengtu, where my Second Brother had his picture taken before leaving for Europe. It was expensive to have a photograph, eight ounces of silver for a united family group. Many of our elders said that the soul of man was absorbed by the machine, and that even if one did not die at once, one became very ill after having a picture taken. But in spite of what they said, every young man wanted to be photographed, and at last in 1907 even our Revered Elder, Taohung, and two other ancestors of other branch clans, each over eighty years old, were photographed. I remember it well, because it was I who arranged for the artist in photography to come to our house and to take this picture, and we had a doctor in attendance in case any harm might befall the Revered Ones. Later, it was I who had the idea of photographing the family documents, and also the scrolls, the plants and flowers in our garden, and the family paintings of our ancestors. For a photograph conserves when the original decays, and after a few years it can be repeated.

All these new and foreign things came in, then, and made us spend money. Some were good, like photography. Others were useless, and helped to wreck us more quickly. I tried everything once, but I did not let myself be tempted, I did not fall; always I would prefer Chinese things, wear Chinese clothes, eat Chinese food and keep my money in China. Never did I put a single copper coin abroad, outside my own country, for I wanted my country to be strong, not sold. If I made mistakes, that was because I did not know how to make the country strong. But in those early years, searching for a way out of the noose which the foreigners put around our necks, I was one of those to realize that it was financial thraldom, economic strangling, more terrible even than armies invading a country. For one can see a foreign soldier, and fight him; but the continuous, silent, secret bleeding, the vampire sucking which went on, is not discerned.

The foreigners were clever. They smelt the wind, they began to sense that we in China were hardening after 1900. Sun Yatsen's Revolutionary League was growing, all the students going to Japan were enthusiastic for revolution, even Elder Brother. Every year there were risings, in spring and in autumn. The foreigners began to talk of uniting against us, "to pursue an efficacious struggle against the growing demands of the Chinese", as they put it in their own newspapers. The "growing demand" was to be masters in our own land.

That is why the famous Consortium was established, a banking alliance of four great banks, the French, the British, American and German, with the power of their governments behind them. The profundity of their cunning was that in so many matters, such as railways, or mines, or the establishment of industries upon our soil, they claimed these ventures to be purely commercial, but actually in each of these they had the military and financial backing of their governments. None of these enterprises was purely commercial, all had political motives. In this Consortium were England and France, America and Germany, and what better control over us than another loan to indebt us for another fifty years.

Looking back now, I can see it better than I did at the time, a surprising thing. Our adversaries were then moving more slowly than we; the temper of our rising nationalism was growing more swiftly then they expected. They were still caught in a mesh of their own bickering over their spoils, which slowed down their alliance. And so it was because they were not united that we could buy back two railways from them, the Peking–Hankow in 1908, and the Hankow–Canton railway. Our joy was great when we bought them back, but it was a warning signal, and it quickened the formation of the Consortium, the British urging it on as they saw more clearly than the others what was happening. And so, by 1909, once again they began to compel the Manchu dynasty to accept another loan for the railways, which would place in their hands the new lines projected, such as our railway in Szechuan.

Meanwhile, all these years there was much talk of reform and of the Constitution we were promised. In 1906 I remember reading a translation of an English newspaper praising the Dowager Empress. "Her Majesty is willing to go down in history as the originator of enlightened reforms," it said. Of course some may have believed this, but many of us already knew what a farce was being perpetrated upon us. We were promised a National Assembly, a Constitution, democratic government; and all the time we knew this was quite impossible, since the material basis upon which such liberal ways can subsist, freedom from want, was not ours. A Provincial Assembly came into being, and many of our Chengtu officials got into it, and great was the talk; but it has all gone, like mist before the sun, for it was only mist. Kang Yuwei's ideas for a time looked like being accepted, and his followers bitterly denounced revolution. But most of us young cadets only mouthed the word reform, and knew no change would come without guns. Poor Kang Yuwei! Like driftwood that becomes strewn on a beach, he was left behind by the current of our needs and desires, until even such youngsters as myself, by no means progessive, accounted him outmoded. He staunchly kept his pigtail when all were cutting theirs, went for a tour of the Balkans and deplored the frequent regicides of these turbulent countries, advising their rulers to build higher walls to their palaces; and ended his life by serving an uncouth and almost illiterate warlord. For history paces with the speed and force of the Great River, and takes no heed of our single vanities, and nothing is more superflous than a conjecture of might-have-beens.

In 1908 the Dowager Empress died, a day after her unfortunate son, the prisoner-Emperor Kuanghsu, and a three-year-old child sat and cried on the Dragon Throne. There had been a reorganization of the military academies all through China, and this was pushed through by Yuan Shihkai, the powerful Commander-in-Chief, who wanted the Army in his hands; while the scholars talked of democracy, he built his own power, and his power was the Army. In 1894 ten battalions had been formed and drilled by German officers near Tientsin. They were under Yuan Shihkai, at that time the hope of his Reformist friends, Kang Yuwei and Tan Szetung, whom he betrayed to the Dowager Empress in that fateful September of 1898. Everything was then put back, including army training: for one and a half years, till 1900, the troops were again drilled in the bow and arrow. In 1903, when Reform became fashionable, Yuan reorganized officers' training centres in some cities. His aim was to create a devoted personal following of young career officers. He sent many to Germany and to Japan. Most of them were ambitious young men, eager for power, a few became revolutionaries; very rapidly they formed juntas and cliques, according to provincial inclination. I became acquainted with a good many when I was sent to the Paoting Military Academy in the north. Crack regiments were being trained there, the core of what were to become the Northern Armies of the warlords. I did not stay very long, however, but was recalled for active service as once again we were threatened: the British were trying to conquer Tibet. They had tried in 1904, sending an expedition to Lhasa. Our Szechuan troops were now called to augment the frontier garrisons. At that time our Viceroy, Chao Erfeng, went out to make the frontiers safe against the British. I was for a year on garrison duty, and I returned in 1909 to teach at the Military Academy in Chengtu.

It was that year on the border which confirmed my belief that there would be no other way out but the way of power, the way of the gun. All the talk of Reform was hypocrisy, meant to delude us. And all these corrupt men who talked of Constitutional Monarchy were defrauding us of the truth. To become strong, we must fight. So I took the way of the gun.

But our family was getting poorer. In 1910 our father died, aged only forty-seven. I resigned my post and went home for the three years' prescribed mourning, chiefly to rescue what could still be saved from ruin. For while I had been on the Tibetan border there was no one able to attend to affairs.

But none of this did we write to Yentung, my Second Brother, in the West, for we did not wish his heart disquieted. I often thought: when Second Brother returns, he and I together can restore the family fortunes. For a great change is coming, and we must prepare for it.

SIXTEEN

FOR some years I had been collecting the memoirs of people who had seen the Revolution of 1911, seeking men of my father's generation who had witnessed its unfolding in Szechuan province. All these memories were now being written down, and it was Puyi, the ex-Emperor of China, who had lost his throne in the Revolution of 1911, who was doing the compilation of these memoirs, at the same time as writing his own.

The most reliable witness I found was Li Chiehjen, the writer, known as the Maupassant of China. A Szechuanese born in Chengtu, he had lived fifteen years in France and in Japan, then returned to Szechuan and written many novels. In his youth he had taken part in the Revolution of 1911. His French was excellent, his love for French literature great. His books, popular before the Revolution of 1949, were being reprinted after it. He had thus bridged two revolutions and two social systems, as active participant as well as observer.

Li gave me his time, his notes, spoke of everything he could possibly remember, a generosity so great from one writer to another that I feel for ever in his debt. We spent several days together, he talking and I taking notes. He was a small, dapper man, with very bright eyes and a sharp face, always dressed in a long flowing silk gown. He looked much younger than his age, and his death in 1963 came as an astonished shock, for in spite of being over seventy he moved and spoke like a young man, and there was not a white hair upon his head. He was actually seventy-five, and looked an incredibly young forty-five, when he died.

You call me eye-witness to revolution; yet what man sees a great turbulence such as a revolution in its wholeness? That is why always man seeks to midget greatness to his own size, enclosing a landscape on a sheet of paper, trees and rocks, a mountain and a lake, in a miniature rock garden, thus giving his heart noble amplitude without feeling overwhelmed. As a writer I am aware of this, and how inexact all words are to represent reality. Especially the reality of a revolution, which seems to give normal time a shove, so that one lives with the feeling of never catching up with events, of having to run hard, hard, merely to remain in place. So much happens, and I have not yet come taut with time myself, I am still bemused, trying in my mind to order the past decades, for only last week it seems it was 1911 . . .

In the spring of 1911 I returned from Japan, along with other students. I had studied law and current affairs rather desultorily for five years; even then I wanted to write, and had written for student magazines, and some of them had been very progressive, especially the *Szechuan Magazine* edited in Japan. There were about five thousand Szechuan students in Japan when I sailed back to Shanghai, and they were accounted more fiery than any other except the Hunan students. This seemed paradoxical, Szechuan being one of the most enclosed and least under Western influence of all our regions. The Szechuan students, precisely because of their feudal attachment to their soil, were fiercely patriotic, and their gentry had very few connections with foreign moneyed interests. They had not developed a middleman merchant class dependent on the West for its own wealth and power, as in the eastern seaboard provinces. And this was important, for a good many of the Szechuan students who returned from Japan, as I did, were convinced revolutionaries, members of Sun Yatsen's Revolutionary League.

I had cut off my queue in Japan, and in Shanghai bought a false queue attached to a cap. As I proceeded up the Great River to Hankow, as a steerage passenger in a British steamer, the rarity of western suits became striking, though in Japan a Chinese in a long gown was a rarity, and most of us had come to wear the Japanese students' uniform, which later was termed the Sun Yatsen suit, and is now spoken of as the Communist garb. Actually, the close collar, jacket and trousers is still today the uniform of Japanese students. I discarded it in Hankow, and wore a cool long grasscloth robe, cotton trousers and cotton shoes. I was re-entering thus into a past self, and the sensation was strange, as if I were stepping back in time.

In Japan, in the university circles, all was effervescence, endless discussions, endless talk of revolution, since Sun Yatsen's League was established in Tokyo. I felt as if I were dipped back into a stagnant, rancid pond, dead water ... but how false this impression was I soon found out. Like an old temple, majestic with paint, the structure of the dynasty, its neverending corruption based on squalor and defeat, remained standing; yet all was eaten away within. I was not the only one to be thus at first deceived. I read the foreigners' newspapers in Shanghai, all expressing satisfaction at the state of affairs. "Never has the dynasty been more popular," they wrote in 1911. They were consolidating their own power, and it looked as if we were not moving. That very spring in the south another insurrection had failed, and the slaughter had been very great.

The first class of the British steamer I travelled on was reserved for white people, and below deck we were all crowded together. Up and down the Son of the Ocean went foreign gunboats. There had been a great famine in the province of Hunan, and the Triple City of Hankow, Wuchang and Hanyang, triangular metropolis astride the River, was invaded by hundreds of thousands of starved peasants, carrying their children in baskets balanced at both ends of a pole slung across their shoulders. The concessions of the foreigners were wired in with barbed wire, Sikhs and Corsican policemen patrolled them, pushing back or beating anyone who tried to crawl through to beg for food. Outside the foreign concessions, every morning they picked up the dead: thirty thousand in a week. Those too weak to move sat in rows, staring at those who passed them; behind their eyes their skeletons looked at me.

At Ichang, where the River leaves the plains and enters the gorges into Szechuan, were the gunboats of the British, patrolling. On the heights above, commandeering the landscape, the English consulate, and a big Catholic church, its spire and cross all white, palisaded with high white walls, overrode the cliffs. Down the slopes toppled dingy, dark hovels, propped on long stilts, where lived my people. And the sight, added to my new consciousness of nationalism fostered in Japan, made the waters of hatred rise, bitter, bitter gall, in my mouth. A slave country, a slave country, everyone's slave.

From Ichang going up river there was now a tugboat, the *Shutung*. It had been started in 1908 by the merchant-gentry of Chungking and Chengtu, and it towed alongside a flat barge carrying sixty tons of cargo and as many people as could be packed into her, generally about three hundred. The pilot was an Englishman. On both sides we passed the junks, still pulled through the gorges against the current by naked men, shrivelled, sunburnt, step by step. On the cliffs I saw ant-big men breaking stones. "They are building the roadbed of our railway, the railway that we, the fifty million people of Szechuan, have dreamt about for years," said one passenger to me, and at once everyone began to speak of the railway, the Szechuan railway. The Administrator of the Railway Company at Ichang, a name named Lee, had about a hundred thousand men working on the roadbed. "Our Szechuan people do not want any foreigners to build our railway." The tugboat *Shutung* had been bought from the British firm of Thornycrofts especially to bring railway material up the River.

But many of the Szechuanese on board with me were critical. And as usual everyone talked and told me freely what had happened. Although the Governor of Szechuan had obtained permission to build the railway in 1903, it was now 1911 but only one hundred and twenty-five *lis*, or about eighty kilometres, of roadbed had been laid in place, going westward from Ichang to Kuifu in the direction of Chungking. It had been decided to build this section, although it was the most difficult of all and therefore the most costly: since it was to span the gorges a good many bridges and tunnels across and through the zigzag of rocky heights would have to be constructed. Many Szechuanese would have preferred to start with an easier portion, building the railway from Chengtu eastward to Chungking, and then from Chungking to Ichang. But there was another difficulty: all the material, including the rails, had to be transported up river by boat, across the gorges, and this was not deemed feasible. By beginning at Ichang, and proceeding towards Chungkind, the material could come up the River on the small barge lashed to the *Shutung*. But no one was pleased with the progress made.

"Look you, the railway from Ichang to Chengtu is three thousand *lis* in length, and we have only done just over one hundred of roadbed. There are three thousand to go, and at this rate it will take thirty years to build the railway. And the cost, five million ounces of silver merely for this. All the silver of the Jade Emperor's realm will not be enough."

Since 1903 money had been collected in Szechuan for our railway. The big shares and small shares among the gentry had gone well, but how much gentry was there? Less than two per cent of the population. Thereupon the Railway Company had had recourse to "rent shares", which were shares guaranteed by the land rent, and equivalent to three per cent of the revenue from land rent. This was supposed to be paid by the landlord-gentry, but actually was passed on by them to the peasants who rented the fields. Further levies for the railway were raised, on salt, on consumer goods (non-foreign), and added to the *likin* or transport tax, and all these were paid by the people. This money amounted to fourteen million ounces of silver, but it was estimated that seventy million would be needed.

"Tell me, how can the matter be given head and tail? There is constant quarrel among the directors of the Company, all of them being gentry, and between the head office in Chengtu and branch offices in Ichang, Chungking. All these directors are putting money in their pockets; and this is our people's money, sweated out by them all these years, and now it is spent on banquets and opium."

I already knew something of this. After its establishment in 1903, the Railway Company had come more and more under government control through official appointees; the shares out of the land rent and *likin* taxes were embezzled. In 1906 the Szechuan students in Japan had already denounced this, and asked that the Company become genuinely a private enterprise, run by Szechuan merchants. As long as there were officials about, there would be outright corruption and funds would vanish; but even worse, the danger of the government going back on the 1903 edict, and selling our railway rights to foreigners, was always there.

In 1907 two students returning from Japan, friends of mine, had attempted a rising in Chengtu, but it had failed and the leaders had been beheaded. But the people were not lethargic. In one way or another, because the levy of money for the railway had affected so many of them, the whole population was aware of the issue, and when the students were beheaded the magistrate who had to condemn them resigned from his post and joined the Revolution.

In 1910, our Szechuan Students' Association in Japan had again denounced the Managing Director who, entrusted with a large sum collected from the taxes, had put it for "safe keeping" in a private bank in Shanghai; that year a bullion scare occurred in Shanghai, and the bank declared itself bankrupt. The money turned to morning dew. Everyone knew the Managing Director had pocketed it; as he was an official appointed by the government, nothing was done.

And so the talk went, on the barge, and all of us made brothers by the talk. And among the two hundred or more passengers on board were members of the Kelao Secret Society; I gave the sign of the teacups, and two of them came over to speak with me. There were also many of them in Japan, and in the batting of a fairy's eyelid we had established our brotherhood. I felt comforted and upheld, knowing the Kelao in Szechuan would support such returned students from Japan as myself. As usual, their system of information was excellent, and through them the Revolutionary League had established a network of messengers throughout the provinces.

But in spite of the comfort of the Brothers, my heart was the colour of sorrow. Oh my country, when will you get rid of devils? Not only the outside devils, but also the inside ones that keep you weak? No one is kind to the weak. Only when we could be strong, like Japan, would no one dare to parade gunboats on our waters, to push our people off the sidewalks of our cities, to garrison troops on our land. "Revolution," I whispered, and looked for an omen. Clouds gathered, a shadow upon the town of Ichang, precursor of night squall.

At Wanhsien, midway through the gorges, a grizzle-haired man, thin as an opium smoker, climbed on board, and was hailed by one of the Brothers with me as Uncle Chu. He was an employee of the Telegraph Company set up in 1907. Cables could now be sent from Szechuan to the outside world. Chu, being a Brother, held no secret from us, and he told us of the projected nationalization of the railways.

"But what does nationalization mean?" I asked.

"It means a sell-out to the foreigners," said Chu. "Prepare yourselves, oh my Brothers, for what we feared has indeed happened."

Actually rumours of nationalization had existed since 1906. It was known that at Court many foreigners – English, Japanese, German – pressed for the acceptance of "loans". Since each loan meant money in the pockets of Ministers, the latter were only too eager to sell the railway rights. But the opposition from the provincial gentry had been so tenacious that they had feared to move. Now, however, the pressures had become irresistible, and the fact that the private companies had been so inefficient gave the officials sufficient excuse.

A Banking Consortium of Four Powers had offered a large loan to build the railways. Once again they had got hold of Sheng Hsinsun, Minister of Posts and Telegraphs, now Director of Railway Building, and some other Chinese officials, using them to get the Manchu Court to accept the loan. I think Sheng was one of the most hated men in China then. He had, in 1894–5, taken bribes from the Japanese at the height of the war with Japan, made another fortune negotiating the Belgian railway contract for the Peking–Hankow Railway, and yet another in 1908 when that line was bought back by the Chinese government against the King of the Belgians' wishes.

Sheng also managed the Hanyehping iron industry started by the Viceroy Chang Chihtung at the Triple City; he managed it so well that a deficit of six million pounds was produced, and soon the company was in Japanese hands; but Sheng remained the official manager, and in every railway contract he signed it was specified that some of the material would come from the Hanyehping works. Not surprisingly, therefore, Sheng urged another large railway loan and foreigners to build the projected railways, and also tried to bring his friends the Japanese into the Consortium, so that again the contract would specify that the steel used for the rails would come from the Hanyehping iron works, the works he managed, which meant another increment to his vast wealth.

The manoeuvring in Peking at Court and between the Powers had been intense, scandalous, and mostly unrecorded. Russia had started complaining, wanting a share in the Consortium, and nagged France for help; England objected to Russia, and France to Japan; then America claimed twenty-five per cent share of the total loan, under a clause of a 1904 agreement, which read: "Should the capital for building the Szechuan–Hankow railway be insufficient, the Chinese Government will so inform England *and the United States of*

America." The capital was insufficient, the Americans averred, and the American Minister had made representations to the Manchu Court in July 1909 that "unless a satisfactory answer be obtained, the Chinese government would be held entirely responsible for any consequences ...", the usual diplomatic gunboat threat. As a result, America had become a solid partner of the Banking Consortium which now agreed to finance two railways, the Szechuan–Hankow and the Hankow–Canton; although the Americans had sold back in 1905 to the Chinese their share of the latter, at that time one-third built, they were now back in the market for the remaining two-thirds.

In order to hide from the people the fact that once again foreign control of the railways was being accepted, for cash, by the government, the word "nationalization" was to be used. Already a six million pounds sterling loan had been approved by the Consortium. Now, by Imperial Edict, on May 9th, 1911, the nationalization of railways was proclaimed, which removed the rights granted to the Chinese provincial companies for financing and building their own railways.

Brother of the Robe Chu had seen the telegrams, ordering the provincial government of Szechuan to prepare for nationalization. "What shall we do? We are all to be told that this is a good thing, that foreigners should build our railways. The railways will be built faster, China modernized more quickly. But all the people are against it, especially our people in Szechuan. Blood will run, and heads fly from bodies. Shall we hand over our land to them with three obeisances in the name of nationalization? I for one would rather die."

As our tugboat struggled up the gorges, the news spread among the passengers, and there were more rumours at each landing stop: that in Chengtu the Railway Company shareholders were holding protest meetings; that in Ichang the manager had cabled the head office to ask what would happen to the hundred thousand workmen and the engineers, who would pay them, were the funds being taken over, was he to stop work until nationalization was completed? All of us knew that it was a farce, there could be no nationalization since there was no money, all the revenue was going to repay the war indemnities and the previous loans and interest on loans. All, all was gone; the customs, and even the *likin* taxes, were mortgaged, and so many other resources. How could the state then nationalize the railways? How could it compensate the shareholders in the companies and buy back the shares from them?

On May 20th, 1911, as I landed in Chunking, I heard that the great Railway Loan contract had been signed between Sheng Hsinsun, as Minister of Communications, Posts and Telegraphs, and the Banking Consortium of the Four Powers, America, England, France and Germany.

You know how our Chengtu is: an old, old city, trees, flowers, literature, old bookshops, a quiet city, proud of its age, its history. But when I returned to it at the end of May 1911 it was uneasy, irritable, anxious, the teahouses, in the public gardens and on the streets exuding unease. An anxious city, poised for rioting.

It is said that of a man the most difficult things to draw are his hands, because we constantly see them and that makes us blind. Fresh from Japan, I opened my eyes in amazement at my own city, Chengtu, marvelling that corpulent officials could still go about the streets with drummers in front, on their heads the buttons of coral, on their ceremonial robes the pheasants and lions, peacocks and leopards, embroidered front and back to denote their civil or military rank. The higher the rank, the more the official seemed in favour of nationalization, whereas the officials of the seventh, eighth and ninth grades kept silent, or sighed in a significant manner. The call: "I buy tea", uttered so frequently in the teahouses, no longer prefaced amicable talk of business, respect to an elder, demand for a favour, or any of those transactions of land or merchandise which are normally done in a teahouse or a restaurant because the home is no place for such mundane matters; it was now practically a clarion call for an immediate drift of diverse loiterers, small groups coalescing into larger ones, some even standing to listen as debates went on concerning the nationalization question and the railway loan; and silently they would drift apart again, then on to another teahouse, to hear another man expound.

And in the beginning it all seemed so quiet, just a few more people drifting lazily, casually about, sipping tea and idling – but the colour of men's faces had changed, there was a certain carefully bland look, hiding the grimness below. And for anyone acquainted with us in Szechuan, the uncommon quietness of these gatherings, the lack of chaff and repartee, the precursor silence falling when officials were about, were heralds of the storm to come.

Even my mother, who had never gone out of the house except in a sedan chair, talked of railways as if she had travelled on one, and her water-pipe bubbled as she inhaled strongly in her anger. On the very day of my arrival, even before our greetings were ended, she spoke: "You have heard of the railway? That Sheng is a rascal! They will not sell our railway! I myself will walk to Peking to petition against this!" She trembled with the outrage, and I was afraid for her health.

It was through my mother's feelings that I noticed that things had indeed changed, though outwardly all was the same, backward as ever. The women were changing. There were families where girls refused to bind their feet. In others the girls did not marry the man chosen for them, had run away, to study, or to join the Revolutionary League, and both were synonymous. In my own family a younger cousin declared she would not marry anyone she had not seen. She demanded to see a photograph first. Each of these things was a great scandal, and the old people talked of the corruption of the young, and called for the old moralities. But when the railway question came up, we were as one. The railway must remain in our hands, in Szechuan hands, run by Chinese enterprise. No fake nationalization, no foreign loan!

Up and down the city the murmurs swelled, a far-off torrent cry; teahouse or brothel, merchant guild or school, morning and evening and at night round the eating stalls, the talk went on, and grew. As in the spring the beehive swells and hums, so did our city of Chengtu, so did our people, preparing themselves against the coming slaughter.

Now the terms of the loan contracted became known: ten million pounds sterling from the Consortium, and a possible further ten million from the Japanese. It was said the interest rate was eight per cent. Also there were secret terms, and it was rumoured that once again ten miles (English) on each side of the railway line would be controlled by the foreign builders of the railway, as this was what the British had extorted from us in previous railway building: ten miles each side, with priority on all natural resources and mines therein ... But it was impossible to get the full text in Chengtu. The whole affair had been carried through without consulting the newly organized Provincial Assemblies, therefore it was illegal. According to the reform measures, the Provincial Assemblies, in existence since 1908, had to be consulted about anything pertaining to their respective provinces, and the Szechuan–Hankow railway was our own provincial railway. We had sweated money eight years for it. More than any other province, we in Szechuan had sweated money for our iron road. Money, money. How much money we had paid out nobody will ever know, but all of us, from the brothel courtesans to the poorest peasant, had sweated money for it. The gentry, who did most of the protesting, had paid the least. As usual, from the poor, the already-ground-to-misery peasant of Szechuan, some millions of silver ounces had come, not only the land-rent three per cent taxes, but the rice tax and salt tax of four copper coins per cattie, years and years of life sweat; and now, would the iron road be taken from us? Even the sedan chair carriers' neck veins swelled when they pronounced the words: "Our iron road, sold to foreigners."

And the craftsmen, the miners and the shopkeepers, and the boatmen and the peasants, all of them who did not know what a railway looked like, all were angry.

Among the returned students the information was more precise. We had our links with newspapers offices, and we tried to find out what the exact terms of the Consortium loan were; but as usual some clauses were secret. It was reported that the American Under-Secretary for Foreign Affairs had said: "The old principle of spheres of influence is being given up; the new system is that of division among the various nations interested." The terms of this new division of China, to begin with the new railways became known: the four big Powers had agreed among themselves that the allocation of mileage, with engineering rights and all other rights, would be, on our line alone:

The British, 600 kilometres;

The Americans, 600 kilometres, of which 400 to be in Szechuan;

The French, 600 kilometres;

The rest to be divided between England and Germany; England was to get a very big share on the other railway, the Hankow–Canton railway.

The purchasing agent, the chief engineer, all rights to allocate posts, hire the personnel, the finance and materials, an option on all natural resources for up to ten miles on each side of the line, were allotted to the nation building that railway section.

Another agreement, for currency reform and industrial development, was in preparation, we heard. Meanwhile, the railway loan was not at par: the Chinese government would receive ninety dollars out of every one hundred dollar share subscribed.

All the main trunk lines, whether built or building, or in the planning stage, would be taken over. Although at first the Szechuan railway had been spoken of as an extension or branch line, it was to be treated as a trunk line, at the request of the British and the Americans.

The Board of Directors of the Szechuan Railway Company called an Extraordinary General Meeting in Chengtu to protest. It took place on June 17th, 1911. The Board of Directors had reasons for protest, not only patriotic. For eight years these gentlemen had looked forward to making money out of a private enterprise, the railway, but in the meantime they had not stinted themselves. They had all had their fingers stuck in sweet candied fruit, and distributed to themselves posts with high-sounding names and higher emoluments. Now Minister Sheng, knowing the embezzlement that had gone on, and to forestall protest, suggested an "audit" of the Company's accounts (one had already been asked for in 1908). But this could not possibly be done, the Company's financial diversions being of such a nature that no accounts could be produced.

Sheng, knowing his own hands far from clean, and not wishing to be impeached for corruption by a subtle manoeuvre, had had Tuan Fang, a Chinese whose family had become Manchus three generations previously, named Director of the Szechuan–Hankow and Hankow–Canton Railways. Tuan Fang was Viceroy of Nanking, reckoned a "modern" as he had visited Europe in 1906 to study their political systems in order to provide China with a democratic Constitution. He was highly acceptable to the foreigners, having sent his sons abroad for education, and was described as a genial and hospitable man, progressive for a Manchu (which he was not), given to good living. On his return from Europe he had presented to the Dowager Empress Tze Hsi an elephant, which had subsequently died of starvation. At the funeral of Tze Hsi two years later, he had allowed photographs to be taken of the cortège, and for this lack of respect had been cashiered and retired. He was now exhumed from obscurity by Sheng, who needed him to deal with the angry merchant-gentry.

The Railway Company premises in Chengtu were at the Yueh Mansion on Yuehfu Street. In front of the mansion a large carved-brick screening wall prevented a rush by evil spirits. It was a very hot June morning, and I went in carried by a big tide of people pushing in the streets, flowing towards the screening wall, there separating, to coalesce again on the other side, and narrowing to squeeze into the courtyard, Invincible water, relentless water, they advanced, very quiet, and where not more than fifty or a hundred shareholders attended, that day over a thousand came. I was floated in by the tide, and while still in the courtyard already could hear a sound of weeping from the meeting hall. Men weeping, worse than anything at funerals.

My friend Lung Mingchien, a revolutionary and a Brother, passed me, pushing forward, saying: "Lend a way, we also are shareholders."

Inside it was stifling, but no one was fanning himself, all fans forgotten, stuck in people's collars. People were standing, haranguing the platform where the Board sat, and there was weeping, though I could not see where it came from. On the platform, behind a long table, the directors and also some officials, bleary with heat and fear. Then someone was shouting:

"Organize, organize, organize a Save the Railway League, everybody become a member ... sign ... sign ... petitions ... don't crowd, don't push, don't weep so loudly, please ... sign ... sign ..."

Lo Lun, a landowner, member of the Provincial Assembly and a staunch defender of the Dynasty, was standing and shouting with the others; and also Pu Peiying, another provincial assemblyman, both worthy gentry: "We are sold, we are sold out, the province is finished, our Szechuan is sold to the foreigners, our country is finished ..."

Others were screaming: "Traitors, traitors. Let us march to Peking, let us march ... let us there demand Sheng the traitor's head."

I looked round. Handicraftsmen, students and landowners, even two Hanling Academicians, seventy and eighty years old, with wispy beards and stumbling walk, supported by their pupils as they were hoisted on to the platform, but their quavery old voices went unheard in the clapping. Then someone, either Lung Mingchien or Wu Yuchang, the leaders of the revolutionary students, shouted: "We demand that the

contract with the Consortium be cancelled, the loan abrogated, our railway rights given back to us. These are the aims
of our Save the Railway League. The League comes into existence *now!* Sign *now!*"

Suddenly, we had a Save the Railway League. The emotion was tremendous. There and then an organizing committee was formed, and a march to petition the Governor in
Chengtu was decided upon. The Board was to go in full ceremonial dress, so the directors and the assemblymen went back
to their homes, in their sedan chairs, to fetch their dresses
and hats and ceremonial shoes; they would announce formally to the Governor of the province the establishment of a
Save the Railway League, and their opposition to the nationalization of the Szechuan–Hankow railway.

By noon the procession was winding through the streets,
at its head the old Hanling Academicians, then the Board of
Directors, the various guilds of merchants, the provincial assemblymen, a gamut of landlords, some young officers of
the New Army, some newspaper writers, many teachers of the
schools and even the Supervisor of the Chengtu Academy,
where my father, your father and your grandfather had studied. Some of the lower grades of officials also joined in;
dressed in full regalia, their emblems of rank on their jackets,
they marched, though not in the vanguard. Behind them came
small shopkeepers, craftsmen and boatmen; a few of our new
policemen to keep order were in front and back of our procession. We had had police since 1905, and the Chief of Police,
known as Chou the Bald, was a very energetic man. He was
really in sympathy with us, but did not dare to show it. Usually
we made fun of Chou the Bald's policemen, for they were all
opium devils and never would catch any thief; instead, they
had struck bargains with these knights of the roofs (as we
call thieves) so that for a certain amount of cash, equally
shared between them, some houses would not be molested.
They loved a parade, and marched with us, joking and laughing, and also shouting: "Protect our railway, save our land!"
lustily.

The following evening returned students from Japan held
meetings, Lung Mingchien and Wu Yuchang among them.
Several decisions were taken then, the chief one being to
collect money and members for the Save the Railway League,
and thus to press forward the revolutionary movement. We
knew that staid monarchists, like the provincial assemblymen,

Lo Lun and Pu Peiying, the landowners and the gentry, were now fighting for the rights of the railway merely because they were involved in the Railway Company's accounts. They wanted their own profit, and were averse to a company audit. But later they might be bribed by Sheng, or by Tuan Fang, into compromising. Our motives were different: we wanted a revolution, the overthrow of the Manchus, an end to foreign exploitation. Most of us, students like myself, drew our inspiration then from the French Revolution, from Garibaldi; Sun Yatsen's Revolutionary League in Japan had fused together every nuance of revolutionary thought, but few of us had any definite programme. We had to learn how to make revolution by making it; among us also would be renegades and traitors, for it is always so, in any revolution, and to be expected. Many start the ascent, few go all the way; but there is constant replenishment, as out of the people arise new fighters. And those who make revolution cannot stop to count those who fall or falter, or betray.

Because postal communications were in the hands of the Minister of Communications, Sheng, it was from the very start nearly impossible for us to communicate with similar protest movements in the other provinces. Any telegram or postal letter would be censored, or simply not sent. A few of us then volunteered to become regular couriers. It worked, but it killed some, who died of exhaustion and malaria and typhoid in that hot summer of the Revolution. Still others were detailed to procure weapons, and to find ingenious methods of smuggling arms and ammunition into the cities. And others, like Lung and another returned student named Wang, went to other cities to organize branches of the League, and also to confer with the Kelao Brothers with a view to organizing murders of officials, and armed risings. Since the revolutionary movement was illegal, and beheading the punishment if caught, only two fields of action were open to us: to make underground alliance with the Kelao, and also to organize secret cells of revolutionaries in the New Army. Both were used in the railway agitation in Szechuan, but at first the main New Army battalions were not accessible, they were at Tatsienlu, the border garrison, as it was rumoured the British might try to invade Tibet once again.

Your Third Uncle was a cadet officer in the New Army, and he will tell you how the cells were organized in the military academies among the young officers. Most of them belonged to gentry families who had bought shares in the railway, so that they were really on our side in their hearts. During the months of June and July, then, we were very active. Couriers kept us informed of what was happening elsewhere.

In Hunan, Hupeh and Kuangtung, all provinces to be crossed by the two railways, there was also much agitation. In Peking Minister Sheng was upheld by a Manchu prince, Duke Tsai Tse, uncle of the Emperor. A revolt of four provinces was something they could not face, and they might have partly given in, had not the foreign lobbies pressured them. All the Consuls were sure there would be no trouble: "A storm in a teacup." What we really felt, the depth of the people's feeling, the foreigners ignored. Thus the Court was reassured.

In order to pacify the protest delegations sent to Peking by the provinces, Tuan Fang had the idea to organize in Peking, at the Garden of the Three Princes, which later became a zoo, a meeting to lecture on "How to Save Our Country by Borrowing Money". The argument was ingenious: "The best way to get Europeans to like you is to ask them to lend you money, and to mortgage something to them. They have too much money, but too little of everything else." The meeting ended disastrously, the staid delegates picking up stones to fling at the hired speakers and calling them "traitors".

Tuan Fang, the Director of Railways, was advised by Sheng to offer each discontented provincial railway company separate treatment. Kuangtung was reckoned difficult to handle. Everyone was afraid of the Cantonese, because they were so fiery, rebellious, and so many had Overseas Chinese connections and the latter strongly supported Sun Yatsen; he had collected two hundred thousand dollars among them for an uprising only a few months previously. The Overseas Chinese had many shares in the railway, but the section of the railway through the province of Kuangtung had been completed by 1910, and all that remained to be built were the sections through Hunan and Hupeh provinces to reach Hankow. Not to antagonize the Overseas Chinese further, Tuan Fang therefore suggested buying back the private shares of the Hankow–Canton shareholders at market value; and since the share values were up, the shareholders would make a profit. "It has always been a failing of merchants, to sacrifice a long-term advantage for a short-term profit," he noted. But the shareholders organized a run on the bank, to withdraw their money in silver. The governor sent orders to arrest them, and many fled to Hongkong. Opposition also came from Cantonese students in San Francisco and in Japan, who set up a clamour; but they were far away, and ignored.

In Hunan the opposition was also strong. Another method was devised by Tuan Fang to split it. The Hunan people were stopping Barclay, the American engineer who was supposed to survey the railway line layout, from entering the province. Many young officers and contingents in the New Army, and in the arsenals, were from Hunan, and there had been disastrous floods in 1909 and 1910, a million Hunan peasants had been affected, and revolt was already brewing. But the railway shares for the Hunan section had been subscribed to chiefly by townspeople and merchants. Tuan Fang decided to buy back the ordinary small shares at the buying price; while the larger shares of the principal shareholders, the merchants, would be exchanged at par for national railway shares, and interest paid upon them from the day they changed hands. The governor of Hunan asked for troops, and these were provided, and thus the rising was temporarily held in check.

In Hupeh province the contributions had been few, the Hupeh merchants were not as keen about a railway as Szechuan was. Hupeh was in a central position, the River, broad and smooth, crossed the province horizontally, providing transport, and already one railway, the Peking–Hankow line, had been built by foreigners. There was the proximity of Shanghai, and foreign industries in which to invest capital. But while the wealthy hesitated, many of the small shareholders organized meetings in all three parts of the Triple City, and sent delegates to protest in Peking. The movement was suppressed, since Wuchang was a centre of the New Army. Hankow had foreign concessions and troops, factories and firms; here the British-American Tobacco Company and the Japanese had established cigarette factories and textile mills; whatever Chinese capital there was, was absorbed in the subservient form known as "comprador" or middleman investment in foreign enterprises. Also many of the railway shares were single, official shares, held by officials, forced to buy from "voluntary contributions" of salary, and they were only too pleased to see their money come back without loss. The Hupeh people were already used to owning national shares from the Peking–Hankow railway, which the Chinese government had bought back in 1908. The government propaganda here was powerful and effective: they were told that unless foreigners built the railways, these would never materialize, and the inefficiency of the private railway companies was also held up to them. The agitation was not as strong as in Szechuan; nevertheless, it did occur, and simmered but did not break out in open riots.

That left Sheng, Duke Tsai and Tuan Fang with Szechuan province to deal with, the most recalcitrant of all.

From Peking our couriers brought us the news. "Leave it to me," had said Tuan Fang, "the Szechuanese are notorious talkers. They will shout, but they will not move. Szechuan rats, who have never come out of their province! Snobs who despise others, but are themselves backwoods savages. Beat them and they will crawl." Because of the prevalence of that voracious animal the rat in all the cities of Szechuan, many people have called us rats.

That the Szechuan people would be ready to fight for a railway sounded fantastic. The Ministers did not realize that here all classes, and not only the gentry, were involved. Granted the Szechuan Railway Company was inefficient, and that there had been disappearance of money: it was a government official appointed by Sheng, not a Szechuanese merchant of Chengtu, who had lost three million ounces of silver in a bankrupt bank in Shanghai. Finally, because of the talk of audit, and no talk of compensation for the shares paid out nor for the work which had already been done, the gentry was determined to resist.

"Not only do they take away our railway rights, but they also want to deprive us of the money we collected."

"They look down on us in Szechuan. Because they have had no trouble with us in the last three years. Their mother's arse. Let us give them trouble. Come and taste our mettle. See how they like it."

In every teahouse, restaurant, barber shop, the talk was of "fighting it out with traitor Sheng".

Szechuan delegates sent to Peking to petition were made to wait outside the petition hall, and insulted. In Chengtu there were more meetings. At the telegraph office every day people asked: "Any news from Peking?"

Meanwhile the Save the Railway League expanded, with branches in every big city. Students wrote pamphlets, and made public speeches. A man called Yang Sulan, an actor, sold his land and brought the money to the League. Another man, named Kuo, drowned himself in his family well, leaving a letter cursing Sheng the traitor.

Jumping into a well was in those days the best form of suicide. A well was clean business, one became a water-borne spirit, and in Chengtu wells were plentiful, each house owning at least one; whereas hanging made a sad, vindictive ghost.

"I hope," Kuo had written in his will, that the League will not be a dragon head with a worm's tail. May my death give it fortitude."

This classical death-rather-than-dishonour gesture caused a tremendous increase in emotion; the whole city became excited. The teahouse waiters organized their protest groups, newspapers quoted great men of old, even the courtesans in the flower quarter wrote verses condemning Sheng and calling for a heroic spirit among their clients. Even the pawnshops put up banners: "Respect our Railway!"

Summer became hotter; the schools closed, students went back to their villages and there agitated so that in a short time branches of the League were established all over the province. Other meetings were held. Thousands of letters of protest were exhibited. Thirteen-year-old girls wrote that they would march on Peking; children gave up their sweets to collect money for the Railway League; people wrote in blood from self-inflicted wounds; even a Canadian missionary expressed his sympathy; he was a Dr. Kilborn, the same man who thirteen years previously protested against the British Consul buying Chengtu land through the proxy of a missionary.

Delegates were sent to the other provinces to tell everyone by word of mouth (the telegrams from the Railway League being refused transmission): "Know that our fight is for our people's rights, it is for the people against tyranny. If we are defeated, we the people of Szechuan, and tyranny reigns to befoul the country, do you think we shall be the only ones to suffer?" A circular letter was signed by Lo Lun, Pu Peiying, and other gentry and officials, provincial assemblymen, and addressed to the Provincial Assemblies of the other provinces affected by railway nationalization. More delegates went to Peking to address the Szechuan Student Association there, to win support among the officials in opposing the Consortium loan, and to make clear to the Regent (for the Emperor, afterwards to be known as Puyi, was only five years old) that the

Save the Railway League in Szechuan was not a rebellion, not anti-dynastic, but opposition to Sheng's schemes which were termed treacherous. It was only too easy for the suspicious Court to deem every movement a rebellion, and once Szechuan was declared a "rebels' nest", massacre would follow. In Kuangtung one hundred thousand people had been killed, it was said, for a rising in 1893; and every year, in suppressing the uprisings which kept on happening, much blood flowed.

But the Szechuan officials at Court were bribed with great efficiency by Sheng. And the manager of the branch at Ichang, Lee, was also bought over. He had been all along in a difficult position. He had a hundred thousand workers on the Ichang sector of the roadbed, and some engineers. He depended on Shanghai for material supplies, on Chengtu for money. At first he had opposed nationalization. Then Tuan Fang sent him a telegram telling him the Ichang section would now be under American engineers, but Lee would remain manager, his salary assured, all the workmen maintained; supplies from Shanghai would be speeded up, the embezzlement of funds would cease. Tuan hinted that Lee might even become Assistant Supervisor of the whole railway. This bribe worked, and Lee opted for nationalization. When in Chengtu the Board of Directors heard of Lee's defection, they were very angry and threatened to dig up his ancestors' graves and scatter the bones. But in the end nothing was done.

By the end of June the Szechuan dissidents seemed isolated. The province itself was neatly cut off, no cables or messages, even private, relating to the railway dispute were transmitted anywhere; no one outside Szechuan knew what was happening there. Had it not been for the Kelao, the students and their couriers, suppression would have been effective.

Sheng himself was worried. He felt now like drawing back, but again the foreign diplomats derided these fears, and pressed for implementation of the contract. Sheng was afraid that the Regent, who sneered at him and called him an "imitation foreigner", might be approached by Szechuanese delegates, and since the Regent was an arch-conservative who wanted no railways at all, the whole contract might be in jeopardy. He thereupon resolved to use force, and ordered Chao Erfeng to go to Chengtu and initiate "severe measures". Meanwhile Tuan Fang went to the Triple City to ready some battalions of the New Army to reinforce the garrison at Ichang, in case of trouble leaking out of Szechuan.

Chao Erfeng, then Viceroy of Szechuan and Sikang, was at that time one of the most powerful men in China. He was known to the British as their most redoubtable foe, his functions as Keeper of the Borders extending to the frontiers with the British colony of India. Your Third Uncle served under him on the Tibet borders, when after the Younghusband aggression of 1904 into Tibet Chao Erfeng put an end to British encroachment for about six years, maintaining troops at all points, and garrisoning Lhasa where he ousted both Russian and British influence. The British suspected Chao of intriguing with the mountain tribes against them. The whole area, annexed by Britain as recently as 1895 and added to India (although ethnically totally different), was full of unrest, its inhabitants the Nagas in perpetual revolt, as they have remained to this day. Chao's main headquarters were at Tatsienlu, an important garrison town commanding the passes between Szechuan and Tibet; it was from Tatsienlu that he moved some troops, including a battalion of the New Army, to Chengtu when summoned to pacify the city in July 1911.

The astrologers in Chengtu were predicting a massacre: "This is the year Hsin Hai, of the Pig. The pig must bleed under the butcher's knife. The butcher, Chao Erfeng, is coming to Chengtu. Beware for the light of slaughter shines in his eyes!"

July was a tigerish heat, so hot, so muggy, with no let-up at night. My body seemed bathed in sweat all the time, yet the fervour grew, and I have no recollection of anything else but this great excitement, swallowing us up and making us insensible to everything else, discomfort, family ties, even hunger or thirst. Everyday there were meetings and speeches, besides meetings at night.

"Let me hit them, and they will grovel," Chao Erfeng was reported to have said. "Look at Chuko Liang of the days of the Three Kingdoms. He dealt harshly with the Szechuanese, and they revere him to this day and still wear white bands of hempen cloth round their foreheads in mourning for him. That is the Szechuanese. I know them. They only obey when they are beaten up; they despise softness, are afraid of hardness. Shout and beat them up, that is the only way to get the Szechuanese down. Even Chang the Yellow Tiger in 1640 found them difficult, ungrateful and quarrelsome; no wonder he tried to kill them all." Chao had massively suppressed an uprising in North Szechuan in 1903 and 1904, and thought he knew the people.

"The light of massacre is in Chao's eyes," warned the astrologers.

When the provincial assemblymen who welcomed Chao the day he arrived, warned him that the people's spirit was aroused, he shouted at them: "Spirit of the people? What *is* the spirit of the people? How much money per pound of spirit? There is no spirit in Szechuan. Those rebels that I executed in 1898, in 1904, in 1907, tell me, did they have any spirit? It's all those students from Japan making trouble."

I saw Chao Erfeng twice. When he arrived, met at the city gates by respectful officials, he alighted from the great eight-carrier sedan chair, in front of him a mounted guard of honour, plumes flying from their hats, embroidered boots, lustrous coats with hoofed sleeves upon their hands, tassels on the bridles of the horses; behind his chair also a mounted guard, and a body of troops, stout, well armed, unlike our own two-gun militia, so called in jest as they used the fan and the opium pipe, but had no weapons. Chao was a heavy man, inclined to fat, a face entirely square, entirely immovable, slightly pock-marked; he moved about slowly, conscious of his power. It was said that he was a homosexual, and did not spare even his best-loved when it came to fighting, but executed them if they lost a battle. His jacket was embroidered with a griffin front and back to denote his military rank, first grade, and he had a ruby in the top of his hat. In his left hand he held two jade walnuts, beautifully carved, which he rolled without stop. His executioners were famous for the speed of their decapitations.

On July 11th there was another shareholders' meeting, which Chao Erfeng attended. At the meeting Pu Peiying, speaking for the Railway Company, told him that "according to constitutional law, no property of a private company can be taken away without the consent of all the shareholders in general assembly", and that "the loan and the nationalization of railways edicts were not submitted to the debate of the National Consultative Assembly, and therefore they are illegal."

Chao was extremely irritated, and read a menacing telegram from Tuan Fang, saying that there were rebel agitators in Szechuan to be punished.

Far from cowing, the message further infuriated the people. Thousands both inside and outside the building began to hoot and to shout. Chao Erfeng, very rattled, left hastily.

The Railway League tried to extort from him a promise that the money in the banks in Shanghai, Ichang and other places, collected by the Szechuan Railway Company, should remain in the Company's name, and not arbitrarily be taken over by the Ministry of Communications. But on July 15th Chao Erfeng circulated a notice that Lee, the manager at Ichang, had been given permission to use the money in the Banks of Communication to pursue work on the railway. This was a move to take over the funds.

Another meeting was hastily summoned; Chao was asked to come, but did not appear, though the shareholders waited until evening, going without food.

Now the agitation became intense. In every street the Save the Railway League members made speeches. By now all the guilds, the craftsmen, the vegetable sellers, the lantern makers, the silversmiths, the silk embroiderers, manure collectors, had their Save the Railway League branches. Even the beggars' guild, the deaf and dumb and the cripples, had their delegates to the League. So had the musical-instrument players, and the waiters in the teahouses and restaurants. Every school, Old or New Learning institute, academy, had theirs. And now a general, complete, total strike was declared by the League.

"Not all the waters of the River of Heaven* can put out our fire," was the League's war-cry.

As I went out that afternoon I heard the sound of the shops being closed. Men stood looking on, wordless, as the shopkeepers put up their wooden shutters; even the children seemed to have stopped playing. Yet it was not yet dark, the parrots in their cages still clung to their water pots, the cats still basked in the heat.

The sedan chair carriers put down their chairs, by order of the Railway League. "To obtain such swift obedience, the League must have the backing of the Brotherhood, the Kelao, otherwise it would not spread so rapidly or so efficiently," the officials reported to Chao, who now tried to get the Kelao on his side, but failed.

Students went about, urging the shopmen to close, and with each one also went a Brother of the Robe, and at sight of the latter the workmen downed tools, the sedan carriers

* The River of Heaven = The Milky Way.

dropped their chairs, so that within two hours the whole city closed down, even the brothels and the opium houses. Only in the small lanes outside the city walls, where shops sell birds in birdcages, the birds were being fed.

And everything was done with discipline and order, quietly. There was no turbulence and no rioting, since Chao had threatened to separate heads from bodies at the least sign of disorder. The general strike also meant no schools, no market and no fair. Only the police were on duty, but they could do nothing to make the shops open again. That evening theatres and teahouses also closed down.

As the movement progressed the gentry, the directors and assemblymen now felt frightened of the hurrying current of revolt dragging them irretrievably onward at much swifter pace than they liked. The strike was announced as: "Mourning for our Late Emperor", and this was written on large bands stuck across the closed shop-fronts. "Loyal mourning for the late Emperor" could not be used as a pretext to start a massacre of the population. The Emperor referred to was of course Emperor Kuanghsu, in whose name in 1903 the railway rights had been granted to the Szechuanese merchants; mourning for him was indirectly mourning for the betrayal of these rights.

The fearful members of the Board of Directors now issued a circular letter, stressing that the matter should be legally settled. The railway could temporarily continue to be in private hands, they said, while the question of the loan should be settled by the National Consultative Assembly and referred to Provincial Assemblies. This was a backing down, the word "temporarily" being ominous. The circular ended: "Should the Assembly decide that nationalization is legal, then even if we the shareholders must take a loss, yet we shall strictly obey, as it is constitutional."

This surrender was the work of a small group under two members of the Board, Wang Wenping and Chou Shanpei. Chao Erfeng praised the circular, and appeared to acquiesce, and told the directors that they must now disband the Save the Railway League, while a peaceful solution was sought.

"You do not need this League, full of unruly hooligans, students from Japan."

Some of the gentry agreed. "Let us wait quietly for the law to decide."

Another meeting was convoked, to report on the success of their peace-seeking solution. Again it was a very hot day, an autumn tiger day, crowds milling round, and it was evident that the unity of June no longer existed. There were two groups in existence. The "moderates", afraid of violence, asking the people to sacrifice the railway for the greater good of the country, reported that Chao praised the Szechuanese for their great restraint, their discipline, their respect for constitutional procedure, held up as a victory the fact that Chao now agreed to present a rephrased petition to Peking. The second, now labelled "extremists", were ourselves, the returned students, and other revolutionaries, who saw in this an abject surrender and would not compromise.

Chou Shanpei told the meeting that Chao had promised to carry the new petition through, or he himself would resign his viceroyship.

"Of course, we must struggle on, but there are ways of doing it. We must use peaceful, legal ways of doing these things. Violence is not right. It is like trying to lift the moon out of water. Let us call off the strikes, restore the markets, open the shops and the schools."

No sooner had Chou Shanpei said this than he was met with howls and shrieks. No one believed Chao Erfeng's promises.

"We won't reopen till we've got our rights back. We won't. All the fires of heaven may drop on earth, we shall not change. Running dogs, slaves . . . running dogs . . ."

The moderates fled. The strike went on.

After a week the strike proved very inconvenient. There were three hundred thousand people in Chengtu, of whom five-sixths lived within the city walls. Water was no problem, for at eight feet down one sometimes strikes water, and at twelve to sixteen feet there is always well water. But well water can only be used for washing, it is too polluted with dirt from the soil for drinking. For drinking there must be live water, mountain water or running water, river water; and river water was carried into the city every day by eight hundred to a thousand water carriers. But now the water carriers were on strike, so there was no good water for tea, and even if the well water was boiled for a long time, the tea tasted of mud.

The Railway League officials finally had to tell the water-carriers: "You are not on strike. You sell your strength to eat, you must not go on strike." Water came in, brought by the water-carriers.

When water from the river was brought in, the night soil was taken out of the city. Until then, for over a week, the night soil had been accumulating, and in the heat the stench was terrible. Now vegetables could come into the city and be sold on the streets; the shops and markets remained closed, but many small stalls lined the lanes and back streets.

The Railway League erected "mourning altars" everywhere on the streets to obstruct circulation, and also in front of the mansions of the wealthy who had not contributed money to save the railway. Bands of students went collecting, and also made sure that shops remained shut.

Another week passed, another meeting was held. At this meeting Wang and Lung, the two student leaders, suggested that the people refuse to pay levies and taxes, and also refuse the tribute in grain and specie, and the *likin* tax, until the railway affair was settled. "This is a constitutional, legal, democratic form of protest, used in democratic countries with a constitution. The French have done this, also the British in their past history." Since China was supposed to get a constitution "soon", the implication was that these democratic forms of opposition could be practised. But the merchants and shopkeepers were addressed by Chou Shanpei, who was by now very friendly with the Viceroy, Chao Erfeng: "Here we have been twelve days with no commerce, you and I are eating our own capital, which is bad for us. We are losing money, but still we go on in this silly way. To what purpose?"

He told the people how the British Consul himself had come in a conciliatory manner to visit him, Chou, and offered to "mediate". Ten amendments to the terms of the loan had been suggested, and the Consul had promised to report to his Ministry in Peking and to obtain some action. Chou Shanpei glowed as he recounted this episode; even the British, he said, admired the discipline, order and quiet of the Chengtu merchants and shopkeepers. He hinted that the British were anxious to come to terms directly with the Szechuan railway shareholders over this railway question. (Possibly the British had in mind double-crossing the other foreigners at this point? Who knows?)

The student Lung, thin and worn out with his exertions of the past five weeks, climbed on to the platform. "If we don't get back our railway, we remain on strike. Without our own railway there is no Szechuan left."

Wu Yuchang, another revolutionary, also rose to talk about

taxes. He started with the agricultural rent tax, and suggested that the people refuse to pay it. "Over a hundred years ago there was suppression of the White Lotus Society, and a levy was imposed on us to fight them, which we paid, and which we have gone on paying. In fact, every year the amount of the levy has increased. It is now bigger than the agricultural land tax. I suggest that every district keep its own money; let us refuse to pay all levies, all taxes; let us stop buying and selling houses and fields, to cut off the sales tax. Let us stop paying the rent tax, the salt tax and oil tax. We shall refuse to contribute any money towards paying the interests on any foreign loans or any war indemnities, contracted by the state with foreign powers, for which we are now paying until we are reduced to paupery."

Such a roar of approval greeted Wu that the Chief of Police, who came to nearly every meeting, looked upset and went away. "Yes, yes, yes! Rather starve than give in! No studying, no buying, no selling. Anyone who tries to stop us is a traitor and we shall dig up his ancestors and scatter their bones . . ."

At last Chao Erfeng knew this was no ordinary protest, nor ordinary uprising, but an organized movement, going deep, extending far. He summoned his military commanders to a conference, and sent secret cables. But through the Brothers it was known he was now calling for some battalions of the New Army, and on the fourteenth night of the strike twice the gates of the city opened to admit many soldiers. A rumour spread that the gates would be kept shut for everything else, no food would be allowed to come in. The people would starve.

"If you cannot go hungry, go and eat Christianity."

"Go and eat rats."

Those who grew apprehensive and wanted to give up the strike had these things said to them rudely. Meanwhile some students, Lung and Wang among them, left Chengtu and went to Tzechow, south of Chengtu, to prepare, with the Kelao, an armed uprising in that small town.

September 7th, All Souls' Day (in the Chinese calendar the fifteenth day of the seventh month), is the day all souls in hell come forth to roam the earth. That morning a great still-ness was upon the city; there were guards in front of the Manchu quarters and government offices, soldiers with raw red faces, unlike the local garrison, border soldiers, New

Army trained and equipped, renowned for their fierceness. I was in Bookshop Street when suddenly I saw a crowd, their pigtails wound round their heads as if for running. They were pushing forward, shouting that Pu Peiying and Lo Lun, the two assemblymen representing the Railway Company, were held prisoners by Chao Erfeng. I went with the crowd, and from all sides people collected, until finally we were in front of the official mansion. We surged into the outer court, past the two stone lions guarding the gates. Soldiers, with good guns, fixed bayonets, also many policemen, lined it. Then we were pushed by the crowd behind us into the inner court, opposite the Audience Hall. On the high stone platform surrounding the Audience Hall the officials stood in their robes and hats, shouting at us: "Get out, get out! Send us some representatives, but the others, get out." But the crowd behind us was too thick, it pressed us forward and pressing forward did not hear, so many people were shouting: "Release Pu Peiying and Lo Lun!" Some young boys and some men were thus pushed up the stone steps to the platform, a few apprentices, holding in their hands the banner of mourning for the deceased Emperor, to show they were not in revolt but only petitioners.

An official screamed: "If you don't get down, we order the soldiers to fire." And then the soldiers did fire. I only saw the muzzles go up, a gleam on the bayonets, and the sound was small, plop plop, not at all a big sound – even firecrackers make louder noise. People who are killed do not scream or shout, even the wounded do not. It is the people round them who scream.

Now the crowd had turned, about-faced, was running out of the courtyard. All the mouths were open but no shout came. And in a few moments the place was empty except for twenty or so bodies bleeding on the courtyard stones and who would never walk again.

Outside the courtyard the soldiers also began to fire upon the crowd. At the gates, with the stone lions looking on, one paw up as if counting the shots, people ran, scattering in the streets, and screaming: "A massacre!" And there was the sound of more firing.

A platoon or two of soldiers had pushed forward in Craftsmen Street to stop the people there from joining the others in front of the governor's residence, and now they were firing on the craftsmen.

And hearing the noise the soldiers stationed in other parts of the city also started to fire on the people.

Later that night it was rumoured that nine of the Railway Company representatives, including the two provincial assemblymen, and the Hanling Academicians, the old scholars Meng and Yen, had been invited to come for a talk by Chao Erfeng that morning, and then detained. Chao wanted to force them to open the markets and break the strike, to declare null the resolution about not paying taxes, levy or tribute in grain and specie. We heard that they were to be executed that evening.

And that was the massacre of All Souls' Day in Chengtu.

The evening before, the eve of All Souls' Day, every household had lit its fires to burn packets of paper money and gifts for the souls of the deceased. In the countryside, all over the fields, paper offerings had burnt in front of the graves. But the gates of the city were shut tight, guards reinforced. No one was supposed to go in or out. The troops and military police searched private houses for revolutionaries.

Our League members met in secret that night. We knew that we had to warn the revolutionaries outside the city. We could not use couriers, two of them having already been apprehended and beheaded. We could not send telegrams or letters. The army was hunting us. It was then that Lung and Wu hit on the idea of the water-messages.

At that time one of our revolutionary group was employed in a timber merchant's shop, and there were wooden boards to be carved with words to commemorate the dead Emperor. Lung suggested we use these boards to write our messages, varnish them with wood oil, wrap them in oil paper and throw them in the river, to be carried by the swift full water down the river to all the towns and villages along the banks. It was the only way we had of making known what had happened. Lung's stratagem was not new. It had been used before in battle; and when I went to France to read literature I found that in the love story of *Tristram and Iseult* the same trick of messages by water had been used.

Twenty-one words were written on about a hundred boards, and we carried them in small packets, and threw them into the river. This took about six or eight hours. It was cock-crow before we had finished, and a miracle that none of us was caught. These were the words we wrote:

Butcher Chao arrested Pu and Lo,
Then massacred the Szechuan people.
In all places, friends, arise, save and protect your land!

The next day I was able to bribe my way out of the city gates, through a cousin who was an officer in the New Army. I went to Pihsien, which is also the district where your family had its ancestral graves, sanctuary and fields.

The Kelao Brotherhood was strong in Pihsien, and as you know they had been anti-Manchu for three hundred years, and even tried to assassinate the Dowager Empress on her return from Sian to Peking in 1901.

The Kelao controlled the boatmen on the River, the craftsmen and small shopkeepers, the manure collectors and water carriers and sedan chair carriers, but they also had adherents among the merchants, the pawnbrokers, the landlords, and now the students. The managing of public cloacae was in their hands, for the "manure head", or headman of those who collected the manure, was a Kelao member, and this was a source of revenue for them.

It is said that men make their own history, but they do not make it entirely as they please, the circumstances under which they make it are not chosen by themselves, but given and transmitted by the past. We had to make history with the material at hand: with the secret societies, with the young officers, with the gentry in revolt, with the misery of our peasantry, with our feudal system; everything would go into making the Revolution. For alone an ideal means nothing, it has to be given physical reality by the means available to man before it can be truly said to exist. And to make a revolution we utilized everything we had.

But we were young at revolution, inexperienced. This crisis of history had forced itself into our lives, and there was no escape from it. Through that gruelling summer all of us were totally involved in actions which, later, we were to remember with surprise, with astonishment. And yet thus it happened.

Already before the massacre of All Souls' Day the Brotherhood had been preparing for armed revolt, in concert with revolutionaries. It had grasped the occasion of a market fair to mobilize many men in this part of the Chengtu plain. There was a fair at Hsinfan, half-way between Pihsien and the stronghold of the Kelao, Kuanhsien, where the Mien River starts its diversion. Crowds attended the fair, old women carrying a clutch of eggs, young men with baskets to sell, men with a bamboo pole on the shoulder and meat to sell at both ends, men driving pigs, all going to the fair at Hsinfan. Coming in small groups, as peasants, as boatmen, as timber-cutters, as loafers, with guns hidden among the sugar-cane rods for sale, with ammunition among the eggs in the baskets, the Brothers came and finally assembled at the local temple, where the spacious courtyards permitted them to quarter.

There were already about two thousand of them when I reached Pihsien. The railway taxes had fallen heavily upon the peasants, and every share-cropper, tenant farmer and small farmer had paid for the railway. The local officials were terrified; one of them, in Pihsien, actually died of fear; his wife and daughter hanged themselves by his coffin.

The heads of the local Kelao in that region arrived. Chang Hsi, leader of several thousand miners of the Pure True Mountains beyond Kuanhsien, where his main headquarters, the Pure True Taoist Temple, reared among gingko trees a thousand years old. Many of his men were ex-militia, now disbanded, unemployed, willing to fight.

Another Chang, a Dragon Head Grand Master, in ordinary life a Supervisor of schools in Chengtu, a mild and subtle man, an opium addict, also arrived.

And finally a third Chang, a pawnbroker, the wealthiest man in Pihsien district. Pawnshops functioned as banks, lending money at ten per cent interest a month. This Chang had contacts with many officials and landlords, he could obtain gifts and solid gold from great families where others would only find morning dew. And Pihsien is a rich district, strewn with ancestors' sanctuaries, the graves of wealthy families, and large landlord houses. Chang the pawnbroker knew them all.

The temple of the tutelary genius of Pihsien, where the Kelao Brotherhood camped their followers, was spacious. The tutelary genius had been an upright official, and even if now disembodied, had right to a four-carrier sedan chair when on the twenty-eighth day of the third moon he was promenaded round the town and through the fields on his annual tour of inspection. His bedroom behind the audience hall was the room where the Kelao heads assembled to discuss strategy. On his bed the three Changs alternated, to smoke their opium pipes.

When I saw the full regalia of the Brotherhood out, with the three Changs representing, of the mountain the military strength, of the school the strategy, and of the pawnshop the finance, of an expeditionary corps, I was impressed. When the three Changs asked me to come and have a talk with them, I trembled as if the Emperor had called me, for they were indeed powerful men, and men braver than I were afraid of the Kelao and their fierce followers, who kept on swelling in numbers, charcoal-burners and woodcutters and timber men, to be called the Western Army, since it was quartered west of Chengtu. Later they were to be joined by about five hundred students, fleeing from the schools and the academies to join the Revolution and to fight for the railway. But the students were young, idealistic, not hardened to work, to fight, to privation; they looked down on the Kelao, and had to be organized separately in a students' battalion because, although full of goodwill, it was difficult to make them obey rules. They talked of freedom, but did not know that freedom must be won. They were critical of the opium-smoking, the gambling dens and brothels which accompanied the Kelao, and the gangster methods were repugnant to their idealism. They did not know how a revolution is made; and mountains lay between their ways and the ways of the boatmen, charcoal burners, timber cutters, of the Kelao. Fortunately there were some excellent revolutionaries among them who understood how to use the Kelao, and fought and died for the Revolution, and led blameless lives. Wu Yuchang, the student from Japan, had most intelligently enrolled two of the Changs as members of the Revolutionary League. This young man understood how to make a revolution. He had already participated in many risings in the south. But I had not. I wanted everything to be clean and noble, and when I stood before Chang of the Mountain and he shouted at me: "What about the red hill?" I was terrified. The term "red hill" means a massacre: slaughter being a heap of corpses, an elevation of bleeding bodies.

Finally I managed to tell them what had happened in Chengtu. But the Kelao chiefs wanted to know how many soldiers Chao Erfeng had brought into Chengtu with him. For they were practical men, and would not risk a battle unless they were sure of winning. But since the soldiers had been brought in secretly, at night, no one knew exactly how many there were, though we guessed about two to three thousand.

After a few days it was suggested by Wu Yuchang, the revolutionary leader, that those among the students who were dissatisfied should return to Chengtu and try to work there. Since I was well connected, and knew some of the New Army officers who would be helpful later, it was a good idea for me to return to Chengtu and try to win one or two officers. Nothing is better than a friend inside the fortress, to open the city gates in time's ripeness.

I went back to Chengtu, but could accomplish little, and most of what was done was done by others, not by me. There was a problem of munitions and guns, which we had to solve. Some of our Szechuan students were most experienced gunrunners, as others were efficient at making bombs. In the uprisings of 1908, 1909, 1910 and 1911, students like Wu Yuchang, who had also been the editor of a magazine in Japan, had gone to Hongkong, and procured guns and ammunition there for the Revolution, smuggling them in many ways: in packets of hair for wigs, even in bridal chairs, under the skirts and red veil of "brides". The Kelao boatmen also were excellent smugglers all along the River. In Pihsien there were only a few old guns, some spears, lances and big knives, and very old cannon of Taiping days on the walls. In Chengtu the students could only find some old weapons, heirlooms of the Ming, kept as relics of the ancestors. One student had joined with nothing but a Japanese pocket-knife on him. Almost barehanded, we began to make knives, and to help in the gunrunning.

A song appeared among the people, who hummed it at work, holding the words back between their teeth, only the melody being heard. "Chao Erfeng, Chao Erfeng, you may be very strong, you may appear invincible. But time is on our side, and we shall beat you down, for we are many, you are one."

And then all of a sudden the countryside was marching. Chengtu was attacked from the east and the south-east, only a few days after the massacre. The wooden boards thrown in the river had done their work. In the district of Huayang, lower down the Mien River, a man called Tsin the Black Mule, a salt smuggler and silk craftsman, Brother of the Robe and a member of Sun Yatsen's Revolutionary League, had recovered one. He had his own intelligence network, and actually had been told of the killings in Chengtu that very night by a runner, and later a boatman brought him one of the boards, picked up from the river. Tsin sent other couriers to towns farther down. There too boards had been salvaged.

He now mobilized the Brotherhood of his district. The drums were struck, and while local officials hid in their bedrooms, Tsin and a thousand men of the Kelao marched out to attack Chengtu. Their levies were armed with staves and lances of bamboo; some had beaten their spades into rough swords. On the way they collected more recruits from hamlets and villages; out of the night and the twisted, flimsy shacks of the fields, came the share-croppers, first to find out what it was about, and when they found out, to join the marching men, and they were another two thousand.

On September 18th and 19th the gates of Chengtu were stormed, but the troops of Chao Erfeng, among them New Army men, came out with their new guns blazing; and the firearms were stronger, the volunteers were routed and died. At the east gate and at the south gate they died, chiefly at the south gate, for there one thousand of them had nothing but sticks. But Tsin believed himself invincible, for the Taoists had told him no bullet could harm him.

The boards still kept going down river, and being picked up. From all the hamlets of the plain rose men, more men, beating gongs and drums; here twenty and there a hundred, all were poor and most were without weapons. And these levies out of nothing swelled, and the whole plain was fighting men, so that no one knew the shadow of tree or soldier, all trees were soldiers too. The people refused to pay taxes and levies to the government, and the Kelao started levying money in the name of the Railway League, and the landlords and the bigger gentry did not like what was happening; and now quarrels began among the various groups of Kelao, some of whom resorted to looting. Wherever the Kelao went, brothels, opium dens and gambling also went. The revolutionaries found discipline foundering.

In Chengtu Chao Erfeng contrived to divide completely the moderates from the revolutionaries; he released a few of the arrested gentry, issued a proclamation separating the railway issue from the taxes and levies issue, promising to reconsider the railway issue but threatening those who refused to pay the taxes.

In the confused, disorderly fighting that went on in the plain, hamlets and towns were taken and lost, changing hands back and forth, and whispers began of another Taiping. Some said that Chu of the Red Lamp, who claimed descendance from the Ming emperors, had risen again. The last time Chu had been claimed alive was in 1900, when the Righteous Fists began.

Chao Erfeng discovered that among the officers of the New Army the revolutionaries had done their work, their loyalty was faltering. His spies informed him of other risings being prepared, and of the merchants of Chungking plotting with revolutionaries and smuggling money to the Kelao for an uprising there. From Chungking weapons were now being taken upstream by the junks; they came from Hongkong and Canton, smuggled by merchants, or brought singly by pedlars or wandering beggars, sometimes embedded in salt. No commander in the world could arrest and search every man, woman or child walking among the fields, inspect every small barge on the River for weapons.

In Tzechow, south-east of Chengtu, where Lung and Wu had conferred with the Kelao in August, the people rose, and another rising took place in Junghsien farther south. At Hsinching also there was a revolt, and this was a serious matter, for near the town of Hsinching was a cantonment of the New Army. The commander of the New Army battalion quartered there, was rumoured to be in league with the revolutionaries.

Looking at the map of Szechuan, looking at these wild fires of revolt, flaring then subsiding, south and west, east and north, like will-o'-the-wisps over a bog, never extinguished, Viceroy Chao Erfeng must have felt himself cornered. But he could not give up. From Peking Sheng cabled to him: "Suppress the rebels."

At the Military Academy in Chengtu some of the cadets were reported to have said they would not fight a compatriot army, nor against the railway rights, which were the people's rights.

Chao Erfeng summoned a council of war. He could be sure of the higher ranking officers, most of them not Szechuanese, for it was dynastic policy not to appoint an official, military or civil, to his own province for fear of nepotism. There were many Hakkas among the higher officers, the Hakkas being thought less prone to local patriotism and local corruption; that was one reason why military command had always come easily to Hakkas in Szechuan. Chao needed more troops. He had about three thousand men, regular, of the New Army. He could count on three thousand more militia. He knew the Kelao altogether numbered fifteen thousand, though poorly armed. Chao sent a telegram to Tuan Fang, the Director of

Railways, at that time in the Triple City of Hankow-Hanyang-Wuchang, asking for army reinforcements in order to put down, once and for all, the "local bandits and their instigators" in Szechuan.

He ordered a commander named Chen, of whose loyalty he was sure, to attack the rebels encamped in Pihsien, and to pacify all the region up to the Taoist Monastery in the Pure True Mountains. The three Changs, of the mountain, the school and the pawnshop, must be destroyed. Commander Chen took Pihsien, Kuanhsien, marched some men up the mountain to the temple and down again, the Kelao levies, the student corps, melting away in front of him; but when he turned back, having pacified the region, he found behind him the Kelao had reformed, and everything he had conquered had again been wrested. Again he conquered, and it was like cutting water with a sword. Long and painstakingly he searched for rebels, and found only ordinary peasants, farmhands bent over the fields, and it was near harvest time and many hired landless toilers were in the fields. It was impossible to tell whether they were soldiers or peasants.

He wrote: "The enemy has no shape, no form, no content. I do not know who is friend or foe. I catch only shadows, not substance."

Chen quartered soldiers in every townlet, every village, but the countryside was not his. He got reprimand after reprimand from Chao Erfent for not exterminating the ragged bandits. Finally he shut himself up in Pihsien, reinforced the walls, barricaded the gates, and every night heard outside the town the horns of the Kelao levies blowing eerily through the night. "I do not know what my troops think." Within a few days his weapons were disappearing; his soldiers were selling them to the Kelao.

At Hsinfan the local magistrate, half-insane with fear, ordered a little boy of twelve, who had let off a firecracker in the crowd, to be beaten to death. This started a riot, the Kelao coming to the boy's rescue, led by their chief of the district, called Rudder of the Barge, or head boatman, for that is the name given them. The Kelao and the people stormed the magistrate's residence, did his retainers to death and chopped his executioner to pieces. Hsinfan was then occupied by the Kelao in the name of the Revolutionary Army.

All these were localized battles, blind, unco-ordinated, hit-and-miss blood and mess, a chaos but with a direction, for

now an East Route army, well disciplined, was formed under
Lung Mingchien, now thin and gaunt with his superhuman
efforts. He joined forces with Tsin the Black Mule, the one
who thought himself proof against bullets, and together they
stormed and took Junghsien, half-way down the Mien River,
an important centre on the road to Chungking.

Whereas Tzechow, where in a bloody day of battle the
Kelao had won the town, fell again to government troops,
Junghsien was never retaken by Chao Erfeng. There the East
Route revolutionary army, strong and well organized, the
Kelao and their gangster methods under control, held the
town against all assaults. That happened on September 25th,
three weeks before the "official" Revolution started in the
Triple City on October 10th. Junghsien was the first place in
China which proclaimed a Republic. Some of us in Szechuan
claim that the Revolution began in Junghsien in our pro-
vince, and that this matter should be more widely known.

Afterwards Lung Mingchien was to die of exhaustion, and
Wu Yuchang took his place and held Junghsien.

On September 24th Tuan Fang, who had received the cable
from Chao Erfeng asking for reinforcements, marched into
Szechuan from the Triple City with two thousand troops that
had been garrisoning Wuchang, crack New Army regiments.
Their departure left the Triple City shorn of defence; only a
weak, undisciplined militia, some raw recruit battalions, already subverted to the revolutionary cause, remained. Immediately the revolutionaries in the Triple City knew that if
a coup was to be attempted, it must be done while Tuan Fang
was away in Szechuan.

Rumours that there would be a great massacre on October
6th had been current in the Triple City. October 6th that
year corresponded to the Harvest Festival, or Moon Festival,
the fifteenth of the eighth moon in the lunar calendar, a
movable date. On that day, eight hundred years previously,
an insurrection against the Mongol Yuan dynasty, founded
by Genghis Khan the Siberian invader of China, had been
mounted and succeeded. The day of the Harvest Festival
was also called Killing the Tartars Day in the Triple City,
and the Manchus were afraid, for they too were Tartars.

On October 6th, however, the revolutionaries were not yet
ready; they postponed the date of their rising till October
15th. But the accidental explosion of a bomb which a student
was manufacturing in a private house forced them to act

on October 10th. In all the history books, therefore, the Revolution began in Wuchang on October 10th, 1911.

Yet on October 8th or 9th the British Consul resident there wrote: "All is quiet. Rumours of a rebellion are much exaggerated. Actually since their defeat in Canton in April this year, the revolutionaries are losing ground day by day ..."

Thus was the Revolution of 1911 made. Had Tuan Fang not removed troops from the Triple City to succour Chao, the viceroy of Szechuan; had the latter not been so obdurate about the railway; had Minister Sheng not signed the contract with the Consortium for a railway loan; had the foreigners not forced him to force Chao to use force ... The Revolution would have happened anyway, in a different manner, but it would have happened.

As it was, from May 11th when nationalization of the railways was declared, to October 10th, when the Revolution occurred and the Manchu dynasty came to an end, five months of the long, hot summer of 1911, the people of Szechuan in one way or another fought nearly every day, peacefully at first and then violently.

October 10th was not the end of fighting. In Szechuan we did not know that there had been revolution in Wuchang, that a Republic had been proclaimed, since all communications were cut. We only knew that Tuan Fang and his troops had reached Ichang, recaptured Tzechow, were marching on Chengtu, and that heads would fall.

The floating, shapeless, see-saw battles went on. The harvest fields were destroyed with a going and coming of soldiers; only opium flourished on the untouched slopes. On October 15th the Eastern revolutionary army, quartered at Junghsien, attacked the government garrison at the salt mines of Tzeliuching; control of the salt mines meant revenue; they fought a pitched battle to a stalemate. Tuan Fang secured Tzeliuching, then took Neichiang, the sugar city. It looked as if he would now move on to Junghsien and destroy the Eastern revolutionary army, our best army. But officers of the New Army were as disgruntled under Tuan Fang, the false Manchu, as under Chao Erfeng. While in the Triple City they had been influenced by Sun Yatsen's League, the appeal to their patriotism. They had no appetite for this butchering of peasants and boatmen and students. The young officers revolted, murdered their commander, Tuan Fang, on November 25th. Neichiang was then taken by the Eastern Army under Wu

Yuchang on November 26th, and Tzeliuching on November 28th.

In Chungking the government garrison also revolted, pulled down the Manchu flag, hoisted the revolutionary flag, and proclaimed the Republic on November 22nd. This was due to a Japanese returned student called Hsia, the platoon leader of a small New Army group in Chengtu. Ordered to reinforce the garrison near Chungking, he marched to Chungking (making a detour to avoid Tzechow, which at that time was still in Tuan Fang's hands), and with two hundred men entered Chungking. Thus within a few hours a city of half a million people fell to a platoon commander. There was practically no killing. The Roman Catholic priests were evacuated in gunboats, but returned a few weeks later, seeing the revolutionaries did them no harm.

Chengtu was still in the hands of Chao Erfeng. He had been the first to know of the October 10th revolt, and at first this had not troubled him. So many uprisings! He himself had put down a good half-dozen of them, this was another "rebel" scare, to be liquidated in blood, with decapitations to follow, easy as mowing grass. By October 15th he was uneasy. On October 17th he heard that the whole of the Triple City was in the revolutionaries' hands, and that a former brigade commander of the New Army had cut off his queue, sided with the Revolution, declared a Republic, and become military governor of the Triple City.

Chao now sought out the very men he had formerly detained, Pu Peiying, Lo Lun, Chou Shanpei, offering compromise and conciliation. These worthy gentlemen were as frightened as he was. Things were going much too far. Chao made Pu Peiying military governor of Chengtu, and established one of his own followers as vice-military governor, proclaiming a military government, later to be called the Great Han Military Government, in remembrance of the Han dynasty. Perhaps he felt that one day, emulating Liu Pei the Han Emperor, he, Chao Erfeng, might set up an empire in Szechuan...

Chao assigned to himself the role of border defence, to keep the troops under his control. But the people of Chengtu wanted true revolution, they were cutting off their queues, they no longer wanted any emperor, Manchu or other. The Great Han Military Government rapidly disintegrated. Pu Peiying fled, a small group of young officers of the New

Army appointed Lo Lun and the principal of the Military Academy as heads of the new government. These were to act as puppets, the young officers hoping to exercise power through them in the classic pattern of army *coups*. Army *coups* also took place in other provinces, as one by one they declared themselves independent of Manchu rule and power fell to those who could handle a gun.

And now the young officers turned against Chao, disarmed and beheaded him on December 22nd, 1911. That was the second time I saw Chao Erfeng, by then only a head, held up by his queue, while a hundred thousand people roared and clapped their hands in the big square in front of the two stone lions, where three months before his soldiers had fired upon the people and killed so many.

And now all was chaos in Chengtu: landlords and upper gentry, supported by gangster bands, the Kelao, the revolutionaries, a medley of intrigues and counter-intrigues and each man for himself. By the end of December 1911 there were two governments in Szechuan, one in Chengtu and one in Chungking. The Chungking one adhered to Sun Yatsen; the Chengtu one was not even pretending to be revolutionary. But neither of them wanted the Manchus back.

For the next twenty-eight years, from 1911 to 1939, like the medieval barons of Europe, the warlords of Szechuan, bred from young officers, Kelao, gentry, all the ingredients of disorder, were to fight each other, town by town, hamlet by hamlet, street by street, for power in the province. Szechuan remained feudal and was not really at peace till 1949.

SEVENTEEN

I SPENT some days with Li Chiehjen, and with other men who had seen or participated in the Revolution of 1911, re-creating those years, with their high exaltation, their sacrifices, their hopes and confusion, and then the swift withering away of these hopes, already doomed in 1913, a little over a year after the Revolution had occurred. Now, of course, the scrutiny of past events permits hindsight knowledge; the aftermath was that long period of internecine trouble known as the warlord decades. Third Uncle summed it up.

"There was one thing we did not understand. We thought that once the Manchus were overthrown our troubles would disappear. And so we compromised with the real enemy, the exploiters who had backed the Manchu, and would soon find someone else to back."

"What did you do at the time of the 1911 Revolution, Third Uncle?"

To this Third Uncle answered with the gentle, candid smile his face produces whenever he is caught by surprise and is going to emit a cautious equivocation. "What could we do? At first we, the young officers of the New Army, were ordered to go against the people. But of course we could not shoot them. None of us from Chengtu could shoot our own people. Soon we too joined the Revolution, but I was sent again to Tatsienlu because the British gave us trouble again in Tibet. Chao Erfeng, the viceroy, was our commander. When he was killed our battalion went back to Chengtu. Things were in the utmost confusion, and no one knew which government was really in power. The British advanced, crossing the Outer Line they had delimited in North India, and arbitrarily drawing the McMahon Line. If the First World War had not happened in 1914, they would certainly have tried to take at least a portion of Tibet. And things with us were as when a stagnant pond is disturbed and a thousand strange monsters leap to the light; we were all fighting each other, and sometimes I thought we would never end."

Third Uncle was back in Chengtu in 1912, and of course sided with the conservative, landed gentry, Great Han military government then set up. In 1913 he was in command of the Chengtu garrison, and later took part in the warfare which developed when Szechuan and Yunnan provinces declared their independence from Yuan Shihkai, in 1916. He was to become an officer under a warlord of Szechuan, the famous Liu Hsiang, who ruled much of the province until 1940, later served under him for some years as financial adviser in charge of opium eradication. It was this career which enabled him to leave the army, to go into business, and to restore the family fortunes.

"Of course, all I did was completely reactionary," said Third Uncle, laughingly, "but at that time I knew no better, did I?"

We were sitting with some Communist writers when he said this, and all nodded. Everything was clear, the past determined, my uncle had written his deeds and been classified as a native capitalist. He had nothing to fear by telling how he had fought against the Revolution; his past was accepted, as he now accepted the present he had fought against.

Though Szechuan had been the fuse of the Revolution, it was not the first to declare its autonomy from the Manchu dynasty and join the proclaimed Republic. It was actually the last to join the southern and western provinces, which had all revolted one by one after the Wuchang uprising and declared their independence from the Manchu dynasty. The local Manchu officials were overthrown; the local Chinese officials, seeing the wind change, all in good time rose in righteousness, proclaimed themselves republicans and followers of Sun Yatsen. And it was precisely this facile turnover, the smooth and almost bloodless rapidity with which this turnabout was accomplished, which was the weakness, and later became the failure of the Revolution. Power still remained in the same class, the gentry-official-mandarin-literati class, now allied to the New Army military commanders (themselves sons of the gentry) who needed guns and money to pay their men. Soldiers of fortune, military men with ambition and cunning, now fought their way to power. And they also needed guns and money, and very quickly both came to depend upon the very same Western Powers which they had sworn to overthrow.

The gentry was the first to try to stamp down the Revolution it had temporarily joined. Ensconced in power, self-proclaimed republicans now hounded the true revolutionaries to death with nearly the same alacrity as the Manchus had done.

Sun Yatsen was actually not in China (where he was proscribed) when the Revolution broke out in October 1911. He was in England, and Dr. Cantlie, his English friend, tells the charming episode where Sun received a telegram, read it and folded it up again, and later, while they were having tea, offhandedly said: "By the way, I am asked to become the President of the Republic of China." He returned in December, and on January 1st, 1912, was proclaimed President of the Chinese Republic in Nanking, the old capital of the Ming dynasty, which had also been the capital of the Taiping in 1853. Like the Communist Party of today, Sun claimed inheritance, spiritual and political, from the Taiping, but also from the Chinese Ming emperors. It was to the graves of the Ming rulers in Nanking that Sun went to announce himself (as it is customary to keep one's ancestors informed), that their spirits might have rest after waiting two hundred and sixty-seven years for revenge. He told them that foreign rule had gone from China, and that China had at last come into her own, free, equal among nations, independent . . .

Come into her own . . . But alas, it was not so, for the Powers had not given up. Already they were undermining the Revolution, and had willing helpers. A country is not truly betrayed to the enemy outside its gates unless there are also traitors within. For money, for power, these can be found. A long list of "strong men", willing puppets of foreign powers, have made the headlines, not in China alone, but in every country finding its way from the feudal past into the present, struggling for survival in independence.

Very soon newspaper articles against Sun Yatsen, gloomily predicting chaos and announcing that massacres could be expected, were circulating abroad. The correspondent of *The Times*, George Morrison, wrote that Sun was a madman, hysterical, imbued with impossible romanticism, a mischievous visionary. In Peking the diplomats of the Western embassies, for a while taken aback, rallied and made overtures to Yuan Shihkai, the Commander-in-Chief of the New Army, a man "prudent and solid" with whom "one could deal with confidence". That George Morrison obtained the post of Adviser to Yuan Shihkai the following year surprised no one.

Sun the dreamer was to be disposed of, and Yuan put in his place, for Sun was inaccessible to corruption and wanted China truly independent, at last taking, in a cliché Sun had probably learnt in England, her rightful place in the sun. "China must no longer be everyone's colony, nay, even less than a colony." He called upon the Western democracies to help China attain her rightful place, that the world might live in peace and harmony. And this was his great foolishness, that he believed he could, with words, with reason, plead the cause of China, and obtain justice. How could this be? To demand from the Powers that they refrain from such a succulently profitable prey? Quite impossible. Sun's appeals not only went unheard and unpublished, but everything was now done to bring him and his Revolution down.

The first pressures applied were of course economic, the long-lived Sir Robert Hart (the same one who in 1885 bullied the timorous Manchus into giving in to the French by withholding the grain tribute) now withholding *all* revenue money from Sun's government, but turning money over to Yuan Shihkai in the North, who also received gifts and contributions from several foreign banks during 1912. The republican government of Sun Yatsen in Hankow and Canton had no funds to pay their soldiers, while Yuan strengthened his forces and was amply supplied with guns. For as always, as today is still alas so true, power comes out of the gun, and the Powers, having themselves used the gun with such success in China, now armed their strong man Yuan to fight for them.

The Banking Consortium took a prominent part in these Chinese affairs. As Cantlie writes in his biography of Sun Yatsen: "A fundamental change had been made in the Banking Consortium. Its political significance, as distinct from its banking function, was recognized by the powers, and because of this, Japan and Russia had also been admitted, thus bringing into the Consortium all of the six powers with any considerable interests in China." This United Front of finance now engaged in a campaign of deliberate subversive activities in China in order to keep the country in its financial thraldom and firmly in the grip of foreign Powers.

The first evidence that the Powers, and chiefly England, were behind Yuan Shihkai, came in the form of rumours of a loan, to be called by the high-sounding name of the Reorganization Loan. The Banking Consortium proposed to lend to the Republic a large amount of money on the security of the national salt taxes, provided these, as well as what remained of internal transport revenue, were brought under the foreign-controlled Maritime Customs Service, a service which already held all of the outside revenue of China, and a part of the *likin*, in its hands. An Englishman was to be controller of the salt taxes, to be assisted by a German. Meanwhile, to tighten the financial hold on China's future, a Bureau of International Loans, somewhat resembling today's International Monetary Fund, under the directorship of a German, with a Russian and a Frenchman as auditors, was set up.

Sun and his Revolutionary Party opposed all this, and to their credit the Americans, under President Wilson, sensing the wrath of the Chinese, withdrew from the Consortium. Wilson announced: "The conditions of the loan seem to us to touch the administrative independence of China itself ..." Unfortunately he spoilt the integrity of his gesture by adding: "Our interests are those of the Open Door – a door of friendship and mutual advantage." Since the Open Door policy was merely an affirmation of equal benefits as regards import tariffs for the foreign Powers, the Chinese considered Wilson's declaration ambiguous, and though there was gratitude at the time, later American manoeuvres did not fulfil Chinese expectations.

Sun Yatsen remains one of history's great men, a truly noble figure, his vision just, his courage beyond praise; but his defect was to think other people as dedicated, as noble and unselfish as he was. He had no time, no place, for meanness, for cupidity. All his life he moved within his own great dream: the overthrow of the Manchus, the establishment of a republic, China free, equal, respected. He went further: he envisaged a united world at peace, in which the nations helped each other along the road to progress, the strong and the wealthy helping the poor and the weak. He was, as Cantlie remarks, "a most gentle person". But he was to die bitterly disappointed not only in the West, which he had believed to be fair and democratic, but also in Japan. Again and again he appealed to the Powers, begging for international co-operation, for understanding. He pointed out that in the Revolution there had been no mob rule, no massacres, that foreign interests had not been harmed. There had not even been large-scale killing of Manchus, though there were three million of them self-sequestered in quarters in Chinese cities, and pogroms could have taken place. They did not. He asked for a chance for China. He spoke of justice, decency, honesty ... He did not get them.

If today China is Communist, it is the Western Powers which forced her into it; and if the peoples of Asia are beginning to believe that nothing can be achieved except by the power of the gun, it is because that was proved by decades of violence. Everyone is conditioned by experience; our future made before we are born. Today the same lesson is being taught to future generations, the lesson that the gun is sole arbiter in the end, and it is still the West which teaches this lesson.

Sun Yatsen's greatest illusion of universal brotherhood, nourished by his deep and sincere friendship with some individual Englishmen and Americans, such as the English doctor Cantlie, faltered and later turned to bitterness. His perplexity, his mental dilemma, was that of my father, that of so many thousands and hundreds of thousands of other Asians yesterday and today, who have to make the same distinction between personal amity, friendship, and resistance to exploitation.

Yuan Shihkai had no illusions, nourished no such dreams of peace and justice. He was of the size of his backers, unscrupulous, dishonest, entirely concerned with his own aggrandisement. For them, he was the ideal ruthless strong man. Not only George Morrison, but an American missionary named Goodnow, diligently toiled to assure him a favourable image in the West. Cantlie writes: "These reports, perhaps more than anything else, besmirched Sun's name in England, and encouraged the subversive activity of the Banking Consortium."

For the sake of unity, Sun early offered to resign and give his own position of President to Yuan, a gesture in keeping with his idealistic character, placing all men on the same lofty plane as himself. Yuan's personal ambitions satisfied, Sun felt he might work for the good of the people. Sun thought that a democratically convened cabinet, a National Assembly, universal franchise, would be safeguards against attempts by Yuan to become dictator. For was it not sufficient in democratic England, in America? Did not the rulers there heed the voice of their peoples in elected parliaments? Sun had little notion of the actual basis of power, even in a democracy, and he certainly did not understand economics, nor the role of finance in politics. He was soon to learn, at his cost. He had not dreamed that Yuan would pack the National Assembly, would fake votes, would get a soldier with a gun to stand behind each representative so as to assure himself a favourable yes ... all tricks now still amply used in other parts of the world going through the same Calvary as China did.

Yuan wanted to become Emperor. His fortune-tellers had predicted for him this glorious destiny. He outwitted or murdered every opponent, real or fancied. He must have thought Sun a glorious fool to offer him the Presidency. Sun's motives he never understood, and the nobly pathetic telegram sent to him by the latter is an historic document:

I cannot bear to see a war between south and north, for our people would suffer so much! If war can be avoided through your efforts, it is only fair for me to give you credit, and yield the presidency to you.

This abnegation, for the sake of the people, seemed to him the acme of naivety. It left Yuan, left the Consortium, Morrison and Goodnow, untouched. Who really bothered about "the people" when imperial interests were the game?

Years later, in 1918 to be exact, George Morrison, who had done so much to discredit Sun Yatsen and to obtain London's backing for Yuan, was to regret what he had done. "Had I known there was much good in Sun ..." he confided to Cantlie. But it was too late.

Ian Morrison, son of George Morrison, who in 1949 became my lover, talked at length about his father, whom he had greatly feared, for George Morrison had married late and was a severe, strict man with his sons.

"He treated all Chinese with contempt, as from a great height."

"He thought Yuan capable, and Yuan gave him a large jade seal. He liked dressing up as a Chinese official."

In Peking the main street going north from the Legation Quarters was named Morrison Street, and remained so named until 1949.

The manoeuvring and trickery that went on are history; the deviousness, the farces enacted, the assassinations, the machinations of the banks and the Consortium, have their full documentation.

Sun's followers were dazed by the turn of events. Some were bought over by Yuan, others gave up in disgust, others again were slaughtered. In the spring of 1913 Sun once more became a runaway outlaw, fleeing his country.

"Good riddance," joyously wrote Morrison.

And now Yuan began to kill Sun's followers on a large scale, and they fled for their lives.

Yuan Shihkai had thus broken China's first attempt at democratic government, with the help of the democracies. From the Banking Consortium money came pouring into his pockets, solid silver, to consolidate his power.

Everything in China was now to be mortgaged, held as security; not only the customs revenues, the *likin*, the salt taxes, but also the mines and the railways, the ports and their installations. Cantlie tells how the Consortium Loan now resulted in a fundamental change in the customs service, the foreign diplomats becoming openly trustees of all revenue, releasing to the government only the surplus after payment of the loan interests.

"As we had predicted in 1911," says the Report of the *Banque de la Société Générale de Belgique* in 1913, "the Chinese government has decided to realize important railway projects. A loan of ten million pounds sterling with our Company" – the Belgian Society for Belgian Railways and Tramways in China, established in 1908 by Leopold II, a subsidiary of the Belgian Bank – "has been signed. An international financial syndicate, to which our *Société* is a party, has made to the Chinese government (Yuan Shihkai) an advance of one million two hundred and fifty thousand pounds sterling, against a loan of twelve million five hundred thousand pounds. This syndicate has interests in the Consortium of the six powers which have just concluded, with China, the great Reorganization Loan of twenty-five million pounds."

In these bland words, in these innocuous financial sentences, the fate of the 1911 Revolution was sealed. China was once again a land full of promise, not for the Chinese, but for foreign investments.

English historians, such as Sir John Pratt and Sir Frederick Whyte, have since deplored what was done at the time, "backing the wrong horse". But wrong horse or right horse, the intentions and the techniques remain; whatever the name, Consortium or World Bank or Aid, today still the financial backing of "strong men" continues, not for the good of their own people, but for the good of imperialist interests. And the end will be the same as in China.

In March 1913, on the very day when the evidence was published that Sun Yatsen's best friend and most efficient organizer had been murdered in Peking by Yuan Shihkai's hired assassins, the contract for the great Reorganization Loan of twenty-five million pounds, for "reorganizing" railways, mines, natural resources and currency, was signed between the Consortium and Yuan Shihkai.

Sun begged the Consortium to withhold payments to Yuan, claiming the latter was using the money to equip an army for civil war, which was true. Four days after a solemn promise to Sun *not* to pay Yuan, the Consortium had advanced to Yuan two million pounds for his army.

Goodnow, also promoted Adviser, was lyrical about Yuan: "He may be somewhat unscrupulous, but we must remember that the Chinese idea of honesty ... is not ours." Goodnow called Sun a rebel, hinted that he was anti-Christian (which was untrue, for Sun Yatsen was a Protestant convert) and made up stories about the revolutionaries being devils let loose from hell, to influence American opinion. He now began the press campaign to make his patron Emperor of China, wrote articles to prove that the republican system did not suit China, that what the people needed was an Emperor; in other words, Yuan Shihkai.

However, the First World War had broken out in August 1914. The Consortium of Banks still existed, but the Powers were fighting out, in a bloody mess, their rivalries; and millions of young men died in Flanders fields, and to what purpose?

On December 12th, 1915, Yuan was begged by a so-called parliament, packed with his supporters, to ascend the Dragon Throne. Immediately sixteen out of eighteen provinces revolted against him. For, notwithstanding the China experts of the day such as Goodnow, who proved lengthily that the Chinese people wanted an Emperor back, they did *not* want an Emperor back. Very much frightened, Yuan gave up the attempt. And now Japan once again saw her opportunity. The Western Powers were busily trying to kill off their own young in a holocaust of Asian scale; this was the time for Japan to conquer the world, beginning with China . . .

Harried on all sides, Yuan asked for money, but the Powers were too busy, they had neither time nor money for Yuan Shihkai. In June 1916, abandoned by his backers and even his advisers, Yuan died.

Now money became worthless, as the bankers even before his death had refused to honour the banknotes of the Yuan government. Silver also disappeared, back into the mint houses and the pockets of provincial officials. The harm was done. All over China each province was on its own, everywhere provincial armies declaring independence; Yuan and Szechuan, Kuangsi and Shensi, each had their warlords now, and soon they were all fighting each other. The Warlord Era had begun.

Of that time, I hold a private testimonial, a letter from Joseph Hers, a Belgian then employed by the Society for the Construction of Railways in China. This company, which worked in harmony with the Consortium, in 1913 finalized the contract for the Lunghai railway, the famous horizontal railway dreamed by Leopold II, from the sea to Kansu province.

Letter from Joseph Hers, Agent for the Belgian Society for the Construction of Railways in China

My dear Suyin,

You have asked me for some of my memoirs. Here is part of my diary of the period you ask for. I met your father the first time in 1913, when he applied for a position with us, and again in 1914, a few months before the War, when he was employed on the construction of the Belgian railways in China.

The time is 1913. The Revolution is over (unless one prefers to look upon it as only beginning). The Manchu dynasty has gone. Sun Yatsen had returned to China, the Republic was proclaimed on January 1st, 1912. Sun had immediately taken up his great dream, to give China an immense network of railways...

In Peking the provisional government under Yuan Shihkai remembers that the Franco–Belgian group has constructed the Peking–Hankow railway and that the railway is paying well. This line, twelve hundred kilometres, built by us (the Belgians), had allowed the Chinese government to break the monopoly over railways which the British and Americans wanted to acquire in the Yangtse Valley and South China. It was to break this monopoly that the Russian diplomats helped us in 1898. But the English have not forgiven us. (Even in 1924 an English newspaper in Hankow was still harping on this question.*) However, they are threatened bôth by the United States' growing power, and by Japan.

On April 1st, 1912, Sun Yatsen resigned the presidency in favour of Yuan Shihkai. Within twelve months two contracts were signed in Peking for the great east–west line, the Lunghai, and another line cutting across the formidable mountain ranges to Chengtu in Szechuan. It seems certain that Yuan Shihkai, an astute military man, will dominate this new era in China. He is ruthless, a consummate strategist.

At the moment China is still in effervescence; emotion is to the fore, Sun Yatsen is the idol and the hero of the millions, not so much because he is a strong leader as because his dream of overthrowing the Manchu dynasty, a dream which appeared completely impossible some years ago, has come to pass. What appeared impregnable as the Great Wall of China has proved as easy as a cobweb to brush off. I am not inclined, as the English are, to qualify Sun as a person who cannot have the confidence of public opinion and whose downfall is certain. Some of my Chinese friends have a low opinion of Yuan: "His ability lies in cheating his own people."

I flatter myself that I know the mind of the Chinese. Often they act in diametrically opposite ways to ours in evincing their feelings, a trait which few Europeans pay attention to. I am inclined to think that those who are anxious to back Yuan may overplay their hand, and bring about another upheaval.

But meanwhile our advantage is to press on with the building of railways, and it is certain that in this matter we shall find Yuan far more agreeable to our participation than the other man. Although Sun dreams of a great network of railways, a hundred thousand miles of them, connecting the plains of China with Tibet

*Addition by Joseph Hers to his copied diary.

and Turkistan to the west, Siberia to the north, and India and
Burma to the south, the nationalists round him would be only too
eager to make the terms for building these railways extremely
difficult for us.

From early 1913, by Trans–Siberian railway, arrive numerous
French and Belgian technicians to help in the building of the
Lunghai line. There are also Italians and Greeks. Chinese engineers,
freshly graduated from universities in Belgium and France, are
also given work. It would anyway be very difficult for them to find
work anywhere else, for in the whole of the Yangtse Valley it is
the British, and the English language, which dominate.

The French Catholic schools of Shanghai furnish the staff for
the offices. These young Shanghai people are not used to the hard
life and the rigorous morality of the people of North China. In
the station of Chengchow they have seen the punishments inflicted
on an adulterous woman and her male partner, as is customary
here. They have been horrified by it, for they are city people.

The small world of the railway works hard and lives hard. The
houses of the Chinese staff are scarcely better than peasant houses.
There are no iceboxes, no electricity, nothing. Once a month we
received the mail, and beer and canned food, ordered in Hankow
or Tientsin for the Europeans.

Between the men working here there is no colour bar. Between
the women, it is quite different. There is first the rivalry between
the European women themselves, French, Belgian, Greek, Italian;
then there is the coldness and disdain manifested to the European
women married to Chinese engineers. These unfortunate European
women are now aware that their husbands receive much less
salary than Europeans. Socially, there is no contact. Together we
work, in the office or out of doors, but after that everyone goes
home. The only place where there is a general meeting is once a
year, or perhaps when funds are collected for the famines which
are almost perpetual. Later civil war in all its destructiveness comes,
but still there is no contact.

Our greatest enemies are the troops of this or that general, who
get on the train free of charge, requisition engines and wagons.
And then there are the bandits, bands like those of White Wolf or
Leopard, who attempt to kidnap people for ransom.

Present and past meet: the recital of my friend Joseph Hers
of the Belgian railways, the reminiscences of Li Chiehjen, of
Third Uncle: all this was part of one panorama, now mine
to view, the beginning of a beginning: the long march to 1949.

And now a final paragraph from Li Chiehjen, the writer.

It was the failure of the 1911 Revolution which made certain that the 1949 one would grow; as in a forest an old tree
impedes the vigour of a young one, until the lightning fells it
or the storm strikes it down.

This failure made many of the young students run away.
Others gave up, in bitterness, became cynical. Still others

died, killed by Yuan. Yuan placed a military governor in
Szechuan after 1913, with the task of hunting down revolutionaries. And the warlords who succeeded Yuan were also
to hunt down those who were suspected of being Communists,
shoot or behead them, even on the streets, without giving
them time to say any word in their defence.

Wu Yuchang, the revolutionary student who with Lung
Mingchien raised the flag of the republic at Junghsien, the
first place in China to declare itself free of the Manchus, had
in 1912 already realized what kind of a man Yuan was. He
went to see Sun Yatsen, and might even have urged him not to
trust Yuan Shihkai, but he could do little, and returned to
Szechuan.

The Revolutionary Party then set up an association, called
the Association for Work and Study in France. Why France?
Because some French officers had helped the revolutionaries
both in Wuchang and Shanghai with gun-running and military techniques; France had made the French Revolution,
and the young students admired greatly the French Revolution. This scheme was to provide young men with a work per-
mit to go to France, where they would both work and study at
the same time.

In 1914 came the First World War, and France and other
countries desperately needed man-power, Chinese workmen
to take the place of the Frenchmen fighting at the front, or
dead. Many thousands of workers and students thus went to
France, and among them were Chou Enlai, today's Prime
Minister of China, and Marshal Chen Yi, Foreign Minister of
China, and Teng Hsiaoping, Li Fuchun and Nieh Jungchen,
all prominent in today's government in China. And many
others, as students or workers or both, went to France, and
returned in 1919 and 1920, bringing back with them not only
the ideas of the French Revolution, but also Communism.

And the two streams, of those who went abroad, and those
who stayed on in China, like Mao Tsetung and Chu Teh, were
to meet, and together to complete the Revolution begun by
Sun Yatsen. And that was in 1949.

Part Two (1913-1928)

EIGHTEEN

In January 1913, with his wife and son, my father Chou Yentung left Belgium to return to China. His grandfather, Chou Taohung, had died in December 1912, and lay in his double coffin, awaiting burial.

Though Yentung did not know it, the family was by now very short of money, and this also delayed the burial, which would prove costly. The tobacco commerce was not doing well. Due to the political crisis the value of money had deteriorated, inflation making prices climb so rapidly that the copper coin was said to fester as it changed hands. The Chengtu government and the Chungking government both issued their own currency. It was fortunate that the coffin, both inner and outer, of excellent lanmu, had been purchased some twenty years before, when Taohung was still a strong seventy. Land also had been reserved for his grave obtained with foresight in the 1880s. Otherwise the family could not have afforded a fitting burial.

Taohung lay in the coffin, awaiting a propitious day for interment; while his grandson, bringing his first great-grandson, sped on a boat, back from the Western Ocean. Meanwhile the family devised ways and means of procuring money for the double event: the burial of the ancestor, and a befitting welcome for the foreign daughter-in-law that Chou Yentung was bringing into the family.

On the steamer carrying us back, it began. Like a monster which had lain in wait for me, patiently waiting many years. And now here it was, for all my days to come to haunt me with its wolfish fear.

Oh great monster, hold back a little longer yet the mountainous dark waters of your cruelty from my shore. For see, I inhabit a little island, almost a paradisial miniature, almost like my toy garden at home with diminutive trees and sparkling pebble mountains and enough water for a cup its lake. Oh, let me have more time, but a little more time.

But time could not be stayed. The destruction of our enchantment began on the steamer, and it did not stop.

No shame is as the shame of being stripped naked before the loved one. Rather a million strangers, than the open, gentle face tautened, the confident eyes gravelled with doubt.

And doubt measured me and found me wanting. All the cloying illusions of memory blown, the haloes of unctuous myth dispelled, our prisoned heads, so dissimilar, now yoked by a bond stronger than love, the stupefaction of our deceit; spirits and bodies had met in a passionate dream, and woke to find the dream itself a chain.

Thus from the window-longing first encounter, through the rapture and the abundance of love, and the somnolent, gentle bliss of a heart full of refuge, of pampered habits that liked us as we liked them, to this raw silence, full of accusation. Like the shadow of rain upon a city, the harm I had crouched to avoid was gathered, and came pouring upon the loved one, bearing her down, streaking with grief her bright devastated hair.

All I could do was to follow her as she grew in her tragedy to its unfolding, to its end, to the narrow death of love.

I became aware of it when I made the bookings. It was an English boat. I asked for first class, and was told courteously that no "coloured person" was allowed in first class on this boat. When I insisted, I was told there was no first class available, it was full.

Marguerite was not with me. I walked out of the booking office a little dazed, only partly comprehending what I had been told. The tone was so polite, close-clipped to such smooth polish, it was impossible to protest.

"What is the matter? Are you not feeling well?" said Marguerite when I returned.

I said it was nothing, that we had only second-class tickets, the first class was full.

"Don't worry," said she. "I don't mind how I go, so long as I get to China. I do so want to see your beautiful Szechuan, and your mother. Do you think she will like me?"

She had asked this so often, I had assured her just as often, with so much fervour and confidence, that my mother would like her. And now there was gall in my mouth as I heard someone, surprisingly me, mouthing words which were lies.

When we went to collect the tickets, the man in the booking office (tall, blond, low-voiced) said to Marguerite: "But, madame, you can go in first class if you wish, but not monsieur. It is the rule."

"Oh," said Marguerite, astonished, "but he is my husband. Of course I shall go with him."

"As you wish, madame." He gave us a second-class cabin, looked at our son doubtfully. "Tall for his age, isn't he? Only four and something, did you say?"

Coming out of the office the sun was darkened for me, but I heard Marguerite laugh, hearty, defiant, reassuring laughter. Her face was a little pink, her hair seemed resplendent, a sun on its own. "Don't worry. Yentung. It is only the English. They have always had a bee in their bonnet about colour. We are not like that, in Belgium. It would not be the same on a French boat. Why, the English are like that even with us. They think people on the Continent are also a lower breed. I was in England, I know."

Poor Marguerite. She had been about a week in London, found it both cold and unfriendly, and since then insisted she understood the English perfectly. I felt better. Of course, it was only the English. They were like that.

"Wait till we get to your country, and you start building your railway," said Marguerite. She always spoke of it as my railway. "And when we reach your province I shall wear Chinese dress, and do everything like a Chinese woman. It is a pity my feet are big, but now they are unbinding the women's feet since the Republic. I long to know all your family. I am sure I shall love them."

That night I swore that never, never would I be parted from Marguerite. I would make her happy, cost what it may. Never would I forget her courage, the way she had laughed. I have kept my promise.

In Singapore we were refused a room at the English hotel, and the Chinese ones were very hot and uncomfortable; there was opium-smoking, prostitution and gambling all round us. Marguerite had prickly heat, and our son cried all night long. Our clothes were all too heavy for the damp, hot weather. I called on old friends, brought Marguerite; she sat in silence while we talked, they stared at her with much curiosity. Soon we all became uneasy, our tongues would not move. We walked about the streets, and to the docks to watch the ships on the sea, a sea like silver foil, hard glitter under the hard sun. I could feel the stares, not malevolent but astonished: a Chinese man, a European woman ... Marguerite soon said she was tired, her feet were swollen with the heat.

"When we get to China I shall dress as a Chinese woman, then nobody will look at me."

Alas, poor Marguerite. Not only was she, once in China, only the wife of a Chinese, and therefore rejected by her own people; but to us she was, she remained always, a European, the white woman, to be followed everywhere by crowds, to be stared at, to be called names: "Big nose! Western devil!" And when, in the riots, the temper of the crowd rose and their anger against the Whites, then she too, like other foreigners, had to stay indoors, to hide, to be evacuated.

There was love between us, passion, and the children, and we did not betray each other. But all around us, all the time, we were not allowed to forget that so much had happened between the Europe she belonged to and the China that was mine, such a hugeness of sombre injustice to redress; by marrying me she had lowered herself in the eyes of her people, and in the eyes of mine she was one of those foreigners who had done so much harm. A maze without escape where, tracked by the evil of the past, we stumbled, yoked together by the lies we had believed.

And thus, returning to reality at last, I do not know which one of us suffered more.

In Shanghai it was agony, for there it was only too plain that in my own country I was nothing but an inferior, despised being. There were parks and restaurants and hotels I could not enter, although she could. I had no rights on the soil of a Chinese city which did not belong to the Chinese; she had rights, by reason of something called skin.

We boarded the English steamer from Shanghai to Hankow; the first class was for Europeans only, and there was no other steamer. Marguerite leaned her arms on the railings and stared at the river. She was in first class, with our son. I went second class. I had insisted it should be so. "It is too hot for you here below."

We stayed in a small hotel in the French concession in Hankow. It was run by a French Eurasian. It was Sunday, and Marguerite went to church. I did not go with her, I stayed to look after our child. When she returned her eyes were red. We waited in Hankow for a steamer up river, but there was trouble, civil war would break out at any moment, so everyone told us, and the troops of Yuan Shihkai were said to be moving from the north to conquer the south and put an end to Sun Yatsen and the Revolution. The Great River was full of foreign gunboats. No tugboat or small steamer went to Szechuan. We would have to take a junk.

That night Marguerite cried: "Yentung, will it be better in your province?"

What could I say? "China is poor, but soon, soon all will be well. You will see. This is only the beginning."

"These beggars, the filth, the misery . . . ?"

"We have had so many wars, so much trouble." And then I added: "It is due to the foreigners, Marguerite, to the white men. They came and made war with us."

"But how can it be," she said, "when we have done so much good, and tried to help? You know how we collected money in Belgium for the little Chinese."

How could I explain to her the hypocrisy of "charity" without hurting her? Even Marguerite had collected silver paper from the chocolates she ate, kept and kneaded the silver paper in a ball, a very large ball, which was then given to the Sisters of Charity to be sold to buy back the soul of a little Chinese girl . . . Everyone did it in Europe, all the girls in school, and they always became so sentimental about Chinese children, or for that matter African children, all dependent on the chocolate silver paper to be saved. How could I hurl at her this ignominy, and all her people had done to us? Especially since Belgium had not been as bad as the others.

I hired a private junk to take us up to Szechuan, since the steamer would not run. The newspapers were full of the forays of bandits, and there was fighting in every province. I was impatient to be back in Szechuan. Once in Chengtu, with my family, all would be much better. Szechuan was capable of standing on its own, still the enclosed kingdom, self-sufficient. I would start working on our railway. Szechuan could be autonomous, independent . . . I hastened our departure from Hankow.

It took us seventy-two days to go up the Great River from Hankow to Chungking. During those seventy-two days Marguerite seemed to age ten years.

We landed at Chunking, and when I saw my younger brother, who had come to meet us, I cried:

"Why did you not tell me? Why did you not write to me?"

He bowed before my sternness. "We did not wish to disturb your studies . . . you are so valuable . . ."

I stared at him. He had been a boy of fifteen in 1903 when I left, and he had entered the Military Academy, obeying the

Family's commands. Now he wore an officer's grey uniform with epaulets. My brother kept his face respectfully averted from Marguerite, as is our custom when we show consideration for a woman. Marguerite thought he was insulting her. I explained, but she was difficult to convince.

Misery, desolation, everywhere. The streets of Chungking were noisome with people in rags. Everywhere we went, like flies the beggars followed, running under our feet, exhibiting their sores. Marguerite screamed as a woman thrust a fetid, stinking bag of pus under her eyes: it was a child, faceless, the nose and eyes gone into one running, putrid sore. The houses crumbled, children ran after rats to eat them. The Guild House, where we were invited to stay, had not been repainted for years. Everywhere the smells were horrible. Corpses rotted in the smaller lanes.

"We could not tell you . . . how could we?"

That night I sat with my young brother, after the banquet. At the banquet some of the businessmen I had met eight years ago, and a few new ones, congratulated me; their speeches were full of praise. Not once did we talk of what was really happening, not once did we falter in a courtesy which consisted in not mentioning the actual.

"Tell me what has happened, Brother. All these ten years."

"I do not know myself how to explain. We are getting poorer and poorer all the time, as you see. And there are troubles everywhere, rebellions. We had the Revolution, but it is the same as before. Perhaps worse."

"I read that the foreigners were helping us now. There has been a big loan."

"The more they help us, the poorer we get."

"And the railway, our railway? I came back to build our railway, in our province . . ."

"Brother, I have so much to tell you. I do not know where to begin."

The next day we left by sedan chair for Chengtu, a ten-day journey. My brother had been thoughtful, he had done what he could for us, for Marguerite. And we talked during those days. I learnt something of what my people had endured, and fear tightened in my throat. Would Marguerite stay with me, in these conditions? Would she leave me? I could not bear her leaving me.

We reached Chengtu on the afternoon of the tenth day, and were home, to be welcomed by my mother, and to pay the last obeisance to my grandfather, Chou Taohung, who had already awaited burial for six months in his great coffin. Marguerite and I bowed to the brown coffin, so large, in the Ancestors' Hall. We bowed to the Ancestors' tablets in their ranks while my mother spoke, called to them and introduced Marguerite to them. And thus my wife entered into the Family.

I was happy that afternoon in Chengtu, home at last, observing how my mother took to her first grandson and how everyone tried to please Marguerite. The fatigues of the trying journey over, Marguerite would relax. Slowly she would adapt. Except for my Elder Brother, who out of respect for my wife did not come (as it is not courtesy to look upon a younger sister-in-law's face), many relatives were there, even of a higher generation, and many friends and their wives, come specially to greet her, including the wives of many officials. In the evening the Governor would give a reception in our honour. My younger sisters had tried to master some French in order to talk to Marguerite, but their efforts only turned to much giggling and they were very shy.

Of course, Marguerite would have to learn restraint. She must curb her thoughtless exuberance. Delighted when riding in sedan chairs, she would lift the curtain, wishing to look out at the street, and this was immodest. If the people knew that it was a foreign woman in the sedan chair, though the curtains were down, they would follow the chair, accounting it something new and exciting. "A foreign woman, a foreign she-devil, let us see her big nose ..." Always we tried to provide an escort for her outings. I would have to explain to her that this was courtesy, tender care; she was impatient of all slowness, the slightest bridling of her freedom of movement.

The first few days all seemed well. Marguerite was a little nervous. The damp, cloying heat, with that perpetual lid of cloud holding the steamy vapours of earth down upon the plain, and the mosquitoes, did not help to make her less irritable. Once or twice she started crying, but would wipe her face hastily, and say: "It is nothing, just the heat. It is so suffocating."

There were many callers. Because my grandfather's funeral would take place soon, many parties to entertain the spirit of the deceased were held. For hours at a time Marguerite would have to sit with the ladies in the women's quarters, while they played mahjong to solace the dead elder. I think this was her worst trial, for women are seldom kind to each other.

Every morning I had to go to the Official Mansion, for I was now given the title of Chief Engineer of the Province, and a salary to be paid in silver; and this was most gratifying, for money was deteriorating very fast, and only silver and gold, solid metal, were of worth. The paper money was now devaluated, five hundred times, a thousand times, ten thousand times, a fall so catastrophic, and seemingly unending, that all measures for curbing prices only worsened it. We had always reckoned money by the price of grain, and in the past our society had little circulating money, much rent being collected in kind. Now there was hoarding of grain, as the harvests had been so bad due to the constant fighting, and the peasant borrowing money found it melt in value. I received pieces in precious silver, and gave half to my mother and this helped a little, for I now found that the Family had lost nearly all its land, property and cash.

There was nominally a government in Chengtu and one in Chungking, opposed to each other. Both governments were bargaining with Yuan Shihkai, and with Sun Yatsen's government, and with each other, and with the governments of Yunnan and Kueichow, the provinces farther south. Much of this bargaining concerned the opium trade.

It was obvious to me that no railway could be built under these circumstances, there was no money, no way of getting material; but every day I had to appear in my office, a substantial and lordly room prepared for me, with a large desk, where I was to draft plans and undertake surveys. It had now been decided to start building the railway between Chengtu and Chungking, since this was entirely within the province. But all the time I knew, and everyone knew, that it was quite impossible even to lay a single tie upon the track. Meanwhile, I was the only engineer in Chengtu; with a magnificent title and a salary in silver, I spent my time chatting with the vice-governor and the officials and drinking tea, and no one knew what was really going to happen. There was nothing to do, except to wait. The military ran things, jockeyed for power; they were arming for a tussle, all they were interested in was weapons, and opium to finance the weapons they bought, chiefly from the French, through Yunnan.

Marguerite began to deteriorate. I cannot say how it began exactly. I returned home in the afternoon to find her surly, everyone else in the house strangely silent. There were so many things that could not be explained, that were beyond explanation. Marguerite could do none of the things that a daughter-in-law should do or could do. And she could not imagine spending the day shut up in a house, only going as far as the first courtyard, twenty steps there, twenty steps back. The most conservative ritual was put in practice, not to spite her, but to protect her, and it was disastrous. When she wanted to go out, it was a mobilization; the whole household would anxiously consult the weather, then someone or other would remark that this was not an auspicious day for going out. When she insisted nevertheless, an aunt, two sisters-in-law, perhaps some cousins, would go with her; but first some younger male cousins would have to be recruited to protect the women, not because any real harm would happen to them, but because it was so unusual. It was no use pointing out that young girls now went out alone, and that my own mother had gone to Kansu; Marguerite was to be looked after, and look after her they did until she screamed with irritation.

For by the time all preparations were ended for this expedition, she was frantic with exasperation, and would say she was not going out, and return to lie on her bed and to sob. Then no one understood why she had changed her mind, and they thought she might be ill and sent for the doctor, and she would slam the bamboo door curtain violently as if slamming a door.

Marguerite also insulted, unwittingly, many friends of the family who came to see her, to pay their respects, but also out of curiosity. No need to say that they were all women, and among them some malicious ones who drooled remarks about her feet, her size, her clothes, her manners or lack of them. Although she did not understand the words, Marguerite was only too ready to suspect everyone of sneering at her.

And then came the question of the ancestors. One day my older brother took me apart, and with as much self-control as he could muster, told me Marguerite had insulted my mother and all the ancestors. However, even that they were willing to forgive, to overlook, as she was a foreigner and in time it would be better. But she must not turn the grandson against the family, and now the grandson was hitting everyone, and Marguerite was encouraging him, and everyone was afraid for he was a very strong little boy although so young.

I do not know why at that moment, myself worried, almost driven to despair by the frustrating days spent chatting, drinking tea and simulating work, I became curt with my Elder Brother. I said China was now a Republic, and that these old preoccupations should change. My Elder Brother stared at me with amazement, then lowered his eyes and left me. He had performed his duty, which was to keep order in the family; he now withdrew completely from me, and that was bad. I had greatly insulted him.

I went into our room, and Marguerite was sobbing. Oh, that sobbing, it tore me to pieces, turned my knees to water, and my belly. Later I was habituated, though always vulnerable, so very vulnerable because of love. Later I devised techniques to shut off the sound of her sobbing, the sound of her voice, to avoid being destroyed. In the courtyard outside our room I knew the younger ones were gathered, a small curious crowd, wondering what was happening, shushing each other. At times the children had poked their fingers through the paper latticed windows to peep at Marguerite, and that enraged her, so that they no longer did it. But their mothers had become unhappy, because when she shrieked at their children they were insulted, and they said sour things to each other about Marguerite.

I drew near to her, reluctant for I dreaded the violence she exhibited so freely now. I shrank from it and the dire wound it made to our love, which her constant mordant anger now threatened with impotence. I loved her: yet now, gazing at her on the bed, when she turned a face purpled with tears and rubbing, and her russet hair – once the glory of her person, now drab and somehow obscene, so unlike our own black hair – wavered, moved on the pillow, oh heavens, I thought, how ugly she is, how repulsive, how foreign! Suddenly I saw her, saw her as the others in the family must see her, big and clumsy, uncouth, all that is wrong and incomprehensible and different. Even her breathing was different, wild, undisciplined. What enchantment had been cast upon me to think her beautiful, and now the spell had gone, and my engrossment revealed for what it was, almost a perversion, an obscenity . . . how could I ever have married such a one?

It only lasted a few minutes, and never came back again, that vision too unbearable to know. She sprang up as, overcoming my reluctance, I put a hand upon her arm. "Don't touch me, don't touch me!" If only she knew how much I felt like not touching her. I sat down again on the chair, facing her. I said:

"Pack up your things. We go away."

"No?"

"Yes. We are going away. Now. This very day."

I walked out of the room, feeling like an emanation of my own limbs, body; not myself, but someone else standing by me and giving orders, to pack, to leave. For the next three days I remained in that protective trance, sheltered from everything and everyone, from bemused reproach, from Marguerite's triumph; a weak man, suddenly obstinate, vacantly hard, in a decision which refused to define or explain itself. Again it was Third Brother, hastily called that very night and riding back twenty miles from military camp, who arranged everything for us.

The manner of our going was shaming, for my mother clung to us, sighing softly, plucking my sleeve, too well behaved to sorrow openly, all her tears appropriately reserved for the old man in his coffin. To protect her, Third Brother invented the story that I was urgently needed elsewhere by the government, and would return soon. But it was Marguerite who refused my mother charity of this pitiful lie. "I never lie," she said, and asked my sisters to tell my mother that we would never return, never. "We Europeans do not tell lies. It is contemptible to lie."

We took with us Son of Spring, Eldest Grandson, and by so doing he became our first victim. And this leaving was a rude death, for we would never return.

All this I did for Marguerite, to save her and to save our love, that sucking darkness with no door, this labyrinth which was to end in my being left, in turn, alone. I was to follow my love into the maze of our years, and in the end desolation more absolute than the one I inflicted upon my mother would be mine. And Son of Spring too was bereft, for when we took him away, we did not know we were condemning him and his children; without the Family, there was no place for him in China.

It is only in the evening, when the shadows ooze into each other, that I remember the day we left, autumn, the cricket grizzling an early winter song, Marguerite's hair coiled upon her victorious head. Looking back now, with the hindsight of history, I can understand it so much better. But understanding is also effacement, a vagueness, which explains, but explains away the minute agonies, the grief that warps a life, which accepts, as a tree, crippled at its root by some voracious stabbing insect and for ever after bearing the mark of the beast upon its unfolding, is accepted in the landscape.

Who was right, who was wrong? There was no right or wrong. She tried, how hard she tried, to become one of us. She was invited by the Protestant missionaries at the hospital to visit them, but did not go, replying proudly that her place was with her husband and his family. But there was no companionship for her with the family, as she could not converse with them. She was alone, against all history, alone against a century of accumulated dislike, against all the unconscious hostilities, assumptions, which saw in her only a representative of the Whites; and all the harm they had done militated against her being accepted. And, on the other hand, she did not understand or accept that she must change totally. How otherwise fit into a feudal family?

No one ever laid a finger on her. She was never molested, never threatened, but the air was not friendly to her. The children shouted insults, they had done so for decades now, I had told her not to care; but how could she not care? And there was a small thing: a young boy of about twelve, perhaps more, hating foreigners (as by this time did so many of the young, especially in Szechuan where the Revolution was still vivid), thought it amusing to try to urinate upon her skirt as she stood looking at some handwoven baskets in an open shopfront. My sisters shooed him away, my youngest male cousin gave him a push. He was a beggar child, a truant, he escaped. Everyone laughed, the crowd, my sisters, my cousin. But Marguerite could not laugh. She cried again, half the night. "Your people don't want me, and I cannot be like them." I reassured her, saying it was the abnormal times, the troubles.

But at other times I could not reassure her, could not explain that the goodwill of one person was not enough to wipe out the gunboats and the troops: "If your people had not done evil to us, we would not be thus." But of this she could never be persuaded, and I gave up. It would have broken our love, our marriage, had I insisted on being truthful telling her historical facts. "What is that to me?" she would say.

I kept her with me many years, but she was altered in temper and in mind, and her hair began to grey.

We reached Hankow. The whole of the Great River basin was still in the hands of the British, under their influence and control. Nothing had changed with the Revolution, nothing

... or so it seemed to me at the time. I had to find a job, to earn money. To get a job one had to know English. No British firm employed one without English, and there were no jobs otherwise, not for an engineer. The Russians in the north wanted people who knew Russian, the French in the South only employed French-returned students.

There was one hope for me: the Belgian-built railway, the Peking–Hankow line. I went to the Belgian Consul in Hankow. He told me to go to the office of the Belgian Society for the Construction of Railways in China. He gave me the address.

I went to the Society. Behind the desk was a tall, very tall man, with a short beard and prominent blue eyes. His name was Joseph Hers. There was no job available on the Peking–Hankow railway, which had been redeemed by China in 1908 but still employed Belgian engineers. No job for a *Chinese* engineer on that Chinese railway! But the Belgians were to construct another railway, from east to west, in the north, the Lunghai railway. The contract had been signed that very year. There might be a job there for me.

I waited seven weeks in Hankow. During those seven weeks Marguerite was offered repatriation by the Belgian Consul. She refused. "I stay with my husband." The Consul spoke of troubles. "Troubles in China, wars, the Chinese have them all the time. They cannot agree among themselves. We advise all European women and children to be evacuated. Although you have a Chinese passport, we wish to stretch a point, as your family is well known. When things are more peaceful, you could return." Gunboats were on the Yangtse; to protect European property and lives; foreign troops would land at any moment.

By this time our love, threatened already in Chengtu, had turned into something utterly different from its first, natural candour. Something which has no name took its place, an utter dependence and a total resentment, mixed with a frightening compassion for each other, unworded, clutching at the stomach. I went out to cry, tears running down my eyes in the street, and never knew whether it was for myself or for her. She went to church every day now. Our son was getting very thin, fretful. We decided to send him back to Belgium, but we would remain together.

And so it was. Between her son and me, Marguerite chose me. Son of Spring went back on a steamer with a Belgian family with three children of their own, the De Vos. He arrived safely in Belgium in December, and was met by his grandfather, George Denis. He was five years and two months old.

"We must not have any more children, Yentung. God knows what the future may be for them."

I knew already what the future had in store for them. My children would belong nowhere. Always there would be this double load for them, no place they could call their own land, their true home. No house for them in the world. Eurasians, despised by everyone ... We must not have any more children.

But we had seven more. The priests who confessed Marguerite saw to that.

One day I received a letter from the Society. I was offered a job as foreman of works on the Lunghai railway. I would have to live on the job, in the countryside, in North China.

I accepted. For the next eight years, until 1921, I was to work on the Lunghai railway under Belgian engineers. I was a Chinese, and would never be promoted to any high job that a European, sometimes far less competent than myself, could hold. My salary would never be that of a European, even when later as assistant engineer I was doing the same work. At most a quarter, a third, of the salary of the white man. As for Marguerite, she was the wife of a Chinese, and the wives of the Belgian engineers looked down on her, and would not receive her. But there was no other way for me, for her. We had to live, to eat. I kept her by my side; we had each other. She often spoke of leaving me, of going back. But all those years she never did. Until the last time, in 1949.

Marguerite Denis walked up and down, down and up. Her slippers fell after her feet, a muffled slap on the floor. Her daughter watched her with the seeing eye which has no pity, the eye better than love, saw her mother's hair streaked with grey, the dandruff on the bent black of the blouse, the gaunt face and the veined hands, and once again saw, with the eye of memory, the stomach through the ballooning skirt, with its tortuous wrinkles coiled as nests of snakes. The child had seen it, the afternoon before, coming suddenly into the bedroom, and been shouted out. But the question, how had Mama's stomach become like that? danced tirelessly on her mind's surface and refused to be felled and dragged down. At six it was well known that children came in the doctor's bag, brought by an angel from heaven to the doctor, who then brought it to Mama in her bed. How and why then did Mama say: "If I have lost my figure, it's because of you," with a look of smoulder and a hand upon her belly?

In response to the silent, impassive watching, the eyes that did not flicker, Mama spoke. That always happened. At six a child remembers everything, especially a child with an auditory memory like a tape recorder, who was later to remember dialogue, scenes, acres of small events adding up to a total story. Mama's every step seconded like a drum the swing of her sentences; she spoke in the rhythm of her own slapping feet, and her child drew Mama walking within the house, the walls curving outwards, expanding to contain the story which shaped the child and made her future predictable. But let Mama not weep again, the child thought. For this I do not like, and I will then go to look at the vine, as Papa does, and pinch the green hard little knobs which will be grapes, pretending to know all about ripening fruit. And my heart shall know what it is not to be one, yet not two, for ever almost, for my house of life has two doors, and the people that walk into it by one door do not use the other, and everything has to be kept apart from everything else. I alone use both, use all, grasping the keys to both to open and shut my house at will. She drew two doors to the house with the expendable walls.

And Mama spoke, answering the strenuous silent watching, for she could not bear silence. Mama had no one to talk to, no one no one no one but her detested beloved child, the one that would not let go of any argument, story, play or work, but always insisted on going on and on, longer than anyone else, always reaching for more, more, making herself sick all the time, till Mama shrieked with exhaustion, or the younger child howled, or someone was hit. O hateful hateful yet indispensable witness for monologue which is also dialogue, for some object to listen while the void is filled with words. Both Papa and Mama talked to the child, but separately, and never never the stories the same, and she remembered it all.

What have I done? My God, my God, I want to go away, but how can I leave now? What have I done to deserve this? Well, perhaps it is a punishment. And last Saturday Father Clement would ask me why I was not having more children, and I told him, "Isn't eight enough with four dead? My health is broken," I said, and he had the cheek to answer: "Madame, you are as strong as a horse." Well, that is the last time I go to his church. Next Sunday we go to the Tungtang Church. It stinks, and the beggars at the gate are awful, but I will borrow your father's stick to beat them out of the way. I don't want to catch the itch or leprosy.

Those priests, they never know anything. If they only had the life I had. If they only had babies, perhaps they would understand. I wish they had my life. Only a little of it would cure them of, "Madame, what is the age of your last child?" And they spoilt it all for me. If it was not for them I would never have had another child.

*

At this the child knew that again the Big Hurt would come, the hurt of her own birth, so unwelcome. She sought the by-pass: "Mama, tell about Brother, Son of Spring."

Mama stopped her up and down rhythm, her face soft all at once. The first-born would be coming, returning to his country, soon, soon, perhaps next year. She sat down, suddenly relaxed, confidential as over a cup of coffee; her hands were quietly restless with a knitting she neither began nor ended for it was always there, and mufflers, caps and pullovers came out of the knitting, but inexhaustible the small mountain of wool yarn protruded out of its workbasket with its crochet wool daisies spread-eagled over the roughness of the wicker strands.

And like the wool in the workbasket, Mama was inexhaustible on this story of her life.

It was seventy-two days, although now many people do not believe me, but anyone who has done the trip in a small boat will know I am right. And there were troubles, North fighting South, just as today; nothing has changed, nothing ever changes, except the names of the warlords. At that time it was Yuan Shihkai of the North fighting Sun Yatsen of the South, and all the Europeans were for Yuan Shihkai, and as usual your father would not say which side he was on. And in Hankow there were so many soldiers in the streets. I went to the Belgian Consul there, and he was rude to me because your father was a Chinese. "No sane person, Madame, would come to China now." He told me that I was Chinese now, and if anything happened to me the Belgian government could not be held responsible. And when I left he did not even see me to the door. Oh, I was so humiliated, so humiliated, and all because my husband was Chinese. And I thought, but what has happened to all these people, all these Europeans who come here, do they think they are born from Jupiter's thigh they behave so arrogantly? I am a Denis, I will tell them my grandfather was burgomaster of Malines. I told your father: "Do something," but he was not even allowed in the concessions, they were for Europeans, and in time of trouble they put barbed wire round the concessions; the land did not belong to the Chinese, there were British and French and Belgian and other concessions, and barbed wire, so thick you could not see through, between them and the Chinese. But I could go in and out, they always opened the barbed wire gate when they saw me, but not for your father.

So we took a junk up the River. It was difficult to find anyone wanting to go up, but we did, we paid well, and oh I shall never forget that trip. I think I was the only European going to Szechuan that year. It was terrible, but I have never seen anything so wonderful. It was not like sailing at all, it was climbing, climbing a mountain of water which came rushing at us, and that is how the boatmen spoke of it, as pushing up against the Great River. Most of the time we were being towed, up up up against the current, men pulling, all naked, not even trousers; they said clothes were more precious than men, and when the men fell in and drowned, the clothes would not be lost.

It was not a big junk, and there were only the three of us and the boatmen, and after a few days I felt I had been all my life on that boat. I was young and strong, and after a few days I wanted to row too, but your father would not let me.

I didn't wear my stays or my corsets, and took off my shoes, and oh then it was glorious, hours and hours on the deck, only the water and the sun. It was April, and the wide hills white with flowers. I did not know it was opium till your father told me.

And then we came to Ichang, and that was fifteen hundred miles from Shanghai where we had landed, but it was an eternity and a world and a half away, for now we would pass the gorges and we would come to Szechuan, and I thought: It will be different there, not so terribly poor.

I tied your brother to a barrel with a rope, so that if anything happened he would float, and put the rosary round his neck with the Blessed Medal of the Virgin to protect him. But I was not really afraid. This was wonderful, wonderful, I had never seen anything like it, not even the ocean, for the ocean is just big and all water, and after a time one forgot the ocean; but here the boatmen were fighting, all the time, every step of the way; the towmen and the boatmen, all through these two and a half months, fought for our lives on that junk, and I knew they were closer to me than my own family, and though I did not row I felt I was a part of them, also fighting the water. They got used to me, and the skipper brought me some vegetables, a chicken, and sometimes when we moored he would bring a small paper toy for your brother, a marion-ette or a small windmill, or a small cake, and I learnt some words like "thank you". When we landed in the evening the skipper would take Son of Spring on his shoulders and play horse to him to amuse him. How he laughed and laughed. And all these days he was not unwell, but happy, and so was I. And the colour of spring in the gorges was marvel, and even a storm we had did not frighten me.

That is when I saw the monkeys upon the cliffs, I could not miss them. Nothing but sea and sky and our junk between the two high walls of the cliffs. And they were green, green. I heard them hoot. And it was like after being dead, going to heaven in a boat.

The boatmen sang. I always knew when we were going to pass a rapid, because the skipper would start, as if talking, but his voice ended on a long note like a call, and he was calling the song, the song to start, and the words got quicker and quicker, and also the rowing, hei hei hei hei, they rowed and sang. And I too would push the boat, tight squeezing my muscles I would push with my mind, fighting pushing the boat through the rapids. Once we were so near a whirlpool I saw the whirlpool's eye, a horrible eye welling in, in, watching me as it caved in. I felt my brain giving in to the dreadful brain behind that eye which will me to give in, to come to it, come to it, dragging the boat and everything with me. You will never know what it is like to fight for your life through the gorges if you go by steamer. That is nothing. And the song went slapping the rocks and back at us, and we passed a cave with a chain across its mouth, to chain the dragon of the water in-side. And all shouted as we passed the whirlpool and it was left, snarling to itself, licking some rocks just pointing a tip of white foam.

At night the junk was made fast to the river's edge, and we would get out and stretch our legs. Always there was something to eat, a small place, a few houses, and people came to look at me, but I did not mind, as I minded afterwards in the city when I could not stand the crowds any more. All along they never did me harm. In one place we stopped there was only one hovel on stilts above the water, most filthy, with a miserable pig, its back sagging, and some piglets so thin it was pitiful, like dying cats, and every kind of dirt. But in the hovel was the most beautiful girl I had seen, a skin so fair, such wonderful eyes. Now I could begin to see the difference in all the faces about me, and this girl – I will never forget her face. They told me her name was Flower on a Heap of Dung, and that was so true, she was so beautiful among so much dirt. And the place was terribly poor, everyone had gone or died, there had been some disease, only this girl was left with some pigs, and they were dying too. She made some food for us out of our rice and some vegetables we had left, and we gave her a little money. I wanted to give her something, so I gave her a handkerchief. She had nothing except trousers and jacket, and no one knew what would happen to her.

We came out of the gorges, and it was three weeks later, landing at a place, quite big, with a church. And there it was all changed, the crowds were not nice. I knew it, though they did not touch me, they never did me harm. But they hated me, I knew, and here was barbed wire and some British and Sikhs, perhaps that was why. And there were two gunboats. It made me very nervous, and from then on I was nervous of the crowds.

Your father's brother was in Chungking when we arrived, an officer in a smart uniform and on a white horse, and at first I thought he was insulting me, he only bowed once to me and then he did not look at me; but afterwards Yentung told me that was the way of his country. Everything is the other way round in China. Everything, from buttoning your clothes to greeting people, is upside down.

When I had had a bath and washed your brother, I looked through the window, and it was most beautiful though very hot. I could see two big rivers meeting, mountains all around, the city like a fortress on a tongue of rock going between the rivers. I thought it such a pity, a lovely land like this and the people so poor, so miserable, everything so filthy, and the beggar children, skeletons with pot-bellies dragging themselves about. Every day they picked up people dead of hunger on the streets. And all this your father had never told me. "Why didn't you tell me?" I said. And he said: "It's your fault, you the Whites." "How could it be my fault?" I said. Then we had a big quarrel. And never again did your father say that it was our fault. Because, anyway, he could not find any work except on a Belgian railway, a railway built by my people in his country. So after that he kept quiet, and now I never know what he really thinks. He is like a deaf-mute with me now.

We went by sedan chair to Chengtu, all over the hills, down and up again, and through the fields, and it was nice. Every hour the four men who carried me would give a shout, and four other men would come running up, switching the poles of the chair on to their shoulders, slipping the poles so that one did not even feel a bump, and all the time they were doing their running walk, so smooth and fast, they did not even stop to put the chair down when they changed. Then the first four would wipe their sweat with the white cloth tied round their heads, and spit and sigh, and they seemed to sigh the tiredness out of them, and they would trot by the side of the chair and laugh and make jokes. Your brother liked the chair, he jumped up and down on my lap.

Oh, the countryside was beautiful, I had never seen anything so large, so many fields going out and out to the sky and back again. And in some places in the hills the coal could be seen, dark seams in the hills, and people would not have to dig for the coal, it was just there, and your father said: "One day there will be a great industry here, there is coal and iron and there will be steel, and we shall make our own rails for our railways." "But that day hasn't come yet, has it?" I told him later.

Everywhere there were beggars, it was frightening. Good that we had men with us for protection. They were supposed to be soldiers, but I could have felled them with a sweep of the hand, they were so small and weak, and they wore straw shoes on their feet, and I am sure they could have become bandits in no time. Every four hours, three times a day, they smoked opium pipes.

At night we stopped in inns. I put your brother on a table top. I always asked for a table top so there would be no rats on him. One night I woke to find a rat running on my chest, though we had our camp beds with us and our own bedding, or we would have been eaten up by bedbugs. We soaked the camp beds in kerosense to get rid of bedbugs.

Then we were in Chengtu. Far out already I could see the gates and the city wall, and we came through the streets and it was just as dirty and verminous as everywhere else.

Then to the house, the family all there; at least, it looked like it, there were so many of them. And a little old woman in front, very small, tiny, she did not even reach my shoulder, I could have picked her up, she was so small, and that was his mother. It was supposed to be a great honour, she had come to meet me at the gate, instead of waiting for me inside the courtyard; that is what they told me. Anyway I thought, now I must do what I can, and perhaps things will be better. So I did everything like Yentung, and bowed, and then the little woman extended her hand towards me and so I shook it, and some people began to laugh. But it was all right, Yentung afterwards told me. "My mother has tried to learn western manners to please you. And they have given us the best room, on the east side, although this should not really be ours but my Elder Brother's room. And they have bought some furniture for you." There was a lamp, and a kind of canvas chair, and a woollen blanket, English, and a carpet on the floor. It was all very poor quality, but then the Europeans sold bad quality things to the Chinese, who did not know better.

I did not say anything, I was too tired. But they really liked your brother. When the old woman saw him she laughed all over the face and drew him to her, but he began to scream, he did not like her. And after I had put him to rest, we had to go to the Ancestors' Hall to be introduced to the ancestors. There was a big long table, and behind that, lined up against the wall, the tablets of the souls, and in a room near by a big coffin, and that was the grandfather who had died. Everyone in the family was wearing white or grey cloth, either a band round the shoes or round the head. As I said before, everything is upside down; white for mourning, they don't look at you when they respect you, and when they want to insult you they are so polite you think they like you, but they don't, they really hate you.

It was your father who would no longer kotow to the ancestors, but I did all I was asked to do by his mother. The little woman put a cushion down and asked me to kneel and to bow, and I did, and she held the incense sticks and put them in the braziers, showing me how to do it, and I did it. And I let Son of Spring do it too. I did not think it was wrong at all. But the priest said it was very wrong, it was idolatry. And when

I went to confession he said if I did not give up bowing to the ancestors he would refuse me absolution. So I told him I would stop, and I did stop. And he said my son must be brought up as a Catholic, and he must not come near any idols. And it made me very frightened, as I did not want your brother to go to hell, or to be refused at his first communion. A child's soul is so important. I hadn't thought I was doing anything wrong, kneeling and just bowing, but that is how they catch you. It's wrong to eat meat on Fridays, and it's wrong not to want babies. It's easier for the Protestants, they don't have all these things. But I suppose they will go to hell, and I've had my hell on earth, I don't want another one.

And one day I caught them at it. All the children together, and my son among them, and the old woman was teaching him to light incense sticks, to place them in the incense brazier. She was not even worried when she saw me, she only smiled and told Son of Spring to call me "Mother" in Chinese. It is their custom to greet people by calling them like that. I was supposed, every time I saw anyone, to remember who they were in relation to me, and to say Sixth Aunt or Third Sister-in-Law or Second Uncle. Of course it was too difficult for me, so after a time they asked me to call them by their names, although this was not done.

But I couldn't let my son become a pagan, so I went and took all the sticks and threw them on the floor and picked up Son of Spring and carried him into our room. And after that your father said we would go away. He wasn't doing anything anyway, just going to drink tea and to eat with a lot of officials, and not doing any work.

Oh, they tried a lot of things, saying we would return soon, and so on, and they gave me a lot of presents. But I threw them all back at them. I know they tried to poison me, otherwise my head would not have felt so terrible, and I also had diarrhoea all the time. And though the little woman pretended to cry, she did not make a lot of noise, only stood there on her tiny feet when we went away. I felt like spitting at them all. I knew they didn't like me. And your father looked awful. His face was so pale, I have never seen him like this. He looked like a dead man.

After that your brother was sent back to Belgium. He would be safer there. Because we had a terrible time getting out of Szechuan, though going down river was much quicker than climbing up the River; but the soldiers were shooting, and we had to lie flat on the deck of the boat, the bullets whizzed past, they shot at all the boats, even at night.

And the next year was 1914, and the war broke out in Belgium and my parents went to England as refugees, and my father was on the *Lusitania* and nearly drowned, eleven hours in the sea floating on a bit of wood. Your brother was at school in England four years, so he will know English, and when he comes here he will get a good job knowing English. He will soon be through his studies, and he will come here to see us. You will see your brother. Very soon. Oh, it will be wonderful to have my son with me again.

It was over. She had exhausted herself, she was calm now. The child was to hear the same story, differently told, to see it written, with a different meaning, in the many years to follow. To remember, to pursue, tenacious, until the day in 1964 when, too late, came the final absolution.

"Yes," said Third Uncle, "I do remember the day your mother came to us."

I had him pinned down at last. It had taken me four years to get Third Uncle to promise: "Tomorrow morning, at ten o'clock, I shall tell you what I remember of your parents' return."

I am nothing if not persistent; persistence is needed when one wants to bare the crippled tree, and study its mishap.

Even in 1964 veneration held us still all clutched in her thick, adhesive fingers, clogging our tongues, sticking them to our palates, but it was not such dense hierarchical reverence as before Liberation. Thank God for the Revolution of 1949, I thought, and for the idea the Communists had of making everyone write out their own lives, write the pent putrid bygones out of their system. It broke down so many inhibitions, brought to light so many closet skeletons, put to flight so many bogeys, dispelled so many myths and avoided so many nervous breakdowns. For the first time the mask of face, propriety, the haughty gentry vanity, the reticence which was not reticence at all, the whitewash, had been washed away in great pailfuls of self writings out. At last people had to face themselves as they were, not as they pretended to themselves to be.

"I shall talk to you of your parents' return in 1913. What I remember." The last three words an escape-hole: Third Uncle has a faculty for forgetting what he does not wish to remember. This, being one of the sacred rights of the individual, I would have to circumvent by questions, off-hand yet cut-crystal.

Ten o'clock next morning was grizzly wet autumn, feathery rain-mist, mist-rain, impregnating yet too fine spread for umbrella. A cocoon-wet Szechuan autumn, damp to the marrow. Only in England is there so much warmish wetness about, splendid for flowers but smothering for brains. I drank some strong Maotai wine, sixty per cent alcohol, and went to see Third Uncle, solid in resolution to find through an old world made explicit a completion of the new; through the story of a return with its ecstasy and horror, the resolution of my own return. When such as I cast out remorse, I thought ... but then I never had cast out anything. Even remorse was useful, well handled.

Third Uncle was in his rattan long chair, made for reclining, but in which he sat bolt upright upon the skin of a leopard of the Snow Mountains. And on the lacquer table were four jars of tea, all different, and four cups, to taste each tea.

"You will have to drink alone now, I can no longer drink tea, my bladder is too weak," he said.

And like a diver on a cold morning, recklessly throwing himself into icy water, he plunged.

It was because of your great-grandfather, Ancestor Tao-hung, that your father returned six months earlier than he was due. Your great-grandfather died in December 1912, and we sent a telegram to your father in Belgium.

Your parents left Europe some time in the end of January 1913, or perhaps early February, I do not know. But there was trouble in many places, the steamer went no farther than Hankow. It was June or July when they arrived in Szechuan.

I went to meet them in Chungking, desiring to look after their comforts, and also to protect them if possible; for all the roads were unsafe, and there was also a child, my mother's first grandson.

The Revolution had been made, in 1911, but in 1913 it had been defeated. Except that there was no longer a Manchu emperor, all was as before, if not worse. Money was no longer worth anything. Each city was minting coin for itself, ours in Chengtu was now of baked clay.

I knew that I must warn my brother, your father. He knew

nothing of the changes that had taken place. I went to Chung-king a few days before they were due, made arrangements to hire sedan chairs, to have a few stalwart men about for protection on the road. I also bought some things I felt my sister-in-law, your mother, might need, European things: I purchased two commodes, with new lacquered wood covers, and as the summer would be hot, the finest mosquito nets I could get. For these purchases I borrowed money from some friends of the family, for we were now very nearly ruined. Three more years, and we would be bankrupt. In 1917 our tobacco commerce, which had lasted a hundred and twenty years, closed down.

I went to the landing place to meet their junk, but they were late, having encountered a storm on the way. I posted men to await them, servants and runners, to warn me as soon as their boat was sighted. I had had a telegram from Ichang, sent through a foreign company (for our telegrams no longer functioned properly) telling of their arrival there.

On the third day of my waiting, in the afternoon they arrived. I was there to meet them nearly as soon as their freight of luggage had been taken down, and your mother, my revered sister-in-law, carrying her first-born, my mother's first grandson, was there. Already there were crowds, to see a foreigner was always unusual for us in Szechuan. It was good that I had some men to make a way for her, to push the crowd off, so many wanted to come near her, to see her clothes and how she walked. It was mere curiosity, but your mother was always very upset by it, and even now, coming off the boat, she stood on the plank, lifting her skirts because of the water purling over the plank at its edges, and she was shouting at your father. I did not understand, but I could see her face, she was angry, and your father came down and saw me, and I called to him: "Second Brother, welcome home," and he said quickly: "Third Brother, can you bring the sedan chairs closer?" (I had the sedan chairs some distance away, behind us), and so I did. And the sedan chair carriers also stared, but I gave them a look, and they turned their backs as is normal when a woman enters the chair, not to look at her. On my orders they immediately heaved the poles on their shoulders and started carrying, and so went up the steps, climbing to the city and through the gates, to the rooms I had prepared for them in the Guild House. And all the way there were crowds following. So many children kept running with the sedan chairs and shouting: "Come and see, a foreign devil woman," and a throng of idlers.

I had read a book about the habits and manners of foreigners, a book I had bought to prepare our family for your mother's arrival. I knew that foreigners are always abrupt, and one must be patient with them. I therefore curtailed the drinking of tea and sitting in the reception room, which I had decorated with flowers as I knew that European women are always given flowers, which is not our custom at all. I had given orders for baths to be ready. A servant maid had been retained by me, she would take care of the child, and another one, slightly older, to look after my sister-in-law. They were both loaned to me by a friend. I was glad to have cultivated so many friends, both military and through business relations.

"Respected sister-in-law must rest," I said, not looking at her.

Your mother went into the bedchamber to rest, and I think she was pleased, though later I was not sure. The place was clean, there were new bedcovers on the bed.

Then your father turned to me: "Third Brother, things seem very bad ... everywhere misery, confusion ... we have had a terrible journey. I knew nothing of this ..."

The time had come for me to tell your father. But it would take some days. It is not possible to say everything at once. "Second Brother, we did not wish to disturb you in your studies. Now I shall proceed to tell you everything."

We were ten days on the road, in sedan chairs, from Chungking to Chengtu. I was glad that I had a small posse of soldiers with me, and that as an officer people were afraid of me and of our firearms. Thus I was able to convey your parents and your eldest brother in safety to the family house in Chengtu. I had sent a courier ahead, to warn the family of certain manners. My respected mother pawned her last jewels to obtain some silks, some filigree silver, brocades for the room in which your mother would stay, and for a small welcome feast. We all did what we could. But it was not enough.

I was not always there, and my Second Brother was busy, and your mother was much alone. There were many of us in the house, and they were very curious to see your mother, a foreigner. Also they liked to touch the curls of your brother, and this made your mother scream and shout, and the shouting frightened some, and others went home in silence but were not pleased with your mother,

So many small things happened, all very small, but perhaps we should have studied more how to please your mother. I do not know what else we could have done. Our circumstances were straitened at the time; never were we so poor. Your mother did not know that the family jewels had been pawned in order to receive her with honour, in spite of the mourning for your great-grandfather Taohung. What more could we do? Somehow we could not please her, and we did not understand her. And one day your parents went away, taking their son, our first-born grandson, with them, and my mother, your grandmother, wept very much for she could not bear their going away, she clung to your eldest brother, to her first grandson. But they went away, and they never came back.

*

They stayed from June to October with the family in Chengtu, five months in which my mother became the person that she would remain all through her next thirty-five years in China: a dislocated, hectic, suspicious woman, doomed to misunderstanding, to fits of rages and tears, and at all times victim of situations even when self-engendered, and sometimes a willing victim because helplessness was in itself a power, a power to exert oneself in active emotion, emotion pointless but satisfying in its very impotence in the large exhibition of physical activity which she needed, which all Europeans, meat-eaters, need, which procured relief, left one spent, tired and at peace through exhaustion. It was a way of smashing what could not, would not, be held in the hand, yield, of breaking the unbreakable cage in which she felt immured and which would never give way, never open. She developed a lifelong addiction to anger, to a flow of words which like a flood submerged those within reach. She spent herself also in enormous letters, a trunk-full. And all this was a great pity, for it could have been turned to use, instead of being wasted and laying waste around her.

It is a pity that never for a moment did the Family round her guess what they were doing to her. Their non-comprehension was equal to hers, their reactions were equally blinded, and perhaps in the final count even more ferocious because they were so absolutely righteous, even their slighting sanctioned by custom, propriety, tradition, her status in the family. A collective is a cruel thing because each member reinforces the other in a course of behaviour, like a pack of hounds pursuing a deer at bay to the last; and yet, they never knew that they were hounding her. They did try their best, forgiving her much.

She rapidly went to pieces in the hot summer, before my father's eyes, and without his being able to arrest either her degradation or the processes of thought and the actions of the family which steadily drove her to frenzy, until she became fixed in her attitudes and unable ever to reason herself out of them again.

It is not big things but small things that precipitate an emotional crisis. A laugh heard behind a door and immediately misinterpreted into mockery, insult, obscenity, malice; a hot afternoon, no fans, and no chair to sit on because all the chairs are occupied by elderly ladies and the young must stand; a dish that turns one's stomach; the irritation especially of never being alone in a big family, never for a moment alone, or so it seemed to Marguerite.

"But you are alone," Yentung said to her, "you can go to your room and sit there quietly. My mother is most concerned..."

"Concerned? They wish me dead. I *know* it. Sixth Sister or Eleventh Niece comes in as soon as I am in the room, wondering why I have gone away, and asks in that terrible French they are trying to learn to please me, so they say: 'Mother is worried. Are you not well? We shall call the doctor. Please come out and talk to us. Great-Aunt will come soon and wishes to see First Grandson.' Why do they always want me to be with them? They kill me, kill me and my son."

"I have told them that sometimes you want to sit down by yourself and write letters, and they said they quite understand, but they are afraid that you might pine and be lonely, that is why they come. All you have to say is that you are quite happy and are writing a letter to your parents."

And Marguerite would flare up. "I can't lie. Why should I lie? All of you Chinese lie all the time. I told them to leave me alone, that I don't want to see their blasted faces any more. That'll teach them." And then she would hold her son in her arms and weep and weep, in a paroxysm of nerves.

There were the interminable mahjong parties, going on for six or seven days and nights without interruption. Twenty or thirty women collected together around the tables set up in every room, and the click-click-click, the eternal click and fall of the mahjong all the time, and the cries of the babies brought in by the amahs to be fed at pendulous breasts, the mother not even interrupting her game while she breast-fed her child, and then handing it back to the servant. Six, seven, eight hours they played, a lunatic passion, sometimes giving their turn to someone else to go to snatch a few hours' sleep. Most terrible of all for Marguerite, prostrating her ultimately, was the noise, the continual human noise, the voices, the laughter. She was always sure they were laughing at her. Sums changed hands, the opium pipe changed hands; although the Mother and her sons did not smoke, opium was provided for the guests. And though the Family was now penurious, yet still gentry, and had obligations, the guests were important guests, for this was Great-Grandfather's funeral, and it was obligatory to entertain him while he lay in his coffin awaiting burial with the noise of mahjong and talk, that he might know all was well.

It was discourtesy not to allow one's room to be invaded thus by the mahjong tables, not to sleep stretched out on a chair or a settee. Marguerite's room was not touched, she was the foreigner, an honoured guest, but she could not sleep. The noise, the perpetual noise, kept her awake. The talk, high pitched loud voices, for Szechuan people talk very loudly, the peasant habit of shouting from field to field even in town; the bawling of children, and especially the curiosity of the children and the small maidservants, giggling and poking their fingers through the paper of the windows to peer at her, the foreigner. It drove her mad. And then they would all touch and fondle Son of Spring, touching his curls (she wound his hair in curlers at night).

One day she put on her hat and walked out of the house, alone, in the streets. She had never been out alone, she had never been out walking; always a sedan chair, and always in company. Now she stepped out into the street, dressed in her foreign clothes, and immediately a crowd collected, augmenting and swelling with children and grown-ups who came running, running from the houses and adjacent streets, to stare at her, and pushed and jostled till she trod upon their feet; and more came, and she trod upon more feet, and became very frightened. She could neither go back nor go forward.

And as usual it was her Third Brother-in-Law who came to the rescue, pushing a way into the crowd, pushing but without violence, drawling loudly but not with anger: "Looking at what? There is nothing to look at. Have you nothing else to do?"

And still the crowd swelled, and then Yentung, her husband, was there, who said to her: "Get back to the house."

"I won't go back," she said. "I won't go back. I want to go home."

"We will talk about this in the house," he said.

And then right there in the middle of the street she broke down and started shrieking, which made all shout with laughter, especially the children. They laughed and laughed and laughed, until the tears rolled down their faces; they thought it was like a scene at the opera, something extremely comical. And Yentung took her arm and tried to push her back, but she resisted, which brought more laughter from the children; and some of the smaller ones, not understanding, began to weep too, which caused more laughter all round.

Third Brother, always resourceful, called a sedan chair, and now he shoved some people out of the way, but still not too roughly, not wanting to cause a riot. "Get away, get away, the lady is ill."

Finally they had Marguerite in the sedan chair, and arrived back in the middle of the mahjong players, who did not interrupt their game. And one or two of the women, throwing their dice, said rudely: "What has happened to the foreigner?"

The Mother was angry, all this was such bad behaviour, but she did not show it. She left the game for a moment to go into the room where Marguerite was lying on the bed, her tears subsiding, but now seized by a trembling fit and yet wanting to laugh wildly, hysterically.

"What has happened?" said the Mother. "Why did our Daughter go away? Why does she not wish to sit by us and learn the game, as we asked her to?"

"She is not well," said Yentung. "She begs you to forgive her, she was going out to find a doctor, the French doctor," he hastened to add. At that time there was in Chengtu a French doctor near the Roman Catholic church where Marguerite went to Mass and to confession.

The Mother's face showed distaste. "But that is a man doctor," she said, "how could she go to a man doctor *alone*? If she wishes we will send for him to come to the house and see her."

"I will arrange it, Mother," replied Yentung.

But at that moment Marguerite sat up and said, loudly and

distinctly, to the Mother: "Get out of my room," and then she repeated it in Chinese, with a bad accent but comprehensible. "Get out, get out."

The Mother turned slowly, walked out, and went back to her game, face calm as if nothing had happened. Elder Brother, who had been respectfully standing by the door, but not looking inside out of respect to Marguerite, followed his mother, and Yentung remained with his wife.

Marguerite was now seized with vomiting. She thought, this is effective, I will vomit. And she did. And now the idea struck her: There is something wrong with me. They are trying to poison me, they are trying to get rid of me. And the idea never left her mind again.

Years later she told her children: "They gave me something to drive me mad, and as they could not drive me mad, they tried to poison me."

And one day her daughter asked her: "What poison did they use?" But even she, in all the scepticism bred of this strange repulsion between mother and child, was impressed, and for many years believed that an attempt had been made by the Family to poison her mother.

Yentung could not do anything. She repeated day after day: "I want to go away, they are trying to poison me." She would not let her son play with the other children. And he, being a mimic like all children, soon took up the hatred which simmered in the air of the close room. "Beat you, beat you," he shouted to his grandmother when she came near him.

And all this the older woman pretended not to notice. But the Elders knew, and were angry.

Thus both sides froze in their misunderstanding, their mutual dislike.

And now the Family left her alone, retired and waited in their rooms, and forbade the children to go near her. And they hired another servant, who had been with foreign missionaries, to cook for her. And Marguerite got autumn diarrhoea, and so did her son, and she was more convinced than ever that she was being poisoned.

Outside the doors of the Family in the city of Chengtu, in all China, there were disturbances, civil war, the disintegration of the old Empire and the rise of a new order through much suffering and pain and horror. Yentung was caught in the turmoil, as was every Chinese in China. But it was not a thing he could discuss with Marguerite. He could never talk of his work, his obligations to the Family, his responsibility, to her. For her, he was her husband, with obligations to her alone. And in front of her, the enormous convulsions which shook his country, the millions dead, dying and to die before chaos could become order, seemed insignificant compared to the convulsions which agitated Marguerite . . .

They went away. At the last his mother broke down, clung to his sleeve, clung to her daughter-in-law, weeping. How had they offended? What must she do so that they would stay? But the agony was a whisper, and Marguerite Denis was a European, and only the imperious gesture, the all-too-obvious victory, the mental obliteration of the Family, the Mother, would do to confirm that Yentung was hers, as she brushed aside the old woman's hand, picked up her son and, followed by her husband, entered the sedan chair.

NINETEEN

CHOU YENTUNG wrote in April 1955:

This morning as I was having breakfast, Hsueh Mah my servant hobbled into the room on her bound feet (one of them gives her pain when autumn comes), bringing the two-pint bottle of milk the government allots me free of charge because of my age and health, and a letter. I recognize the angular, sloping hand running diagonally down the envelope at the same slant as upon the foolscap; Marguerite always put the paper sideways when she wrote.

"Ah," says Hsueh Mah, "it is a letter from the Venerable Lady to the Old Gentleman. Oh, that it may bring us news of her speedy return!"

The fiction that my wife will return is kept up by Hsueh Mah and by myself, she to me, I for her. We both know that she will not come back, but it is kinder for both of us to pretend she is merely having a holiday abroad. Sometimes we both half believe it . . .

I do not open the letter, though Hsueh Mah hovers, skipping on her good foot, gingerly putting the other one down on its single toe. It is nearly six months since I have had a letter. She is in Europe, the stamp says *Italia*. I place the envelope in front of my morning bowl of boiled millet. I spoon the millet, and my mind cries: Oh, come back, come back, Marguerite. I am so alone, so alone ...

But the moment passes with strong breath, for I remember to breathe in deeply, to stop myself from self-pity.

I take the letter, unopened, to the office with me. There, I cannot break down.

Marguerite has always written very long letters. Nearly every day she would write one, all through our years together. The way I remember her is sitting at a table running her pen, body projected into the slanting, sloping line upon the paper. She found letter paper too small, I supplied her with large foolscap sheets from the railway administration office; a small theft, of course, but otherwise no paper was to be had, and she chafed and paced without this cathartic. With paper she would be absorbed for some hours, silent. She wrote and she wrote, and in the evening: "Yentung, I need more paper tomorrow." Somewhere her letters must be kept, stored by her parents to whom they were addressed.

My friend Poh Hungwen is already at the office. Poh and I are in the same Department of Engineering. He was in Paris when I was in Brussels, he came to see us there twice, after our marriage. He stands in the middle of the room, warming his hands over a glass of tea, explaining to Comrade Lu how enlightened he feels now that he has read Marx. He expounds to Lu as if Lu, the seasoned Communist, knew nothing of Marx, and Lu nods, listens, never restless or impatient, and then he says to Poh:

"Comrade Poh, it is indeed a pleasure to hear you talk. How devoted you are to learning. I hope you continue in this excellent way. We must all learn more and more, it is indeed good to find you so enthusiastic now." The slight emphasis on the "now" does not escape me, even if it escapes Poh.

Poh beams, he thinks he has made a good impression upon Fathead Lu, as he calls Lu when we are alone together. It is not my feeling that Lu is a fathead, but I never argue with Poh. Poh has always done well for himself, he is a good talker.

I sit, letter in hand, at my table lengthened with blueprints. Comrade Lu sees the letter in my hand, and looks away. Then he leaves the room.

Dear Yentung,

I want to tell you that *that woman* came to see us yesterday. Arrogant as ever, with her daughter who has tuberculosis and whom she promenades all round the world, a chit of fifteen who cannot open her mouth. Came with some sweaters and things for us. Of course, I did not speak to her. I do not change my mind so easily. Afterwards we threw all the things in the fire ... we don't want her things full of germs ... that woman is like her brother, heartless ... I cleaned the room after she had gone.

Marguerite is in good health. Such verve in hate, such pursuit of resentment, can only point to one thing: she feels well. And I am glad, for I still worry about her wellbeing. In her last letter she said she would not live long, and that was six months ago. This one does not contain a word about dying. She will outlive me, and I am glad. I hope she will not be alone, as I am. She has our Second Daughter with her, and a grandchild. On and on goes the letter, all about the grand-daughter. "We find it difficult to get peas, but the doctor says the child must have peas, otherwise she may become constipated ..." Tireless as always, all trivia recorded. I am glad.

"What a nice stamp," says Poh. He is on his morning round, self-appointed cheery fellow, going to all in the Department, saying a word or two. He calls this: Preserving good relationship and a good style of work with fellow workers. "May I have it? Italy? Your wife is lucky, enjoying herself in Italy." Poh's French wife died many years ago, he then married a Chinese woman by whom he has several children. I have never seen her, but I understand she is capable and he is afraid of her.

Comrade Lu comes in again with a glass of hot green tea, the leaves uncurling, unfolding, like green flowers, at the bottom. First-class tea. He tells me that his cousin from Hang-chow has just brought some fresh Dragon's Well tea straight from the Co-operative there. Would I try a little? "You look tired, Comrade Chou. Would you perhaps like the morning off, to rest? I shall order the car to take you home."

I refuse. I have always refused a car, although my age and my standing as Consulting Engineer entitle me to a car. Never have I had a car in my life. I am not going to start using precious petrol now, in my old age. Our country is too short of petrol to waste it on me.

"I am well, it is nothing," I reply, a little shortly.

Lu goes out again, to cancel the car, meek as a son, and again my heart is wrung by something like affection. I give the stamp to Poh. I put the letter back in my pocket and my hands to the blueprints, while my mind seeps, returns to the time, the misordered time when Marguerite conceived this resentment for our First Daughter, whom she now calls *that woman*; the dreadful time when our son, Sea Orchid, died because he was Eurasian.

*

The story of Sea Orchid was embedded in the silken evenings of autumn in Peking, as an embroidered flower is embedded in smooth shine. Evening time, after the tiger heat of summer, before the frost dwindled the time of open windows; the time round the new lamp, because the old one had broken moving from one place to another. This new lamp was brass and did not smell like the old one, though sometimes the wick went sprouting a long long flame like hair, like Mama's hair when she was young, hair which licked and blackened the glass funnel in sudden fury, and Mama screamed, turned down the wick, and sometimes the lamp went out. Evening went softly padding by, back and forth, with a swish of silk, watching from outside the window, and sometimes snub-pawing into the house like a cat wanting attention.

Sea Orchid, Second Son, was born on the railway, The Lunghai railway, in a new station because the train was just going through. It was in the yellow plains of Honan; not far from it, the Yellow River had burst its dykes and gone flooding once again, and there were many displaced peasants and also bandits and soldiers, the latter more than the former and more to be feared. The little station was safe, however. There the Big Engineer, whose name was spoken of with indrawn breath and a small pause of respect because he was a Belgian and had a large salary, stayed in a new brick house constructed specially for him on a small hill. Mama and Papa lived in a small Chinese house of earth walls on the other side of the railway, about two miles away from the hill, in the town. On the same hill was the doctor's house, and the houses of the assistant engineer, the accountant, and two Belgian technicians. The doctor was French, and looked after the Belgian staff and the French and also the rest of the railway personnel. Altogether there were six families of Belgians in this station, the rest were Chinese. Mama and Papa were half and half, and so was another family, but that other family was the other way, Belgian father, Chinese mother.

Sea Orchid was born, and when he was born the doctor was away on the railway line, so that Sea Orchid was born with a Chinese midwife to help, and Mama was angry with the doctor, which he did not seem to mind. However, the doctor's wife minded; she was French, and Mama did not get on well with her. She was only a butcher's daughter, said Mama, but she gave herself airs. Mama always preferred Dutch and Flemish and Germans, she said the French were not trustworthy. Mama never went up the hill either to see the pure-blood Belgian families. "They think they are gods."

There is a photograph, mauved by the years, showing Mama in a white blouse and black skirt on one side of a table, Papa with boots on (he had to wear boots, rushing up and down the line, because of the snakes, the mosquitoes and the mud, and always pushing on with the railway), and Sea Orchid, a fat baby, bundled in the Chinese way in a flowered blanket, is in Mama's arms.

That was one thing about Mama: she liked to dress her children in Chinese clothes when they were small, and she herself, in winter, wore Chinese clothes and always wore Chinese soft slippers on her feet.

When Sea Orchid was born Mama was very happy; her first-born, Son of Spring, was at that time in England with his grandfather and grandmother, for there was war in Europe, and it had come so quickly that many Belgians had not returned to their homes. The work on the railway was going very slowly, because of the war and no money. Mama loved Sea Orchid, he was the most beautiful child in the world, and she named him Gabriel, Messenger from Heaven. He was baptized by the priest, who also went up and down the already built section of the line to celebrate mass for the Catholics.

One evening Gabriel Sea Orchid, who had been gurgling all day, dribbled a little milk, and Mama noticed that one side of his face seemed to pucker, pulling up, then letting go of the rounded cheek, the eye closing in a terrifying wink. He had been teething, had had a little fever for a few days. She had taken him to the doctor two days before at his morning clinic, which was for Chinese and people like herself, married to Chinese. The Europeans did not come to the clinic; the doctor stayed in a house on the hill with them, they could see him at any time.

Half an hour after that first tic, Sea Orchid had a convulsion, twisting his body, and then he started to wail. Then he had another convulsion, his body arching backwards.

Papa was not at home, he was out on the railway with the workmen, out at another station, a very small one where there had been soldiers going through and they had taken the railway ties away, and Papa had to inspect the damage and try to put new ones back.

Mama did not know what to do. She walked up and down, up and down the beaten earth floor of the small mud house, singing to Sea Orchid, and her servant, the cook's wife, looked at Sea Orchid's face, and started an "Aiyah, Taitai, the little lord is sick . . ."

At the third convulsion Mama wrapped Sea Orchid in his blanket, and called the cook to go with her, and both walked through the night across the sleeping town, up the hill, to the house of the doctor across the railway line.

There were the usual scavenger dogs about, looking for food. They ran barking after Mama's black skirt, and the cook who carried a lantern grew terrified and fell back, screaming with fear because of the dog pack at his heels, so Mama went on alone, picking up stones to throw at the dogs.

The doctor's cottage was dark, the garden gate locked, but she knocked, and slowly the doorman yawned it open, seeing this European woman with a child in her arms. The house door was locked. "Open, open, doctor, open!" she shouted, knocking at the door with the flat palm of her hand. The doctor's Alsatian, which was let off at night, was barking, and Sea Orchid had another fit, she could feel his spine bending in her arms.

"Who is it?" A window opened upstairs. It was the doctor's wife, Madame herself disturbed from sleep.

"It is I, Madame Chou," replied Mama. "My child is sick."

"Oh, it is you? What an idea to come at this time. The doctor does not see patients at this hour. Come to the clinic tomorrow, Madame."

"But my child is dying, he has convulsions. Madame, for the love of God, let me see the doctor."

"Certainly not, Madame. Don't shout like that, it is ridiculous. There is nothing wrong with your child, only teething. The doctor cannot see you."

"My baby is dying, my baby is dying," screamed Mama, striking the door more violently, hurling her weight against it.

"Get out, you and your filthy halfcaste brat, get out of my house," shouted the French woman upstairs. Then Mama heard a man's voice, and again the woman's: "I forbid you to go. Do you hear, Pierre? I forbid it. I will not have you kill yourself for the sake of a halfcaste throwdown."

"Open open open open," Mama went on.

The woman shouted words, Mama did not hear them, though the servants did, and later came to tell Papa, many days later. Mama hurled herself like a butting ram against the door, one two three bang, one two three bang. She might have kept on like that all night, all the time her mouth was shouting, "Open open open, for the love of God," for by now she was a little mad, when the door opened.

It was the French woman, in her nightgown, mouth froth-flecked. For what Mama did not know was that Madame the Doctor's wife was also mad; she had crises of nerves, which the doctor treated, and she used to beat her husband, she was a very strong woman. She was much more nerve-wracked than Mama was at the time. A good many European women do get nervous breakdowns in China, and the Lunghai railway line was not exactly restful. Behind his wife stood the doctor, expostulating: "Voyons, voyons, Amélie my dear ..." But the woman was big and strong. Mama thrust an arm through the open door to reach the doctor, the woman pushed her back, pushed her and threw some pills on the ground. "There, take that, take that, and don't come back." The door shut.

Mama went, walking back across the railway lines to the town. The dog pack barked and snapped at her heels, one snapped a piece off her skirt. The next morning Sea Orchid was dead.

Mama went drunk, drinking brandy, drinking Chinese wine, which she bought in the shops of the town, and she slapped the cook and the cook's wife, but they knew she was a little off her mind and stayed on and looked after her. She stayed drunk on whatever alcohol she could get for some weeks.

Papa returned, and Sea Orchid was buried, in a coffin of white wood. The servants looked after everything, they fed and washed Mama when Papa was working. The doctor did not appear, nor did anyone else from the hill.

Afterwards, the Chief Engineer and his wife told Papa they were desolated, they knew nothing, absolutely nothing about it. No one had told them anything.

And then Papa and Mama's First Daughter was born.

She was, I am told, a long thin child who came screaming her lungs out, and Mama refused to look at her. "Take that halfcaste brat away. It is not my child."

Mama refused to look at her daughter for a whole week, and the baby became more and more yellow, partly from the usual baby's jaundice, partly from hunger, for she was fed with rice-water by the cook's wife, and a little condensed milk, diluted. And she refused to die, and yelled all the time.

"Die, die!" shouted Mama, who kept on drinking and calling for Sea Orchid.

On the eighth day Papa slapped Mama hard, hit her and put the child in her arms. "Are you going to feed her or not? She is your child."

The priest came to baptize the baby, and she was given a long string of names, all the names of the Denis family, and her grandmother Matilda Rosalie Leenders' name as well.

But Papa called her Meme, Little Sister, from the very beginning, for it was on the Harvest Festival day that she was born. Papa had a photograph taken, in which he held his daughter in his arms, bundled in the flowered blanket which had been Sea Orchid's blanket.

And then Mama recovered after the slapping, though she never forgave it, and she was a good mother, and often told this story, at evening time, round the lamp. In the silken evenings round the lamp, she told her daughter how much she had disliked her birth, and how she had been slapped for it. "That was the first and the last time your father dared to hit me, and it was because of you."

But Mama never really forgave her daughter for having taken Sea Orchid's place. She tried hard to love her, and she did her best. But no one can escape the unconscious, unexplained resentment for which only circumstance is responsible.

A year later another child was born, then another, and another. One in one station, one in another, all along the railways which Papa was helping to build, Mama had her children. Only the last was born in a big city.

And all along the railways Mama wrote, of the bandits, of the warlords, of the soldiers, of running away at night from raids, of the death of her children; for, out of five born on the railway, only two girls survived.

In November 1964 Joseph Hers, the man who in 1913 first knew my father when he applied for a job with the Belgian Society for the Construction of Railways in China, wrote to me:

I scratch my head, trying to find out what I can tell you about that period ... all I can tell you is that for the Belgian wives of the Chinese personnel, their hearts must have been full of bitterness, but WE NEVER WENT OUT OF OUR WAY TO DO ANYTHING ABOUT IT.

Old man, do not worry and do not regret. For it is too late. And do not think that I, my mother's First Daughter, whom she hated, shall now hate you for telling me this, so late, too late. For you too are a victim, a victim of the old piracies, just as she was a victim of a history she never made. Do not worry, old man, and rest in peace, absolved. For although the tree was crippled, it has gone on living, and who knows but that its fruit shall be sweeter and better than that of any other?

TWENTY

"WHAT is it like," asked Li Chiehjen the writer, "to run after one's own childhood? I also have wanted to do it. We all do. But the Revolution of 1911 captured me, and I found myself unable to go forward or back from that event."

I felt no basking satisfaction, nudging the child I was. Only a need to set it down, because if for Li Chiehjen the 1911 Revolution had been so all-compelling that his creative work had become centred round it, for me a far more drawn-out process, involving a large number of disparate experiences, had left me uncentred, and conditioned my writing. He belonged to only one culture, had moved with it, was carried by it, and never overleapt it. Few writers outreach the bonds of their own climate. But I had been tossed about by contradictoriness since my birth. And in 1960 his experiences and mine met, joined by circumstance to form part of the same story. In all his books Li Chiehjen had written of Szechuan, the Szechuan of 1911 and after, of the secret societies and their role in the Revolution, and later he had written of the warlords. He had depicted a whole era; this era was part of my early years, had moulded the life of my generation.

The warlords of China: they lasted from 1916, when Yuan Shihkai died of apoplexy, until 1937, when the Sino-Japanese War began. Today in many parts of the world the same historical paradoxes which gave birth to the warlords of China are reproduced in other countries, scarcely disguised under other names, juntas, military governments, Young Turks, officer cliques; from Latin America to South Vietnam they breed, and like weeds grow long, then fester, sustained by the same causes which gave rise to them in China of yesterday.

So often today, in 1964, reading of Brazil, or of South Vietnam, thinking of India in a not too distant future, of Indonesia perhaps tomorrow, I have been brought back by similarity to China's warlord decades: the rule of the feudal robber baron, whatever verbal accoutrement he may wear, of the military dictator, in whatever uniform paid by a foreign power he may find himself. For armed power dominates, and the battle of the peoples for the right to their own destiny is a dual one, against foreign exploitation, but also against their own corrupt and repressive systems.

Yuan Shihkai was the first of China's warlords; it was he who set in movement the subsequent chaos in China. In 1917, after the death of Yuan, one of his military commanders, Chang Hsun, had attempted to restore the Manchu ex-Emperor, Puyi, who had ascended the Dragon Throne when three years old, in 1908, and abdicated in 1911 when he was six. This move to restoration of Empire was supported by Kang Yuwei, the one-time Reformist, one-time rebel with a price on his head. Poor Kang Yuwei, victim of his own stead-fastness, who had not moved with the times, and still clung to the illusion of reform through orderly, superior intellec-tuals like himself, when it was already too late, far too late, and when Destiny, or History, or whatever the unnameable law which governs mankind's fate, like the Great River at floodtime, went rolling forwards, little heeding the admoni-tions of superior intellects like his, carrying the mantide of China forward into a future all unknown; and all the strata-gems of strong men, and the calculations of banking consor-tiums, were to be swept away, finally, in this elemental and irresistible process.

Chang Hsun and Kang Yuwei, the one an illiterate warlord, the other a great scholar, futile ghosts of a past that would not return, had both kept their queues, symbol of their loyalty to the Manchu dynasty. This extraordinary alliance made Puyi return on the throne for two weeks, and the financial backing of this restoration was Japanese. And then the pan-tomime was over. Puyi was kept in cold storage by Japan for fifteen years, to be used later as their puppet when the imperial troops of Nippon took Manchuria in 1932. In Peking today Puyi, ex-Emperor, now a happily married citizen, author, botanist by hobby, and Keeper of Archives, recently elected member of the Peoples' Congress, is a busy and useful man in charge of collecting the memoirs and documents of his own period, having himself written his own memoirs, made his penance, and re-entered the destiny of his own people.

In the ten years between 1917 and 1927, when Chiang Kai-shek came to power, more than fifteen hundred military chieftains, warlords big and small, devastated the land. A few became powerful, having beaten in battle or bought over at conciliation banquets their adversaries, and for a time they reigned, over two, or four, or six provinces; each in turn shot to prominence as the future "strong man" in the Press of whichever western country was paying and supplying him with the extra ammunition and guns left over from the First World War of Europe. And this provided a bewildering kaleidoscope of scavenger-dog fights between military adventurers whose huge armies grew or vanished overnight.

Today no one of the younger generation in China remembers their names; only old men, busily writing their memoirs for the historians.

A few of these warlords are still alive. Some are in Peking, having turned over and "chosen righteousness" in good time, made their penance, sometimes served jail sentences, and been pardoned. In the National Congress of 1964 sixteen of these are members of the Consultative Assembly, or even occupy posts of importance in the government in a new channelled usefulness. Others are in Hongkong, in America, or in Formosa; but not even the Central Intelligence Agency of the United States can use them, they have so flagrantly outlived themselves. They await death, but the door of China is always open to them, should they want to return to lay their exile-weary bones in the land of their ancestors . . .

Such people as myself, the generation between forty and fifty years old, remember the warlords, and say:

I remember . . . when Yen Hsishan was the strong man of Shansi, and the English and the Americans and the Japanese were giving him guns and trucks and money . . . He was the wiliest and the most long-lived of them all, he made calamity money out of U.N.N.R.A. food for refugees in 1946 and 1947, before he left for Formosa . . .

Wu Peifu, now he was rather a grand one . . . He nearly succeeded in taking over the north; he sat astraddle the Peking–Hankow railway, and controlled all the rolling stock. He shot a lot of workers in a railway strike on the Peking–Hankow railway, the first big railway workers' strike, in 1923; and he came a cropper because the warlord Chang Tsolin, who was paid by the Japanese, took Peking and beat him. But he never collaborated with the Japanese, though he lived in Peking when they occupied it ...

Chang Tsolin ... lord of Manchuria, puppet of the Japanese, until 1928 when the Japanese made a deal with Chiang Kaishek and then they had to get rid of their erstwhile strong puppet Chang Tsolin, and they put a bomb under his train and blasted him to heaven ... for such is the fate of unwanted puppets, whether they are Chang Tsolin yesterday or Ngo Din Diem today ...

Tuan Chijui ... for him too Peking bedecked herself in triumphal parades and arches of paper flowers, and for a time he too got a lot of money from everyone ... where is he now? No one can remember how he died. For a time he had the support of some Reformist intellectuals, who believed that he could institute moderate democracy ... He received two billion dollars from the Japanese to agree to their demands, and he sold a lot of China to them ... and killed a lot of students and peasants ...

Feng Yuhsiang, the Christian general, at one time military commander and warlord of Honan, who commanded a stretch of the railways and moved his troops on them, east and west, south and north. He was the warlord who came to dinner with my father and mother and prayed before eating, and my mother was so excited she gave him macaroni instead of Chinese noodles ... He was the best of a bad lot, a man of some honesty, a good commander to his soldiers, but personal ambition made him short-sighted and he fell.

Sun Chuanfang, most powerful Overlord of them all, absolute ruler of five provinces at one time, whom I remember only because his daughter, in the last years of my own husband's life, tried to supersede me and to become his wife in 1946. Sun Chuanfang killed thousands of people, his soldiers went about cutting off heads as easily as mowing grass; anyone who wore something red, or carried a book, or even had a kerchief with some red colour, was killed on the spot by his men, decapitated or shot or hacked to pieces. He was the most deliberately cruel of them all ...

Then there was Chang's Tsungchang, the "three don't knows" warlord, who did not know how many soldiers, how many

wives, or how much money he had. There were Feng Kuo-
chang, and Tsao Kun, Hsing Kehwa, Teng Hsihou, Liu Hsiang
and Liu Wenhui, the two latter nephew and uncle, fighting
each other in Szechuan for many years.

So many names, so many army cliques: the Chihli clique
and the Anhwei clique, the Paoting faction and the Tientsin
faction, the Kiangsi warlords and the Chekiang warlords ...
Province against province, and within each province smaller
warlords fighting each other, district by district; the railways
all divided up, each warlord occupying a stretch, grabbing
rolling stock, taxing the peasants, kidnapping and press-
ganging men, confiscating food and fodder. And behind each
warlord and his clique, his guns and his half-starved armies,
a foreign power subsidizing, pressuring, instigating; Japan and
England, America and France, keeping the mêlée going, all
fighting each other and only united in one thing: suppressing
the nationalist movement, suppressing the unsuppressable Revolution which once again was beginning, killing and killing
revolutionaries and true nationalists; and thus making more
sure of the final apocalypse. The blood of the martyrs is the
seed of the Church.

For, as in Europe the roots of World War Two were
planted in World War One, so the Revolution, defeated in
1913, began again to grow. And, as the Americans in South
Vietnam with indiscriminate slaughter have succeeded in making Communism appear to the people the only salvation, so
the destructive chaos, abetted by the Powers, nurtured the
Communist Revolution of China and made sure of its spread.

Strange are the ways of history, where no single thing
abides, but all things flow into each other, fragment to fragment clinging, growing new wholeness. To understand any
event, in any country, one must go back three generations.
A century ago sprouted the seed, root of today's tree, whose
branches cast their spreading shade over our heads, whose
leaves may fall in a storm only to be replaced by a myriad
other leaves.

*Extract from the memoirs of Joseph Hers, Agent for the
Society for the Construction of Railways in China*

It was in 1919 that I stood on the main road at Loyang,
together with George Morrison of the London *Times*. We had
not seen each other since before the War, and how much
blood had been spilt since then! Morrison was as sprightly

as ever, scarcely changed. He was on his accustomed beat again, China, and he spoke of going up to Shensi province where he wanted to interview Feng Yuhsiang, at that moment gathering his forces there.

In front of us passed an endless flood of refugees, men, women, children, some with hand-carts which they pulled themselves, others with a mule or a donkey, probably taken by force from the Chinese peasants; these refugees were White Russians, fleeing across Siberia into China after the Bolshevik Revolution of 1917. Manchuria was full of them. They fought to get on whatever train would run, heading for Shanghai, Tientsin, Peking.

George Morrison and I watched, and four hours later they were still pouring across. He said: "This is the end of an era . . . for us."

We were back in China, after a messy four years of killing each other in Europe, and we had to hurry. For us, the Belgians, the most important thing was to keep our hand in, not to let the Japanese or the Americans take away our railways and our interests. My mission was to report on conditions, to try to maintain Belgian influence and interests: all our work of the previous decades could not be wasted by a lack of effort now.

The French and the British have suffered greatly, and their influence is on the wane in the Far East. The balance of power has changed. England is beset by trouble at home, and is losing her supremacy. For all of us a spectre haunts the horizon, the rise of Communism in Russia. The Germans have been knocked out of China by war, the Russians have gone out of China by their Revolution. But on the horizon of the Pacific the two new powers that have emerged, America and Japan, are causing us anxiety.

Where our railways are concerned, it is at the moment Japan we fear, more than America. And the same preoccupation inhabits the mind of George Morrison. The British have suffered heavily. Their far-flung Empire will now prove a burden, they lack manpower to keep it, they will not be able to launch into acquisition of new territory for some decades.

"Just imagine," said Morrison to me after dinner, "supposing one day China were to become Communist?"

We both laughed heartily at this preposterous idea. We know the Chinese people, they will never be Communists, although the Bolshevik idea has done its work among a section of the returned students and the workers recruited during the war to work in the factories of Europe; Chinese workmen have been digging trenches, manning the public utilities, students have been in the factories, and have become infected with Communism. But the whole of Chinese culture, the family tradition, is against their turning to this creed.

After dinner Morrison told me he might have misjudged Sun Yatsen; there was good in the man. England might be more favourably disposed towards Sun, if he could provide a moderate alternative to anarchy. Morrison intended to do a walkabout of several hundred miles, going around China, feeling the situation.

Meanwhile the chaos here is indescribable. To control the provinces Yuan Shihkai before his death had appointed *tuchuns*, or military commanders, in each province, with both civil and military power, selecting trusted officers, his erstwhile students, for these posts. But when he tried to become Emperor they turned hostile. The first province openly to go against him was Yunnan, which proclaimed its independence on Christmas Day of 1915. The Yunnan soldiers were without food or money, but the French sold them some guns and they marched into Szechuan, where Yuan had his most trusted commander, Chen Huan. However, Chen also turned against Yuan, and proclaimed Szechuan's independence. It is said that when Yuan received the news he had a stroke, from which he died three weeks later.

Before the death of Yuan Shihkai, Japan had launched her offiensive Twenty-One Demands upon China, while Europe was busy in her slaughter; she seized her only chance to control China, and thus to be a World Power. It was a maladroit attempt, fortunately for us, otherwise the return of the West to the Far East markets might have been very difficult. As it is, Japan has taken Shantung province from the Germans, and established herself there. During the war Japan has very much expanded her industries, consolidated her possession of Korea, extended her influence in Manchuria, and is enjoying a business boom, since her textiles and goods are now in demand in the East. But the resentment aroused in China by Japan's action is enormous. The most widespread and organized demonstrations yet seen by the populace against Japan are taking place, including boycott of their goods. The students are demonstrating against the Peace Conference at Versailles, where Japan has been confirmed in her claims to

Shantung. It is imperative that we should profit from Japan's unpopularity to represent ourselves once again as China's best friends, and thus secure our aims and interests in railways and mines.

Unfortunately the ire of the Chinese is not only directed against Japan; it is also against the West, and chiefly America and England for their treachery at the Peace Conference of Versailles. The newspapers report that both these Powers, in 1917, secretly agreed to recognize Japan's special rights in China, because they want to use Japan as a counter-weight to Bolshevism in Asia.

Manoeuvring Japan against Russia is not new; it has been practised by England for some decades, it has led to the tacit as well as overt Anglo-Japanese alliance of the past, giving Japan a free hand in Manchuria against Tsarist Russia, and now an even freer hand against Bolshevik Russia as well. No better battlefield for working out these grand games of politics can be found than the wide helplessness of that weak colossus, China.

Our Peking–Hankow railway, contracted for in 1898, constructed by us and terminated in 1905, was bought back by China in 1908. The line is still dependent upon us and the French for technical advice and personnel, for supplies and deliveries of all sorts.

Our Lunghai railway line: a portion of it, called the Pienlo, 185 kilometres long, was contracted for by our Company in 1903 and ended in 1909. In 1905–7 a loan of 41 million francs (gold) was contracted for the building of this railway.

In 1912, after the Republic was proclaimed, our Company negotiated and obtained from the government of Yuan Shih-kai the prolongations, to the east and to the west, of this line, which were to form the Lunghai railway as originally blue-printed, extending from Lanchow, the capital of Kansu province, to the sea, near the port of Haichow. Thus the Pienlo is really a mid-section of 185 kilometres of a much longer, 1,800-kilometre, line. A £10 million sterling loan at five per cent, which would include reimbursement, to begin with, of the loan of 41 million francs, was necessary for this project. In 1913 a new loan for the Lunghai railway was floated in Belgium and France. The work started immediately, but the war of 1914 interrupted much of its momentum.

Now, in 1919, due to the needs of reconstruction in our

own countries, French and Belgian capital cannot be exported. This difficulty must be surmounted in other ways, and approaches by a Dutch syndicate have been made to us. It is, however, necessary to study on the spot the possibilities of development.

The railway line from Sian in Shensi province to Chengtu in Szechuan province, which we and the French also contracted for with Yuan Shihkai in 1913, cannot be undertaken at the present moment due to the situation in Szechuan. I wonder whether Morrison's trip to Sian, ostensibly to call on the local warlord there, has anything to do with this projected railway? Certainly if he can obtain for England at some future date the possibility of cutting us out in a railway deal in this all important hinterland, he will not hesitate.

Meanwhile this year the construction of the Lunghai continues: 551 kilometres will be in operation by December, and the profits, so far as I can make out, will surpass the sum necessary for the servicing of all anterior loans.

Though new financial arrangements will have to be concluded, we are distinctly hopeful, in spite of the situation. At the moment our Lunghai and Peking–Hankow railway lines cross the territories of several warlords, and the former will also advance into Japanese-occupied Shantung. Delicate negotiations will have to be undertaken if the project is to be carried to an end. It seems that a reorganization of the Banking Consortium, which had worked so well in the period of 1911 to 1914 before the War, might be attempted at some future date. Our Society forms part, ever since its inception, of the Belgian group which had a share in the Consortium, although not nominally a member.

TWENTY-ONE

MARGUERITE DENIS lay in the swaying darkness, hearing the hacking striking flat regular geegalup, geegalup, geegalup, tatarap, tatarap, of the moving train, letting the regularity take her up into a firmness, an affirmation of her will to leave, to go away. She would do it as soon as they reached Peking. She had had enough, enough, enough. As long as the train moved she felt carried by her resolution, pistoning her forward, but when the pulsing motion and its sound faltered, slowed, when the train came to a standstill at a station, and the compartment, coffin-still, immured the four of them in a would-be sleep, while outside voices and hasty cloth-shoed steps, the cries of beggars and sometimes a quarrel, only increased her sensation of undersea immobility, and lights filtered greenly through the dirty green cloth curtain in front of the train window: when happened thus a stop in moving time, then also her will faltered, seeming to turn back into her, weight in her breast, clamp of her limbs to the bunk, paralysis manacling her to this country she hated, to the people she hated, manacled by her husband and her children, aliens, aliens to her, in this alien country where she had suffered so much.

"I suffer, I suffer!" she had screamed so often to Yentung, her husband. Along the Lunghai line, station after station had heard her scream.

Yentung stared at her with the middle-distance fixity of eye she hated, at her and also through her to a point just beyond her right shoulder, so that sometimes when he looked at her she turned her head nervously, looking over her shoulder at what he was staring at.

"I do what I can," he replied. "I do all I can."

"I was a fool, a fool to marry you ... I thought you were a prince, you said China was so beautiful, so wonderful ... palaces and pagodas and people in silk and embroidered clothes, and I believed you ... and look at me now. Look at me."

She had run her hands through her hair, thinning, white-streaked, disaggregating dandruff. Often thus she had paced to a mirror, to look with fierce flecked eyes at face, figure, gaunt yet slack-breasted in the cotton blouse, with the strong red V of the neck where the sun had burnt her skin.

"Seven children, seven children, and look at me now. And I was so beautiful once, so beautiful ..."

Now, lying in the dark train lurching across the endless plains of North China, she felt the familiar bitterness well up, rhythmic as the train motion, propelled in regular gusts of striking iron, acid-like regurgitated bile lapping plop plop round her heart.

"A wasted life, varicose veins down both legs, my stomach all wrinkled and streaked folds, my hair, my teeth – I lost so many teeth, only the front ones are still good. Look at me. Who would want me now? Even he does not want me. He is always tired, always tired, with the railways and the workers' strikes, and the warlords and this one great hell of a country with these oceans of beggars in it. All of them rags and filth and beggars, saying nothing, looking at me, crowding in the streets and laughing and shouting: "Foreigner! Devil from over the ocean!" I want to go back, I want to go back. When we get to Peking I will pack and go. I will take Tiza and go."

She heaved on to her side, irritated by the short sheet that could not cover her entirely; a mosquito had bitten the uncovered sole of her right foot, it was the worst place to be bitten because scratching gave no relief. Tiza and Rosalie were sleeping, one at each end of the lower bunk, her husband on one of the top bunks. She looked where, love piercing the darkness and delineating the form of the little girl upon her pillow, Tiza lay, calm, gentle, so pretty. "That one I will take with me," she thought. "The other can stay with her father, she will be all right." The other was tough and strong, but Tiza was delicate and needed her, would always need her. Tiza and she would go back to Europe. "As soon as we get to Peking, I shall pack and go."

"Tell a story, Mama, tell a story."

Around the lamp at night, with the work-basket on the table, domestic happiness such as in the picture albums which came at Christmas from the Europe Mama cried for, longed for and always said she would go back to, the children would crowd, Rosalie asking for a story, imperious, unquiet, hopping on one foot till she got her way. But Tiza would climb on Mama's lap and put her head against her breast. Tiza was the child Mama had breast-fed for a long time, because she was so small, so delicate at birth.

"What story do you want?" said Mama, knowing the answer.

"The story of when you were a little girl."

"Like me," said Tiza, burrowing in Mama's breast.

"Like me," screamed Rosalie. "Like me, like me, Mama." And pulled Mama's hand, hard.

Mama took her hand away. "Stop screaming," said Mama. "And stop moving. You drive me crazy, moving all the time."

Mama lifted a sock, and looked at her own hands. She had had beautiful hands, the hands of a lady. Everyone admired her hands at the Conservatory in Brussels where she had studied singing and piano. Her fingers tapered, tips delicate and pointed, as in the Holbein paintings. Now the skin was

freckled, big veins ran on the back, a geography of pain.
"Who sees his veins, sees his own pains," said Mama. "My
hands, spoilt with work now." But the fingers remained delicate, the long oval nails, the tapered tips.

"When I was a little girl," she began. Ostensibly the story
was for Tiza and Rosalie, but it was not for them she spoke;
it was for Yentung, the for ever Silent One, who sat in his
armchair looking into space, or became a bent back over-
hanging the flowerpots lined on the veranda, always dreaming
of something he never told her. She never knew whether he
heard her or not. It was a way of punishing him, telling him
what she had been. There was no way of reaching him, except through the children, in the evenings round the lamp.
And she was never to know whether it hurt him or not, for
he never showed any emotion. When the children gave up
asking for stories, there was no way left to reach him at all.

"And when I was eighteen I went to church in an enormous
hat with big, big red roses on it. It was a very expensive hat."

"White roses," said Rosalie. "You said white roses last
time."

"White or red, it doesn't matter, don't interrupt me," said
Mama, "or I shan't tell you stories any more. Why are you
always so wicked?"

"I remember you said white roses."

"My God," said Mama, "I could die, and you would still
be arguing with me."

"You said white."

Mama got very angry, and the Wicked One went off to
bed screaming. Papa walked out to inspect the forsythia in
the blenching dusk, and Tiza wept.

Mama said: "It's the Wicked One, *your* daughter."

Another evening, the story went on: "I went to school at
the Ladies of the Sacred Heart Convent. It was for aristocrats only. All the girls were noble, except me."

"What were you, Mama?"

Mama sat straighter, winding wool. "I belong to the bourgeoisie. We have no title, but it doesn't matter. Some of these
noble families are not as old as we are. That is why I have
these hands. Not peasant hands. Not like Madame Poh, that
one has hands like a boxer. Some of the nobility, they had
hands like butchers."

The nuns at the Convent of the Sacred Heart were aristocratic too. The Mother Superior was of noble family, one of

the princesses of Hesse. Mama's schooldays were bedazzled by aristocracy. She recited their names.

"The Doutremont, the Gaiffier de la Haye, the Mainboche de Beuve de Wartegue, the Mezier de la Roche . . ."

It was also bedevilled by religious filth and bad food.

"We bathed once a week, in cold water, with our chemises on and reciting the rosary. To take off our chemises was immodest."

Mama had been a rebel, and had taken off her neck-to-toe, long-sleeved, flannel chemise, and been nearly expelled for it.

The food was also designed for saintliness. "Dishwater for soup, prayers aloud throughout the meals." Mama was so hungry she wrote home for food. Crystallized fruit and buns and chocolate came from her mother. She ate them at night in her bed. Angélique de la Haye shared some with her, but Thérèse Doutremont, who was a beauty with brown hair and a most aristocratic profile, turned up her nose at these manners.

"She is not of our station of life," she told Angélique de la Haye.

Mama was hurt, but others were not as proud as Thérèse, and shared the hampers, all save Suzanne de Wartegue, who wanted to be a saint, and drank the water in which the dishes were washed.

Mama learnt to embroider and to curtsy; singing and copperplate handwriting. She went to the Music Conservatory to learn the piano, and continue singing. When she walked to church on Sundays a maid walked behind her, carrying her prayer book and a fresh pair of gloves. "And look at me now, look at me now! My dowry gone into these bricks, to build this house. And your father, never a word out of him, except about his railway. The railway, that's where my life has gone. Oh, if only I had the money, I would leave tomorrow!"

There were many stories of Mama's life, told round the lamp. Her children were enveloped in them, carried by them, floating in the stories of Mama on the railway, Mama in Belgium, Mama in China . . . Rosalie shut her eyes and listened. It was like being in a train, listening to the train which also told stories. The lamplight hemmed them into its startled universe, the world globed in a drop of vision around Mama's lap.

But to Marguerite Denis, lying in the moving darkness of

a train, her life belonged elsewhere; gone out of gear, it was
not in this country. Only Tiza really belonged to her. All the
rest was China, the big, monstrous, poor, indifferent, illimit-
able and, with beggars, and war, locusts, starvation, and flood,
and someone shouting "foreigner".

"I want to go back, to go back. I shall take Tiza and go
back."

"To go back, to go back," sang the train, endlessly galloping
forwards, never looking back.

And Rosalie, eyes shut, heard the mocking-bird song of the
train, pounding its heart out in its journey towards the horizon.

"Rosalie, Rosalie."

Rosalie, who did not want to be named Rosalie, crawled
still farther away from the house with its calling voice,
crawled into the spiky grass that was not as all-protective as
it had looked. Her back bore the sun's heat, the strings of her
straw hat cut into her neck, and there were flies, persistent,
more prickly than the grass, lurching at her legs. "The princess," she continued, "started swimming away from the castle.
She swam swiftly, the clean cool water soothing her
wounds . . ." She made swimming strokes with her arms and
legs, flat on her stomach. It was very uncomfortable. She
removed two pebbles from under her, and continued swimming.

"Eldest Miss, your mother is calling Eldest Miss."

That was another voice, the voice of Liu Mah the nurse,
who was fat and had the smallest, the most pointed bound
feet that Rosalie had noticed. In fact, because Rosalie had
been fascinated by Liu Mah's feet, she had jumped on one of
them only a few days ago. Liu Mah had sat sewing on the
veranda, one of her legs with its dainty foot encased in a
neat black cloth shoe resting upon the other thigh, one foot
on the ground, in the way peasant women sit when they are
sewing. Rosalie, looking at the foot on the ground, had
jumped on it with both her feet. Liu Mah had screamed in
agony, holding her foot in her hand, big tears rolling down
her fat cheeks, suddenly ashen with pain. Now Liu Mah wad-
dled towards her on those two small stumps which supported
her ample weight, her trousered legs stroked aside the grass,
and Rosalie could see how each stone under the tiny soles
made Liu Mah stumble. Liu Mah tried to raise the little girl.

Rosalie threw her arms round the legs in their black padded trousers. "There loomed the saving rock, and the princess reached it, and threw her arms around it." Oh no, corrected Rosalie to herself, rocks would be all spiky, hard. The princess couldn't do that, it would hurt. She ceased clutching Liu Mah, who was laughing, nearly falling, disengaging herself from the child's arms.

"Big Miss, didn't you hear your mother calling you? Go quickly, or Taitai will be very angry with you."

"She's always angry with me," said Rosalie. "And I don't like my name, Rosalie."

"It is a very nice name," said Liu Mah, "Lo-sa-lee. Go quickly, Taitai is waiting with Second Miss. Second Miss is already dressed, and look at you."

"My mother loves her, she doesn't love me."

This was Rosalie's big dolorous secret, among those she held clutched, a secret half disbelieved at times, at others only too obvious. Now she gave it to Liu Mah, because she had hurt Liu Mah by jumping on her foot; but Liu Mah did not acknowledge the gift. People seldom knew when one gave them something. Even Liu Mah, whose gentle patient fatness was all the tenderness Rosalie was to remember, did not know she was being given something . . . She dusted Rosalie's dress.

"You must not say this, Big Miss! Of course Taitai* loves you. And your father, Laoyeh,* loves you best of all. But you are so wicked at times."

"Papa is always busy."

"Ah, but Laoyeh is a great gentleman. Without Laoyeh, there would be no rice in our bowls, no stick to our fire, no warmth under our beds.† Look at the railway, all of us depend on the iron road to eat rice.

Rosalie went back with Liu Mah through the grass, up the slope, to the house. The house she was to remember as a large building on top of a hill. Below the hill was the railway station, the rails like a small maze, and the trains. All around, flat flat, the loess plain of Honan, flat to the sky's limit. The house was red brick. It had been the house of a Belgian engineer, but now Papa had taken his place, the Belgian had gone, another one would come, and they would move to a small house. At the front door with its broad stone steps she

---

* Laoyeh, Taitai: Master and Mistress of the house, respectively.

†Under our beds: Because of the intense winter cold, beds in North China are plat forms of cement with a stove arrangement below. One sleeps on an oven top.

turned to watch the glistening tracks dancing in the heat haze, and laying in wait upon the tracks, alive and understandable, the trains, grey smoke like breath couched upon them. At night she woke to listen to them, the pounding, the hoots, rending night with soft deliberation, like Liu Mah tearing un-bleached cotton into long strips with which to bind tight her aching feet, every night.

"Ah, there you are at last," said Mama, tying big white satin ribbons sent by Grandmama on to Tiza's pigtails, "and dirty as usual. One would think you love dirt, dragging your-self in the mud."

"Dirt is clean," shouted Rosalie, enraged. "Anyway, cleaner than you."

Mama caught her a slap intended for the face, but it slipped on her hair instead. Rosalie, screaming, was led off by Liu Mah and put to bed, while Mama went off with Tiza, to call on Mrs. Belloni, the wife of the Italian engineer, who lived in the next house.

For years Rosalie was to remember the desolate width of the bed that afternoon, with the two big lumpy pillows (one hers, one Tiza's) which she now drew over her face, hiding in the crevice between them, her nose a little out to breathe, but otherwise buried in plump whiteness, while she sobbed and knew the enormous, endless sorrow of childhood; while Liu Mah sighed as if she, Liu Mah, had also been punished, and rocked herself on the hard small stool by the bedside, and once in a while put out a patting hand to pat the pillows, not the child; and the gesture was more solace than any closer touch, for Liu Mah knew that the child detested being touched or hugged. Rosalie in bed thought she would scream, and ex-ploded in such a paroxysm of screaming that she became frightened at the spasmodic clutching and unclutching within her breast, and stopped. As her loud sobs became systema-tized and rhythmic and somehow appeasing, Liu Mah patted, and in the interval she caught the smell of Liu Mah, the aroma of garlic and sweat which she was to recover, time and time again, in China, in China, only in China; it was the smell of love, selfless and detached, which made her go back and go back to China, for nowhere was it like that smell; recapturing through this smell the trance of childhood, more potent than any after-coming love, was coming home, coming home to love and security.

"Oh, you naughty child, naughty Big Miss," crooned Liu

Mah, lullaby rather than admonishment, "you have made Tai-tai so angry. And now you scream yourself ugly. And there is no one here but me to see you. What will Taitai say?"

Rosalie, tranquil now, wept normally. "Liu Mah, I am bad, bad, everybody says I am bad," and had another fit of sobs as she remembered Liu Mah's foot.

Together they saw the room darken with evening, and Liu Mah crooned and washed Rosalie's swollen face and changed her clothes, meanwhile keeping up the soft burr of her voice, so soothing. And then she brought Rosalie downstairs, holding her hand, the child reluctant but keeping step, for to be dragged behind Liu Mah would have been shameful; downstairs to the living-room with its brown wooden floors, with the round table covered with a white table-cloth, and the big lamp with its alluring blue glass body, and round glass funnel with a soft cream shimmer, which flung into faces shadows of not-themselves, transfiguring all.

Already Papa sat at the table, his boots in one corner, standing by themselves, like another Papa ready to tread the iron road, to make rice fill the bowl of Liu Mah, and twigs for the fire under the beds. The boots were black, long to the knee, there were straps below the knee-caps, and they had their own smell and their own boot sound when they walked. Papa was ladling out the soup, beef and turnips, and it smoked a little white cloud upwards from its tureen, and inside the beef broth swayed oval big and small oil globules upon its surface, like many eyes staring up. "Eyes of sea-serpents," thought Rosalie, starting on her self-told story again.

"Ah, there she is," said Mama. "Did I tell you" – she addressed Papa – "what the Wicked One said to me today?"

The Wicked One began more tears, they rolled down cheeks wooden with crying. But inside herself she was not weeping, she was tired, and she waited, her eyes upon her father. Would Papa too be against her?

Papa sighed, it was a sigh much sadder than Liu Mah's. "You've told me. Now, why are you so wicked?" His voice was monotonous with tiredness. It was the warlords that made him so tired, they kept on stealing the engines and the carriages from the railway.

"Sit down, sit down, Big Miss, now you must eat," clucked Liu Mah, and then her bulk was gone, leaving a sudden emptiness, and Rosalie was swallowing her soup and licking her mouth sideways to catch a saltiness of tears.

Tiza sat across the table, the loved one, still with her ribbons on, looking mildly at her big sister out of candid brown eyes. Mama cut bread and knifed butter on it, cut it in two and gave half to Tiza and half to Rosalie. Rosalie did not want to eat it. She was hungry, and had another plate of soup.

After supper Liu Mah undressed the children and put them to bed, and Mama came to the bed Rosalie and Tiza shared, the same one that Rosalie had rolled and screamed on in the hot afternoon. The nights were still cool, but the thick winter quilts had been changed to thinner ones, and there was a green and silver pattern on the top quilt. Liu Mah had sewn the quilts for the family in the previous autumn, laying a large white cotton sheet down upon newspapers on the floor, and on that placed the cotton wool wadding, padding it even by hand, tuft by tuft, flake by flake, until it was like a small snowfall upon the ground. Her ugly daughter, who had a very thick pigtail and only one eye, the other was an empty shut eyelid, having been put out by a blow from her father, helped her, picking out of the tufts small seeds or flecks of dirt left over by the carder. On the wadding they had then spread the silk top, six foot by four, tucked the cotton sheet round it, and sewn the two together with the hand-made thread of Honan, spooled by hand, thread which smelt so nice, twisted together, and waxed to make long-burning wicks. In the late spring Liu Mah would unpick all the quilts, wash the cloth lining and the silk separately; and the cotton wool padding, now matted, went to the village carder to be washed. The carder, with a great bow and metal string that went zing-zing-zing, sifted the newly washed matted lumps to make it all fluffy again, and then rolled it up and put paper round it and a twist of rope, and there it was, ready for next winter's quilt.

Tiza's hair was done up tight for the night in pigtails, because the next day was Sunday, when her hair, which reached below her shoulders, would spread out, waved stiffly for the morning service, which was only prayers, since there was no priest as yet, on this sector of the railway. Mama brushed and plaited the hair herself, and now the pigtails were in place upon the pillow, and she bent down, kissed Tiza, with her finger drawing a little cross upon her forehead, whispering: "God bless you and keep you safe tonight." Rosalie hardened herself as Mama came round the foot of the bed to her side, tucked the quilt in, and made a small cross on her forehead and said: "God bless you and keep you safe tonight."

Rosalie's hair was short and straight, ribbon always slid off it, even before the garden was reached. At night there was no brushing to make it shine, no plaiting for the next day. Once, long ago (so it seemed to her at four), she had said to Mama, who was brushing Tiza's hair: "Brush mine, brush mine, Mama." Mama had given it a few strokes, bringing the brush down hurriedly upon Rosalie's head, and there had been this feeling of hurry and distaste, and no pleasure; not the pleasure which made Tiza's eyes rounder and rounder, as with long slow strokes Mama brushed her hair. "You never keep still, how can anyone brush your hair?" Mama said to Rosalie.

Tiza had many ribbons. "When we get to Peking Papa will buy you a carved box for your ribbons," said Mama to her.

The dark was around them, tucked like a quilt about them. In the dark a train hooted, melodious, comforting, half asleep. The big cupboard opposite the bed grew into its familiar night dragon shape, an embattled dragon keeping watch, and Rosalie picked up once more her story of the Princess. "She drew herself out of the water, upon the beach, and out of the sea after her came Faithful Dragon. And before her eyes was a knight in armour, flashing gold, his sword one solid diamond."

Thus Rosalie gave her unforgiving mind its rest, rocked to sleep, but not to forgetfulness, by the distant pounding of a train.

It was a turgid, hot afternoon, on the slope. Blurred with the heat that wavered upwards from the ground, the railway station hopped up and down; in the plain, parched and brown with no rain, minute figures, like motes in a sunbeam, emptied of solidity, were about, peasants at their fields. Rosalie stood on the slope, and saw herself standing, straw hat with white string upon her head, chequered pinafore, cloth shoes made by Liu Mah upon her feet. She looked up, and the sky was a hot blue roundness, the horizon line erased as it met the earth. Liu Mah had said: "It is too dry, there will be a heat wind-and-dust dragon upon the plain tonight." And, of course, there it was, the dragon, gathering itself between the sky with its smouldering light and the slack, laid-down earth, cracked and furrowed with dryness. And Liu Mah had said:

"No rain, no grain." Who am I, what am I? thought Rosalie. What is to *be*? But there was no one to answer.

She had just left Mama sitting at her desk, writing a letter. The desk was made by carpenter Wu of the village, on the other side of the station and the railway tracks. This was Hsinyang, a big station, and the carpenter's shop was a happy-making place, because of its smell, and the sounds of the saw almost as good as train music. Two men moved the six-foot saw, one standing on the log, one kneeling below it, and they pushed and pulled smoothly the long saw clean through the wood, and that made planks; the railway needed planks, and ties. The curly shavings, blond and fragrant, of Wu the carpenter using the adze to smooth the planks, wound round a little girl's fingers, could be pulled out in the long sausage curls of a princess. Rosalie sometimes made up a story that one day she woke to find long curls upon her own head.

The desk was smooth and smelt of wood, and Mama sat and wrote at it, while Rosalie sniffed and tried to pull the drawers. Then she stood still, watching Mama write; the pen scratched on the white paper, a sound somewhat like the saw when it started to bite into the wood. Already some sheets covered with writing lay on the desk, and Mama went on, hand moving, face bent.

"Mama, when you write, what does it mean?"

Mama frowned. She did not like being interrupted when she was writing letters. "I am writing to your grandmother. Go and play."

Rosalie persisted: "But how does Grandmama know what you want to say? How is it that you do this" – she moved her hand – "and the letter goes, and Grandmama sees it, and she knows what you want to tell her?"

"Go away, you are asking stupid questions," said Mama.

This did not hurt Rosalie, because Rosalie knew that most questions were stupid, and it was part of her wickedness to ask them. Mama gave nicknames to everybody, and they were always right, even Papa used them. Going away then to play, the Wicked One saw herself for the first time, not as in a mirror, where images of self were only colloquies for the fitting of dresses, a tiresome process anyway since it was connected with putting on a lot of clothes that so soon became dirty on her, while Tiza remained so clean, or for having one's hair cut, another boring stillness inflicted. She saw herself, a

speck between sky and earth, felt the earth under her feet
solid and real, and said aloud:

"This is Hsinyang in Honan, and Papa is Chinese and Mama
is Belgian, and I am Rosalie or so they call me, but really I
am not Rosalie, I am me."

And who was me? Under the large elm grass smelt better,
not so dusty brown, and she immediately lay down on it. But
there were many ants out walking, big black ants and fiery
smaller red ones, rampaging in the dry heat, and they were
bringing out their small dot-white eggs from the anthills, as
if they were afraid of a disaster. Like the peasants before some
terrible warlord or flood, they were moving. Rosalie got up
and went back to the house. Some day she must find out who
Me was. And Liu Mah gave her a round date-and-honey cake,
round like the sun.

And here at Hsinyang Papa had much trouble with the
warlords. So much that for a while they had to run away from
the red brick house.

Suddenly one night, after the great heat, Papa appeared all
dressed, with his boots on with those straps on top which always Rosalie wanted to finger because it seemed such an expert and skilful trick to make the boots secure, the leather
thongs through clips, neat as a belt. He looked as if he had
come out of a story, to do something important and wonderful yet just now lost sight of, as one lost sight of shadows,
shadows moving away inexplicably even if one put one's foot
on them. So Papa appeared, and then Mama and Liu Mah,
and Liu Mah was saying: "Get up, Big Miss and Second Miss,"
and though it was so dark, not the right time to get up, they
were out of bed and Liu Mah dressed them, which was also
different because she did not first wash faces, but dragged out
the tin chamber pots and while they sat she whistled, as she
always did, so that the obedient liquid trickled out, warm.

"Don't move, I'm taking off your ear-rings," Liu Mah said.
She took off the little gold rings which were in Rosalie's ears
to keep the holes open.

And then shoes were put on, and they were the leather
shoes that were beginning to hurt so Tiza and Rosalie both
complained, and Tiza cried. "Oh, let them keep their slippers," said Mama. They went downstairs, and there were
bundles in bedsheets, looking like the fallen people after the
shooting that had taken place that afternoon in the village,
a shooting which Rosalie had seen because she was out with

Liu Mah to buy white thread in twisted skeins; and there on
the wasteland where the village ended, before a pond newly
dug in front of the railway station's grey brick and green windows, were the soldiers, all in grey, and all of a sudden Liu
Mah said: "Aiyah," and drew Rosalie towards her, putting
her face firmly against her knees; but she had turned her face
and seen the men fall, crumpled in their blue dresses, men
who had been standing there, and they lay as these bundles
now on the living-room floor, boneless.

The candles moved excited shadows on the walls, so Rosalie
tried hopping up and down in time with the candles, and
Papa said: "Hush, stop that," and then: "Come, let us go."

The cooler air slapped her forehead and nose, like a soft
cold paw, a little wet. Rosalie put out her tongue to taste it.
There were stars, like flowers, pushing themselves out of the
sky-garden, and there was the River of Heaven, pouring itself
across their way to the Bellonis'.

Papa led, Mama carried Tiza, and Rosalie followed with
Liu Mah, who never pulled on her hand, so that it was nice
walking with her, one did not have to pull away. And by that
time Rosalie was happy, wide awake, and her feet felt light
walking the glow-worm colour of night earth.

Their place of refuge was the house of the Italian engineer,
Mr. Belloni. The Bellonis lived in another red brick house
similar to theirs, but a little distance away, back of the hill.
Mr. Belloni was not really an engineer, he ran the repairs
shop. Mama said Mrs. Belloni could not write, but he got
three times as much money as Papa, because he was European.

"They are Europeans, so the warlords and the bandits won't
touch us here, but your father is only a Chinese," said Mama
later, speaking of that night flight away from the red brick
house.

This was something Rosalie understood early, that the only
protection was to be European. In fact Mama invoked this
protection all the time. "They can't touch me, I am European." Because Papa was Chinese and Mama was not, they
would go and lie on the carpet in Mr. Belloni's sitting-room.
Things happened to Chinese which did not happen to Europeans, like shootings, and no rice in the rice bowls, and having
to run away; and they could not stay in their house, and had
to go because Papa was a Chinese and not a European.

There were the soldiers of the warlords, men in grey, some

with guns in their hands and others with great cutlasses swinging on their backs, and sometimes so many, so many of them, ike a horde of great locusts, and Papa: "Sun Chuanfang's soldiers ... they are bad ... they slit open a pregnant woman the other day to see..." And Rosalie, very excited, saying: "What is pregnant, Mama? Mama, why did they?" And Mama, with a terrible look upon her face, turning round and crying: "Hush, never ask these questions, it is indecent."

And many times, in other houses, from other railway stations, they left at night; and when they came back, there was no furniture left, and many people were crying, and there were coffins of wood laid in rows, and Papa went away all day, and Mama said: "Don't go out, do you hear?" And even Liu Mah would not let her go out.

There was the morning, honey sun, syrupy air above the hedges, with Mama sitting sewing in a rattan chair in the garden, and Tiza and herself perhaps playing (Rosalie was not sure), and then, a Punch and Judy show suddenly emergent from behind a hedge, two soldiers in grey, with rifles, and one of them only half a face, because the middle of it was a hole where the nose should have been. And that night again they slept and then woke, and got on a mule-cart, and went away.

When they were not busy running away from the warlords, Papa and Mama welcomed them, occasionally, very seldom. In Rosalie's mind one warlord remained, a good one, Feng Yuhsiang; no one ran away from him or his soldiers, who were disciplined. Her first picture of Feng Yuhsiang was of an army encamped one morning, rows and rows of grey tents in the plain that lay below the hill, grey men, like the ants round their eggs, moving about; and that evening, of a very tall man with a round head, in grey uniform, sitting at the table eating, and Mama had herself prepared all kinds of things, including macaroni. "It's just like Chinese noodles," said Mama. Rosalie was called out of bed to see General Feng, and she remembered that she was made to sit near the General. Outside the house, four soldiers with large cutlasses slung on their backs stood guard. In the morning Papa went down with her to the tents, and a photograph was taken, which forty years later Rosalie was to find again. And afterwards Mama said: "Funny, isn't it? – but he said prayers. That is because he is a Christian General." And when later they were in Peking, Feng Yuhsiang was there, and he remembered Papa; and later, much later, Rosalie was to see him again.

Of the Bellonis Rosalie remembered two girls, Helena and Maria, who played with a swing in the garden. One girl was darker and fatter, the other was blonde, and the dark one loved to swing. The Belloni father was tall and thin with glasses, and Mama had a nickname for him, the Astonished One, because he was always saying: "I am astonished, really astonished . . ."

And so Papa on the railway had worries and troubles because of the warlords, and did not speak, and this sometimes enraged Mama. "But answer me," she would cry, "answer me! Why don't you open your mouth?"

And he would say: "I am thinking."

"Thinking? You are always thinking, you think of everything and everybody, but not of me," said Mama, and then a sob came up from her chest, and she took Tiza in her arms and went off into the bedroom.

And the lamp, and Papa and Rosalie would stay in the silence, eating the evening soup. And Papa looked up, and Rosalie loved him strongly, with her eyes giving him her love. But he did not look at her, and never knew.

There were the ear-rings.

Tiza had fleshy lobes, Rosalie had no lobes, but both were taken to a Greek Dr. Tonakis, when for a brief while they were at Chengchow, which was a very big station on the railway, to have their ears pierced. Rosalie was held down by four men, and screamed and fought; afterwards she remembered the fighting and kicking and screaming, not the actual operation. For weeks she wore a bandage round her ears and head, and Mama said: "Your ears have become infected." After a while they healed, and two little gold rings were run in by Liu Mah, but they had to be removed whenever the warlords came again. One day the rings could not be found and the holes shut themselves and Rosalie never wore ear-rings again. "Anyway, you have no lobes," said Mama. And so Mama gave the little turquoise ear-rings to Tiza to wear. They were the ones she had worn when she was a child. Rosalie pretended not to care.

There were the insects.

Bedbugs, encountered first on a pillow in the train, when they travelled down the line with Papa who had so much work. One night Rosalie felt an acute burning in her neck, woke up to find under her fingers what felt like large lumps, hot; Papa turned on the light. On the pillow paraded a small procession of bedbugs, their gait and colour vivid in memory when so much else had faded: a fat, darkish bug in front, three smaller ones behind, just like a family, the last one bright red, brilliantly coloured. Their smell was unforgettable too.

There were mosquitoes, to be slapped at night when they zing-zinged inside the mosquito net which stifled one in the summer, so that Rosalie wept and said she would sleep as Papa did, on the flat roof top. Papa used a red-and-black lacquer Chinese pillow and a mat for coolness up there on the roof, and fanned himself with a palm-leaf fan. But the next summer there was no roof top, and it was at another railway station, a place called Stone Family Hamlet, where Rosalie and Mama and Tiza all got dysentery.

There were ants, flies of all sizes and descriptions, midges which ran along with one in a cloud about one's head in the evening, ladybirds that could not be hurt because they brought good luck, butterflies, to be netted, they said, and collected. Papa one day caught a butterfly for Rosalie, a beautiful yellow-and-black butterfly, and stuck it with a pin through its middle on one of Mama's spools of thread. For hours it beat its wings slowly up and down. Rosalie was supposed to be pleased, and went to look at it several times, dying; she wanted to take out the pin and let the butterfly go but she thought Papa would scold her. The next day it was dead, which was good, it was no longer hurt. Rosalie buried it and then said she had lost it, and Mama said: "You lose everything."

There were locusts in great clouds one year, so that it became very dark in the afternoon, and Mama prayed aloud. All the windows and doors were closed, and the locusts went over the house and many hit their bodies against the glass panes and the sound was like hail falling, a terrible sound, and Liu Mah moaned and rocked and said: "Aiyah, aiyah, heaven, oh heaven, we shall have nothing to eat." Papa that night was more silent than usual, although Mama wanted to talk about the locusts; and Mama wrote a long letter the next day, and then a few weeks later she was weeping because Grandmama and Grandpapa in Europe did not believe about locusts blacking the sky till it was moonless midnight at noon.

And there were the Others: a hedgehog, a lamb, cats, puppies to be picked up in the villages, brought home to be fed. But they died so often the next day, possibly of eating too much. Flower-keeper Wang buried them. Rosalie had a row of graves behind the house, crosses of wood and tombstones of gravel. There was the wooden horse Balthazar, also known as Feiyun. When he was Balthazar and European, he went rescuing princesses; when he was known as Feiyun and Chinese, he overtook warlords and allowed the noble general on his back (Rosalie, now become Kuan Kung, God of War) to cut them down with a sword made of one piece of jade. In her mixed dreams, confusing tales told by Liu Mah with tales told by Mama, galloping knights of medieval European castles and charging generals of Chinese fortresses, princesses (looking like Tiza) wrung distressed hands towards the sky; Chinese maidens about to be kidnapped by dragons lifted similarly delicate appendages heavenwards. These epics kept Balthazar-Feiyun rocking rocking rocking, until one day, in a more than fearsome skirmish in which Rosalie became a warlord and led her troops (represented by the two Italian girls, Tiza, the one-eyed daughter of Liu Mah, and a pair of boys from the village) to battle, he lost his tail, which could never be found again. Afterwards one of the boys was accused of taking it away by Mama, and Liu Mah beat her daughter for not looking properly after Big Miss's property.

This sent Rosalie into one of those paroxysms of grief which Mama tried to shout down, Papa avoided, and Liu Mah alone could soothe. "Rosalie never weeps for sorrow, she always howls in anger," Mama said. It was true except for Balthazar-Feiyun's tail. At night she woke sobbing, and rose in the morning, hoping that during the night a miracle had taken place (for had not Mama prayed with her to St. Anthony, and also Liu Mah burnt a stick of incense to Kuanyin the All-Merciful, for a new tailpiece to Balthazar-Feiyun?); but there was he, the dappled steed, forlorn, in tailless immobility.

Liu Mah tore up strips of cotton to bandage the unsightly hole which Rosalie declared was bleeding. Tiza, always softhearted, started weeping at this and went off to Mama sobbing that Rosalie's horse was bleeding and was going to die. Mama appeared, throwing her arms up, saying: "My God, my God, what shall I do with this child? There, don't cry, I'll find a tail for Balthazar." She started to rummage in her

work-basket, among spools of various colours, socks, a
wooden egg to patch sock holes, and pieces of cloth for patch-
ing Papa's shirts and making cloth shoes. Liu Mah made all
the cloth shoes of the family, sticking all the pieces together
by boiling them into a sort of glue and cutting them out into
soles, layer by layer, and then with a thick long needle threading the layered sole with regular stitches, until the whole was
firm, and then on top of that she basted the top of the shoe;
and sometimes, when she was at leisure, she embroidered two
little flowers on the front, roses for Rosalie and snowdrops
for Tiza who had been born in winter.

But there was nothing resembling a tail in the work-basket,
and Rosalie started a fresh bout of wailing.

"Oh, Holy Virgin," said Mama, "when are you going to
stop?" And in a fit of exasperation she went to her room,
followed by Rosalie, and opened her cupboard. There,
wrapped in white cloth with moth balls, she kept her foxes,
furs she had brought with her from Europe and still kept,
though she never wore them; and twelve years later she still
had them, worn with keeping in their wrapping of naphtha-
lene and cloth. Mama was in a rage by now, possessed by the
fury which later would not let her go. She seized a pair of
long scissors from Liu Mah's table, grasped one of the foxes,
cut off its tail and handed it to Rosalie. "There," she said,
"there's a new tail for your horse. And now leave me in peace,
I can't stand the sight of you any longer."

Rosalie was left with the tail in her hand, and for the next
hour supervised Liu Mah sewing its end on to a piece of cloth,
then ramming the cloth with soft paper into the hole with
glue. Balthazar then stood in the sun to dry until well-tailed
again.

The hedgehog, grunting love, was bought in the village
where he was being tortured by some children with sticks.
Rosalie again burst into one of her fits and would not be
pacified until Papa, as pale as he could become, either from
weariness at Rosalie's tantrum or because he too was moved
at the hedgehog's sufferings (but that could not be, because
Papa had no sentiment about animals, and neither had Mama,
nor Tiza; only Rosalie had to suffer, for years and years,
of this unreasoning passion for the Others, those that could
not complain), purchased it and it was led home. The carpenter made a cage for it, Rosalie fed it with shreds of cabbage
and carrots and sweet potato, and even tried rice pudding

(which she detested and now saved up 'for my hedgehog'). It had an iron ring through its nose to which a string was attached; now it was to have the ring removed. This was done, and the hedgehog lay still on the pathway, bleeding from its nose, with Rosalie sobbing until taken away to eat. When she returned it had gone, and this led to another burst, until Mama said: "He's probably been taken up to Heaven by the good God."

This stopped Rosalie's tears immediately. "Is it true, Mama? Do you *know* he's gone to Heaven?"

"Of course."

That night Rosalie prayed to die and go to Heaven; and even thought of waking Tiza and telling her that she would give her her favourite doll, and she would give Balthazar to Liu Mah because Tiza was afraid of the rocking horse. For many years these words of Mama's entertained in her the firm conviction that the Others, which meant all animals, when dead went to Heaven, which was both logical and just, since they suffered much on earth. And when this illusion was destroyed (and by a priest, of all people), Rosalie too lost whatever faith she had managed to retain, and did not go to church any more.

There were picnics, organized by Papa, on his trips on the railway. One Rosalie remembered was on the banks of the river; it was just below the big bridge over the Yellow River, the water running between white sandbanks as far as her eyes could grasp the edge of sky-earth, horizon which enticed her heart out of her so that her feet would walk following her heart. Papa washed his feet in the water, then came a train running over the bridge, with a long call, clattering all its wheels with hurry, and Papa took out his watch and said: "The 10.45, right on time." And the heat, coming up from the sand, the river water, so cool, the smell of the iron bridge, and the train appearing on it, overhead, its cry in the silence of noon, all was a splendour in the sun, a greatness. For always there would be the trains, and the railway, that was eternity.

Papa silent, Mama strident, workers coming to the house with banners, Papa talking, Mama shouting: "You want us to become beggars, giving away money to these beggars." And sometimes she came out and shouted to the workmen: "Go away, go away!" And they went away, silent. And only later Rosalie knew that this was a strike of the workers on the railway.

The railway, the long whip of the railway across the plain, to the far-off threadline, sky-earth. One day she had started walking towards it, and was never to reach it, for they came running after her, shouting that she was lost.

The trains at night, answering each other with different voices. The long, deep call of trains, swinging along the night plains of China towards the unlimited, undefined, over-there. Over there Liu Mah's dragons danced, coiled in the dancing dust. Liu Mah said that was the end of the earth, and Kuan-yin the Merciful Goddess there caught you in her hand, and all was Peace.

Then one day Papa dressed, but without boots, the boots were packed. Suitcases and bags came tumbling at the door, and even the lamp was put in a crate. Tiza cried with her head on one side. Everyone got in the train, except Liu Mah and Wang the flower keeper and Li the cook and Liu Mah's one-eyed daughter. They stood in a row waving, Liu Mah weeping, weeping, running after the train weeping and waving her hand, running on those two stumps with their pointed single toes.

"Where are we going, Mama? Mama, are we coming back?"

"We're going to Peking, then you can go to school," said Mama. She turned to Papa. "And as soon as we get there, I will get a divorce because I want to go home. I don't want to stay in this hell of a country any more."

The train took up its song and sang it along, and along, and clattered by stations, and pebbles sometimes flew under the wheels. As long as they were in the train, Mama would not go away. There was no way out of the moving carriage. The landscape slid by, and some peasants in the devastated fields, all naked without trousers, stood to see the train go by, running across the war-weary land towards Peking.

TWENTY-TWO

"A SISTER, a sister, it's a little sister!"

Shrieks from the bedroom were a little sister. Why Mama had to go to bed for a little sister was not clear. The doctor had come, a doctor from the French hospital; Mama hated all the French, since a French doctor had killed Sea Orchid, her son, but this doctor was a Greek; Mama said the Greeks were gentle, and good doctors.

The Greek doctor had an elongate black bag, a small beard curving over his chin which bobbed when he spattered talk, so that Mama called him the Goat, and his hair grew fiercely, very shining and curly. He had a big, pale, damp-haired daughter who had just been married to a French clerk in the French bank. Rosalie and Tiza had been to the wedding in St. Michael's Church in the Legation Quarters. A few days later, Papa talking to Mama had said something about this girl being "barred". Rosalie was excited, especially when Papa had added, laughing, that she seemed "to have a bone there". A bone where? Why was she barred? From what? The bone, the beard, the doctor's bag and the French doctor who had killed Sea Orchid, were jumbled in a trance of words, and it all ended into the fact that Sea Orchid had died because he was half-caste. Rosalie knew that she too was half-caste, and the big, pale, doctor's child was a half-caste too, but much less so than Rosalie, because her father was Greek and therefore European; her mother, who was Chinese, was kept hidden in the house, so that her daughter's chances in life might not be spoilt. In that way, it made her less half-caste. Everyone said the mother was so right to hide.

But this new little sister brought by the Greek doctor, what was she? Would she be Greek, or French since she came from the French hospital, or half-caste too? And in that case would she die? Not only Sea Orchid, but after Rosalie and Tiza were born, another little brother, another little sister, and yet another little brother; all had died, because they were half-caste, which meant the doctor might or might not bother to come. And a Chinese midwife delivered one brother, and dropped him on his head, so that he died two days later; a little sister had been infected with abscesses all over her body, and died screaming; and another brother became blue and died, and Mama had nearly died of bleeding too. That was when Papa was working, up and down the railways. Up and down, and right and left; first on the Lunghai railway, to push the line east from Hsuchow, west from Kaifeng. Rosalie knew all the names of all the stations along the Lunghai railway. This Papa had done for years, from 1913 to 1919. And then on the Peking–Hankow railway, down to Hankow on the Great River, up to Chengchow on the Yellow River, on to Hsinyang, and then to Changhsintien, and finally to Peking in 1921 or 1922.

Peking was a city, a big city at last, and Mama said: "Now I can be looked after properly by a good doctor."

Since the others had died because they were half-caste, how could a doctor prevent this new little sister dying? Doctors were wonderful people, like magicians in the stories, like the wizard Chuko Liang, like Wah Toh the clever physician who removed arrows without pain. Liu Mah was no longer there, but there was a Wang Mah now, thin and small and never smiling, her hands always dry, big feet because she was a Manchu, and very cheap, eating very little. Wang Mah also told fine stories: of a boy walking to find the sun which had gone away in hiding, and fighting demons of the darkness on his way; another one about a girl who had a magic flute and people who heard its sound forgot their worries; and another about a woman who was really a beautiful white snake and who died for love. Wang Mah said that doctors were good spirits, the same as Buddha, and she herself believed much in taking medicines. Often she had headaches and appeared in the morning with little round pieces of paper stuck in her temples, and smelling of ginger.

The new little sister might live, with the doctor there, and in a big city. Rosalie and Tiza were taken into the bedroom, with its disinfectant smell. The candle flickered a hollow flame in its white enamelled candle-holder, which had a bit chipped off its round saucer bottom, showing the black iron underneath, the bit Rosalie thought nice to rub against her finger. Rosalie thrust her head against the mosquito net, which had a cottony smell and feel, and made a music when rubbed, as a comb did, a weak cicada noise. Everything had its own smell and feel and look and sound, and that was why it was good to be; and suddenly she was happy because there were so many things to feel and hear and smell and look at, like the mosquito net, or the smell and shape, colour and size, sound of this new thing, a little sister, a long red thing shrieking and black hair on its head, and the smell different from any other, and by its side Mama lying down, almost as if it was nothing to be brought a new baby. Why did she have to lie down because the doctor brought a baby in his bag? Rosalie eyed the bag, decided it was too small to put a baby in unless the baby was folded up inside. Folding things did make them smaller. She tried it with her doll next day, and it worked. Then for a while she had to play at having a baby, and folded herself into a large water jar in the courtyard, and was both baby and doctor, while Tiza became Mama and was made to lie down.

Tiza stared also at the little sister, her breath coming gently in and out. Tiza was so pretty now, and she wanted a kitten, and Mama had promised her one. She looked at the baby and said: "Marianne."

That was the name of her doll, with dark curly hair and a biscuit tint to her face. So the new sister was Marianne. Rosalie's doll had had her nose cut, her face washed, was so much the worse for it, and could not give her name to the new baby.

And now in the rickshaw, to go to the park in the morning, there was Mama carrying Marianne, and Tiza and Rosalie standing by her knees on the footrest, a heavy load for a man to pull. The carriage was a secondhand one, bought when they had arrived in Peking. Feng, the rickshaw puller, was handsome, muscled shoulders most beautiful, skin like golden silk, hairless, and he pulled for six dollars a month. In the morning, for two coppers, he bought himself unleavened wheat bread, a big flat round slab of it, and ate it with a stick or two of raw garlic, and drank hot water. In winter he wore a padded gown that Mama had made for him. There were two copper lamps to the rickshaw, swinging on either side of the shafts, a bell underfoot with a push button of copper that Rosalie pressed her foot on and then it went ding-a-ling ding-a-ling, clearing a way along the dusty small intestinal *hutungs** of Peking. The rickshaw seat was padded, there were slip covers of white cotton with frills which Mama ordered Wang Mah to wash and change once a week, because of the fleas and lice, Mama said. Mama did not allow Feng to sit in his own rickshaw seat because of the lice, he was to sit on the footrest, but that was comfortable enough because there was a small carpet upon which the feet of the sitter rested. No rickshaw owner allowed the rickshaw man, the man between the shafts, to sit in his own rickshaw seat because he might dirty it. Only outside rickshaws, those who did not have private owners, who rented their rickshaws from companies and prowled the streets for passengers and haggled over a copper, those sat and slept in their rickshaws, because they had no home, there was nowhere else for them to sit or sleep. They huddled in their rags in the

* *hutungs:* the narrow streets of Peking are thus called.

winter, and Mama said their rickshaws were full of vermin, and one would catch the plague, bitten by lice, if one sat in a common rickshaw.

Remembered best after Liu Mah in after years was Feng, the rickshaw puller, remembered to the last detail because Rosalie knew he was beautiful. She looked at his back, saw the skin slide upon the slim strong muscles, the colour of the skin, and it was something to look at all the time, because Feng pulled off his top jacket to run; he sweated, and then it was more beautiful, like the sun going into rainpools. And yet it was never spoken of, and there was no way to say this beauty. Feng pulled smooth and fast, outdistancing other rickshaws, mocking them with his swift feet from which the dust flew, the rickshaw wheels with their shining spokes leaving two skipping fountains of dust behind them. Feng was even better than Balthazar, even better than a train, for he went singing, "Going north," when he turned a corner, or "Make light, make light," when he passed another puller.

And because of Feng, there were all the rickshaws of Peking, all the possible Fengs. Through Feng all the other pulling men were seen, felt, heard, smelt, because they were, they existed, they did not disappear, like stories one could not remember the next morning because of a piece missing and no one to tell what was wrong. They made a world of fleet misery, beauty and squalor, a world running by on swift feet, or stumbling in rags, a brightness of bells and brass or a dingy broken-down panting; always a horror and a fascination, their backs, their backs naked and quivering, bones counted, flesh sweating its life out running. Never could one see their faces, and as they ran between their shafts one could shout, "Faster, faster!" or stamp up and down to make them run. Their backs were terribly alive, and sometimes Rosalie thought: What would I do if I pulled a rickshaw? And she did, putting herself between the shafts, trying to lift and to pull, and Feng laughed softly, and stopped her, taking the rickshaw back to its shed. He slept on a plank behind the shed. He was lucky, Feng, being young and strong, and hired by a family for six dollars a month.

And alongside the gazelle (for so Mama called Feng) shuffled and limped and dragged all future Fengs, wizened, bent, smelly old men pulling carriages as ruinous as they, pulling as they had pulled since they were young like Feng, pulling towards a cold, verminous and wheezy death between the shafts.

One day Rosalie refused to sit in the rickshaw. It was because she had seen the death of a rickshaw man, so ragged that in death he seemed to come to pieces. A common death between the shafts, while Feng ran by. This rickshaw man was ahead of Feng on the way back from the East Market, and suddenly he toppled down, falling into his own heap of rags, and on him fell his passenger, a man in a long gown with a scarf round his neck and a felt hat square upon his head; and Feng coming behind nearly ran into them, only braked himself in time, skidding on cloth shoes, shouting 'Wai!' to warn himself and others, and the shafts of his carriage he lifted up so quickly that Mama and the children fell backwards in their seat. Feng was so well built, skilful and careful, that the carriage did not topple entirely backwards, and they were only a little shaken, but Mama screamed and screamed, and immediately many people collected, and the man who had fallen on top of his dead puller also was shouting, and a crowd gathered to look, and then they turned the puller over, and someone said: "Dead, he is dead."

"Go home, quick, quick," shouted Mama.

So Feng picked up the shafts again and lifted and ran past the dead man, and a little along he laughed and said: "He died, Taitai."

"Don't talk. Run, quick, home," shouted Mama.

And Rosalie pressed on the bell button with her foot and shouted: "Kwai, kwai," – quick, quick. So they ran homewards.

The next day Rosalie did not sit in the rickshaw, and the night after Tiza woke screaming in a nightmare. But after a while it was over, and they went as usual in the rickshaw.

The Central Park was a favourite place for children to play in, and Mama went there nearly three times a week, sometimes four times, in the short spring, after the dust storms, and in the early morning of the hot summers, through the autumn until it became too cold. There stories became games, acted out as they were talked with Tiza, with other playmates.

To get to the park, after coming out of the maze of *hutungs*, grey, dusty, uneven between the loping grey walls of houses, one emerged on to the old imperial way, paved with enormous blocks of stone diagonally set. The main gateway of the red-walled Forbidden City was the Gate of Heavenly Peace, facing the midday sun; and from there a paved road led straight to the Temple of Heaven. In the great square before the Gate of Heavenly Peace there were soldiers, soldiers with cutlasses on their backs; and not only there, but everywhere about Peking were soldiers, and in the Legation Quarters were foreign soldiers, each in front of their own legation gates. Everyone made a wide detour, well before reaching any soldier of any kind, for it was not good to get too near a uniform, any uniform. There were very few cars, and if one came, klaxoning, lunging on the road, everyone got out of the way quickly, for it was sure to be a warlord or a warlord's underling, and if one were run over nothing could be done about it. Standing on the footboard on both sides of the war-lord cars were hired bodyguards, revolver at the hip, and sometimes, if they thought someone in the crowd was looking at them, they shot at him, or at the passers-by if they got excited, and no one could say anything, one merely ran for cover. These bodyguards were not Chinese, but so often White Russian, for it was a fashion of the warlords to hire White Russian bodyguards, and they were even worse, being more excitable than others.

When Papa returned home in the evening from his office with news of yet another warlord entering in triumph into the city of Peking, and when Peking prepared to receive the warlord with archways of paper flowers, and the citizens were stopped on the streets by soldiers for money for welcome gates and soldiers' comforts, when klaxoning cars ran the streets shooting and shouting, then Mama would tie a little flag, the red yellow black flag of Belgium, her own country, upon the rickshaw carriage when she took her children to the park.

And one day as they alighted in front of Central Park a European man leading a child by the hand stopped to stare at them getting out of the rickshaw, and said, very loud, look-ing at the flag, then at Mama carrying Marianne, at Rosalie and Tiza: "Look, Peter, these are half-castes."

Rosalie stared at him, and he was European, and the child was European too. Mama said: "Come, my children, come," and they entered the park. Across the flat sandy space where acrobats and shadow boxers practised, to the pine-planted man-made rocky hillocks where they played so many wonder-ful stories, Rosalie heard the word, a noise not to be smelt or palpated, no sound or look about it, the word. She knew it already, but somehow it had become new, the way the man had said it. And it made Mama different: Mama clutched her hand tighter as they walked, and it was the tight clasp of something fierce and gentle, like love, and suddenly Mama said:

"You look European, my children, you look like me."

And the sun kicked the grey slate tiles of the pavilions among the rocks, and a grey-blue Peking magpie flew away.

And that was all it meant: half-caste, and Sea Orchid dying, and all the others dying. It was Papa being Chinese, and to be a Chinese in China was wrong, only being European was right. So Rosalie took the rickshaw's Belgian flag in her hand, and led troops to fight the dirty Chinese that day, since she looked European, she looked like Mama, so Mama had said.

TWENTY-THREE

THERE was Church, or rather two churches, the European and the Chinese one.

The European was St. Michael's, in the Legation Quarters where the European legations were, and the European soldiers, and the Japanese. It had two sharp pointed towers, each bearing a cross; above the main door was a plaster statue of St. Michael, piercing with a lance a writhing serpent with a man's horned head, which was the Devil. Rosalie always looked with great satisfaction upon the serpent's head, it had such attractive curls above its horns. St. Michael's head was not half so good-looking as the devil's, the nose was too big; but his wings were beautiful, how did they grow out of the shoulder blades, and how could St. Michael put his vest on properly with those wings?

At first they went every week, and later about once a month, to the European church, 'to show them we are not dead,' said Mama. It was quite an occasion, it meant wearing one's best dress, and of course that meant in turn urticaria, for all best clothes made one itch.

At the time Rosalie had a dress of white cashmere wool, made to last for years, with a deep hem to be let down, sleeves with cuffs to be lengthened when the child within the dress grew, a collar, an embroidered sash. It itched, round the neck and the sleeves and the bodice and the skirt, from top to bottom and back again. "It's pure cashmere, how can it itch?" Mama said. So Rosalie wriggled and scratched, looked at the devil's head, clutched her rosary, sniffed the incense smell, and, Mass over, on the church porch with its flagstones and people shaking hands with each other and talking, stared at the Greek doctor's daughter with the bone in her, noticing her pink dress, silk stockings, and wondering where the bone was.

The Legation Quarters, she knew, were reserved for Europeans to live in. No Chinese could live there, and outside it Japanese soldiers quartered in tents on a bare space near the Legation Quarters. "One would think there are more Japanese than Chinese in Peking," said Mama.

The other church, the Tungtang or East Church, was hideous because of the beggars. Not that the beggars were in the church, they were not allowed inside. They waited outside, and that was awful. One ran a gauntlet of monstrosities, fighting one's way out, through a clutching, moaning seethe of beggars.

The church was called Eastern Church or Tungtang because it was in the eastern sector of Peking. It had rounded domes, cross-mounted. Above the altar the vaulted ceilings formed a little paradise of blue paint with golden stars. The pillars were high and foliated, the windows of red and blue glass complicated with saints. The large altar was marble with veins, and arched sculptured woodwork with gilded heads of cherubs formed a screen; in its middle, under a canopy glittering with gold, stood the Host, enclosed in a marvellous sun of gold, and the tabernacle had a curtain of woven gold. It was altogether much more costly-looking than the European church. The priests were Irish Catholics, young and red-faced; the congregation, all Chinese, sang hymns in nasal, high-pitched choruses at the tops of their voices. The men sat on one side, the women on the other, not mixed as in the European church. At communion the altar was crowded, where in the European church not more than one or two communicated. There were spittoons at the end of each bench. The collection was done by Mr. Hsia, a Catholic who owned several pawnshops and was very wealthy. He wore silk padded trousers, a large silver watch chain, spectacles and a drooping moustache.

To this church Mama now went three Sundays in the month, sitting in one of the front pews. There were very few Europeans, only a Belgian couple, young and very pious, who lived near by, and found it convenient. The man had a habit of picking his nose, and then making small pellets of whatever he found in his nose and putting it in his mouth.

In a reserved pew, caparisoned in purple velvet, knelt the family of Wong Hsutong, the wealthiest man in the east sector, a banker. He was paralysed in his legs, was carried to church in a chair, and departed the same way. He had twenty children and three wives, but only one came to church with him, the Big Taitai, and she had jade ear-rings and always wore black satin; the Second Taitai and the Small Concubine stayed at home.

Outside the church was a very large empty space with flower plots, which was the church garden. One walked through it, and then came the other gate on to the street. On both sides were lodges for the gatemen, and this formed a short gorge through which the faithful went in and out from the street. It was this tunnel which was lined with beggars, three deep. One had to thrust through them, push them away, beat them off with sticks, meanwhile holding one's handkerchief to one's nose, for their smell was terrible. There was one beggar worse than all others, and always in the front row: a woman with a devouring ulcer of the face, from forehead down to lip, covering eye and part of the nose; her hands hooked into people, her smell came in gusts, until one day, the litter of Wong Hsutong going by, she clutched at the sleeve of the rich man and received from Mr. Wong's cane a great blow upon her face, and fell back upon the other beggars.

Then there were the blind, children with white stones for eyes turned heavenwards. They smelt the worst, rancid pus, they moaned the loudest, their trousers were shreds, showing their legs and their private parts even in winter.

Through this Rosalie and Tiza fought their way with handkerchiefs round nose and mouth, moving in a phalanx of the faithful hurrying out of church, trying if possible to get behind the litter of Wong Hsutong, which like a wedge of armour drove on, relentless, because the chair-carriers hit and prodded with steel-tipped staves; and after the old woman with the ulcer had nearly got at his sleeve, Mr. Wong hired another two bodyguards, hefty giants from the north, Mongols, to go before the chair, striking the beggars out of the way. They kicked one blind boy out of his niche between a man with stumps for arms and a leper with no hair, rolling his body right into the street with their leather-shod feet, kicking him all the way.

And after one or two times like that Rosalie, like everyone else, felt angry with the beggars. "One good machine gun would finish the lot," said the Belgian man who ate his nose pickings.

And all these things went through Rosalie, as if she were transparent, receiving all, reflecting nothing, accepting as glass or mirror takes images, and nothing to show in return at the time. Mama said the East Church was awful, but going to the other church was too far, it took half an hour by rickshaw, and the sermon which came in the middle of Mass was too long. At the Chinese church the sermon took place before Mass, so one could arrive afterwards. And Mama had quarrelled with the French priest of the European church, Father Clement, because of the baptism of Marianne, which had not been well done, or so Mama said.

Rosalie thought it was not because of Marianne's baptism Mama was angry, but because of the books. Father Clement had a small library of novels, plays, and lives of saints, and Mama borrowed books. One day Father Clement gave a book to Mama, saying: "Reading this you will unite the useful with the agreeable." Mama was hurt, and retorted: "Everyone of my days is useful. I want my reading to be agreeable only." She said the church had not put out enough flowers for Marianne's baptism, and yet they had paid for many flowers. And so-and-so, who was pure European, had had many more bouquets for the same money.

The day came when Rosalie refused to go to church any more, because of the animals, and the babies. In childhood there had been the Others on the railway line, and the Others were at first all animal, hedgehog and lamb, puppy and kitten; and then there were also Feng and all the other Others, a host of Others, who did not seem to exist in the world of St. Michael and his piercing spear, or the heaven above the altar only two hundred yards away from the human putrescence at the gates. It was so confusing, because somehow it made people laugh (and being laughed at was terrible) when one tried to talk of the Others. And as if it was not enough to carry about in one's self all these unexplainable things, there came along another Thing, which was the babies of the baby room at the Sisters of Charity Orphanage.

The Sisters of Charity, the Little Sisters of the Poor, went on the streets two by two, and in the *hutungs* in the winter collected the babies, thrown out dead or dying, and brought them up to embroider such things as wedding trousseaus, or to make lace, tremendous quantities of it, or fine drawn work on linen handkerchiefs, or petit point handbags and spectacle cases.

Their workshop was a long room in which nearly two hundred girls sat on benches, embroidering frames in front of them, from eight in the morning to six at night: they made lace on spools, picked threads out of handkerchiefs to make borders with minute stitches; and they sang hymns, and they filed in and out. They were not allowed to get up to relieve themselves while working, because that was immodest.

The odour was foul in the workshop, all the windows were closed except in summer; but one did not smell it any more when one stayed long in the room. While Mama talked to Sister Mary of the Angels about buying some embroidered baby shoes for Marianne (because Marianne was now a year old and Mama liked her children well dressed to go with her to have tea with Mrs. Poh, a Frenchwoman married to a Chinese who had a son whom Rosalie always managed to hit at least once during tea, or with Mrs. Lautens, a Dutchwoman married to a Dutchman who had no children), Rosalie went round the girls at their frames, six to eight girls in a row. Some bent low on the frames, through which their needles went up and down, down and up; they kept one hand above and one hand below the frames, their noses nearly touching the flowers that grew between their hands.

Click clack went the spools of the lace-makers, and the tense silk of the embroiderers said tut tut as the needles came sharp through. The fingers of the girls moving the bobbins were so swift, it was hard to count them. The floor had little eddies of white threads among the spittle.

Sister Mary of the Angels was a small Chinese woman, with red round cheeks. The coif sat on her, as an enormous white bird sits on an apple. She had a heavy wooden rosary with a cross dangling from her waist, and one day Rosalie seized the cross and kissed it because she had heard in the sermon the Sunday before Father Clement talk about kissing the cross, and Sister Mary of the Angels laughed, and threw her hands up to her coif with laughter.

When they went back to collect the shoes, they met the Mother Superior, who was a European. She had a very big nose and a very pale skin, a pale moustache blending into two deep folds which were her cheeks lapping over the corners of her mouth. Mother Superior asked Rosalie and Tiza what they wanted to be when they grew up. Tiza blushed and looked like crying, she was always very shy, holding her head on one side. Rosalie answered promptly: "I want to be a veterinary."

"Ah," said Mother Superior severely, "and why, my child?"

"Because animals suffer so much."

"It is best to be a nun, it is a blessed state," said Mother Superior. "Souls suffer much more in hell than any animal can suffer on earth, my child."

She took Mama and the two girls across the garden. "Come," she said "'see how we save little angels for God." And while they walked she told Mama that the whole of the wedding trousseau of the doctor's daughter had been embroidered here in the workshop. And again Rosalie thought of the bone. They passed the chapel, in front of whose stucco grey façade they made a genuflexion. Two anxious-looking white-robed angels raised wary scimitars on either side. Mother Superior's beads went click clack, as the bobbins of the lace-makers. They came to a building, a corridor, entered another large room, not filled with frames and girls, but with small cribs of woven rushes, the kind that one bought for a few coins apiece from the maker of brushes and brooms and sieves, and in each crib lay a quiet baby, clean wrapped in unbleached cotton cloth.

"Little angels," said Mother Superior softly, "little angels of God." She bent tenderly over one, and so did Rosalie, looking with interest at the pinched blue face, grinning widely in the pull of dying. "This one won't be long," said Mother Superior. "It will join God tonight."

"My God," said Mama, "how many do you get a day?"

"Two, three a week. More in winter, sometimes ten a week," said Mother Superior. "We always baptize them immediately, then we wait twenty-four hours. If they do not join God, then we give them milk, because we know it is the will of God that they should live. If we find them dead, we still baptize them, in case. We only have twenty-three at the moment," she said, looking round. "It has been a bad year, madame, as you know. We have so little money, not enough for milk."

Mama immediately recognized what she called "the touch," and said hastily: "Ah, how true, Reverend Mother, how very true. It's getting worse and worse. My poor husband, for instance, he has not had his salary paid for three months now, because as you know there has been fighting on the railways, and a big strike. My husband was always too generous, he gave money to the workers who I am sure had no gratitude for it. They are all Bolsheviks, Reds. But whenever they come to him with complaints, he still gives money. We are living at the moment on a shoe-string."

As they left the baby room Rosalie turned to sniff, to remember: once smelt, always there, readily exhumed from memory, however long the wait. She sniffed the tepid, quiet smell of the babies, a sweet sourness of diarrhoea, disinfectant, and something quiet and accepting which was perhaps the dying. I was a baby once, she thought, a little girl. They're all little girls. And she skipped out, skip-skipping into the sun-sprayed afternoon.

And after that the babies, the puppies, the beggars, the rickshaw pullers, so many things became One heaviness inside, as if there was a hedgehog twisting about in her chest. So she skipped and hopped all the harder, and was very wicked, and refused to go to church: "It smells, it smells."

But Mama spoke of Hell, and though Rosalie did not go that Sunday but was allowed to stay with Wang Mah, expecting any moment the Demon with his attractive curly hair to come for her, she went the next Sunday, and all seemed as before.

The beggars and the babies haunted Rosalie, but they did not seem to haunt Papa or Mama, or anything else that was grown up and knowing. They talked of them in injured tones, as if the beggars were guilty to be beggars. They did not talk about the babies.

When Mama told Papa about the girl babies in the baby room, Papa said, chuckling as if it were a good joke: "Yes, females. Nobody wants girl children. It costs too much and brings in so little."

This made Rosalie worried, because she too was female. She was going to cost so much, and Papa was already so poor, there was no money. This was to be made good one day, one day. One day no babies would be thrown out to die on the streets, wrapped in bundles and staring and grinning blue-faced into one's face . . .

That year Papa was breeding carnations on the enclosed veranda of the house. Their sharp, clean scent stabbed through all other smells and made a lucid air. Carnations were spare, slim flowers, no lush flim-flam of leaf about them, their

colours rioted quietly, and Papa had some wonderful ones:
white with dabs of pink, yellow, near-black purples, and one
almost pale green. In winter the frost painted great white
landscapes on the window panes, and the carnations bent towards the mountains and valleys of the cold, the unearthly
beautiful shapes of the frost, and it was such beauty one
shouted and jumped for happiness.

Papa, bending over the carnations, with the white pale glare
of the sun through the frosted windows, could not be spoken
to about the beggars who were stiff and blue-black, dead of
cold, behind the house. Neither could Tiza, who had to be protected because she was delicate. Neither could Mama, so
much noise would follow. At school of course one could not
speak about beggars. Only with Simon Hua. But Simon Hua
also was busy, he stood at street corners, and gave handbills
to people; he was dressed in Boy Scout uniform.

These handbills said: "Down with British imperialism.
Down with Japanese imperialism. Down with unequal treaties. China belongs to the Chinese."

In Rosalie's mind this was not related to the beggars or the
babies. All she knew was this profound physical disturbance
that went on growing and growing in her in spite of herself,
something which became so strenuous that she cried out in
her mind: "When I am big I will do something so that there
will not be a beggar left in China, and no child will be blind.
One day each child in China will have an egg a day." An egg
a day, according to Mama, prevented blindness.

One day, on the way back from school, she saw yet another
beggar. This one was an old man in an epileptic fit, a foam,
a bleat, a writhe in the dust, an amused small crowd paralysed round him, in a small hutung undulating between two
grey walls only five feet apart.

This beggar suddenly became, there and then, all beggars.
Something had to be done, and could be done. She pushed
her way through the crowd and stood by him. He was now
stertorous, the fit over. The watchers laughed, some went
away; Rosalie shook him, he did not move. A rickshaw went
by, empty, drawn by a middle-aged man, who stopped to
look. Rosalie hailed him. "Look," she said, "this poor man is
sick. We must get him home."

"But he is a beggar," cried the rickshaw man. "Little Miss,
what do you want with him?"

"I want to take him home," said Rosalie, feeling ashamed

now; but there it was, she had spoken, it was too late to change.

"You cannot lift him," said the rickshaw man. "It is better to leave him there."

"Put him in your carriage," said Rosalie, "and we shall take him home."

"Me?" cried the rickshaw man. "Little Miss, I tell you he is a beggar, how can he pay my fare?"

"I will pay your fare. Put him in and pull him there."

The rickshaw man looked at her and burst out laughing, and made as if to go away. And then suddenly he put the shafts down, and he and Rosalie lifted the old man into the rickshaw. The old man was coming to slowly, his head lolled, he dribbled words.

"I know where he lives," said the rickshaw man. "He begs round here, and he lives where all the beggars of this district live, in the garbage fields near the wall."

They began to walk, Rosalie by the rickshaw, the old man sprawled in it, half asleep and muttering to himself. The rickshaw man walked slowly, laughing and asking Rosalie questions, delicate and inquisitive. "I am a poor man too," he said, "and it is very far to the wall."

"I will give you a dollar," said Rosalie. She had a dollar upon her, earned by being first in class for the third month in succession. She had meant to change it into coppers. Four hundred copper pieces one got for a dollar, and with that she would buy coloured pencils for drawing a picture for Mama's birthday. Inside her a voice said: "I'll tell Mama, perhaps she will give me another dollar." During that walk Rosalie saw herself partly as a saint, and partly as a guilty, almost a criminal, Wicked One. It was wicked to do things that Mama would not approve of, and Mama would *not* approve of this; yet at the same time in the church they said: "Do charity." Someone, somewhere, must reconcile the two.

And there was a second voice, which said: "I cannot stand this much longer. I do not want to see beggars like this. It is not right. It should not be."

And a third voice began mocking: "Rosalie, there are so many beggars. What can you do?"

And Mama's voice said: "They all cheat and steal, they are lazy, that is why they beg."

The rickshaw turned into a bigger street, and there was a policeman, young, with cloth shoes, his legs in puttees, a yellow uniform and a baton. He stopped the rickshaw, and said: "Where are you going?"

"To the wall," said the rickshaw man. "The Little Miss has hired me."

The policeman got terribly angry. He suddenly hit the rickshaw man full in the chest, so that the man dropped his shafts, and then he went on hitting him, his face rigid with anger, his eyes protruding. Rosalie rushed forward. "Stop," she cried, "stop. Why do you beat him?"

"He does not answer properly," said the policeman. "I will arrest him."

By that time the usual passers-by had stopped. Rosalie was shouting: "Stop, it's me, it is a beggar, the rickshaw man was helping me."

The rickshaw man groaned, hit in the chest and belly.

The policeman pulled the old man out of the rickshaw, and the old man fell in a heap on the ground, but that was perhaps because he was a beggar and used to ill-treatment and he knew that the sooner he collapsed the easier it would be for the other person to stop beating him. The policeman did not kick him, because by that time Rosalie's shouting had convinced one of the passers-by and he intervened, and as he was fairly well dressed the policeman stopped kicking and listened while he said: "Please do not be angry, it is this young miss with a kind heart, taking a poor sick man home, the rickshaw was only obeying her."

The policeman (he was young, new, only wanting to assert himself) changed his face from anger to severity. He said: "Well, of course, I must do my duty. How did I know this rickshaw man was not doing something wrong? It is not customary to see beggars in rickshaws."

"Of course, of course," said the passer-by quickly, and some other passers-by echoed. "Of course, you have a serious responsibility. It was your duty to find out the yes and the no of the situation."

The policeman melted some more, he nearly smiled, he looked suddenly very kind. The passers-by lifted the old man back into the rickshaw, the rickshaw man picked up the shafts, Rosalie and he walked on.

At last they came to the wall, or rather they began to see its bricks and the battlements. There were no houses, only a vast dumping ground, a large space covered with all the things no one wanted: not manure, for human manure was precious, but cinders, ash, rotting vegetables, everything putrid, scavenged and refused. Upon such dumps in Peking pullulated hordes of beggars, the unwanted; armed with small sticks with a hook at the end, they ransacked this waste, desperately searching for what could still be used: all bits of wood and paper were precious, bits of cloth of any size and any kind. They fought over partly burned charcoal which could be used again. There was never anything edible thrown away ... who could afford to throw a particle of food away? The restaurants had their hordes at the back doors, and after the waiters and cooks and their families had fed on the remains, the beggars were given the plates, to lick them clean ...

And there were the scavenger dogs, to take care of everything else.

So the heaps along the wall were refuse of refuse, and among them the beggars lived, in hovels made of perhaps one piece of rotten wood, very precious, debris of mats that others had thrown away. Here the old man lived; who now revived, indicating feebly by moans and hand-waving the direction; and since there were no roads, only cinders, he had to walk, supported by Rosalie and the rickshaw man; and was greeted by other beggars, young and old, some deformed and some all naked, who obviously knew him, a company of the maimed, the crippled, the poorer than poor, next winter's corpses on the streets ... Joyfully they crowded round, not understanding. The rickshaw man explained, and they looked at Rosalie, who felt very foolish again. From among them was extracted an old woman, and this they said was the old beggar's wife. She was deaf and dumb, she smiled, she had no teeth.

Rosalie and the rickshaw man left, and the rickshaw man said: "Climb in if you wish for a little way," and trotted with her in his carriage till the main street, and then they parted, and Rosalie gave him her dollar.

Rosalie went home walking, and she wanted to tell her mother, but she knew it would be difficult because of the dollar. And at home Mama was in bad mood. She had had trouble with the woman who came round to sell eggs. She bought a hundred eggs for a dollar, at that time, four coppers each. It was the cheapest thing to buy, said Mama, and it was good for the eyes. But now she said the eggs were much smaller than they had ever been, and she had been cheated by the egg woman. So Rosalie never told about the beggar, there was no one to tell.

TWENTY-FOUR

FROM the start was duality, an other life, a saving otherness which was also self. One could and did become someone else, at different hours of the day. And the exact, concrete imagination of the child, stretched by the knowledge of this identity of contraries, finds its own order and discipline among the materials of chaos.

Even meals were like that. Meals could be European breakfast, Chinese lunch and again European supper, or one went out, the whole family together, to eat in a restaurant, always Chinese; or one went with Papa and ate all kinds of new things. And sometimes Papa cooked dishes from Szechuan, and that was always wonderful. No wonder Mama had mixed macaroni and Chinese noodles for the warlord, Feng Yuhsiang. After a while no differences were left, one's palate was eager for new savours, though appetite could only be satisfied with rice.

Breakfast could be coffee and bread, eggs and bacon, at one time Quaker Oats porridge because Rosalie was so thin (but porridge was always a sticky mess which Rosalie refused to eat, as she refused blancmange, jelly, anything gooey and bland because it made her feel sick); or it was millet and sweet potatoes and Chinese steamed buns. Lunch was rice and meat and vegetables, huge quantities, belayed into the mouth with chopsticks. Dinner could be brown bread with cheese or sausage and tea, and no milk because milk was too expensive and only Tiza had to drink it being weak, though the smell of milk made both the girls vomit; in that way they shared a Chinese disgust. Millions of Chinese could not stand the smell of milk at that time, only Europeans, half-castes, some westernized Chinese intellectuals drank coffee with milk in China in those days. People drank hot water, or tea, or beancurd milk which tasted of beancurd but not of cow.

Schools were like meals, two of the kind, Chinese school in the morning, French convent in the afternoon. For Chinese school one put on Chinese clothes and took along a brush, an ink box of metal with a sponge of silk wadding inside to soak the ink, the lid engraved with a landscape, an ink stick, a small black plate of polished slate on which one made ink by rubbing the stick on a little poured water, paper with squares, and Chinese books with paper covers. In the first Chinese book were pictures, and under the pictures characters: man, dog, big, small, much, little, eye, nose, mouth, one, two, three. It was very easy, because after a time there was so much rhythm to it all, a swing of word, sound and also writing. One repeated the characters, all together, when the teacher pronounced them. Later came sentences, also learnt by chanting, repeating after the teacher. Still later one could read several hundred characters, then one thousand, then suddenly one could read, truly read. This was a heart-lifting, magnificent day, when Rosalie stood with Papa at the newspaper board on the street and actually read aloud to him the big characters of the titles.

SEVEN COMMUNISTS FOUND IN CAVE: IMMEDIATE EXECUTION OF THE VERMIN. COMMUNIST INSPIRED STRIKE OF RAIL WORKERS BROKEN: LEADERS ARRESTED. MARSHAL CHANG TSOLIN ENTERTAINS JAPANESE DELEGATION TO DINNER. JAPANESE CLAIM INDEMNITY FOR SOLDIER MURDERED BY COMMUNISTS IN SHANTUNG.

One had to ask Papa about Communism. "Papa, what are Communists?"

Papa plucked the sparse hair on his chin, and said: "Young fools."

And Mama, who was standing too, asked: "What does she want?"

Papa said: "She is asking about the Reds."

And Mama said: "The Reds? They would murder us all in our beds if they could. In Russia they took little babies and threw them on their spikes in front of their mothers. They kill priests and nuns and they murder their own mothers."

"They're advancing," said Papa soberly. "The south is full of them."

"The south is always full of troubles," siad Mama. "The Cantonese, they are like monkeys. But they will not come here. It's too cold for them."

"Borodin is with them," said Papa. "The Russians are helping them."

"If they come," said Mama, "I'll go away. You can stay in this terrible country if you like. You'll probably like the Reds.

But I'm not going to be murdered and see my little girls killed in front of me. I shall leave."

Papa plucked at his hairs on the chin, and Rosalie made a mental note to find out about Communism.

Father Clement of the church in the Legation Quarters came to the European convent for catechism every Thursday afternoon. The convent was much farther away from home than the Chinese school and Rosalie at first went by rickshaw when Feng was still the puller. Later she walked to school and back four times a day. The uniform was blue and white, and she had a canvas case slung round the shoulder, a pen, pencils in a wooden pencase with a painted scene from a frosted European landscape of snow and sleighs and bells (Rosalie, wanting to find out how the paint got on to the box, managed to scrape it off, and it never grew back again, whereas Tiza's box kept clean and beautiful). Almost as fast as she got into school she was put into catechism class, because of Holy Communion that was coming. She was six, and learnt to read very quickly, so that after six months she was put in a higher class, and in another six months into a yet higher one.

"The child is too quick," Mother Superior said to Mama, and she made it sound like another wickedness, which was now called SIN. Mother Superior was a tall woman with very blue eyes and a very soft voice, and she was Canadian, and beautiful too. No hair about her mouth.

Mama replied that they had no money, and school was expensive, and Rosalie also had Chinese school, and the sooner she was through her studies the better.

So Rosalie doubled classes about every six months, and came out first almost every month, bringing home a beautiful pink card with her trophy for being first, a holy picture. And every time she was first Papa gave her a silver dollar, with the fat head of a man stamped on it, which was Yuan Shihkai, the warlord who wanted to be Emperor.

It was Father Clement who gave Rosalie the grey catechism book with questions and answers. He asked the questions, and one gave the answers. He also gave them a talk about Jesus afterwards. Rosalie looked up Jesus in the dictionary, and then she read a Bible which had been Mama's, and as she took everything literally, suddenly she became very upset because people were not as the catechism and the Bible told them to be, not at all. People who were Catholics, that is. Not people like the cook, or Feng the rickshaw man, or Wang

Mah. And this was very puzzling. There was, for instance, the injunction: "Give all thou hast." But no one did. Rosalie felt guilty, because both she and Tiza had a drawer in which they kept their things, books, boxes, ribbons, brooches, pencils, toys, glass beads, marbles, and their money in a box with a slit, which made it easy to put in but hard to get out. Tiza had many things in her drawer, but Rosalie decided that she must give all hers away since it said so in the Bible. The dollar to the rickshaw man who had pulled the beggar home she now felt was not enough, so she gave another dollar to the collection in the Eastern church. Nobody ever gave a dollar, not even the very rich Mr. Wong. Mama often gave a button, because she said that is what her uncle used to do, the very wealthy uncle in Antwerp with South African diamond shares. Then Rosalie was so ashamed of having given away a dollar, because Mama said that squanderers would die "on the straw," that again she could never tell anyone, though she comforted herself with the fact that Papa gave her a dollar every time she was first in class, and since she was nearly always first it would only take her to the end of the month to make it up, and Mama need never know.

Then Rosalie went to the cinema one afternoon with Mama and Tiza, and it was a picture on Jesus, called *The King of Kings*. This was most disturbing. She wept all night, she could not stop weeping. The impact of Jesus in the picture, realization that around her no one at all was like Jesus, that people did not even try to be like Him, engulfed her in tears. She was puffy-eyed and exhausted the next morning from crying, but again told no one.

She now began to apply everything exactly as Jesus said, reading the Bible and not the catechism, and the dictionary for all words not understood. Each child in the catechism class was prepared for Communion, being slowly brought up to a boiling-point of fervour with extra prayers, stations in front of the Host, stories of Jesus, scapulars around the neck, and weekly confessions in the little chapel of the Convent School. The first time in confession Rosalie had not had much to say, but now she knew better, and made lists of sins, by categories: anger came first, lying close second. To remember their sins, the children were issued with cards, and enjoined each time they committed a venial sin to prick a small hole into it with a pin; a mortal sin rated a hole in a black square drawn in the middle of the card. Rosalie found to her horror that her card had more holes than anyone else's, and even a mortal sin had to be pricked in one day because she had had impure thoughts, having looked up in the dictionary under p for pregnancy to find where babies came from, though it was communism she was looking up at the time, but pregnancy had been read about too.

A recurrent sin was that she did not love Mother Superior, nor Father Clement, nor any of the people she was supposed to love, except Papa and Mama and Tiza. Since she did not love Father Clement, she decided she must be specially nice to him, and speak to him, and one way to learn to love him was to ask him about communism. But first she asked Simon Hua, because Simon Hua always knew everything.

Simon Hua was four years older than she; they often met and sometimes played together in the park, because Papa and Mr. Hua, Simon's father, worked together in the same railway office. Simon wagged his head solemnly at Rosalie, and said: "You don't understand, you are only a girl. Communism is Revolution. I will be a Communist, and then I am going to make the Revolution."

"I," Rosalie retorted, "will feed one egg to each child in China every day, and no one will be blind. I hate to see blind people. I'm scared of blindness, it's like death."

"You," Simon retorted loftily, "don't understand anything. If there is a revolution there won't be any more blind people. That is communism."

Rosalie went bounding away. Simon used long words, like revolution, and Rosalie disliked long words if she did not know what they meant. That night she got the dictionary down from the shelf above Papa's desk and looked up the word revolution. And then she read the history of the French Revolution, and Danton and Marat. But at the Chinese school there was nothing about revolution, or communism, because this was also a Catholic school and no questions could be asked at all. Questions can be answered, she thought, out of dictionaries and books, but people either did not know, or even if they knew they would not tell what they knew, not the way the dictionary told it, and that was the way she could best understand it.

Simon talked long words, and they were words in the dictionary, one could look them up, but even so he could not really make it clear to a six-year-and-a-little-more-old. Simon's mother was what Mama called "a Jewess", and his

father, Mr. Hua, was Papa's best friend as well as colleague
in the Railway Office. Mr. Hua had studied engineering in
France at the same time as Papa had studied in Belgium. Mr.
Hua was very nice, no one was afraid of him, but Simon and
his sister Leila always acted as if they knew everything, and
snubbed Rosalie, who pretended not to care and bounded off;
yet she always ran back to Simon.

Mrs. Hua was strange, fascinating, and a little frightening,
and Simon was much like Mrs. Hua in his face. There was
always a clear connection between mother and son, so that
she could distinguish in Simon's gestures, tones of voice,
laughter, that part which was his mother, a certain bend of
the profile, a curl to the nostril, but most of all holding the
head very erect, though Mrs. Hua was short compared to
Mama.

It was Mrs. Hua's nose that made Mama say that she was a
Jewess. Mrs. Hua invited them to tea twice a year, and it was
always a solemn affair. She wore a long velvet dress with folds,
a long necklace of amber dangling down to her stomach, her
hair coiled on top of her head, and tea was served in the garden on little tables. Rosalie gazed about her in awe, afraid
to break anything. The house, the garden with its rose bushes
and lilac, and the living-room with an embroidered tapestry of
dragons, amber and scarlet, appeared to her very grand and
rich. Under the tapestry was a couch on which Mrs. Hua
sometimes reclined, upon cushions of yellow satin which to
Rosalie were the acme of beauty, and somehow confused with
the gold veil upon the Host in church. Against another wall a
Chinese rosewood whatnot with many tiers held curios, jade
figures and ivory elephants, and it was all very precious because Mama immediately said: "Don't touch anything, do
you hear?"

Mrs. Hua wrote books, so it was said, something else which
was spoken of with bated breath by several of Mama's friends.
But Mama, returning from tea at the Huas', snorted to Papa:
"That Jewess is full of herself. Books ... I'd much rather
make good soup." At the tea parties one had to sit and sit,
while Simon played the violin, and then clap hands, though
one hadn't heard anything except some noises which were
supposed to be music. And then one trooped into the living-
room, and Leila played the piano, and one clapped again.

And one day Mama said Mrs. Hua was a Communist, and
would be decapitated. All Communists were having their heads

cut off. Rosalie knew it, she had seen executions already, Wang Mah had taken her to see them. At street corners the photographs of the tortured and the executed, all Communists, were fresh every few days. One she remembered, a man, or rather what remained of the man, with no arms and legs left but only bleeding eroded stumps, held up for the camera's picture by two soldiers on each side, his rib bones showing where the skin and overlaying flesh had been chiselled off in chunks. It was the slow torture, before the head was cut off. Reserved for bad Communists.

Rosalie pictured Mrs. Hua in her satin gown held up like that, but the picture would not come true because Mrs. Hua had very short legs with rather fat feet in pointed shoes emerging from under her skirt; in fact, she suddenly resembled a dachshund with nose instead of muzzle most salient in her face.

"Certainly my mother is a Communist," said Simon loftily. "So am I. It's the only thing to be. Don't you see the state the country is in?"

Rosalie looked round her. The park lifted preening slopes of artificial rock gardens; pavilions with red columns stood among willows; and she knew the park was beautiful with its alleys, its old old trees, the swoop of grey magpies in the air. Then other pictures intruded: the beggars, the blind. It was all so unfair, and she had no right to be here, playing, when there were other people who could not play here. So back she went to the dictionary, to find the word communism; and it also said that communism was a belief created by a sect of anarchists, and anarchy meant killing, and throwing bombs, and murder of royalty. And revolution, according to the dictionary, meant the French Revolution, or the earth turning round the sun.

"Communism?" Father Clement hunched upon his folds of grey-red fat. His face was winy-red, with bristles on head and chin and down the two dewlaps of his cheeks, his nose was round and red and pitted with holes, and in her frequent sinful moments Rosalie longed to stick a pin into the holes to find out how deep they went. "My child, who has been talking about communism to you?"

"I saw it in the newspaper," said Rosalie, who could not betray Papa and herself in that Other World of Other Words, standing together to read the Chinese newspaper pasted on the wall, and mentally she thought this half-lie possibly deserved half a hole in her card ... venial sin, it was only a small lie, she decided, since she had actually seen "communism" in the Chinese newspaper.

Father Clement then told her about communism, how it was the most frightful thing, how it made one kill one's own father and mother, was against nature, against God, in fact, an invention of the Devil himself. He added: "Some foolish people, my child, take it up, and you see the result, this country of China, devastated. It is God who made the world, and He knows what is best for us. Pray to Him, and to the Virgin Mary, and have faith. Then you will understand."

So that was that, Father Clement said it was bad, and Simon was wrong; he was more than wrong, he was in danger. Rosalie felt that she must go and convert Simon, and also his mother, and save their souls from communism and certainly their heads from decapitation. For she knew it was Communists who were being killed, beheaded, shot, maimed, flesh ripped from thigh and belly. After school, instead of going home, she told Tiza to tell Mama that she was going to the French Bakery to have tea with Vera Thassounis. Mrs. Thassounis, who sold cakes at the French Bakery and occasionally sold Mama a cake on Sundays (and always gave Tiza and Rosalie an extra small pastry), had a daughter Vera, a very pretty little girl with lovely tumbling curls, red-gold, and beautiful manners, who took ballet dancing and wore silk stockings, and whose sister, a girl of sixteen or so, was reported engaged to an Englishman who worked in the English Bank, and Mama said the English were masters of the world, and to work in a bank was a very good job, and how lucky to marry an Englishman! That was really to be safe for ever after. Mama said to Papa: "These are the people you ought to know." Actually the friendship between Rosalie and Vera was founded on an edible arrangement, whereby Rosalie did Vera's homework for her, because Vera could not do any sums at all, and Vera paid for ever-hungry Rosalie's help with two pastries and a cup of cocoa. In later years Rosalie was to exploit Vera's weakness in brainwork to extract from Vera's mother as payment, an occasional dinner, in return for coaching. But that was some years later, when Rosalie needed money desperately, and Papa and Mama did not give her any.

From school to where Simon Hua lived, in the Hutung of the Unmeasurably Distinguished Gentleman, was twenty minutes, and there was a stiff spring wind with volleys of pelting sand, the dry, intolerably irritating wind from the Gobi desert which crimps the skin with sand; not only the pores but all the openings, the tender place between one's legs, the mouth with its gums, the corners of the eyes.

Fighting the wind, Rosalie arrived at Simon Hua's house near to crying, half with the thought of the task to perform, half with dust-anger. The red door ensconced in its grey wall had a doorbell handle, an intriguing bronze snake that one pulled, when a bell rang in the house. One listened to the house door open, and the advance of footsteps on the stone walk crossing the garden diagonally. The garden had lilac and rose bushes, a Judas tree that went rioting crimson late in the spring, a large porcelain tub with goldfish, but now the goldfish were indoors because it was so cold. In the middle of the goldfish tub was a rock with moss, similar to one in the hothouse at the Central Park. Rosalie always thought that rock a most lovely thing.

The white-robed servant who opened the door said that the family was not in, and invited Rosalie to enter and rest. She sat alone with a cup of tea in the room, and thought it most beautiful, noticing again the couch, the tapestry, other things that to her spoke of luxury then, for at home there were no carpets on the floor, no pictures on the wall, no cushions upon the chairs, the furniture was sombre and full of edges that one bumped into, especially if one was as awkward and clumsy as Rosalie.

The white-robed servant, who was to grow old in the family's service and to be found again, an old man, when Rosalie returned to Simon Hua's house thirty-three years later, said that the Taitai and the Young Master and Miss were preparing to go away, they were going to Europe for a holiday and would be back perhaps after one year or so. Rosalie said oh yes, her own mother was going back for a visit too. This she said defensively, it was a deliberate lie, yet not a lie since Mama always and still threatened to leave, but now there was Marianne, and Rosalie had stopped worrying about Mama going away. Mama herself said Marianne was too small to leave.

The next day converting Simon and his mother from communism did not seem so urgent, and in a week Rosalie forgot because when Simon and she met in the park there were other children, including Pao, whose father was very rich, and he was playing a war game, and suddenly Rosalie forgot about everything but the old days with Balthazar the horse, and was fascinated with Pao, who was arrogant, and had two servants to look after him in the park. Pao was so witheringly clever and sure of himself.

Pao pulled her hair, they fought each other behind the artificial rocks, and that only made him more real. They scarcely exchanged words, they were too intent on physical feats, running, pummelling each other and whipping up imaginary horses for gallops. With Pao Rosalie lapsed back into brute childhood, muscular, raucous, and was happy as the spring, turned mild then sultry, when flowers begin, pert on still leaf-timid trees, and the artificial hills went pink, disdaining the dry earth ready to swivel dust at any moment.

Simon Hua went away to Europe, he and his sister Leila, and did not reappear for some years.

With Pao, as at Chinese school, it was the Other World, a world in which one spoke Chinese, religion did not exist, nor cards to prick for sin; a much less explanation-requiring world, in which other things were done or not done, and it made Rosalie wince when Mama did not know them, as happened when Pao's father invited them all to dinner one night.

The Tang house was a palace of many courtyards, because Pao's father was a Big Official, at that moment working under the Big Overlord Wu Peifu. He did not have a rickshaw, he had a carriage with horses, and a motor car with bodyguards on the sidesteps when he went on official business.

The main gate was bright red with knobs painted in brassy gold. Two stone lions on each side reared from pedestals, three ferocious red-haired chow dogs threw barks and fanged the visitors, restrained by the door servants, tall Northerners in long blue robes with blue trousers underneath, with white socks, black cloth shoes, and black silken bands at the junction between sock and trouser. They went through the first courtyard, as usual barred by a screen of brick, carved with lotuses, so that no devil could enter the house since all devils travelled in straight lines.

The entrance was a little way to the left; on through another, and then another courtyard, with pots of porcelain planted with pomegranates, and peonies; on both sides the rooms, with their latticework windows behind which one could hear people laughing and talking and the rattle of mah-jong. Into the main hall, to be received there, and Rosalie was immediately frightened and Tiza burst into tears because Pao was lying on the floor howling, round him a crowd of women stood or knelt, and servants ran to and fro. Pao's father seemed not to hear or see his son as he received his visitors, and shook hands with Mama, and that is where Mama said: "What a spoilt child," very loud, which was so rude, and there was a freezing hush, except for the screams from the male child upon the rugs.

Of that dinner Rosalie remembered an agony of shame as Mama did one wrong thing after another. Papa, seated at another table with the men, seemed not to see, and in fact did not see her. For once Papa was having happiness, he was quoting verse. Though Rosalie could not understand it all, she knew it was poetry because of the wonderful way chills ran down her spine with the words, and the way all the men applauded ... Papa was the hero-scholar tonight, and it was obvious that he received homage, that others listened, bursts of laughter and applause wafted from his table as in his Szechuan voice, with its resonant gong-like reverberation, he spoke lines of poetry or told a witty story. Papa was a poet, Rosalie knew, because she had found lines in his thin writing, and though her Chinese was not advanced enough for the sense, she could make out the sound by looking at the words, and it was poetry. But he wrote these on slips of paper, then twisted them, and sometimes buried them at the root of his carnations in the earth of the flower pots.

Rosalie and Tiza and Mama were at a women's table, and Mama was doing everything wrong: dropping pieces of food back into the main dish, refusing wine, eating too much of the first course, and then when one of the women, a slight small one with hair like smooth lacquer, who turned out to be the Third Concubine, put a small piece of fish on her plate she did not eat it. It was not so much what Mama did, it was that every gesture, every move, every word, was wrong, excruciatingly wrong. And her Chinese sounded so bad, she put all the accents the wrong way, and it meant something quite different from what she meant, and the women tittered round her. They were stupid women, Rosalie knew, eyes encased in fat; except Third Concubine who was still slim and very pretty, the others were lazy, cruel, stupid, fat women. And soon Rosalie found out that Pao was actually the concubine's son, and there was no other; none of the other wives or concubines had produced sons, and that was why Pao's mother was well beloved. And she also knew that Pao's mother now had to fight for her life, for she could be supplanted, or thrown out if intrigues against her, by the unfavoured jealous ones, succeeded.

After dinner everyone went back to their mahjong game, and Mama sat and watched, and did not play; Pao also played, destroying the games he did not like, sweeping the ivory pieces on to the floor, and immediately half a dozen servants picked them up, laughing as if it was an amusing thing he had done. He was fondled all the time by the women; everyone spoke of his good looks, and Rosalie could understand this, for he had polished skin, hair blue-black like his mother, and all his movements were swift and light. He made some rude remarks about Mama, and Rosalie felt her cheeks burn, but Mama did not understand and took the laughter to be goodnatured, and smiled happily, showing the hole on the side of her mouth where she had lost another tooth.

TWENTY-FIVE

AFTER the fervour, the kneelings, the sinful deeds with unheroic ends in a guilty pin-pricked card, suddenly devotion went, ebbing tranquilly away just before Holy Communion. A new harshness sauntered into Rosalie, a cold vision of the two worlds she lived in, the two beings she had to be, both unreal to herself since both varied with time and place. The two communicated, one sitting back and telling the other: "Go ahead, your turn. Say yes madame, curtsy, hold a fork, laugh at things you don't think funny at all." The other being, more fierce, went in a silent roam about the streets with bread for dogs and coppers for beggars, and rage rage rage for self because there was no end at all, like the dust, like the dust, no end to the misery, the abject squalor; and yet proud, clutching a sense of wanting to be part of this squalor, in spite of Mama.

Now was born another conflict, brought about by Papa and Mama. It started with Mama once more wanting to go away, back to Europe, and even rushing off in the rickshaw with Tiza one afternoon while Rosalie was told to look after Marianne. Mama went to the Belgian Consulate to get a passport, and returned downcast, sobbing into a handkerchief, because the Consul told her that she had Chinese nationality now and would not get her own passport back.

There followed some days of inexplicable hurt, because both Papa and Mama separately told Rosalie things about each other that Rosalie at seven could only understand in small pieces.

Papa complained to Rosalie about Mama's temper, about the vulgarity of her ways. He told her how white people, away from their own lands, from the restraining influence of their own laws, deteriorated into barbaric desert islanders. White people, he said, coming out to China, turned into vicious, brutal beings; back in their own country they behaved so much better. Mama had also changed, he said. And he told how she had changed, though she had been, could be, charming and wonderful. And to prove Papa's words followed headlong two unpleasant episodes, one with a beggar (that relentless pattern of beggary which haunted Rosalie's early years), one at the cinema.

The beggar was an ambulant horror, boy of fourteen or sixteen with leprosy, wrapped in a jute sack full of holes, tied with a rope round his chest, his feet bound with old newspapers, old newspapers round his purulent bald head, and he pursued Mama with moans as she walked with Rosalie and Tiza one afternoon, returning home, because Feng the rickshaw had asked leave to bury his grandmother, and he was gone for two days, and Mama had fired him, and tomorrow another man would come to pull their rickshaw. If Feng *did* try to come back, he would be told that no one could wait for him and his grandmother, so many thousands were waiting for a job, a good job as a rickshaw puller, Feng could "die on the straw" for all one cared, as did all those who squandered, buried grandmothers, were lazy. When Mama spoke that way Rosalie knew that she too could be included in that lot, since she could not accumulate dollars because at times she was seized with the utter folly of giving dollars away.

As rickshaw-less they walked back to the house that day, they met this boy, who pursued Mama, moaning and chanting in a stange shrill voice, and holding up stumps of hands, and Mama shouted: "I have no money. Go away, go away." Rosalie and Tiza turned and also shouted: "Go away." And then the leper was seized with madness, lifted his newspapered arms and struck Mama's back as she walked away from him, and screamed: "Go away, go away, go away ..." parodying her accent, so wrong with Chinese words.

Mama ran, screaming, holding Rosalie and Tiza by the

hand, and at the turning corner of the lane was a policeman (there were many of them in Peking in those days), and she gestured, pointing to the beggar. The policeman, with stick twirling, advanced eagerly upon the beggar. They did not stay to see what happened, but heard the howls, heard the blows, a dull, damp stamping, diminishing as they quickened their steps, ran home.

And whenever Mama told this story, in her own way, in later years, Rosalie would run away, run from the story and its recurring horror.

A week after that came the cinema episode.

The cinema was called in Chinese the True Light Cinema. It had a brown gooey façade, and at that time looked enormous; it had suffered, forty years later when Rosalie returned to stare at it (renamed The People's Theatre, and with a grey sticky façade), the shrink that all revisited childhood monuments suffer. The True Light Cinema showed chiefly American pictures in the 1920s, because there were no Chinese film companies. The films were all galloping horses, villains, and usually a buxom girl, with long fair hair, who was constantly getting herself tied to railtracks and rescued in the nick of time from a rapidly enlarging locomotive belching smoke that blackened the screen and dimmed the cinema too. An orchestra of White Russians in the pit made appropriate music with drum beats for revolver shots. *The King of Kings*, and *City Lights* with Charlie Chaplin (which Mama did not think funny), Rosalie would remember for many years; also a film, *The Birth of a Nation*, which showed hooded horsemen clad in white sheets riding down ugly black men, and the same fair-haired, buxom girl, throwing herself down some rocks because a black man was running after her and smiling. It was at this film that the incident occurred.

Someone in the audience (while it was dark and musically solemn because a house was being burnt with the white-clad horsemen ranged round watching) got up and started to shout. There was immediately a commotion, lights were switched on, policemen appeared from the four corners of the hall where they were always posted, and the young man who had shouted was dragged away, the usual sticks plying upon him quick and fast while he strove to cover his bleeding face with his hands. And it reminded Rosalie of Charlie Chaplin, though this young man was Chinese and had the scarf round his neck which indicated he was a university student.

While the young man was being dragged out, Mama turned to Rosalie, who was not sitting in the same row as Mama and Tiza and Papa, but alone behind, because there had been only three seats in the row. The young boy who occupied the seat next to Tiza had left it to run to the aisle, as many others did, to get closer to the young student whom the policemen were dragging away. "Quick, now," said Mama, "sit here with us."

Rosalie obeyed. She sat next to Tiza, in the seat left vacant by the boy.

But the boy now returned, and said: "This is my seat."

Mama indicated the seat in the row behind, which Rosalie had left. "You can sit there."

The young boy began to shout: "This is my seat, my seat."

And all the people in the cinema now crowded round them, round Mama, Papa, Rosalie and Tiza.

Then another young man with a scarf began to shout, and the young boy suddenly raised his fist and screamed: "Down with all white devils from over the sea," and there was a noise like a train approaching quickly, and it was the whole cinema, all the people there, together making this noise. They stamped, clapped, whistled, and suddenly they were all shouting, in time: "Down with the colonists, down with the imperialists," and singing.

The policemen reappeared, and again they began to use their sticks, but they were too few, and they crowded round Mama and the girls and got them out of the cinema, and Papa stayed behind. Then he too came out, and he was so pale, Rosalie had never seen him that colour before.

"Back home," he said, not looking at Mama. For the first time Rosalie heard him raise his voice. "It's your fault. You don't understand. You are a white woman. You cannot insult us all the time."

"Just try," Mama said, "just touch me. My government will send an army with guns and kill you all off. Remember the Boxers."

"You are my wife," said Papa.

And Mama screamed: "I will go back, I don't want anything to do with this vermin, these yellow vermin of yours." And as usual, as was nearly automatic now, as soon as they were inside their own house, she wrapped Tiza (who was crying just as automatically) in her arms and swept into the bedroom, pursued by Rosalie, who held her skirt, tugging, and saying: "Mama, Mama . . ."

But Mama looked at her with a terrible face, as the police-man had looked at the beggar, and said: "Go away, you, go to your father."

And so Rosalie was left with Papa in the dining-room, and Papa sat down. He began to talk to Rosalie, first with a big sigh like a "han", like the "han" that the coolies exhaled when they lifted loads on to their shoulders, and then staggered on, walking in single file, catching breath with a "han" now and then, singing: "Oioyeehoh, han, Oyoyeehoh, han, Ayayeyaha, han, Ayayeehaha." The song of work, the song of heavy loads to be carried, unendingly, till dead, dead between their spine-breaking load and the dust, the never-ending dust.

And that "han" was also like the breathing of old rickshaw pullers, those that could not run fast any more when they pulled, those always out of breath, having blown their lungs out with a lifetime of running.

"Han ... han ... hoho han ... han ... aiyah ... han ... han."

So Papa "han'ed", and then began to talk, complaining about Mama, and Rosalie remembered the words, the sen-tences in small pieces, though in the middle there was an emptiness, which Papa left untouched, which Rosalie could not understand. In the days that followed there was happiness with Papa, because he took Rosalie out walking with him, going to look at things here and there, but chiefly to the flower and plant markets, staying out late in the afternoons. And all the time he talked about Mama.

And for Rosalie it was happiness, but also agony, because listening to Papa was going against Mama, and one *had* to love Mama, there was something so hateful and yet so much to be pitied about Mama. It was a grievous sin not to love Mama. Mama complained about Papa too. But then she always complained, it was not so serious. Whereas Papa com-plaining, saying these things, Papa out of his silence, was a terrible thing, almost as bad as the leper boy.

And so one day, between remorse and headache, a feeling that she wanted to vomit and another strange feeling of power, of making herself into something important, Rosalie opened her mouth, and told Mama what Papa said of her.

She did not tell everything, but only some of the things Papa had said. And Mama grasped Rosalie's shoulder, and said: "You are my daughter." And Rosalie felt once again accepted, back into safety. But it was only for an hour or so.

Mama could not keep her tongue still, though she had promised Rosalie not to tell Papa. A day later, walking to the flower market, Papa said quietly to Rosalie: "It seems that you too are like a sieve, everything goes from you."

And Rosalie knew Mama had betrayed her, but said righteously: "You shouldn't say things about Mama, because she is my mother."

And Papa said: "Perhaps I shouldn't," and they went on to the flower market. But it was not the same as before, and they never spoke of Mama again until thirty years later.

The day of Holy Communion came round. It had been delayed for Rosalie, to wait for Tiza, Mama wanted both of them to have it together. Though Tiza was under seven, it had been proclaimed in the church that, by special permission, any child who loved God could take Communion, even if not yet seven. Tiza did not even have to learn much catechism, and anyway she was an angel, everyone said it.

On that day all was gone from Rosalie, all piety, all emotion. Everything was dry in her, dry, acerbic, burnt; dry as the cinders on the garbage dumps where the beggars rotted their lives away. Though she tried, Rosalie could no longer find the remorse or the ardour that she had associated with *The King of Kings*. The tears at night, the card with its pin holes, all that had made flame inside her was gone, would never return. Other images remained. Puppies, and babies, and the fierce longing that made her walk, walk, looking at beggars. On the very morning of that day she was wicked: in church, trying hard to feel the promised ecstasy on the absorption of the small, difficult-to-swallow, dry round wafer, without savour or smell, which stuck in her throat and melted slowly, without pleasure or pain, she said what she had been taught to say, "Thank you, O God, for this great favour," but she felt nothing at all. Throughout that day, though the other little girls managed to look so happy, so radiant, in white gowns with veils and crowns of white artificial flowers pinning the veils in place, all to be good and happy for ever, she felt nothing but a grim gritty lassitude; and looking at the devil's head, familiar with that prostrate demon and his curls, she began to smile, a secret, conspiratorial grin, as at some infamous joke, never to be betrayed.

TWENTY-SIX

WHAT does a growing child know of its own growth? A measurement, triumphant, along a wall; a reaching up for things, a clambering, a trying on of mother's clothes; a joyous shout when a dress becomes too short; an exuberant muscular will to run, to leap, to play games, an avid demand for knowing, in spite of the refrain: "When you grow up ...", "Don't ask now," "Don't be wicked," "Don't, don't, don't ask," "Curiosity is a sin," "Why do you want to know all this?"

And so the child is brought back to self; a growing self, weedlike, ugly, stubborn, quarrelsome, disturbing, unstill and full of dreams.

In Rosalie a fragmentation of the total self occurred, each piece recreating from its own sum of facts a person, each person functioning separately, withholding itself from the other, yet throughout maintaining a secret vigilance, boneless coherence, fragile as the thread that guided Theseus in his labyrinth. Others born like her of two worlds, who chose not to accept this splitting, fragmentation of monolithic identity into several selves, found themselves later unable to face the contradictions latent in their own beings. Consistency left them crippled for the world's incoherence.

In Rosalie the necessity of knowing mutually contradictory truths without assuming any one of them to be the whole truth, became in childhood the only way to live on, to live and to remain substantial. And she was astonished that others were unwilling to accept the discomfort of always being partly wrong, of never knowing a total answer; they became so sure, believing one thing only, preferring a cosy semi-blindness to the pricking clarity of doubt.

Of course, thought Rosalie, it is more comfortable. It is like never moving the furniture about.

She saw Meiling, her friend at the time of acute friendships, riding in her rickshaw through the street, her eyes shut. "Because I don't like to see those ugly poor people," said Meiling to Rosalie, smiling an enchanting happy smile. Meiling was pretty and rich, being the daughter of Mr. Hsu, who took collections in the Eastern church. She was Rosalie's schoolmate at Chinese school, and loved Rosalie, and Rosalie for a while forgave her for not *wanting* to see, because Meiling was so pretty to look at. But only for a while; only as long as Meiling enchanted her. One day the enchantment stopped, Meiling began to bore her, and her closed eyelids in the rickshaw provided the excuse for breaking their friendship.

Rosalie loved many friends, made many friends, but the friends fell off, like fruit ripening on a tree, in their time. Sooner or later, dry-eyed, screaming abuse where she had loved with torrid passion and given gifts with earned dollars, Rosalie threw another love away, shaking it off her tree of life. Plop, it fell off her, and took days to heal the scar, though she had done the wound to herself. She sobbed in her pillow, as usual loudly, pouring her momentarily unoccupied emotion into grief, but even as she wept, someone else, who was also Rosalie, sat back watching her weep, sneering: "Look at yourself, you stupid, crying ... you *know* it will stop hurting one day ..."

"That's just it," said Rosalie to Rosalie, "that's what will happen. One day I won't feel anything at all." She sobbed louder.

"You know you could have gone on. You did not have to call her big fat cow just because she won't come walking with you round the park."

"But the park is beautiful. The wistaria is beautiful. And I love her."

"You stupid cow yourself. Who cares about your wistaria? Its hung beauty will be there next year. Next year you can go."

"Rosalie," said Papa, "come and see the wistaria with me this afternoon, next week it will be over."

And Rosalie jumped up, and followed Papa. Though she had betrayed Papa, was now listening to Mama speaking ill of Papa, it made no difference to the wistaria. And only Papa knew how to look at them.

And one day growing up became a great bound, outstripping years of unrelieved plainness, the lotuses in the Peihai Park of Peking. No one had ever told Rosalie that Peking was beautiful. The first shock of beauty was the lotuses in the park, and from that day she really knew that the vibration, like the long cry of summer cicadas, along her wrists and up into the shoulders and down the back, was the recognition of beauty.

And Peking was beautiful then, so beautiful; harsh, cruel beauty to live and die in. Beautiful and hard and cold, harsh winter, with its eddies of dust, each particle solid, gritty cold, hammered out of Cold itself. And after the snows, ice bears down upon the flat city, and everything turns to frozen stone. Icicles, twenty feet high, droop from the roofs, and bodies stone-hard are picked up in the streets, some with their heads between their knees. Then comes spring, the worst season: winds from Central Asia, sand-laden, the sky bronze, all the hutungs corridors of sand, a yellow-golden dusk upon the city from day to day, walking impossible; and only the rickshaws, ghosts of sand, pulling, pulling ghost-yellow carriages in the blur of sand. Then comes a beautiful three weeks, the short pre-summer, when the blue Western Hills are flower-blanketed, when lilac sprouts in the courtyards of the houses, and the battered grass jumps up in the parks, grass immediately, vengefully, to be charred by the sudden summer tramping towards its iron heat of July, an iron lid of heat which clamps down upon the city. Then everyone loses temper and weight, and the Europeans go to the sea-side, and at night there is no sleep. But it is the time of lotuses.

The lotuses bedded in the lakes prepare their outburst in tens of thousands. A foot across, a foot above the water, mastondontal pink and white, they fill the lake and the old canals dug round the Imperial City, and through them a lane must be cut for the gliding small boats, the boats of those who have come to "savour the lotus", poling their craft between the blossoms. With Papa, who was so enamoured of flowers, Rosalie saw the lotuses. She stood on the marble bridge spanning the lake, and beauty came, no longer word-in-dictionary, and became another elemental fierceness, choosing itself always, choosing itself and nothing else.

This is how beauty came, to hold together, with delicate thread, through the dust of make-believe and the dullness of words, through the impotent rages, through the ugliness and the horror, all the Rosalies, all the different Rosalies-to-be. And she knew that Papa also knew what beauty was, and for a short while she thought she understood his silence, his refuge of silence, the great silence of an immobile father looking his heart out at the flowers. She began to understand that one must keep beauty secret, a sharp thing, hedgehog of the heart. Everything began to hurt more, so that she went out raging through the hutungs at dusk, raging because everything was now touched with beauty, everything was infected with this loveliness which was constant pain, a discomfort at times so overwhelming that one had to do ugly things, to say ugly words, to drown the hurt in ugly, trivial laughter, to obtain surcease from the heart pounding of beauty. So many people ran away into ugliness, and made it their home, calling it cosy, and pretty. But beauty always crept in finally, all the more terrible for having been kept out. And beauty was also the beggars on their rubbish dumps, and Feng the rickshaw man, and the dying babies, and the frozen dead. Oh terrible terrible the big merciless hedgehog restlessness on its bed, the heart.

And then the thought of Mama, the love of Mama, began to hurt more, because though she saw, she did not look; when she looked she began to talk, saying: "Look, it's nice," and this hurt too, because when things are beautiful there is no word. The beggar with the fit had had a beautiful face, but Mama would not have called it nice, or anything. She would have run away.

For a while Rosalie clung to the silence of Papa, and with it and the lotus, so sure in swaying loveliness, one side of her grew, waiting while other Rosalies shouted and screamed, hurt and were hurt, wore out fierce loves and broke them, not careless, but because there was, in the end, no compromise with the lotus, the silence, the beauty that was horror, to be seen and smelt and felt.

Every month Papa took Rosalie with him to the Lungfusze Fair. Every ten days a fair was held, but Papa only went once a month. It was a fair that had gone on through many centuries at the temple, and like all temples it was both Taoist and Buddhist at once. In spite of the warlords and their wars, the people of Peking came to the fair to sell and to barter, to see and to haggle, to loiter and to look at the magicians, the wrestlers, the man who broke stones with his wrist, the child acrobats, the goldfish and the flowers, the birds in their cages, the embroidered shoes, the secondhand gowns and coats for sale.

"Goldfish are flowers," said Papa, "flowers that move."

They stood in a small crowd around the old man who with his wrist broke stones, a thin, very thin old man, his left wrist bandaged in a small grey rag.

"Look, look, old masters, young masters, all, see what this old bone can do, with one flick of its wrist, pah, pah, this old one" – pointing to his nose, as Chinese do to designate themselves – "shall break this stone. For my wrist is stronger than an iron hammer, yes, and this I will show. See!"

The bone of the forearm, with its companion blue vein,

came down upon the stone, a round river-worn small boulder, which split in two.

The small crowd threw a few copper coins on the ground, the old man bent to pick them up. All his spine bones could be counted. Rosalie tugged at Papa. They left. She felt Papa knew it hurt her to see the man so old, and what would he do tomorrow, when the stone would no longer split under his blow? And the circle of onlookers had suddenly reminded her of the execution ground, when with a great flash the heavy curved knife had whooshed through the air and only half through the neck, and the semi-severed head opened its mouth but no scream came, the windpipe severed through.

But perhaps Papa did not understand. There was in him, as in so many around Rosalie, in kind, gentle and good little girls, like Meiling, like Tiza, a determination of not-seeing, so that the seeing ones were ashamed of themselves for seeing.

The fair could not be contained within the courtyards of the temple, it overflowed into the adjacent hutungs, and these twisted as usual, so that at each smudged corner there were new things to see, chicken and ducks, geese straining their necks to snap, paper whirligigs, coffins, smelling good, of camphor wood, lacquered leather boxes. But Papa always walked towards the plant section, and only after he had bought some oleanders or midget willows, did they go slowly round. One day Papa bought forsythia for the garden; they blossomed the spring after, throwing tentacular boughs covered in yellow stars, and this again was beauty to watch by the hour. He bought dahlias, enormous, shaggy blossoms, and chrysanthemums for the autumn, pomegranates to place at the entrance to the courtyard, and carnations and roses. He liked to walk slowly, and Rosalie walked with him, proud to walk thus, and the silence now helped her to see. And thus for a short space she learnt to accept through sense what brain did not clamour to know, and Papa made it inevitable, and somehow right, that one should be Rosalie, in Peking, and that Peking should be beautiful, too beautiful for words. But only for a while. Later the relentless zest drove her on, and all this too was to be relinquished, as the tree launches its summer-bearing branches away from the patient, everlasting root.

Growing up involved also simpler, direct kinds of griefs and hurts, which fell neatly into categories, so that after a time Rosalie knew exactly how the hurt would happen, when, and how long it would last. The other Rosalie, the double who carried on that self-dialogue without which loneliness would have been constant, used to promise itself: "Rosalie, it won't last more than two days, a week, a month. The only thing to do is to wait."

Physical pain was bearable when self-inflicted, but unbearable even a light touch when inflicted by others. The hurt of those ear-rings put in while four men held her down carried down the years, reverberated into howling frenzies whenever anyone else touched her, even with affection. The solacing arms, the tender hand upon brow, made her always wriggle with unspoken annoyance. "Don't touch me, don't you dare *touch* me!" she screamed, and very soon Mama left off all physical contact, and the estrangement, always latent, widened.

She went through a season of boils; the largest of all was on her left wrist, prolonging its swelling into the hand and up the arm. Iodine was put on. Mama believed in iodine for everything, and a bottle of strong iodine resided in the family medicine chest. But the boil got worse, throbbed into an abscess. Rosalie could bear it no longer, yet could not bear anyone else's care, so took Papa's penknife from his desk and plunged it into the turgid grey white top, meanwhile sobbing to herself aloud: "Oh, it hurts. Oh, it hurts," then squeezed the matter out, still howling. Thus she cured herself, in delicious relief.

Another time, having invented a game of jumping over a pail, she cut her leg on the rim. It was an old and rusty pail, its bottom was worn into jagged edges, and these went deep into her shin. The blood ran, Rosalie went to the chest, got the bottle of iodine and poured some on the wound, again sobbing with the hurt. But it hurt less to do it oneself than to call Mama, because Mama would have begun by screaming, then scolding, then would have trembled, then complained to Papa, then Tiza would have wept, the iodine would have been put on anyway, a bandage cut out of the soft old cloths Mama kept for this purpose. Rosalie got a roll of it and wound it round her leg. And that was that. She did not tell Mama about it, and only ten days later, when the wound festered, did Mama know of it. And it was the same with a thumb, the nail torn half away; but it grew back.

When the doctor tried to look at her throat (because, with the winter wind, Rosalie coughed every winter nearly all the winter through, until she blew her ribs out slightly, a deformity remedied later in life by self-imposed postural exercise), Rosalie went into a fit of weeping, threw herself back in the chair. Afterwards Mama said she behaved like a baby, and was silly, and Rosalie felt much shame, and for half a night made up stories in which the doctor cut off her arm and she, Rosalie, never said a word but calmly smoked a cigarette while he chopped away.

There was also the pain of being told so repeatedly that she was ugly. At first it had not mattered; then suddenly it did matter, because at the same time Tiza was called pretty and beautiful, as well as good, by everyone.

For much of her life Rosalie, never an angel, was jealous of Tiza's good looks, although in the end she recognized that being told she was ugly had saved her from going the way Tiza did, and Marianne did, who were both told how beautiful they were. Rosalie had to wait many years till at last she realized that her ugliness was only in the eye of the beholder, Mama, and that actually she too was good-looking, in fact possessed a long-lasting handsomeness of body and feature which was to outlast her sisters'. But for years it was a corroding thought, because in Mama's definition the ugliness of Rosalie was allied to her wickedness, and made nought of any other quality she may have had.

"Of course you must work hard and be first in school, you will never be able to get married, you are too ugly. Look at you, how ugly you are. You'll never catch a man. You'll be lucky if someone marries you for your brains. But men don't like brains."

And it was worse when Elder Brother came, and said the same thing, although later he was to say: "You are the most beautiful woman I have ever seen."

At not quite nine Rosalie was convinced of her ugliness, which lasted until at fifteen everyone began to say she was beautiful, and by that time ugliness was bone-conscious knowledge and she could not believe in her own beauty. She grew out of awkwardness, pimples, and a dark, nervous, student thinness, but not out of the defiant, challenging attitude, her defence, so that whenever and wherever Rosalie was things happened, hectic quarrels, arguments, tears, exhilarating insults, strong games like playing battles and getting dresses torn. No one could be in peace with her, nor she with them. Meanwhile, another Rosalie compensated for her taunts and rudeness by saving money and buying presents for

Mama and Tiza; by colouring pictures for Mama's birthday;
by writing small plays to be acted by herself, Tiza and Marianne for Papa's and Mama's birthdays and for Christmas.
Also, at Christmas, one did not ask Father Christmas for
pretty things, since pretty things were for beautiful people
like Tiza: one asked for books. Everyone would have laughed
if one asked for jewels, or ribbons. "What for, with your
face?" Mama would have said. In one's made-up dreams in
bed before falling asleep, in the stories told to oneself by
oneself, one therefore became a boy, a young man, a man.
It was one way out. Since one could not pretend to grow up
into a beautiful girl with corkscrew curls and large candid
eyes, one had to be a man and strong at fighting. I don't want
to be a woman, I want to be a man.

Another way out was to be nasty to Tiza and Marianne.

Tiza was beautiful, but even more than that she was delicate,
haloed by envy-making weakness. Actually she was fatter,
taller, heavier than Rosalie, and pretty soon Rosalie was wearing her younger sister's cast-offs. Rosalie consumed herself in
violence in all ways, remained thin and shorter than her sisters. She was dubbed a bad influence at school, for at play
during recreation she began war games and would get other
girls to play war games. One day Mother Superior forbade
the games, and also forbade Rosalie to play at all, so that during recreation she was made to sit in a corner, and no one was
allowed to speak to her.

Then the glands in Tiza's neck began to swell, and remained
swollen for some months, and Mama spoke darkly of heredity,
because Papa's eldest sister, Aunt Number One, who lived in
Peking with her husband, Uncle Liu, an engineer like Papa,
and their eleven children, had suffered from swollen glands
in the neck in youth, and these had broken down into sup-
purating abscesses. Mama spoke of this happening to Tiza, so
that the whole family seemed to wait, watching fearfully Tiza's
swelling neck, watching for the bursting of the glands, the
dripping beads of pus and the long sinuses, like wrinkled
drains, which deformed Aunt Number One's neck. But this
did not happen, after some months Tiza's glands subsided.
However, Tiza's delicacy was again confirmed by her acquiring trachoma, and also vomiting a large worm one afternoon.

Trachoma was very common in China, at least forty per
cent of people had it at some time or other; it was the cause of

much blindness. But where and how had Tiza caught trachoma? Mama said it was at Chinese Catholic school, and this was to be used against any more study in Chinese. But Rosalie had been to that school for eighteen months, while Tiza had only been there for six months, yet Rosalie had not caught trachoma. "Even the devil won't touch her," said Mama with light venom, hating the Rosalie who never could die, while Tiza was always ill of something or other.

Tiza's trachoma was being treated, when suddenly she vomited a worm. Worms were also very common in China, the doctor said that ninety per cent of children in Peking had worms, round worms, big and white. Rosalie, who went walking in the fields, saw them, lapped in the neat coils of faeces which people who relieved themselves left on the edge of the pathways; or in the city, walking in the hutungs, lined against the back walls of houses, even at the back of their own house, where in the morning a row of men squatted, labourers and rickshaw pullers, depositing neat fuming piles of man-manure in a row. This was collected by the collectors of manure, to be taken to the fields, for fertilizer was expensive, and precious. And Papa said that in his native province of Szechuan whole families lived in idleness, which is the sign of wealth, on the dung of public privies.

Often in these encountered piles, smoking yellow, or brown, or dried after a time into crusty odourless whorls, Rosalie saw the worms, pink fat sausage bodies or white long bodies, some moving yet.

When Tiza was de-wormed, Rosalie was de-wormed too, though Mama said that because she had too much acid in her stomach anyway there would be no worms. And Rosalie was partly elated not to have worms, and partly sorry, because this was another proof that she was neither delicate nor to be looked after, but wiry and wicked, evil, even her stomach evil, lethal to worms. No one could ever pity her, or croon to her; no one would ever really like her.

Worm pills were of two kinds, and the occasion of some dissension between Papa and Mama. For Papa, told to get worm-medicine, brought home thick, round waxy balls, and cuneiform small pyramids, pink, to chew. But Mama said that was Chinese worm-medicine, and would not get rid of worms. However the children did swallow them, and the next day they swallowed the European kind of worm-medicine, far more expensive. The mornings were exciting, as worms were expected, but none of them passed worms, not even Tiza.

Rosalie began to persecute Tiza and Marianne, bullying them, tearing their things and stealing the holy pictures of Mama's albums which she had given to Tiza. Everything Mama had had when a child went to Tiza, jewellery, a bracelet, holy pictures. Everything. And Rosalie became more and more evil, and she also beat other children at school, slapping and pulling their hair. And yet she loved Tiza; watched her from the bed, heart full of love; touched her long lashes, delighted with their curve; in school she beat a little boy who pulled Tiza's pigtails and made her cry, beat him so badly that his mother complained (Rosalie had swung her bag, full of books, and struck him on the head with it). The doctor said he could have had a cracked skull. "Serves him right for teasing my sister," Rosalie replied, virtuous.

Finally, she stole a dollar from Tiza. One Sunday the family went to the French mission of Trappist monks just outside Peking. The monks made wine, planted vegetables, orchards, and also made cheese. Mama for a time had her jewels stored with them, because of the warlords and the sudden raids in the city by deserting soldiers. Every time the city changed warlords Mama and Papa went out at night into the garden of the house (whichever house, that is, they happened to inhabit, for altogether they lived in four houses in Peking), dug a hole and put the jewellery in it. One year Mama decided to leave the jewellery with the monks of the French mission. However, this did not last very long, because after two months Mama said she could not trust the French, they said nice things but they did not mean them, and they might steal the jewels from her. So she took the jewels back, and again started hiding them in the garden.

It was May, bright sun; Papa wanted some shoots from the French fathers to plant a vine in the garden. The vineyards were in the charge of a very old, bent little monk, Father Michael, with a limp and a beard, who chuckled all the time. That day, besides the chickens and sandwiches they brought themselves, Father Michael gave them strawberries from the gardens and also goat's cheese.

Rosalie always ate like a ravenous, famished beggar, bolting her food and finishing before anyone else. She bolted the chicken, the sandwiches, the hard-boiled eggs, some strawberries, and the goat's cheese (which she did not like). It was packed in strawberry leaves, and Mama said it was delicious, and Rosalie ate some to prove she also liked it. Then she took out her skipping-rope and started to skip. Returning in the hot afternoon, Tiza and Marianne rode in the rickshaw, but Rosalie, being the eldest, walked all the way, which was about four miles, to the city wall. When they got home she was already sick. As usual with Rosalie, this was immediate drama, with high fever, much vomiting, and delirium. She never knew what it was, except that the doctor said afterwards: "You are lucky to be alive." It lasted about three weeks, and when she recovered her unpleasant, imperious temper immediately reasserted itself. She now wanted to count her possessions, all of a sudden become miserly after years of profligate squander (as Mama said); a stock-taking urge, as happens to those who have been through a crisis, possessed her. During this spell of illness she had seen the concern about her: Papa getting up at night to hold the basin in which she threw up, Mama exclaiming: "You are saved!" when the thermometer registered a drop in the temperature. The Greek doctor said that she had had a meningitis, and that "it was a pretty close call", caressing his moustache, and Mama replied with emotion: "You have saved her life," and he said: "Well, madame, doctors must do what they can," in a self-satisfied way. To round off the close ring of affection round her bed, she must now count her belongings, the freight of her lifetime.

She and Tiza owned each a drawer in the chest of drawers in the bedroom, two side-by-side drawers. Tiza's drawer was so full that she could not open it, Papa had to open it for her. Rosalie's drawer was half empty, things rattled in it. But this did not worry her too much. She had her money-box, and she had been saving money, money earned by being first in class. Tiza also saved money, because whether she was first or not Mama gave her money, as much as Rosalie earned, and when Rosalie did not earn any Tiza still got money from Mama, but secretly, though Rosalie found out one day. Tiza's money box was at the bottom of her drawer. Both girls began to count the money they had, and Rosalie was sure that she had at least seven dollars. But it turned out that she had only two. Tiza, on the other hand, stopped extracting the money after the ninth dollar, although Papa and Mama both stood round excitedly, highly pleased with Tiza for being so thrifty.

"The tin box is still heavy," said Papa, enchanted, weighing Tiza's. And so Tiza put all the nine dollars back, and put the tin box back, and would not take it out again. And Rosalie, with only two dollars in her hand, began to cry, and there and then decided that an injustice was being done to her. Only two dollars, after months and months of being first ... it was impossible. She had given away, but not so much. She began to weep, silently for a while, the tears rolling down.

"But you're always giving it away," said Mama. "You must have given more than you thought. You'll die on the straw, you'll see."

But Rosalie decided that someone had stolen money from her, and she must steal it back.

The next morning, while Mama was out with Tiza and Marianne, Rosalie opened Tiza's drawer, found the tin box, extracted one dollar and put it in her own tin box.

But the operation now embarked her into a long train of complexities. To begin with, after taking the dollar, Rosalie did not feel as happy as she thought she would become. That night she watched Tiza asleep, round face upon the pillow, long lashes sedately bent, and a surge of love came upon her. It was wrong to take money from Tiza, delicate, weak Tiza, even if she was fatter, and taller, and more beautiful ...

Next morning when they were washing, she turned to Tiza: "Tiza, promise you never stole any money from me?"

"No, of course not," said Tiza, round-eyed.

"Because I stole a dollar from you yesterday," said Rosalie.

Tiza began to weep, the large tears rolling without any effort, and Mama came up and all was known, and two minutes later the dollar had returned to Tiza's tin box.

"Now you've become a thief as well. I told you you'd die on the straw, or in jail," said Mama.

TWENTY-SEVEN

THE Chinese school was a small private school attached to the Tungtang Church. Mama had not wanted to send her children to an ordinary Chinese school, although at one time Papa had said something about it, but Mama had replied:

"I don't want my children to grow up as Communists and cut my throat one dark night!"

The spectacle of Mama with throat cut in bed agitated Rosalie for at least a week.

Papa gave in, and Rosalie and Tiza went to the Catholic

Chinese school; every morning there was half an hour of Bible story, and in this version St. Joseph and the Virgin Mary were Chinese, born in Shantung province.

Rosalie asked: "How can this be? The Western School says born in Judea, and the family were all Jews."

"That's what they say, but we here believe it is in Shantung," replied the Chinese lay-sister who taught Catechism. She was always dressed in grey cloth, she was not to become a real Sister of Charity till seven years later.

Rosalie was not happy, and talked to the other children about it, and three days later Mother Superior sent for her after school and told her to stop asking questions.

"You must understand, my child, that the others don't know any better. They are Chinese. You are here by special permission, because your mother is a Catholic, and you must go to a Catholic school."

This made Rosalie angry. "But you are telling lies, it is a lie, the Virgin Mary was not born in Shantung –"

Mother Superior pushed her gently out of doors. Mama was summoned, and she returned in a temper, partly against the Mother Superior, "I told her my daughter was right," and partly against Rosalie.

Mama cried, Rosalie cried, Papa said "Will you please stop all this noise?"

But when at the end of the month Rosalie had very bad marks, and no dollar came for her from Papa, she stopped wondering about the Virgin Mary's nationality, and was almost docile for three months; and then she tried also to love this Mother Superior, but was stopped by the sight of her moustache.

Much as she was clumsy at writing in European school, so did Rosalie excel with the Chinese brush. It was Papa who discovered it first, looking over the words she painted in the small squares of her copybook. He got excited, more so than she had ever seen him.

"Look," he said, in his typical understatement, "it is not bad." He took up the brush himself, holding the paper away from him, sitting straight and lifting the brush. He made little circles round the parts of ideograms he considered specially well done, the strokes sure and precise and balancing well into the square which they filled. And then he began to teach her, how to lift the wrist, and write from the shoulder; how to SEE the total ideogram before writing it into the square, and later how to imagine the square even when there was no square to write in. And how to get the right consistency (not too watery, not too thick) for the ink.

Then he took her with him to the Eastern Peace Market, and to the Liulichang Market outside the Front Gate of the city, and they spent several afternoons selecting proper ink sticks, smelling them as they lay, black and beautiful, in rows; an old pewter box to store the ink in, with its own silk waste wad to hold the ink so that it did not run; and a smooth black polished ink stone with a design of bats, a brush holder with a design of plum blossom, and a wedge-shaped toothed stone like a range of mountains, green, expensive and beautiful, to rest the brushes upon; and then brushes, thick ones, fine ones, each with its own metal top, fine-bodied bamboo or wood with carved words of wise exhortation to study, and the most expensive ones with a neat small bone cap at the other end from the brush. And it was like entering an unknown garden, and Papa was happy, talking of his childhood. "Now I will try to get an orchid for your desk, when you write."

But he never did, because when they returned home, and Rosalie started making ink, Mama insisted she must wear a pinafore, "She'll get everything dirty," and somehow all the joy went away, even the ink stick lost its scent, and the brushes looked sad; and the next day Papa had forgotten about the orchid.

Then followed weeks of coming home from school to do calligraphy, getting up early to do calligraphy. Papa spoke of his young days, of his own talent, in short brief sentences. He extracted some of his own writing, preserved in a drawer, unseen till then, even by Rosalie, who was a most uncommon pryer and who had discovered nearly everything in every drawer, including Tiza's, the most difficult to open, including a small box of male contraceptives, kept by Papa on the top shelf of the main clothes chest (she did not know what it was, until many years later, and never asked, having learnt prudence). She knew Papa kept his things there, papers, clips, pencils, rubbers, and then this box.

Now Rosalie went to Papa's office at lunch time, and the two ate dumplings in his office, and Papa showed her writing to Mr. Hua, Simon's father. Mr. Hua was quite alone these days, because Mrs. Hua and Simon and Leila were still in France, where the children would study. Rosalie looked attentively at Mr. Hua. Doing calligraphy made one look more closely at everything, because every person and object was also Word, Ideogram, with lines and spaces, planes and curves and hooks, thick or elongated limbs or moustaches, each placed into its own square or oblong, drawn as itself, itself with all its meanings, within the framework of itself. Mr. Hua was such an object-person-event ideogram, reducible to a painted abstraction, elliptical meaning, tall, small moustache, thick glasses, square head, thick hair cut short and standing straight up because so thick, firm mouth, clothes always neat, stiff white collar and a curiously long thin tie that swung in front of him because he stooped, concavely. He had long legs, an entrancing habit of shaking hands: his hand started upwards from his hip in a parabola, he brought it up, then down again towards Rosalie to shake hands, and the second movement was of a pouncing magpie. And he had a kind, tired voice, the same voice as Papa, and when they talked together there was happiness in the office, so that a little girl could put up her legs, tired and aching with walking, and listen, and draw beautiful words. Thus Mr. Hua, his person, *was* the poised ideogram, his surname himself redrawn in a name right for him, Hua, meaning Glory. In that, all that Mr. Hua said and did, all that he was, a wholeness making sense, a pensive, unshowy glory, sprang to the eye.

And Papa's name, Chou, with its bronze incense-burner heaviness, was honest and right too, right in his world, a temperate world of strolls in the markets, fragrant ink sticks, and the courteous burr of voices discussing formally, with long silences to fill the thoughts between. But it became shrunk, came unstuck, in that other world, that of Mama. Glory and honesty went out of Hua and Chou in Mama's world.

Thus happiness was created in Papa's railway office, a small room so cold that in winter Papa worked in his overcoat, so hot that in summer Papa lost many pounds in sweat; for a brief while was happiness secured, anchoring the child Rosalie to sureness, that of the written word.

Ideogram and the object it represented, the action or event enfolded in its strokes, became comprehension. At least, it looked like comprehension, until Rosalie realized that it was an intensification of description and observation which was produced in her through this connection between symbol and thing symbolized. And then came its corollary, to shatter sureness: she began to realize the frailty of states of being. Thus, in the word "run" written in Chinese was a whole configuration of legs leaping, feet stamping, and a will above it all, directing the action, directing a heavy body, dragged by the willing legs and feet. "Walking" was a stately stalk, difficult to write out with that long, graceful lope of the robe swinging in the ideogram, like an old scholar in the theatre's classical plays, the wind lifting his robe in a forward skirmish. Oh, wonderful and twice wonderful was the word, the word the world, in movement and in pause, a reflection, a knowledge, a comprehension, and a making, all in one. And how frail the states of one's being, indescribable, when compared to the fixity of the word. How anxious to be, a transience, one's words immortal.

Calligraphy held her in enchantment, as it had held her father, and from calligraphy to Chinese poetry was ascent ordained, though difficult. But it did not occur. The trance was stopped, the mood broken. It was Mama who broke it, unknowingly. And for the best of reasons.

For after eighteen months in Chinese school Rosalie was made to start again, in the first year of Chinese; again she sat, to do dog, big dog, small dog, as on the first day. At first she thought: "This is wrong, it cannot be." Then she told Mama and Papa, and after four days Mama, hatted and coated, went to see Mother Superior, this time with Rosalie. Rosalie cleaned her white shoes, tied the shoelaces, her heart beating hard. She hated the Mother Superior of the Chinese School much more than she hated the Canadian one at the European School. The Canadian one had a beautiful face; it made a lot of difference to Rosalie.

At first Mother Superior said she did not know anything about classes, perhaps Rosalie had not been a good pupil? At this Rosalie almost burst with indignation. "It's not true, I can even read the newspaper ... and Papa shows me some poetry."

Then Mother Superior said: "Ah, Madame, we have nothing more to teach your daughter, nothing more. This school is for the daughters of our Catholics, pious families, who wish their daughters instructed. It is not for geniuses, Madame, we form character here, we do not intend our pupils to become anything else but good Catholic wives ... Goodbye, Madame."

And so it was. The school did not teach more, and so Mama came home with Rosalie, the latter with a hollow sensation in her. "You can always keep up your Chinese at home," said Mama.

There was now no possibility of Rosalie going to another Chinese school. The European convent classes occupied both morning and afternoon. For a time Mama spoke of a Chinese tutor three times a week at home; but that was ten dollars a month. And meanwhile it was decided that Rosalie should learn to play the piano. She had suddenly wanted to learn the piano, the idea having grown out of a mixture of emotions at Leila Hua playing the piano and being shown off by her proud mother, and Mama saying she had learnt to play the piano and had a talent for music. "Me too, me too," clamoured Rosalie, who at that time wanted desperately to learn and chiefly to be talented and brilliant, and who had already developed a consuming envy of any achievement by anyone else. She saw herself playing, and hosts of admiring Leilas clapping their hands, while Mama poured tea with her beautiful hands, and said: "*My* daughter."

Between piano and the European school, Chinese was dropped. Mama said: "With Chinese you cannot earn a living." It was seven years before Rosalie was to start studying Chinese again.

TWENTY-EIGHT

It was Suchen who remained longest as friend to Rosalie, the only one whose friendship did not end in a rending quarrel. Perhaps because Suchen's large house was not far from Rosalie's, perhaps because Suchen was a cripple, perhaps because both of them went to Chinese school and to European school, except that Suchen's Chinese school was a very good one, and not a Catholic primary which stopped after two years. Suchen also had five private tutors, one to play the flute, two for Chinese classics, one for poetry and calligraphy, one for German. She studied French and English at the convent. She began courses in mathematics with the German tutor. Suchen was the daughter of a Manchu ex-prince and princess.

In later years Rosalie understood that Suchen had had poliomyelitis when very young. One of her legs was shorter than the other, her right hip was deformed. She wore a heavy boot with a high heel, but she was extremely active and often insisted on walking home with Rosalie. Suchen was always pushing herself, mind and body, and that is why they re-

mained friends. She was a vigorous girl with round face, black
shining hair cut in a fringe to her heavy black eyebrows,
beautiful teeth, a tongue sharper and far more witty than
Rosalie's.

Suchen talked much, which was soothing for Rosalie. She
knew a good deal, and lectured steadily, lucidly, in a voice unaltered and unalterable, pedantic and beautiful. She spoke the
most wonderful Peking Chinese, spoke it beautifully, it was
delight to listen. No language was so lovely to Rosalie's ear as
Chinese spoken in a woman's voice, full, round, alto, the consonants resonant as gongs, precise as the taps of a dancer's
heels, the laughter and the emotion of words held in, each
sound so full that the mind saw at the same time an image
and its ideogram, so true that one read the word in one's
mind at the same time as hearing it in one's ears. All Suchen's
sentences were structurally faultless. There was never anything sloppy or half-thought; each word was sharp and shining, fresh created as she spoke it. Suchen wanted to be a politician and a revolutionary, If it had not been for her leg and
for her mother the princess, she probably would have become
famous.

"I tell you," said Suchen to Rosalie, "I often want to die.
But I cannot die," She said this smilingly; it was not courteous
to be sad-faced when sad-hearted.

Her mother beat her, made her kneel on the courtyard
stones with a big stone poised on her head. If the stone fell
off, she was beaten again. "That is because my mother is a
princess. She wants absolute obedience," said Suchen.

Suchen read enormously, and brooked no contradiction.
Her peremptoriness was accepted, however, because she gave
reasons for it, and Rosalie was content to listen, overawed by
her friend's knowledge and also by her audacity. One day the
two went to the cinema together; it was called the Pavilion
Cinema, and it was more or less "for Europeans" or for
wealthy Chinese, because it was more expensive than the True
Light Cinema which had shown *The King of Kings*. The
Pavilion was near the Legation Quarters, and many Europeans
went to it. Suchen and Rosalie sat in the best seats, reserved
for Europeans although nothing was written anywhere to state
it, but it was so: Chinese just did not sit there, and Europeans
naturally sat together. But Suchen bullied the clerk into selling her two European tickets by saying in a loud voice:
"And why should we not sit upstairs in the best circle seats?

Is this my country, or is it not?" The clerk immediately gave her two tickets; anyway, it was afternoon when very few Europeans went to the cinema, they usually went at night.

Suchen and Rosalie sat totally alone in the European seats. On all sides were seats, empty, expectant, curving sedately right and left, concaving forward and backward. A feeling of exaltation kept the two girls sitting straight, unlolling, a stance interrupted by the advent of a solitary European man, who saw them and came to sit by them, to the left of Suchen. "Take care," said Suchen, between her teeth, in Chinese to Rosalie. "If he is rude to us, we must shout resolutely. We must not allow him to molest us." And she continued rigid, staring straight in front of her. Rosalie was awed. What was it like to be molested?

The European turned his head to look at the two little girls, astonishment on his face, in the still greyish electric light; the film had not begun, the musicians were tuning up. He spoke to Suchen in English: "Do you speak English?" Suchen did not reply. He swivelled his neck back, but it seemed he could not leave the matter alone, and he tried again, in very poor Chinese: "You speak English words? Yes?"

"No," said Suchen in English, very clearly, "we do not speak English."

The man burst out laughing. "My, my," he said, "what a clever little girl you are. How come you two are sitting here all by yourselves?"

"Mind your own business," said Suchen, in English again. "We are ladies, and you should not speak to us unless requested by me."

"My my," said the man, his jaw dropping widely with mock terror, "my my. Here, I'll give you a dollar," he held it in his fingers in front of Suchen, "I'll give you a dollar if you say that all over again."

Suchen took the dollar bill delicately between her fingers, spat upon it, rolled it up as a ball, and threw it into the auditorium, lobbing it like a ball.

At that moment the bell rang, the music began, like a curtain fell the darkness from extinguished lights. The man slumped in his chair. Triumphant, holding hands, Rosalie and Suchen sat staring at the picture, which Rosalie could not remember afterwards; she could only remember the loud drum in her ears. At the interval the man went to sit somewhere else, the little girls remained, savouring their triumph, walked home aureate with glory.

"I think he was American," said Suchen, "otherwise he would not have offered us a dollar."

The first time Rosalie went to Suchen's house was an occasion she never forgot, because she was made to wear her best dress which itched all the time.

"Suchen is Princess Dan's daughter," said Papa to Mama.

Mama's face smiled. Princess Dan had been one of the ladies-in-waiting to the old Empress Dowager, and had written a book on the Empress, a book which had been sold in England and America and had been extremely popular because the Europeans all loved the Empress Dowager, although she hated them and had tried to kill them through the Boxers. But then Europeans were like that, they said she was a dear old lady and could not have instigated the killings, although every Chinese knew she had.

Princess Dan had travelled extensively over the world, finally to settle in Peking. Mama had not at first known that Suchen was the daughter of Princess Dan. "Why didn't you tell me before?" said Mama to Papa, and Papa said he had not thought about it. He had not. His family was like that in Szechuan, they spoke scantily about relatives and relationships because these things fell pat into their lap, and they assumed that everyone else knew all this, since it was a self-evident pattern. But Mama never knew, and Rosalie later was to spend years making up this knowledge, since it had not been passed on to her by Papa.

The gate of Suchen's house had nothing ornamental about it, not fierce dogs nor the tall striding northern guards in blue, nor the brass-nailed red doors, nor the brick screen carved with a fan-shaped happy omen of flowers and fruit, which were the entrance to the house of the Tang family of Pao. The house did not seem high, yet it was very extensive. It was, as all houses in Peking are, a succession of rooms arranged round courtyards; sculptured and painted galleries went from one to the other, zigzagging gracefully amid a landscape of smooth willows sweeping branches down to the ground, rock gardens, pools with lotus and fish, lilac and forsythia, walls with windows each shaped differently, the glass carved with birds and flowers, each one a different scene. It was a real palace, and into its ample and graceful loveliness Rosalie and Suchen walked, until they reached the room where

Suchen lived, with its high bed carved with birds in black
and gold lacquer, with drawers underneath the bed, a heap
of quilts of satin neatly folded upon the silk sheets. There
were thick carpets on the floor. Everything smelt good, incense, the fragrance of nasturtium, the scholar's favourite
spring perfume.

Suchen had everything. A library with books, a beautiful
antique desk with the most wonderful assortment for calligraphy: a turquoise brush stand with a gold knob, and a
little frog carved on one side, a Ming porcelain blue-and-
white scroll holder with old paintings; chests, and in their
drawers so many lovely things, small carved bottles of crystal,
jade and agate, kingfisher feathers and coral. She also had a
camera, a gramophone and records which she played for
Rosalie. A maid came in on felted feet, a young girl with hair
drawn tight in plaits, and served them tea in cups that were
so thin one could see the shadow of one's hand through them.
After a while of looking at Suchen's things and being slightly
jealous (there was so much, it was all so beautiful to feel, to
breathe, to touch, to look, and at home much was so ugly,
and what Rosalie had was ugly too except for calligraphy,
and now time for calligraphy was shrinking), another servant
came in and said softly that the Lady would receive them.
They went through more galleries, with red columns on both
sides, open to the garden, with a covering roof of green glaze
tiles, beams painted each with a different landscape as at the
Summer Palace, zigzagging to prevent devils from following
since devils only pursue straight lines, to another room, with
bronze incense-burners outside making in the still air a further
stillness. The servant lifted the fine woven mat over the open
door, and they walked into the room where Princess Dan
sat on a modern sofa, and motioned graciously while Suchen
bowed and introduced Rosalie, who by now was stiff with
shyness. The girls sat, feet together, hands together, scarcely
breathing, on chairs. The Princess Dan did not say anything,
her gaze wandered over them; then she took her flute, and
began to play.

Princess Dan was lovely, a delicate oval face like a melon
seed, very purely drawn, a small nose, thin, slightly hooked as
some Manchus have, eyebrows sweeping well away, very dark
dark hair. She wore long nails, the ring and the last finger
nails were about two inches long. She was made up, not too
obviously, but still in Manchu make-up fashion, with much

pink-and-white powder. Chinese ladies did not make up so
much, only concubines did; but the Manchu ladies always
painted their faces into masks.

More and more beautiful grew the Princess playing the
flute, as Rosalie looked. Her beauty was in her gestures, in the
way she breathed, cast her eyes in a side glance that was courteous and noble, distant and knowledgeable, with a detach-
ment that kept Rosalie tranced with reverence. The music
ended, and the Princess put her flute down, with a gesture like
a flower being bedded, upon a small table.

Then tea and cakes were brought, many small cakes, many
kinds. Rosalie was very hungry as usual, and she ate. Suchen
nibbled, and the Princess just looked, and then the Princess
said: "My daughter tells me that you are intelligent," employ
ing a diminutive diminishing word for daughter which was
courteous towards Rosalie, as if Rosalie were an older and
wiser person than Suchen. Rosalie was not used to so much
courtly language, her other Chinese friends were more
straightforward and spoke the ordinary, not court, language.
Only Papa could have withstood the elegant diction of the
Princess.

Rosalie could not answer; then, horror of horrors, nodded,
mouth full. She had not meant to nod acknowledgment, she
had meant to shake her head in vigorous denial as was correct,
to say: "Oh, I am very stupid, it is Elder Sister Suchen who is
so intelligent, Revered Princess," but the words did not come
since her mouth was full of sesame-seed baked cakes, the ones
she liked best of all.

The Princess made more elegant conversation, saying:
"What will Miss Chou intend doing after school? Which university will she attend?"

Rosalie said: "I want to be a boy." Again she felt as if she
had got up and smashed some precious porcelain in front of
the Princess. Why, oh why, was she saying all the wrong
things, doing all the wrong things?

The Princess laughed. "All women want to be men," she
said. "When I was young I also wanted to be a man, a boy,
so that I should not be oppressed." Her mouth twisted its thin
lips into a curve, one side up and one side down, again a
lovely movement to watch, and so expressive, like a theatre
bitterness, so much more real than real people who are often
silly when bitter. The Princess affected one all the time, she
played on one's nerves and brain as on her flute, easily,

negligently. She looked so fragile and lovely, and Rosalie knew she must be very cruel, capriciously cruel, like so many lovely, fragile-looking women are.

And then the Princess said: "I will show you something," and gave an order, not turning her head, and almost instantaneously two servants came running in, and she said: "My baskets," and they said: "Yes Lady, yes Lady," precipitately, and ran away and soon ran back with other servants, bringing in baskets of lacquered wood and bamboo close-woven, covered with red brocade silk, blue and orange brocade silk, their lids topped with knobs encrusted with coral. And when the Princess lifted the lids there were marvels to see, turquoises, pearls, jade, gold, and other stones of which Rosalie did not know the names. Jades of all kinds, pale or deep, light apple-green tender bamboo jade, and deep dark-green jade like emeralds, some near-black, some pieces carved, others uncarved, rings and bracelets and necklaces, brooches and earrings like drops of green light, and others like round moons. There were turquoises, sky-piercing blue and with wonderful names like Wing of Morning, See the Sun, Frozen Delight; pearls, baskets and baskets of them, seed pearls so small, pearls mounted by the thousand on head pins and diadems, bigger ones like tears, with downward droop, large round ones. There were rubies and aquamarines and sapphires, but there were few diamonds, perhaps because there are no diamonds in China; only some diamonds that the Princess had bought at Cartier's in Paris on her trips, solitaires unmounted, which she kept, and now playful she rolled them on the carpets, and they flashed sleepily.

When Rosalie went home Mama asked about the Princess, but Rosalie was monosyllabic and said she had eaten cakes and played in the garden with Suchen. "With all that money Suchen will surely find a nice man to marry," said Mama, "in spite of her leg."

Mama was already grooming Tiza to marry a rich man. It was her conviction that Tiza would be rich and marry well. And the idea of marrying a rich man, or a man with a good job, was Mama's idea of life for her daughters.

But in the midst of all this wealth Suchen was not happy, though her face did not show it and never would. Her face was not constructed for sorrow, it had no angles, no points, no creases. Everything in it was made for hilarity, love, tenderness; she was never to know any.

"Chou Moon Guest," said Suchen solemnly to Rosalie, calling her by her Chinese name, "I will now tell you my very great secret, because you are my friend. I am adopted. I come from a healthy and poor peasant family, and Princess Dan bought me. The Manchus are effete, and degenerate with sloth and disease. The Princess knew this, and she adopted me, because she wants me one day to marry a Manchu nobleman so that I can improve the breed of her family. But now I have this trouble in my leg, and all her plans are undone and so she does not like me and is horribly cruel to me, and I want to die."

Rosalie never saw Princess Dan again, though she was invited. Because she was afraid the uncontrollable wickedness in her might make her sick, for the thought of the baskets, with their great loads of plunder, made her feel like vomiting. She never returned to the Dan palace.

There were other friendships, sudden and capricious ones, going and coming as winds blow, with European and Eurasian girls at the convent, and so many of them turned sour, their linking and their disjoining a recklessness, trial and assay of the wild, greedy spirit gobbling up chunks of living. But her friendship with Suchen took on the pattern of her father's friendships: unstrenuous, continuous through the years, undemanding, less emotional, but in the end shaping her life and not discarded among its odds and ends.

Suchen was stuffed with education; even doing Chinese callisthenics to improve her posture and breathing, and the art of judo to defend herself, and flower arrangement from the Japanese tutor (she now began Japanese), did not diminish her ardour to educate Rosalie. When Elder Brother arrived, and started to do mathematics with Rosalie, Suchen became interested; she wanted Rosalie to tell her what Elder Brother did, and the two conversed of logarithms, and the differential calculus, grave as mathematicians, pure with the pure logic of children.

Fanju was another friend, and she introduced Rosalie to the world of space, the universe and its stars. She was a thin, small, eager, bespectacled little Chinese girl, also stuffed with knowledge, who devoured space fiction in her spare time, and Rosalie soon became as engrossed, going to Fanju's house once a week to read as many books on astronomy as possible. And this affected her daydreaming, the steady outpouring of stories she told to herself. Elder Brother now obtained space-fiction magazines, sent to him by post from America, and for nearly two years he, Rosalie, Suchen and Fanju nourished themselves on space-travel stories, besides trying to learn Esperanto, calculus and geometry. One day Fanju became ill, and stayed in bed. Rosalie went to give her a book to read, and herself borrowed one from Fanju, and said: "See you next week." But the next week Fanju was dead. Her father, who was a lecturer at Peking University, told Rosalie, when she returned the book.

Fanju had been so shy, so colourless, that she was well near to physical invisibility. She remained by echo, a prolonged awareness of her ideas, her muted enthusiasms, more vivid than her self. Years after Fanju's death, Rosalie, too preoccupied at the time with her own chaotic contradictions to ponder, became conscious of the areas in her mind influenced by Fanju's colourless little voice, spectacles, small body and enormous awareness of China and what was going on in China. There was nothing left of Fanju, except this music of the future she had started in Rosalie and which did not end.

Leiwen was different. She wanted protection, sentiment, a concentration upon herself. She was probably stupid, but with a retentive memory, so that she always got good marks at school, and later at the university. She treated Rosalie as if Rosalie were a boy, make to look after her, to bring her things. For a time Rosalie played this game, but after three months it became tedious, and she partitioned off an occasional hour to see Leiwen, and no more. Leiwen had collections of small jade ear-rings, and ivory miniatures. In winter she was wrapped in wool from head to foot. While Rosalie devoured everything edible in reach, she picked daintily and was never hungry. Her family liked Chinese opera, and took Rosalie, who had not been taken before; and after that Rosalie went on her own, fascinated with opera, content to sit at first, not understanding the sung words, but determined to understand, absorbing the gestures; and this also remained with her, and the music of Chinese opera became more accessible to her than the piano pieces she made herself play. Her musical education upon the piano bought for her lasted four years, and came to an abrupt end, leaving her as unmusical as ever.

And then there was Hualan, who was Eurasian like Rosalie, so that she was also known as Sophia. Hualan was supposed to be a slow, dull girl, and in school Rosalie had not noticed her until one day after a fight with a European girl (unremembered, totally gone), while Rosalie stood breathing hard in a corner, Hualan came to the same corner and turned round Rosalie, inspecting her slowly as if she were some animal on show.

Rosalie would have said to her: "Am I a tiger to be stared at?", but Hualan spoke first. "I hear," she said, "that you are clever. Everybody speaks of your cleverness. But you will die young with that bad temper. My mother says people with a bad temper die young."

"I don't care," said Rosalie, "I want to die young. I'll kill myself at thirty, anyway" – thirty to her being incredibly old – "I don't want to lose my teeth and have many children and a stomach like a bag of worms" – here she thought of Mama – "and become stupid."

"Neither do I," said Hualan, "but I was born old. I speak six languages already. My father is an ambassador, that is why."

"Get out of my way," said Rosalie rudely, "I want to go to pee."

Later they sometimes caught sight of each other, unsmiling took stock. Rosalie was three classes above Hualan. Hualan did not make friends, she stood in corners, blinking slowly, produced a small book from her pocket and read out of it. One day a girl bent over the book and said: "Oh! What is it?"

"Pushkin," said Hualan, shutting the book and putting it in her pocket again.

In the convent there were White Russian girls too. Most of these were boarders, not day scholars like Rosalie. There was an obvious apartness between them and the Eurasians, the Europeans and the Chinese girls. The latter were a minority, some from Catholic families, others like Suchen extras, come for six months, to habituate themselves to English or to French. Between these groups friendships were individual, took little account of racial differences, except in sudden fights when race would come up. But the White Russians everybody looked down upon, because they could never leave the convent, they were boarders, they had no money, no one could invite them out.

Rosalie did begin a friendship with a girl called Gala, very pale, with enormous brown eyes, long lashes, hair thick and curly and always damp. She was sixteen years old, very much older than Rosalie, but they became friends.

"I have tuberculosis," said Gala, "and I have not long to live."

She devoured novels on love, sitting in the black pinafore and white collar of the boarders (hers were seldom washed, and because Gala perspired so much from her tuberculosis, they were always damp and sour). She lent to Rosalie, with solemn words because Rosalie was her best friend for life and she and Rosalie, looking into each other's eyes and saying "Cross my heart and hope to die" (which to Gala represented the epitome of solemnity), had sworn to eternal friendship, *La Dame aux Caméllias,* extracting a promise that Rosalie would read it and return it secretly and never let anyone know, for in the convent such books were banned.

Rosalie read and understood very little. She had lapsed, where inquiry was concerned, into a disregarding ignorance, a state of non-curiosity about plain living, owing to the much more entrancing star travel fiction which now made human sentiments seem affected and boring. The death scene struck her as silly, and the whole story unscientific. Her chief hero of the moment was busy exploring Mars, and had no time for love. She returned the book to Gala, saying it had been inter-esting, and Gala said: "I am like her" – meaning the heroine – "and I shall die like her."

"But first," said Rosalie, punctiliously logical, "you must find a lover like her."

"Ah," said Gala dreamily, "I already have one. I love him ... oh, how I love him, and I think he knows. As soon as I am out of this prison I shall go to him. I know he knows it. He is waiting for me, as I am waiting for him."

And again with a "cross my heart" secrecy, Gala told Rosalie that on Sundays, when Gala was led to the church in the sub-missive crocodile of boarders that wound its black-pinafore uniformity along the street from the convent to the Legation Quarters church and back again, she had noticed this man standing on the sidewalk watching. He was, of course, a Euro-pean. Gala, being White Russian, despised and looked down on the "natives", the Chinese. She called them "the yellows", "the Chinks" or "the punks", as did nearly everybody else, including the Eurasians. Gala also looked down on Eurasians, but only when she was in her Tsarist moods, and they did not last too long.

"I know he is waiting for me," said Gala, "because in church he comes in, after us, and sits on the aisle opposite. I love him, oh how I love him!"

Gala did not last long, because after a time Rosalie was bored with stories of this wonderful man, and at the end of the term the holiday came, and afterwards Gala had gone from the convent. Rosalie was not to see her again until many years later. Gala then was in Shanghai, a dancer in a nightclub. And it was true she had tuberculosis; she coughed, and blood came into her mouth when she coughed. And she told Rosalie many things which were sad and terrible, and then a man came to touch her shoulder, and she smiled up at him, and rose to dance with him. And Rosalie, who could not dance at all, looked at Gala's back, above the man's hand, and the spine bones could be counted, as she had counted those of the old man at the market fair breaking boulders with his fist.

TWENTY-NINE

ALTOGETHER, from 1921 when they arrived in Peking, till 1935 when Rosalie went away, the family lived in four houses in Peking.

The first was a rented house, very small, with a small paved courtyard, and rooms with earth floors on which were laid thick straw mats. In winter a stove in the middle of the room kept it warm. The windows were lattice wood with pasted paper instead of glass, and two small stone lions with worn faces kept watch at the door. They lived there only a few months after arriving in Peking, and it was there that Marianne was born. Rosalie liked the house, because coming out of it and walking down the hutungs one reached the main road, and opposite it was the great red wall of the Forbidden City, where the Emperors had lived. The house belonged to a eunuch, who had been in service at the Palace before the Revolution of 1911. The rent was only ten dollars a month.

The second house was in the Manchu district, and to Rosalie it was the best house of all, the most lovely and enchanting one, for many reasons. It was at the end of a cul-de-sac, and it had two enormous stones in front of the entrance door; one could sit on them in the evening, fan oneself and eat peanuts, meanwhile watching other people come out of their houses and fan themselves on their doorsteps. There were only three houses in the cul-de-sac, and apart from the evening hour they presented only a closed front door and walls. But the front doors of the two other houses were beautiful because they had painted guardians of the doors, with red and white faces and weapons of scarlet and gold, and feet in riding boots. In both the other houses the families were Manchu.

"Manchus," said Papa, "are lazy and degenerate." He did not like the Manchus. Rosalie knew the Manchu rule had ended in 1911, in a welter of folly amid a motley of eunuchs. And then had come Sun Yatsen, and China was a Republic. And on the silver dollar in her money-box was stamped the bull-neck profile of Yuan Shihkai, who had tried to make himself Emperor, and died. There was no money with Sun Yatsen's face on it.

The Manchu ladies never came out before the afternoon, when they left their houses to pay visits to friends. Their feet were not bound, they wore embroidered shoes with thick cloth soles; in the middle of the sole was the heel, square and high. They were tall, in long robes of satin, with short jackets of black silk; on their lacquered hair they wore the Manchu head-dress, an enormous butterfly of black stiffened gauze, with many pins of gold and jade and lapis lazuli and king-fisher feathers and small agates and cinnabar and pearls. Their faces were painted white and pink, with painted eyes; the paint stopped abruptly at the edge of their high stiff embroidered collars. The insides of their hands were powdered a pale red; they held a chiffon handkerchief, canary yellow or bright pink or primrose or mauve, in the left hand as they walked out to their sedan chairs. They still went out in sedan chairs, carried by two men, one in front and one in the back, the rickshaw was too modern for them.

When a Manchu man met a Manchu woman, he genuflected (and so did she) by lowering himself, slightly bending the left knee, hands folded and placed upon the right knee. It was a very pretty movement, and immediately Rosalie saw it in the calligraphy of the Chinese word genuflect, which had a component in it indicating exactly the graceful motion of the body thus taking three bends.

The Manchus did no work at all. Papa said it was because in the old days all of them had received pensions from the Imperial House. All their lives they had been paid not to work, and this had gone on for nearly three hundred years, and now they did not know how to work. It was not quite true, however; Rosalie discovered that, out of a family of twenty-five people, there were three men engaged in private tutoring, semi-scholars now turned teachers. But they mostly pawned their things; jewellery, clothes, went regularly out of the Manchu houses to bring in money. And thus they lived, waiting for the day when nothing would be left. "Then they will take an overdose of opium and die," said Papa, laughing.

The house here was rented from one of the two Manchu families, and the courtyard held two lilac trees planted by Papa. In string the lilac burst, filling the courtyard with white and mauve. Rosalie became breathless looking at the lilac, and Rosalie and Tiza took great bunches of it to school to give to the nuns who were their teachers.

Another reason why this house was lovely was because one could fly a kite easily from the cul-de-sac without having to go far, carrying the kite, to an empty space. And the last reason was that Elder Brother came to this house when he first arrived from Europe.

The third house they moved to was not so exciting, and they only went into it in 1925. It was in a hutung, and its only advantage was that it was near to the residence of Princess Dan. It also had a courtyard, but the ground was so hard that nothing grew well; Papa bought pots of flowers to put in the courtyard, and that is where he started his collection of carnations. This house was remembered because it was the house in which Aunt Number One refugeed herself when her husband, Uncle Liu, wanted to give her baby number twelve, and she did not want another baby. But she went back to Uncle Liu after a few days, and died some years later of baby number fourteen.

And the last house of all, the fourth, they were to move into in 1927, when Elder Brother had already left. Rosalie never liked it.

Returning, so many years later, she was to look for the houses, each one of them; but only the last, the ugliest of all, remained of her childhood; the others had been torn down to make new, wide roads for the city.

THIRTY

ELDER BROTHER was anguish to live with for years, ache all the more compelling for not being understood, suffering outside reach of transforming, shaping, doing something about; friendship, end to loneliness, awakening of intellect; defiance tempered and shaped by watchfulness.

A boil on the arm can be made to disgorge its pus, to become whole flesh again, leaving a scar, explainable. Pain occupies its verbal niche in a construction of words, building a life after it has been lived, for what is lived is encountered in a retrospect of sentences made to fit what happened, shaped by what was. Elder Brother escaped sentences for a long time, obfuscated by the reticence of pain renewed; like a small nightmare, he remained without the building gestures of a life, with no logical proposition to compact his existence into architectural sum.

Elder Brother began with his name, Son of Spring. The death of his younger brother, Sea Orchid, had made Mama dislike Rosalie. Rosalie was Moon Guest when she was Chinese, just as she was Rosalie when she was, not European (she could never be European, that was understood by her, if not always by Mama), but a half-caste, a Eurasian, in Peking. She was Moon Guest and Chinese when she went out with Papa to markets and to fairs, and in his silence, for he never called her Rosalie except in the house because of Mama; he disliked the name as much as she did, and so called her Little Moon.

After Moon Guest-Rosalie, Snow Orchid-Tiza had been born, small, delicate and in the winter. Mama had forgotten her grief for Sea Orchid, begun to wean Moon Guest, and was ready to love a child again. She loved Snow Orchid-Tiza with a passion made logical by what had occurred. None of her other children did she love as much; Precious Orchid, Lovely Orchid, Autumn Orchid, were born and died, and their deaths were recited round the dry-eyed evening lamp.

"After that," said Mama, "I told the priest, no more children. Not even if I went to hell for it. But then I had Marianne. "She looked at Marianne, who was red-haired and called Moon Orchid.

"Why –?" Rosalie began. But she stopped. It was mortal sin not to have children, but why? Aunt Number One had run away from Uncle Liu her husband because of having too many children. And why had Mama complained that her stomach looked like nothing on earth because of the children, when she had denied that they came from inside her? Rosalie had had an argument with Mama about it, but Mama had looked at her and said: "Curiosity is a sin. You will know after you get married." And Rosalie had replied: "I will never get married because I am a half-caste," knowing that the word half-caste hurt Mama.

Son of Spring, Elder Brother, the first-born, was coming to Peking, returning to the bosom of his family. He had been all these years in Europe, where Mama had left him, because of the shooting when she and Papa had fled from Szechuan in 1913.

"It was a small boat, we were lucky to get on it. It was through the Belgian Consul we had a place on deck, and the bullets went whizzing across from the banks as our boat crossed the rapids. The soldiers were firing at each other across the river, we were in the middle, and it was night, but the boat kept on going, it had to, the current was so strong. I tied your Elder Brother to a barrel with a rope. I tied myself to another barrel. We went through. When we reached Hankow we sent my son back to Europe, to my own parents, for safety. They would bring him up and I would have a son in Europe, and not here in this terrible country where he would have died. Then your father and I went on to the railway, and all of you were born."

On the railway ... Beneficent dragons champing docile impatience on the iron tracks, insides of fire so still, hooting melody of the night proclaiming life, life roaring, life waiting to pounce. And the night waited too, listened and waited, all the earth seemed to wait, giving no sight but this brief warning hoot, no sight of what was really going on, each man's heart in the darkness a dark shell enrobing hidden fire. And one day the world's heart would explode, the great dragons would roar, the night would be bright with leaping fires ...

So, listening to Mama, Rosalie dreamt, and heard the call of the engines, dragging so many lives, carriages packed full, across the immense plain.

"Elder Brother does not know life on the railway," said Mama. "He is lucky."

In 1924, aged sixteen, Elder Brother was coming to China, returning to his parents at last. He had arrived by boat in

Shanghai in the autumn of 1924, and there he was stuck, unable to travel, because some local warlords were campaigning against the north, and everyone said they were Reds and it was dangerous to travel. The foreign gunboats blockaded the Chinese ports and landed their troops, and the rolling stock of the railways was nearly all gone, divided between the fighting warlords, and there were bandits everywhere. But somehow or other Elder Brother got on to a steamer, and arrived in Tientsin, and one evening, in February 1925, he reached Peking.

He had been expected all afternoon, but the trains were up to twenty-one hours late from the port of Tientsin, where he had landed the previous week, and this was the second train in a week that could be put together for passengers; he had not been able to get on to the first one. There should have been a train a day, but now the trains worked only to carry the soldiers of Warlord Wu Peifu, then in control of Peking. All these days Papa had been telephoning and sending wires down the railway line. The wires were sent in Morse. Rosalie had gone with him the day before to the railway telegraph office. She had seen the key which the man in the office kept tapping with his finger, long, short, short short long, making a buzz of flies. That evening Rosalie looked up in the dictionary the Morse code, studied it, and decided to build herself a telegraph set. She had built for herself a telephone with two perforated tins and some wire, and had also tried to assemble a radio set, but no one was interested in talking through her telephone. Mama had been reciting the rosary every night, for a novena of nine days, to bring Son of Spring safely home to her.

That evening Mama sat waiting by the lamp in the living-room, but Rosalie and Tiza and Marianne were in bed.

"I'll get you up when he arrives," said Mama.

Papa had gone to the railway station some hours before, to wait for the train. He had not come back for supper.

"Everything will be cold," said Mama, who had prepared beef broth, and cooked some chicken and a rice pudding.

Rosalie was half asleep. It was very cold outside, and also very cold in the bedroom. Then noise came into the courtyard with a leaping of kerosene lamps, and Mama, opening the door of the living-room across the courtyard, said: "You are there, you are there, my son, my son!"

It was Elder Brother, at last.

How tall he was! Much taller than Mama or Papa. So tall. Rosalie stood up in bed, and watched through the only glass, in the window's centre, watched Elder Brother standing in the living-room. But only half his head could be seen, and he was turning from Papa to Mama, smiling; his front teeth stood a little apart from each other, butterfly teeth, like Rosalie herself. She could not see the top of his head, the window lattice hid it.

Mama called out: "Come, my children, come to meet your brother," and she strode across the courtyard to the bedroom, she did not even put on her coat. Bundled in their camel-hair dressing-gowns the two little girls ran back with her across the courtyard; Rosalie flung herself into Elder Brother's arms, hitting with her body against him because he was so tall. And Mama also hugged him, throwing her arms round him, her head only reaching his shoulder top, saying: "My son, my son, I have my son back with me."

At breakfast the next morning Elder Brother sat drinking coffee and talking with Papa. "Of course," he said, "I want to learn Chinese and go to a Chinese university here, that's why I came back."

"Chinese?" said Mama. "University? You want to study more? But you are seventeen, my son."

Elder Brother looked up at her smiling and his eyes crinkling, he really loved her, or rather he loved the mother he had imagined all these years, all these years he had spent in Europe waiting to come back to his own father and mother.

"Yes, Mama, I want to be Chinese. I am Chinese, of course," he said, laughing happily, looking at Papa.

"You will never have a future if you are Chinese," said Mama. "Don't you see? Your only future is to be in an English firm. The English are very powerful here in China. The Russians, the French, they're all small potatoes now. The English have so many business firms, banks, here. They are the rulers behind the scenes. All the warlords take money from them. The Japanese are also strong, but the Japanese will never accept you. The English need people like you in their banks and their business companies. Don't be stupid like your father and go on the railways. There is no future on the railways. You don't need to tell people that you are Chinese; you know English, you've spent four years in England. They need people like you in the banks here."

Elder Brother looked at Papa, and Rosalie looked at Papa,

and there was only silence from Papa, who was plucking his chin as he did when he was thinking. And then Rosalie as usual picked up the challenge, thrusting herself bodily into a battle which had nothing to do with her.

"We are half-castes," she said, "Eurasians. That's what we are. But I want to be Chinese, like you, like Papa."

Mama, face blushing with anger, gathered herself for battle, eyebrows and mouth and lift of the spine all springing at Rosalie at once. "There you are again," she shouted, "vicious and wicked. Look at yourself! You a Chinese! You will never be Chinese, and let me tell you why: the Chinese will not have you! Never, never! They won't accept you. They will call you 'yang kueitse,' devil from over the ocean, as they call me. They will call you half-caste and mixed blood, for that is what you are. But not your brother. He looks European."

And Rosalie, also bright-red with anger, shouted: "I hate you, I hate you. Why don't you go back, why don't you go away where you came from, and leave us in peace? I hope the Communists come and cut off your head."

"Yentung, Yentung," Mama said. Suddenly she was calm, nearly happy. Her voice had dropped to normal, and it had the effect of a whisper. "Do you hear what your daughter said to me?"

Papa rose, and slapped Rosalie across the table.

Rosalie screamed, ran out to the bedroom, and put on her hat and shoes, screaming and the tears rolling, took her books and went to school, crying all the way. At school her eyes were red and puffy, and she had forgotten her handkerchief; and then she had to go to the toilet, but this was forbidden in the European school, it was considered immodest to ask for the toilet in school hours. So with a bursting bladder she started the arithmetic lesson. Mother Claire, who took the class, looked at her once or twice, but did not say anything.

After arithmetic came the history quiz, history of France, and the class lined up in front of Mother Claire's rostrum. If a girl could not answer a question, another girl was allowed to raise her hand and reply instead. Rosalie lined up with the others, and since she had been first in class she was first in the line. She answered the question Mother Claire asked her, then came the second girl's turn. Surreptitiously, while Mother Claire asked questions down the line of girls, Rosalie pretended to hitch up her skirt ... in reality she pressed her hand against her pubis, firmly, which would ease for a while the urge to pass urine.

Mother Claire saw Rosalie's hand pressing on the unmentionable portion between her legs, and she frowned. Rosalie scratched herself a little to the left of the cleft between her legs, as if she had an itch. Scratching was permitted. The lesson went on, and again Rosalie felt that she could not stand it any longer, she would disgrace herself, so again she firmly pressed on her lower stomach, and this time Mother Claire exploded.

"Back to your desks, all of you, except" – she glared at Rosalie – "Rosalie Chou."

The girls clattered back to their desks, from where they stared, alert and beaming, at Rosalie.

Mother Claire shouted: "Come here," and Rosalie ascended the rostrum and stood near Mother Claire, nearer than she had ever done. She immediately became engrossed in the texture of Mother Claire's skin, sallow-white with evenly spread pores, middling large, an oval brown mole on the chin, a hair out of its middle. Looking at Mother Claire's skin might ease her bursting stomach.

"Why do you do these impure, sinful things?" said Mother Claire. "It is . . . it is terrible . . ." Her lips quivered. "Will you say ten Hail Marys quickly with me, right now."

"I . . . I . . ." Rosalie's eyes filled with tears, but she did not dare to sob because an inhalation of breath to exhale a sob might be catastrophic. She murmured: "Itch . . . hurts me . . ."

Mother Claire's face changed to concern. "You have pimples there?" she said quickly. "Have you told your mother?"

"No." Rosalie shook her head carefully, too vigorous a shake might be dangerous. "No, I haven't."

Mother Claire's features softened. "Aah, my child, I see you are truly modest, after all. I will not punish you. Offer your suffering as a sacrifice to the Holy Virgin Mary, whose modesty is beyond compare."

Rosalie sat down, and Mother Claire, her voice altered to a burr on some consonants and a long pause between the sentences, with profound emotion told the class the story of a saint, a child of fourteen, who in all her young life had been so modest that from the age of four she had refused to take off her clothes, as she could not bear, in her purity, to look at herself or to let anyone look at her, and she had died a martyr in the Roman amphitheatre, where she had chosen to be suffocated by a bear rather than torn to shreds by a lion because, once again, modesty forbade her to show her body and that might have happened with a lion. Her remains, piously collected, worked many miracles.

Something like a scream issued from Rosalie, but it was a shout of laughter, provoking the irrevocable. Rosalie ran out of the classroom to the lavatory, a hut erected high up several stone steps, standing all by itself, austerely raised and very obvious at the end of the courtyard, its lackpaint door knobbed by string. She squatted over the hole between the two stones, the seatless toilet, and watched the urine flow, steady warm stream, soothing sound, gurgling down, down the hole to the pit beneath, a little steam coming up from it in the cold air. Comforting, delicious release. This was to remain one of the best moments of her life, passing water, thinking of the lion and bear story which somehow was irresistibly comical.

She came out of the lavatory to face an irate Mother Claire, to face punishment, loss of marks, impiety, an hour behind the blackboard, a hundred lines in her best writing. But it did not matter.

"My Elder Brother has come home," she told Suchen that afternoon, "and he wants to be Chinese, like me. I told my mother that the Whites must go away."

Suchen looked at her calmly. "That is good. One day we must stop being beggars, and become people. But my mother says only an Emperor can do this. Of course, she is a Manchu."

They went to the East Market and bought marbles, bright coloured ones, green and blue, pink and white, for Rosalie's Elder Brother.

Elder Brother also had a European name, which was George.

"Do you like your name?" Rosalie asked him three days after his arrival.

Elder Brother's trunks had come, and he was taking his books and his clothes out of them. The second evening Rosalie, overcome by shyness after her breakfast outburst, had not spoken to Elder Brother, who sat quietly talking with Papa. A family is a burial mound of its own doings and sayings, and no one had referred to the morning's argument.

Elder Brother had been given a room by Mama, a room which had been kept for him. It had a cement floor with little white stones embedded in the grey opaqueness. Rosalie thought the room particularly fine, but it faced north and

Elder Brother found it terribly cold. Rosalie knew he felt cold, though he did not say so. Later he was to complain to her bitterly about the cold room, but now he was still living up to the happiness he had expected.

"Do you like your name? Do you?"

Elder Brother looked at Rosalie. They were not yet acquainted, though later they were to love each other deeply. Later Elder Brother was to say: "You have always been the one woman I have truly idealized, to me you were always beautiful," but that was years later. Now she was a child, and the way to final understanding would be long and difficult, made up of so many different Rosalies and so many Elder Brothers, each transformation sloughing off the previous one on the way.

"No," said Elder Brother, "I don't really like my name. But then, one doesn't choose one's name, or one's parents."

"That is true," said Rosalie, putting her head on one side as if very wise, a trick she had learnt from Suchen who was so wise. "That is very true."

After that there was not much to say. Rosalie hovered round Elder Brother, examining him. He would one day be six foot two; Papa was only five foot six and something, Mama five foot eight, both seemed pathetically shrunken when he stood up with them. Elder Brother stooped over his trunks. His hair was cut short, he kept his eyes crinkled, peering at his clothes narrowly, stooping to them. He looked more European than Chinese, more European than she did, Rosalie decided. It was his gestures, his size, his feet, which were large in heavy shoes. But his eyes were Chinese eyes, his hair was black, and he had no hair on his hands; most Europeans, like the Greek doctor, had hair on the backs of their hands.

But Elder Brother had to shave. In fact, every morning the cook would boil water for his shaving, whereas Papa shaved only once a month at the most. Elder Brother was very proud of having to shave.

On Sunday all the family except Papa went to Mass. Mama wanted to show off Elder Brother, advancing proudly down the aisle of St. Michael's Church on his arm. Of course they did not choose the Chinese Eastern Church with the beggars to exhibit Elder Brother, they went to the European Church in the Legation Quarters, Mama at that time was having a feud with Madame Poh, the French wife of Papa's friend, Mr. Poh Hungwen, and at the same time with Mrs. Blievermann, her

Dutch friend. What the feuds were about remained opaquely wrapped in meaninglessness, but anyway Mama got her own back, showing her handsome, tall son to everyone.

Then there were parties, a few. Mama invited some people, and people invited Mama and Elder Brother back; Papa took Elder Brother to his office and to call on his Chinese friends. Rosalie did not go; and afterwards when she asked Elder Brother what he had eaten, he said he could not remember.

Elder Brother began to study Chinese, and he studied it three times a week with a tutor. He had already studied Chinese all by himself in Europe. He had also studied German and Esperanto. His sojourn in England had made him proficient in English, but he did not like the English. Elder Brother said the English were strong, but the Germans were much stronger, and it was such a pity the Germans were beaten in war. He was very pro-German, and he said in Belgium all the Flemish people were pro-German. He also announced that the Russians would one day be as strong, if not stronger, than the British. Everything he said was exactly the reverse of what Rosalie was taught, what Mama and Mama's friends said. But Elder Brother was like Suchen: he always gave reasons why he thought this or that, and that made everything interesting.

"The Russians are Communists," said Mama. "God will punish them." She said everyone in Russia was starving, it was well known. And soon the Tsar would be back. She knew. The laundryman, who was a White Russian, and had very good manners, had told her so.

There were about ten thousand White Russians in Peking, and they were all refugees, they had run away from Bolshevism. Many claimed to be dukes or princesses. They opened laundries, restaurants, bakeries and also dance halls. They had a leader, General Horvath, who was living in Peking. He had been the director of the Russian-built railways in China, and he was now the head of the party that would put the Tsar back in Russia. There was also a Russian Church, and the laundryman, who was very pious, always crossed himself before entering the house with a pile of clean sheets on his shoulder.

Elder Brother said the Tsar would not come back. But chiefly he told Rosalie stories of his time in England, including the brutalities he had suffered at the hands of English schoolboys. One day three of them had amused themselves digging a pair of pointed compasses into his buttocks, again and again.

"Didn't you report them?" asked Rosalie.

"Oh, no," said Elder Brother. "They threw me in the river also," he said reflectively. "But we never told on each other, you know. Not in England."

When he went back to Belgium, after the war, he thought all the European boys at school were cry-babies after the treatment he had had in English schools. For the Belgian boys complained and reported on each other.

"I learnt to box, I boxed all those who had hurt me, one by one, before I left England," he said. "They liked me for it. They still write to me."

Elder Brother was a genius, but a tender genius, the hot-house kind, a plant easily shrivelled in the cold, easily flayed by angry blasts of non-love. Genius can only emerge if it is backed by courage and tenacity, by stupendous, stupid self-confidence. Elder Brother had shown courage and tenacity in England, but he had grievously injured himself: he had loved in absence, loved Mama and Papa with the fierceness of a lonely little boy's heart. Now he was here, with Papa and Mama, dangerously, witheringly unlike what he had loved. He did not recover from this self-induced attachment. It really killed a good deal of him.

Elder Brother now studied Chinese, eight hours a day, and very quickly could read and write. He wanted to be professor of mathematics, and could solve many intricate problems, but he had no lead to himself. It was on a common fascination with mathematics that he and Rosalie established the relationship they never lost; it was because he could not solve his personal equation that they lost each other.

It started slowly, so that Mama was at first unaware of their liking for each other. Rosalie and Elder Brother went out together to visit the parks, the palaces, the museums. They went to the Summer Palace, and to the Peihai Park. They circled the city wall, climbed to the Observatory. In the Western Hills, fragrant with summer, they sweated torrid afternoons, heat-drenched, later watched autumn flush the slopes with scarlet. Elder Brother walked fast, he had big legs, big strides, and he talked, talked about many things, all the time. Rosalie trotted by his side. Never had she been so thin, so sunburnt, so tired, and so interested. The only trouble was a minor one: Elder Brother was so keen to take photographs that there was no time to look at anything properly, except in splintered moments, moments away from giving attention to his comments, remarks, explanations. Elder Brother knew the dates of everything, read every inscription, copied the ideograms on stone tablets and translated them. "Chinese culture is enormous, I'll never get to the end of it," he exclaimed. And in the evening he would teach mathematics to Rosalie. And though he never met Suchen or Fanju, Rosalie carried his knowledge to them. It was a hectic, extraordinary, unreal time, and the space fiction they read enhanced their unearthly trance.

Elder Brother thus was verbose, happy, excited, the first summer and autumn, and he walked Rosalie to exhaustion, walking her all over Peking and the surrounding countryside; and he drove her mind too, opening book after book. Thus they became known to each other, the little girl and the adolescent young man, and it was something Mama did not like. But she could not stop it, until she discovered one day that Elder Brother was short-sighted but had not worn glasses because he was afraid they would spoil his looks.

This discovery of Elder Brother's myopia, made one afternoon by the Greek doctor when he came to tea and cakes, immediately became with Mama drama, tragedy, a fatal defect. How could her son, *her* son, be short-sighted? Elder Brother looked drained as her mournful, tragic phraseology poured itself, filling the house and the courtyard, and he then began to hate her. He never got over this hatred of Mama. "If I am what I am, it is because of Mama, the way she spoke about my being short-sighted," Elder Brother was to say to Rosalie, decades later. He did not know how to compound his love and his hatred of Mama. And yet Mama was truly innocent, feeding her children well, watchful for their physical security. It was not her fault that she was in the wrong context both of geography and history, not her fault that she clothed her overweening emotions in the white anxious robes of wrathful angels, not her fault that she never stopped to think of her children as people.

Mama stood in the living-room, the tragic statue she became when making a shattering statement. Rosalie had returned with Papa from his office. She had been to fetch Papa in a renewed splurge of affection, surging like the tide, going and coming in forever renewed efforts at finding an outlet for all the unworded confusions which accumulated within her.

"He is myopic, he is myopic."

"Who?" said Papa, voice clipped to weary cautiousness. Papa drew a tent of brevity over himself when he came home to find Mama in what he called her "state of nerves".

"Your son," said Mama, and became nearly drawable as an ideogram meaning Terror. She was drawn up to an unmoving full height, but looked as if she might fall at any moment under yet another blow of destiny, Elder Brother's myopia being of course willed by the Malignancy that had pursued her through the years. "Your son, at seventeen, can scarcely see. He is purblind. He will be blind at twenty-one," cried Mama. Because he was myopic, Elder Brother was now Papa's son.

Elder Brother sat by the window pretending to read the Chinese newspaper in the twilight, apparently unconcerned, as if deaf as well as purblind.

Rosalie was terrified. In her unrelenting good health (sickness was a *weakness,* a to-be-despised confession of failure; Rosalie might cough all night, but she was *not* ill, coughing was a sign of lungs growing bigger, not of infection) Rosalie, so afraid of blindness, blinked at Elder Brother, imagined him blind, blind like the blind beggars, two stones for eyeballs.

Elder Brother now became the Short-Sighted One. Both Rosalie and Tiza teased him. "Hoo hoo, can you see me? Hoo hoo, blind as a bat." For though Rosalie loved him, when she was with Tiza she was another Rosalie, who made fun of Elder Brother to please Mama.

"I can see better than any of you," retorted Elder Brother, who meanwhile had read a book on optics and one on ophthalmology sent to him from Belgium. He had also given Rosalie a lecture on light waves. He did not seem to mind Rosalie teasing him; perhaps he too was becoming several different people at once. When they studied together and when he taught her, she did not tease him; and when she was a child among the other children, he ignored her. Their alliance grew, instead of dwindling. When he acquired spectacles, Papa going with him to the optician to fit him with a pair, he put them on and cried: "I see very clearly now," naïvely delighted.

One day, in the wide plain where they had been walking among the cotton fields of the villages outside the city wall, seeing the cotton pods burst their white pompons, he exclaimed: "I saw clearly, for a moment." He did not have his glasses on. He was happy. "It is the air," he said, "the air in China is doing me good."

Thus a spring, a summer and an autumn came and went. Mama knitted two woollen jackets, a purple one for Rosalie, a green one for Tiza. The sisters stood among Papa's enormous dahlias, blazing red and saffron, mottled against the chalky wall, vibrating with the colours of autumn, with the wood-smoke and dry-leaf smells of autumn, and Elder Brother photographed them. Upon the Western Hills the sun was still hot, yet in the tree shadows it became cold. Fuzzy mist hung about the morning, and at sunset the sky became magenta and gold, fused into one big shiningness which transfigured faces. When Rosalie combed her hair, sparks flew out of the comb in streaks. Everything one touched gave a shock, because of the dry cold. It was easy to get violent and emotional in such an air, with the sudden midday heat and the cold sparkling nights, the moon incisive like a silver knife. Rosalie burst into tears, and would not cut the dahlias because flowers should not suffer. Even Elder Brother laughed at her for this.

And now Elder Brother became unhappy. He wanted to continue studying at the Chinese university, but Mama wanted him to work; she said he had lazed enough, all of eight months, since February.

"What is the use of studying? You are already half-blind with too much study."

"Your father is getting old. His job in this railway doesn't pay. We have no money. University? All the students are Communists. What will you learn there? They are always on strike, making demonstrations and shouting and being shot."

"Do you think we are going to feed you and clothe you for years and years for nothing? You have studied enough. Why not take the job that Mr. Blievermann offers you in the German bank?"

"A job in a bank is a good thing. It has a future. If you are polite and hardworking, that is. You can even become an accountant, or even the sub-manager. It is a safe job, with no uncertainty at all."

Every day she talked thus, and Papa never said a word. But Elder Brother did, retorting, fighting for himself, at first politely, and then less politely, more roughly, and then with long spells of silence and sudden outbursts of violence, smashing his fist on the table, and walking out, to his cold room, alone.

Mama won, of course, because there was no money to study, because Elder Brother had no friend, no one to help him. Also, he began to see China as it was, the beggars, the misery, the filth, the hoplessness, the strikes, the warlords, and chiefly the dying, the dying. He had, after all, been brought up in Europe, and naturally he found China horrifying. At first he had tried to keep it picturesque, taking so many photographs of old walls, and monuments. But one had to be more than purblind not to see the squalor and the horror. And gradually he found it impossible to *be* Chinese. And nothing else was left to him, but to cling to the small world of Eurasians in China that Mama offered to him.

For all these reasons he found it impossible to go against the inevitable pattern, and so fell in with the choice Mama made for him.

Elder Brother was Eurasian, half-caste. He could not be Chinese. He could not be European. But he could work *for* a European firm and secure a higher salary than if he had been all-Chinese; he would be able to have people *under* him, even if he had to accept people *above* him. And though a Chinese father meant that he was Chinese on his passport, he would be paid better than a Chinese, better than his own father for a similar job. Had Elder Brother insisted on becoming all-Chinese, it would have meant to him becoming despised, going down in that unreal hierarchy of race, down among the anonymous, faceless crowd he saw round him, begging, hungry, to become of the millions and millions, beasts of their own fields, fields without end, hunger without end, misery without end; to become a poor student in a university, march the streets demanding release from exploitation and be shot at. That very year many students had been shot, and there had been monster demonstrations.

Elder Brother would have no "future" at all, no visible, safe, peaceful future. It meant working for a very small salary, like Papa, even though Papa was a good, experienced engineer, while some lordly White, much younger and without a diploma, earned ten times his salary and ordered him about . . .

It meant cutting himself off from what he knew, taking a lonely, lonely road, perhaps ending in death. It meant abandoing a known superiority for an evident inferiority.

It meant degradation, contempt, ridicule. "Don't tell me you have the nostalgia of mud, like your sister," cried Mama. For it was known that Rosalie had the nostalgia of mud, that she could never be happy with the right, the respectable, the correct people, although she had stopped picking up puppies. Rosalie had just signed with a flourish the testimonial of her ever-growing wickedness by kicking the Mother Superior of the European Convent, and she had been thrown out of school.

It had taken Mama two weeks of going to see Mother Superior, a session on her knees (so Mama said, whether figurative knees or otherwise Rosalie did not know), to get Rosalie re-admitted on conditional terms and in the English class, where for a while everyone was horrible to her, and she then achieved the impossible, by hitting a diplomat's daughter. Fortunately the diplomat's daughter was English, and hit back. They became friends, a friendship based on pugilistic proficiency, and later though not friends, because there was nothing in common between them, Rosalie did not suffer for it. The diplomat's daughter had to be withdrawn from school for immorality; she had circulated love letters written by her boy friends among the girls. But she did not forget Rosalie, who went to tea with her some years later, when she told an aghast Rosalie about her many lovers.

The predestined end of Rosalie, according to Mama, being a pallet of straw placed upon mud, where Rosalie would finally expire, having squandered her last dollar, Elder Brother must be insured against that end. And so, in November, he entered the German bank of Peking, as a Eurasian bank clerk, at a salary three times the salary of the Chinese clerks, who did exactly the same work and had been doing it for twenty years, and only one-fifth the salary of the young German boy, straight from Germany, who was supposed to "oversee" the work of the native staff (including Elder Brother's work), though he knew nothing at all about banking. "He cannot even spell German properly," said Elder Brother bitterly.

"Mr. Blievermann has done his best for you, you are getting the highest salary as a beginner," said Mama. She was pleased. There was Elder Brother settled, earning money. In the second month she asked him to contribute forty dollars of his hundred and twenty dollars for his food, and another twenty for laundry and wear and tear. Elder Brother paid.

Elder Brother was a bank clerk in the German bank for two years, and that was when he fell in love.

The Boisvaux family were also a Belgian railway family. In Peking those who had worked together on the Belgian-built railways, the Lunghai, and the Peking–Hankow, went on knowing each other, Chinese with Chinese, European with European. The railway on which Papa worked had been built with people like Emile Boisvaux, who received a salary five times that of Papa's, and was also given a house, and was supposed to be an engineer; he had been only a station-master back in Belgium. The Boisvaux were Walloons, from the depressed areas of coalmining in the French-speaking part of Belgium. The family invited Papa and Mama to lunch once every two months, and Papa and Mama invited them back. They had two sons, with whom Rosalie played, and one daughter Liza, who had returned from school in Belgium to Peking when she was sixteen, a year before Elder Brother.

The Boisvaux lived in a large house in Goldfish Street. They had carpets on their floors, pictures on their walls. Mama had only two pictures on the wall in the dining-room at home: one a portrait in oils of her Dutch grandfather, Matthias Leenders, who had a long thin nose, a small thin mouth, and sharp blue eyes, the whole topped by curly russet hair and emergent from an enormously high white collar; the other was of an angel guarding two children in a storm. The Boisvaux had at least a dozen pictures, and they also had ivory elephants, some Fukien red lacquer vases, and on their piano an old piece of embroidery; all these things were Chinese, because Mr. Boisvaux collected Chinese curios, he was going back to Belgium to sell them when he retired. Every time they went to lunch there were some new purchases which Mr. Boisvaux wanted to show to Papa. He would ask Papa what he thought of them, and laughed at Papa for not collecting his own country's curios. Papa looked, and did not say anything except "Yes ... yes." Back home Mama would say to him: "If you had the salary he gets, we could also waste it on curios." Mama looked down on all antiques, pictures and curios. "They collect dust."

But Mr. Boisvaux always said that the Chinese did not know how good their own things were, and that he bought these things dirt cheap, and in Europe they would fetch five or ten times as much money, so it was an investment, not a waste of money.

Liza Boisvaux had long hair, blue eyes, a big nose (so Rosalie thought, but then to her at that time all European noses were too big), and she was called a nice girl by everyone. She played the piano, and sang in church. She was twenty when Elder Brother was nineteen, and one day after a year of going to lunch and listening to Mr. Boisvaux telling about his latest buy in curios, Elder Brother when they were back in their own house, sitting to supper, said: "It's taken. It's gone."

"What do you mean?" said Mama.

"My heart," said Elder Brother. "It's taken. I am in love."

Mama stopped ladling out the soup. "In love? What are you talking about?"

"Liza," said Elder Brother. "I am in love with her."

After a week or so of talking it over with Papa, it was decided that Mama should approach Mrs. Boisvaux and start sounding her out about Liza. Would Liza marry Elder Brother?

After all, argued Mama, it was not as if Elder Brother was not a European. He was very nearly a European, and Papa, that negligible Chinese quantity, was after all an engineer; and, said Mama, she knew that the Boisvaux in their own country came from a village in the coalmining area, they were not of good family as she was. They would never have been accepted by *her* mother and father, but here in China it was different, one had to be friends, even with people like that, otherwise one never saw anyone from year's end to year's end, except the Chinese of course, but in Mama's eyes they were background, nothing more. Elder Brother was making one hundred and twenty dollars, and later he would get more. He was still very young.

Having argued herself into courage, Mama put on her best hat, the light winter coat with big black and white squares which was really so chic but so extraordinary because no one wore that kind of coat; Mama, tall and gaunt, with that coat on looked like an ambulant chequer-board, but somehow it was pleasant to Rosalie's eyes. Mama climbed into the rickshaw, and went to call upon Mrs. Boisvaux, having the week before written a letter:

My dear Jeanne,
I would like to come to talk to you about a certain matter which concerns both our families, and unless it is inconvenient to you, will come on Thursday, a week from today, to see you, about three o'clock in the afternoon. I hope, my dear Jeanne, that you will give me some of your precious time.

"As if she ever did anything," said Mama aloud, when she read the draft of her letter to Papa and to Elder Brother.

At a quarter to six Mama returned from her call on Jeanne Boisvaux. Elder Brother was not yet back from the bank, he worked till six, but as soon as he was back he rushed up to Mama: "What did she say, what did she say?"

"I think," said Mama, with an uncertain look, "that they will think it over."

"But what did *she* say?" replied Elder Brother, meaning of course Liza, the daughter.

"Oh, of course I didn't speak to her, she was not there. That's not how things are done. Do you want to spoil everything? I spoke only to her mother."

Weeks went by, and there was another lunch at home. Rosalie watched Mama clumsily manoeuvre to get Elder Brother and Liza to sit next to each other at table. But it was no use: Liza only spoke to her own mother and to Mama.

Elder Brother was hopeful. "I think she likes me, and as for me, there will never be anyone else for me."

Rosalie listened and watched. How could anyone fall in love with Liza, whose hair smelt bad, to begin with? But then it was one of those things that were so unreal, and however much one tried to catch hold, they remained unreal, fluid, not there; present but not there, a hover, like the painted sky in church, like the ceiling above the mosquito net because one always wondered how ceilings held up, and no one explained. It was one of the things to be known in the future, when one grew up, and the growing-up epoch was itself mysterious, uncertain, impalpable time, since the morrows came so quickly to become yesterdays, but still one was not grown up.

"Love is a bore, I shall never love a man," said Rosalie to Suchen.

And Suchen said: "Of course not. All men are disgusting."

Elder Brother and Liza, his looking at her, her laughter so quick and forced; Mama pulling her gloves off, returning from her visit with that look of her eyes as if looking back at herself rather than at Elder Brother; all these things could not be used to fit into a story, they could not be touched or smelt, they belonged to that unreal grown-up world, so boring and so joyless.

At the next lunch, which was at the Boisvaux', Mr. Boisvaux was effusively hearty. He drew Papa aside with loud laughter to show him a porcelain stool he had just bought, which he claimed had been sat upon by a member of the Chinese imperial house, and which he had picked up for under two dollars in a crumbling shop outside the Gate of Peace. Everyone laughed a lot, and Liza played several airs on the piano, and Elder Brother listened and clapped again and again, and spoke to her, and she blushed until her neck in front and at the back was a hot pinkness.

In this unsatisfactory, unget-at-able way, things went on for several weeks, and Elder Brother would not take Rosalie for walks any more, until one afternoon when, punctually at three, Mrs. Boisvaux arrived, arrayed in gloves and hat just as Mama had been, and the two women shut themselves up in the bedroom. Rosalie, who was doing sums because she was supposed to practise scales on the piano but was bored with piano-playing, listened at the keyhole and could not hear a word.

Ten minutes later the two women emerged from the bedroom. Mrs. Boisvaux loudly kissed Mama three times, dispensing that moist smack which Rosalie was to endure later from her own relatives when she went to Belgium. Smack smack smack, repeated three times, right cheek, left cheek, right cheek, and sometimes the whole process done again, left, right, left; never could one kiss less than three times, or one was accused of cold unfriendliness. Then Mrs. Boisvaux went away, after kissing Rosalie three times and Tiza three times. She even kissed Marianne, which was quite a feat because Marianne always pushed her head deeply into her chest and pulled up her dress so as not to be kissed by Mrs. Boisvaux; she said her teeth smelt bad.

When Elder Brother returned from the bank, Mama had to tell him: "Mrs. Boisvaux was here this afternoon, and she says no, it can't be done."

Elder Brother sat down and ate his supper, making no more noise, or less, than usual. Rosalie watched him. What did one do when Mrs. Boisvaux said no? What exactly had she said no to? But these questions were not to be asked, because Elder Brother was unhappy.

But Mama went on arguing with his silence. "If I were you," she said, "if I were you . . ."

What exactly she proposed to do if she were Elder Brother Rosalie neither understood nor listened to, and there was only this silence to fall in between the "If I were you . . ."

Next Sunday Elder Brother did not go with them to church. He said: "I don't want to see her."

Mama said: "You are a softy, you should come. What does

it matter? The Denis would not have looked at the Boisvaux, they are low class, Walloons, hypocritical. It's only here, in China, that we know them. Why, this girl has no education, she never went to a good convent school as I did. Your father is much better educated than Boisvaux," finally remembering Papa.

A few months later Elder Brother said one day: "I am going away."

"Where? Where?" asked Mama. "Going away where? Leaving us? Then who will pay me the sixty dollars a month that you pay for food and laundry? You know we cannot make ends meet, and there is your sisters' education. Luckily Rosalie will soon be out of school, and she can go to work. But what about Tiza, what about Marianne?"

Elder Brother said: "I have found another job, in Tientsin. I don't want to stay here any more. I don't want to see you ever again. I don't want to see any of you again. I have suffered enough, I have put up with enough. I shall not come back."

Mama burst into tears, then she sobbed, and when Papa came back from the office she ran to him before he was in the room and started shouting, and suddenly Elder Brother was also shouting, just as Mama did. It was frightening, for Tiza shrieked, and so did Marianne, and even Rosalie found herself crying at last. And then Elder Brother was packing, and Rosalie thought, I won't have any more space fiction to read, but perhaps wherever he is he can post some magazines to me.

Elder Brother's trunks were packed and put out on the veranda to be taken away in two rickshaws, and the cold room with cement floor where Elder Brother had lived assumed that wide, blank look which rooms have when you take out the furniture, like the stare of a suddenly opened eye. By that time Rosalie knew Elder Brother was truly going, but when she tried to talk to him, he said: "Leave me alone. I don't have time for children like you." And this was terrible, because until now they had been together, and he had never called her a child; and suddenly her mind leapt back to autumn, last autumn with Elder Brother walking, walking in the countryside, in the fields, the smell of the fields, and going to the peasants' houses and being barked at by their dogs, and smelling that lovely smell of garlic and sweat associated with Liu Mah in childhood, the smell of work, and all the furrows grey-grown, quietly shuttered in for early winter; the long, long walk back in the so quiet afternoon, and Rosalie so

tired, legs aching, but keeping up with Elder Brother's paces;
the sun going down, drowned in its own magenta, and the
blue Western Hills, like petals of a flower looked at sideways,
and one's legs so tired, so tired one could weep but did not;
the little man by the roadside with his long bamboo pole,
carrying at one end a stone and at the other end a small chest
with bowls and a teapot, and putting the whole thing down
for them and giving them hot scalding tea for one copper;
Rosalie burnt her tongue, and the burnt tongue remained all
night, but it was somehow lovely, drinking scalding tea, and
the sun drowning, and the little man was so beautiful, so
beautiful his face, furrowed and quiet, like the earth; and
Elder Brother spoke of the sun and the moon, and why the
sky was magenta, and he took a picture of Rosalie standing
in the field, her back to the dying sun.

All this was a not-been, since Elder Brother took it all away
from her, calling her a child. And now there were more scenes,
ugliness, horror, he cursing his mother, cursing the day he
was born, saying: "I will never look at you again, I don't
want you as my family. I shall make my own way. I don't
want any one of you ever to cross my life again."

No one went with him to the railway station. He left in a
rickshaw, his trunks had gone two hours before, with the
cook to look after them.

Rosalie said: "I am going with him," and went out to call a
street rickshaw, and took out her money-box, which luckily
still had some coppers in it to pay her fare.

Mama shouted at her: "You can stay out too if you go
with him." And she slammed the door behind Rosalie.

But at that moment going to the station after Elder Brother
was the only thing to do, and Rosalie's rickshaw was swift
and caught up with Elder Brother's rickshaw. He saw Rosalie,
and said: "Ah, you have come." And then he stopped his rickshaw and she got out from hers, and paid him, and climbed
into Elder Brother's rickshaw, though it was a heavy load for
the rickshaw man to pull, Elder Brother being so tall and
heavy. And so they went to the station. And sitting on Elder
Brother's knee she suddenly remembered Papa sighing, but
he had not moved. He had stayed with Mama, letting Rosalie
go alone.

At the station Elder Brother showed his ticket, and bought
a platform ticket for her. They went into the compartment
of the waiting train, and sat down side by side, and it looked

for a moment as if Rosalie would go away with him. But she knew that could not be. She foraged in her pocket, and brought out the present she had prepared for him but which she could not give him in the house because of Mama, because of being laughed at, a little silk purse made in the shape of a lotus flower, with orange and grey alternate petals, and a string round its mouth to shut it.

"But that is pretty," said Elder Brother, as if he had never seen anything so pretty before, "did you make it?"

"Yes," said Rosalie, lying, because of course she had not made it, she would never be able to sew anything as pretty as that. It had been given to her by Suchen, who had many lovely things given her by her mother Princess Dan. It was one of Rosalie's most precious belongings, and she had to give it to Elder Brother. "It is to put something in," she explained. Suchen had kept scented wood chips in it, but Elder Brother would not understand about scented wood, he was not Chinese enough. "You can put money in it, if you want."

"I will of course put something in it," said Elder Brother.

Then a whistle blew, and Rosalie got up and said goodbye. Elder Brother stood at the window as the train glided away.

"I'll write to you," he said. "I will write. And you write to me."

And then Rosalie went home, and Mama pretended not to see her return.

THIRTY-ONE

EVEN the very young knew that Peking was the city of the Northern warlords, and that often the name of the warlord changed: Chang Tsolin, Wu Peifu, Feng Yuhsiang, Tuan Chijui, they came and went, fought each other, and all of them fought against the South. For in the South there were the Southern armies, and especially the armies of the Canton government, under Sun Yatsen. And though Sun Yatsen had died in 1925, his armies were marching against the Northern warlords. The warlords of the North said that the Canton government armies were Communists and Reds, that they killed everyone on their way. Mama again buried her jewels in the courtyard of the house. They were jewels she had brought from Belgium with her, heirlooms, large rubies and sapphires in rings, diamond pendants, emerald and diamond ear-rings. Then Mama felt the courtyard unsafe, so this time she took the jewels to the Scheut missionaries. They had a locked strongbox, and the jewels would be safer there. Scheut Flemish missionaries were by now all over North China, their missions studded Mongolia, and their headquarters were in Peking.

In 1926 the Southern armies began their march to the North. All the warlords cried out "Communism!" The Legation Quarters put up barbed wire, and Japanese soldiers manoeuvred on the plain in front of the Legation Quarters. Papa said there were military advisers from France and England and Germany come to help the great warlords of the North against the South. The Japanese were giving ten million dollars to the chief of them, Chang Tsolin, to fight the Southern armies of the Kuomintang. Special battalions, mercenaries recruited from the White Russians, paraded with guns supplied by the foreigners. They toasted the Tsar and broke wine glasses, crashing them against the walls of the dance halls in Hatamen Street. Warlord Chang Tsolin's soldiers drilled on the waste spaces in the city, and in the parks; their grey uniforms lined the city walls, stood guard at the gates, tall Northerners making the people walking by afraid to look at them lest they be shot as Communists. And all about the city many died, supposed to be Communists in league with the Southern armies of the Kuomintang.

There were always troops when one warlord went away and another came in triumph to Peking, but this time the Legation Quarters put up entanglements of barbed wire, and many foreign soldiers were landed from gunboats at the port of Tientsin, and this had never occurred when only warlords fought each other. Truly it seemed even the powerful foreigners were afraid of the Kuomintang and its armies of the South.

So many times Peking had been bedecked, in expectancy of another conqueror; the gates with streamers and painted arches, smothered in a profusion of paper flowers, pink, yellow and blue, forming a design of slogans: "Long live our Victorious General...", "Saviour of the People", "Successor to the Heroes of Old", "Ten thousand generations will recall your Glorious Name". Beside these arches soldiers of the new ruler kept guard, for often during the night the fulsome praises were torn down, and the red walls of the Forbidden City would be plastered with other slogans: "Down with

General ... who sells the country to the Imperialists", "Blood cries to heaven for revenge – we shall revenge our country's wrongs", "Long live democracy", "The people will rise and overthrow their tyrants".

So many times Rosalie had watched triumphal processions, with two or three bands of musicians, each playing a different air, to open the road; their uniforms varied as did their tunes; their bright brass instruments out-noised each other. Behind them solid phalanxes of soldiers in grey, high-stepping like small horses, brought down with a soft thump their feet in cloth shoes, and up jumped the dust in gay puffs. Lorries, filled with more soldiers with guns, followed them, and then came the Big Knives squad, executioners and special body-guard. A regiment of cavalry, little Mongolian ponies with shaggy manes, preceded a file of motor-cars, with soldiers standing on the runningboards of the armour-plated, bullet-proof vehicles. The crowds waved, shouted dutifully, paper flowers distributed to them pinned to their chests. Not to wave and cheer was dangerous.

"Never get to the front of the crowd, stay well back," said Papa. He and Rosalie stood well back against the shop wall, Papa having pinned to his coat button, well in view, the flower he had been given to indicate his loyalty to the war-lord of the month.

For sometimes amid the docile rejoicing a small eddy of turmoil rose; there would be thudding blows, the sound of panting, and plainclothes men would haul someone away, a young man, sometimes a young woman. "Students," whispered Papa. "Communists." Then Rosalie felt her body objectionably protuberant, incredibly large, and understood Papa as they both attempted to sink into the walls of the shop behind them, while round about them people seemed not to see, not to hear what was going on, the whole scene invisible while, mysteriously, a way opened, a rift in the crowd allowing the prisoners to be dragged away. To look was dangerous.

Daily came tidings of war. The Southern armies had left Canton, were halfway to the Yangtse River, marching on the Triple City, Hankow. Mama said: "They won't come North, the North is safe. The English will send their gunboats and shoot all of them." Mama's regard for the English had grown with the years. They were powerful enough to stop anyone, and they did what they liked in China. In fact both in Canton and in Shanghai foreign troops had opened fire and shot at

Chinese crowds. Mama disliked the Japanese, and now there were so many Japanese about, but she said the English would put down "the upstart Japs".

The Japanese were giving money to the Northern warlord Chang; photographs of Japanese generals who were to help "fight Communism" appeared in the newspapers. Outside the large hotel called the Peking Hotel, a building owned by the French and which inspired Rosalie with great awe and fear because only Europeans and big warlords were allowed inside, motor-cars were stationed, and out of the largest of them came Japanese generals trailing long shining scabbards in the dust. The big glass doors swung open to reveal red carpets on the floor.

The armies of the South came nearer to Middle China, and repeatedly the name of Chiang Kaishek, their military chief, was mentioned. He was a Red, a Communist, he had been to Moscow. He was much to be feared. And now the Middle Provinces fell, and the Triple City was taken by the Southern armies. Soon it would be the coast, and Shanghai. If Shanghai fell, all the Europeans would send gunboats and troops to protect their people, for Shanghai was their city. Mama spoke of taking refuge with the Scheut missionaries, who already harboured her jewels in their strongbox.

At noon every day Rosalie and Tiza walked from school in the Three Measures Street to Papa's railway office in Two Measures Street. They returned home with him, and in the afternoon stayed at home. There was no school in the afternoon because of "the troubles".

"We cannot go on like this," said Papa, sighing, to his friend Mr. Hua, who occupied the next room in the office. "The country is going to pieces. Each one takes a piece, and the Japanese most of all."

"Have patience," said Mr. Hua, and he raised a thin, aristocratic fist, full of desperate dignity, "soon it will be over. The wolves will be put to flight. Do not fear the Southern armies. I will be glad when they come."

Wolves, thought Rosalie, seeing the character for wolf, lean with slim running legs, altogether a predatory word to write.

Papa smiled, sipped tea. At home Papa was all silence; in his office, with Mr. Hua, he talked, he even talked a lot.

"When you and I were young," he said to Mr. Hua, "what hopes did we entertain, what lofty thoughts of saving the country! Now here we are, two middle-aged men, trying to keep a few trains together, to keep the railways running. Our lives are at the whim of scoundrels with guns. How often have our hopes in such-and-such a man been set to nothing? You revered Sun Yatsen. I met him. But he died, we saw his funeral, and here we are, worse off than before. I don't think the Cantonese armies will win. And if they do, then we shall have the Russians ruling us, and that is just as bad."

Mr. Hua said: "You are wrong. Sun Yatsen was a nationalist. The Southern armies have a programme. They must win, and then China will be united."

"There are too many Communists," said Papa. "I do not like it. Do you not think the Russians will cheat us too? They are directing the Southern armies."

"No," said Mr. Hua, with energy, and again his fist came up. "Russia has had her Revolution. Remember what they did: they abrogated the unequal treaties, gave up all their rights which Russia had acquired in China under the Tsars. They promised to give back the railways in Manchuria. The Russians have treated us well, as equal human beings. All the others are hypocrites, only selling guns to back one warlord against another, to make money and to keep us fighting amongst ourselves. I believe in the Canton government. I believe in Chiang Kaishek, their military commander."

"Sun Yatsen," said Papa, "died too early."

"China must be for the Chinese," said Mr. Hua.

"I hope so," said Papa, "I hope so, but I don't know, I am not sure. There are all kinds of people in the South, good and bad."

"Chiang Kaishek," said Mr. Hua, "is a very good man."

"Yes," said Papa, "but I don't know ... money corrupts even the best people. I have seen it happen."

"Chiang Kaishek is good," said Mr. Hua. "He is our hope and our salvation. He will sweep the Europeans into the sea, where they came from. He will liberate Shanghai. You will see.

"Why," he added, laughing that high, stuttering laugh he had all to himself, a staccato sound that made Rosalie, when she wrote his name, Hua, poise the brush as if for a punctuation mark, in order to convey his laugh, "do you know why there is no more red cotton cloth in the Peking markets these days? Because everyone has been buying it up, to make new small flags, red flags, when Chiang Kaishek comes here."

And Mr. Hua went out, humming to himself a martial tune.

Papa went home with his children, stopping on the way to read the Chinese newspaper pasted on the board in the street. Rosalie read the headlines, tracing with her finger in her left palm the characters as she read them. This habit she had kept, clinging to it as she felt the words slip from her, building a wall of thin, insubstantial characters to remain with Papa, in that world of Papa and Mr. Hua, writing in air to conjure that world's existence, to build a wall and shut out Mama who had shut out Elder Brother.

Rosalie remembered that grit-cold March day in 1925, and the funeral: it had been the funeral of Sun Yatsen. Papa, Mr. Hua and Rosalie had stood in the street with a million others, watching the draped coffin go by. And now she remembered Sun's face, for she had seen it, in a students' procession, an enormous portrait, mild-eyed, borne by a tidal wave of people. Most of them had been young, men and women marching in their thousands, long rows of boys and girls, in blue cotton gowns, with scarves round the neck, and singing. How many times the columns of students had marched, shouting slogans, singing songs, bearing banners, only to be charged by warlord soldiers and police, and shot at? And not only by warlords, but also by the foreign troops. Often there were executions on the waste empty ground by the Forward Gate, beheadings and shootings and hackings; and yet the blue columns formed again, to march and to sing. Futile it looked, so many laughed at them, including Mama and Papa. "These students should study, they should not meddle in politics," the newspapers wrote in big characters. The students marched, and there was more shooting, and so it went on. And now it looked as if Sun Yatsen, though dead, was winning. Though he was in a grave, his armies were marching on, shouting his name.

Rosalie remembered last year, the soft month of May 1926, when the students marched again; June came hotly, and July, and still they marched. "The British have shot workers in Shanghai, that is why the students are marching in Peking," said Papa. On and on went the usual arrests, draggings off, executions. Mama spoke of returning to Belgium with Tiza and Marianne, and even packed one trunk ready to go.

Rosalie stood straight, reading the newspaper with Papa, and now it was 1927. Once again a cold, cold March, and no more red cloth in Peking because all the red cloth had been bought for flags to be put out, the red flags of joy and hope and deliverance. Or so said Mr. Hua. The people walked about, quiet and soft, on cloth-shod feet, colourless their faces, their shadows unhurried after them, crowds quiet as destiny. Mama said: "Look at them, look at the Chinese, they are as dumb as cattle. They don't *want* revolution, they only want money and food. It's only those students, with their Communism."

"Look," said Mama's friends, Mr. and Mrs. Blievermann, "look at those soldiers, who fight and die for a copper and a bowl of rice a day. Give them rice and they'll fight, they do not need to know why, they wouldn't understand it anyway. But they will fight if you give them food and money."

Round the Legation Quarters, where the Europeans took shelter when there was "trouble", as they had taken shelter during the Boxer "trouble" twenty-seven years before, the Japanese now established a ring of troops and carried out manoeuvres on the waste ground, deliberately kept denuded, the ground where the British played polo in the afternoons when there were no "troubles". Rosalie watched the Japanese children on their bicycles going back and forth to Japanese school, very near the Quarters. They all wore hygienic white masks on their faces to keep out the dust, and to keep out encephalitis, for there was an epidemic and many children were sick or had died.

Fifty thousand men had left Canton, fifty thousand strong soldiers marching North to unify China, and the great Northern Expedition went on growing and swelling in numbers on its way, and although in Peking the newspapers printed every other day that the Southern army and its Communist supporters were "disintegrating" and that Chiang Kaishek was beaten, everyone knew this was not true, for on they came.

And now other names besides that of Chiang Kaishek, the commander-in-chief, were in Papa's mouth. Wang Chingwei, beloved of many people in Peking, because in his youth he had thrown a bomb to try to kill the Regent; and there was also a young man called Chou Enlai, who had been training young officers in the Military Academy near Canton; he had been to France, and it was said he had learnt Communism in Paris.

And Rosalie, who knew nothing, yet felt the dark unmoving move, felt the darkness unworded heave, and her heart beat, and she could not understand why she too waited for the South to come. She heard of the dreadful things that were being done by the Communists, according to the newspapers, and also according to the nuns at school. All the men shot, the women shared out among soldiers, children turned into Reds and made to kill their mothers.

Mr. Hua was happy. "Nonsense," he cried, "you will see."

Mrs. Hua now returned from Europe, but without her children; Simon and Leila remained there, to study. Mrs. Hua also wanted the Revolution to come, and the armies of the South to unify China. She told Mama she had seen the students in France, in 1919 and 1920, and the Communists were good, she said. Mama crossed herself, and left, saying she would never enter Mrs. Hua's home again. Now more students were killed, and the word Revolution was forbidden on pain of death.

And then, in April of 1927, all was ended.

"Chiang Kaishek is a good man," said Mama.

Mr. Hua came to Papa's office one afternoon when Rosalie was there, and he and Papa sat for a long time facing each other, not speaking.

Mama went to see Mrs. Hua again, and came back triumphant. Mrs. Hua had looked haggard. 'She didn't dare talk to me of Communism,' said Mama.

The barbed-wire entanglements came down from around the Legation Quarters. Next year Peking would welcome the new victor with arches and paper powers, streamers and the new flags, the white sun on a blue background, the flag of the Kuomintang. And everyone said that China would really be able to get on, and the Blievermanns and the Lautens came to tea. They said that Chiang was a good man, he was not a Communist and so he would not make a Revolution. Instead, when he had marched upon Shanghai, the workers of the city had risen and fought to help him, but suddenly he had turned the tables on them; he had made an agreement with the bankers and the businessmen, the British, the Americans, the French in Shanghai, and had shot thousands of workers, and stopped the Communists, and everyone said he was a genius. Now China would be stable and at peace.

So Mama went to the Scheut Mission to reclaim her box of jewels. "All of them are for you," she said to Tiza, as she brought them back and put them as usual in the wardrobe chest. But she took out a gold locket pendant on a gold chain.

It was round, and had a spider with a pearl for the body and two rubies for its eyes upon its top. When the locket opened, inside it were two photographs, one of Mama and one of Papa. She gave this to Rosalie to wear on great occasions.

And it was after April 1927 that Mama decided that Rosalie should learn English full-time. Everyone now suddenly began to study English, and without English there was no good job to be had. The new government was very friendly with English and American banks and businesses. "You must learn English, so that you may be able to work in an English bank, for you will certainly not be able to marry, not with that face of yours," Mama said to Rosalie.

And the nuns also now changed. For the first time, they would have English Overseas Examinations. The first were to be held in December 1928, and Rosalie would be one of the three girls competing for it, the other two being a Eurasian and an English girl, both about fifteen years old.

THIRTY-TWO

A SEA of cinders, and upon its surface, clustered like ticks in the coats of scavenger dogs, the beggars squatted to sift treasure out of the garbage: bits of cloth, paper, wood, metal, chips of unburnt coal; precious refuse for the pullulating refuse of earth. Rosalie stared, while Papa and the contractor talked. Soon upon this expanse, to be later tamped smooth with stones lifted and let fall again by chanting men, would their new house be built.

The old wall that squared the old Yellow City had come down. Peking was built like a four-square box, containing other four-square boxes; at its heart the Forbidden City, purple walls and yellow roofs, and then round that the Imperial or Yellow City, and to the north the Manchu City. To prove that they were modern and progressive, each warlord in succession tried to improve Peking: they put a fence round some public park, or took one off, erected a monument to themselves, or rifled a palace to the ground. The wall round the Yellow City had now been pulled down by some forgotten Northern warlord, and along its now vanished base, in the deep rute where it had stood, the winter cinders of the city's coal fires were dumped, along with much other refuse. Later this land would be sold and houses built upon it.

Papa drew the plans of the house himself; Mama looked on, giving advice, for the rest of her dowry (so she told her children later) would go into the bricks and stone of that house. Papa bought bricks cheaply: there were many to spare, from old walls being pulled down. When the house was built, it had an imposing gateway of concrete, with a triangular top, framing the wooden door which was painted dark red. Two brass knockers in the shape of lion heads adorned each leaf; from the corners of their mouths hung the ring-shaped knockers.

After a while Rosalie thought the gate quite hideous; it looked so out of place, staring with its pointed cranium, red face and bright brass eyes at her when she walked towards it.

And in front of that gateway, with its lofty seriousness, ran the mule and camel track, which had always run at the foot of the wall. Building houses where the wall had been had not changed this track; it was of earth, turning to churned dust in the dry season, to churned mud in the summer rain, to frozen ruts in winter. All day the carts went by, laden with produce for the city: vegetables and coal, and salt, and in winter a padding procession of camels, ringing their elongate bells with calm deliberation. For so it had been, and now it still was. And the worst of it was the whip cracking: the mules and the little donkeys, with their beautiful patient eyes, being whipped in front of that big twin-knockered gate of the house, and sometimes a man whipping whipping whipping away a poor mule covered in sores, and Rosalie would shriek with it, and say: "Stop, stop!" and then run away, but not inside the house, but outside, anywhere, to make it stop.

Rosalie regretted the last house; in fact, she was still enamoured of the one-before-last house, the one in the Manchu City, with those large square stones in front of the gateway, polished smooth blue with sitting; that would remain for her the most beautiful house of all, with its small courtyard bursting lilac, and the spirit screen of carved brick, and the Manchu ladies going in and out next door. Then they had moved to a house in the Street of the Small Grass Plot, and that was also a beautiful house to Rosalie. This new house, at the Road of the Yellow Wall's Root, was bigger than either of the last two, and yet somehow they were more crowded together than before. This house was not built like a Chinese house, a four-room arrangement, long and low, like the sides of a box, round a central courtyard with trees and flower plots. Here the garden was in front of the house, and behind it all the rooms were together, one opening into the other, as in a European house. The garden was much larger, however, and there was an enormous jar from Shantung, with dragons and phoenixes on the outside, and some goldfish in it. Papa planted several lilacs, a vine and four acacia trees for shade, and there were forsythia, pomegranates and dahlias, and chrysanthemums in clusters along the garden walls.

As soon as they had moved in, Papa and Mama bought some new furniture: a big wardrobe of polished cherry wood, and a large cheval-mirror. One room became the parlour; in it Rosalie's piano, the big mirror, a few good chairs which were reserved for guests, a pair of lacquered vases, the gift of Papa's friends, three bronze figurines stiffened it. Only Rosalie was allowed in it, to practise the piano half an hour a day. But there was still only one bedroom for the three girls, and one for Papa and Mama. There was one bathroom with a flush lavatory, and this was new, as they had no bathroom in any of the older houses, and the dung-removal man had come every morning to collect the night soil, with his elongate wooden cylindrical barrel upon his back and his long spoon. The floors in the new house were not stone, but wood, so brown and shiny at first that Rosalie did not dare to walk upon them. And in the kitchen Mama placed a large iron stove which had come all the way from Belgium, a gleaming thing upon four bow legs that squatted and took possession. Mama could now make pancakes and wafers of almonds, butter and sugar, and every morning she rose early to grind the coffee beans in a coffee grinder which had been with her ever since she had come to China. And now, because the rooms were all one in another, the coffee scent was wafted from the kitchen through the eating-living room and the parlour and at right angles into the bedrooms. Rosalie could smell the ground coffee beans, which was a different and a better smell from that when the coffee had been turned into a brown liquid.

"Now we must invite them," said Mama. "It is better to do it now, and get it over with."

By "them" she meant First Aunt and her husband, Uncle Liu the Lolo, and their children. First Aunt was pregnant again, and no one knew then that she would die of this last, fourteenth child. Their first son, who had been studying in a university in Tientsin, was home; he would soon be going to America, Papa said.

"It's wasted money. He won't learn anything in America," said Mama.

"The Americans are giving him money to study," said Papa.

Three years previously, when they were still living at the Street of the Small Grass Plot, First Aunt had come to stay with them. She had run away from her husband, Liu the Lolo. I do not know now how Rosalie then found out (perhaps she eavesdropped) that First Aunt had come to stay with them because she did not want any more babies. But perhaps this was not the true reason. In any case, she had stayed in the spare room, and was so quiet and still, only coming out for meals, and then taking up so little space, that Rosalie only remembered her as a very white, small, pointed face with beautiful glistening black hair and sad, long-drawn eyes. The eyes she was later to recognize, and the face: the same face and eyes that belonged to Grandfather, Papa's father, who had died long ago. First Aunt wore trousers of grey silk, and tiny black leather shoes upon her bound feet, which were so small that the shoe was half the length of Rosalie's hand. She was altogether small, at that time being scarcely a head taller than Rosalie. After a few days Uncle Liu the Lolo had come to take her back, but Rosalie was at school then, and all she knew was that First Aunt had returned to her family, and after that there had been another baby.

Uncle Liu the Lolo was thus named by Mama because she said he was an aborigine, the son of a Lolo feudal landowner, called a Tumu, of the Lolo tribes who live in the mountains in the north-west of Szechuan. But Uncle Liu persisted in denying this: he said he was not of Lolo race, but of Han or Chinese race. Uncle Liu was an enormous man, fully six foot four, with a laugh and a voice that made all the windows shake. Tiza was terrified of him, and always hid in the bedroom to weep when he came.

Uncle Liu had been one of the students from Szechuan selected to study engineering in Belgium at the same time as Papa. He had returned a year earlier, carrying a letter from Papa to his family. And this letter had led to his being received by the Family, and to his betrothal and marriage to First Aunt, Papa's sister. Papa had three sisters, Rosalie knew, the other two had married in Szechuan and remained there. Only First Aunt, following her husband, had come to Peking a few years earlier. Mama said she was lucky, not having been

in the small stations on the railway, but always in a big city
like Peking.

On the appointed afternoon the Liu family arrived, Uncle
Liu's voice and laughter preceding him a long way ahead,
like gong beaters in a music ceremony, or the music bands
before a warlord's entry. He was followed by First Aunt,
and behind them their children in procession through
the door, from the eldest son, Yusiang, through Yuchen,
their eldest daughter who giggled at everyone and was
very fat, down to the last four toddlers carried by their
amahs. They filled the veranda, and two of the toddlers
opened wide mouths and let out deep, deliberate screams
when they saw Mama.

"They are not used to foreigners," said Uncle Liu.

The amahs took the small ones into the garden, where
they passed water on the tomatoes Papa had planted in rows
in the first plot, nearest to the veranda. Mama loved tomatoes, and in every station on the railway line where she had
lived, there was one garden or courtyard with a small plot of
tomato plants.

First Aunt could hardly stand, and sat down in the parlour
on a best chair. Rosalie examined her carefully, for now she
knew about babies. Son of Spring, Elder Brother, had told
her, and how they were born, and Rosalie had felt nearly
sick when Song of Spring had also told her about how men
and women made a baby together, but now she had grown
used to the idea, and so looked judiciously at First Aunt and
verified the fact that babies were stored in their mothers'
bellies. She had not told Mama that Son of Spring had instructed her in these matters, since Mama would not have
understood, just as she did not understand space fiction. Actually, space fiction was far more interesting than learning
about babies. There was the baby, bulging out of First Aunt's
dress, as she dangled helpless thin legs below the protuberance,
dangled tiny feet, like the heads of match-sticks, at the bottom
of her straight bony legs. Sitting on top of this enormous
nestling egg was First Aunt's small flat chest, and above that
her face, very pale, very thin. From the collar of her dress
rose her ravaged neck, with its runnels and cords of flesh, all
twisted from the disease which Mama dreaded for Tiza, the
swollen, soft like turtle-dove glands, rotund as turtle-dove
breast, warm, and which later broke down and streamed, not
blood as a dove would, but pus, yellow and thick, ploughing

the neck into these ridges of skin and flesh which no collar could hide.

"She has the scrofula," Mama had said, and the word, looked up in the dictionary, also yielded the picture of a French or an English king touching a row of beggars; for only the royal touch could heal the disease, and no king was available to touch First Aunt. No wonder Mama had feared for Tiza's neck. Even now, at any moment, the dread swellings might return. And Rosalie, who had been singularly bullying towards Tiza for the last week, now felt remorse, and resolved to mend, but not for long.

While First Aunt sat, as if guarding her giant egg, her husband boomed away. He spoke of what Mama called politics, and he often turned to his eldest son, Yusiang, who nodded and politely did not speak, letting his father do all the sound. Both Uncle Liu and Papa wore the buttoned garb that Sun Yatsen had worn, and which was now customary for all government officials, railways now being under the Kuomintang government. It was said that Generalissimo Chiang Kaishek was wearing a Sun Yatsen garb at his wedding to Soong Meiling, daughter of that Christian businessman, Soong, who had made so much of his money in America. Now that Peking was no longer under the Northern warlord Chang Tsolin, both Papa and Uncle Liu and all those who worked in the railway office, including Mr. Hua, wore the Sun Yatsen garb, and every Monday congregated in the reception hall of the railway administration where the director of the railway department read out loud the will of Sun Yatsen. It ended with the sentence; "The Revolution is not yet completed." Now Uncle Liu made fun of this.

"Completed? If you ask me, there has not been a Revolution at all. Only one gang of carpet-baggers replacing another."

He made particular fun of the last séance, held by Mr. Chu, the supervisor of railways, who had come from Hankow recently. Mr. Chu was known to be as oily round of soul as he was oily round of body; round as a ball-bearing, able to fit into any system, surviving all changes, and everytime getting more wealthy. Mr. Chu had made a speech, with tears flowing down his cheeks, admonishing his employees to be upright, honest, incorruptible, hardworking, loyal to Chiang Kaishek, and refusing to harbour evil and corrupt thoughts. "These thoughts come from abroad, from foreigners. They are not of our Chinese tradition. That is why we must fight the Communists, who would destroy our country, China. Long live the Leader, Chiang! Ten thousand years to Leader Chiang Kaishek!

Uncle Liu mimicked him, and all the windows rocked and reverberated. Tiza had long ago disappeared to weep. Mama said: "Walls have ears. You should not make fun. After all, Chiang has saved us from the Reds."

But Uncle Liu was not happy. "Wait and see. They say many fine things now, but already their fingers are nimbly groping for the sweets of office. And this idea of removing the capital from Peking to Nanking! That means the North of the country will be neglected. They are concentrating everything round Shanghai and Nanking. Of course, half the government is made up of Shanghai people, and they want to be near their banks and their businesses."

Uncle Liu had recently bought a house in the Street of the Goldfish; and both he and Papa were afraid that with the change of the capital city to Nanking, many families of government employees would leave Peking, and many houses would become vacant. Both Papa and Uncle Liu were trying to find tenants for the houses they had bought, Papa's in the Small Grass Plot Street, and Uncle Liu's in the Street of the Watercarts. But now every day families left for the South, and even the name of Peking was to be changed. It was to be called Peiping, or Northern Peace, instead of Peking, Northern Capital.

"Peiping," said Uncle Liu. "What a disgrace! These Southerners don't trust people from the North, and they won't spend any money on us. I am thankful that at least our own province of Szechuan is not letting Chiang Kaishek come in."

"Szechuan is always different," said Papa, with a little laugh, secretly pleased.

"Yes, that's true," said Uncle Liu. "We are different in Szechuan. We won't let these carpet-baggers from Shanghai with their susurrating hisses dialect come in. Why, they might try to change the names of our cities in Szechuan as well!"

"I hope you don't have any Communists there," said Mama. "Here the schools and universities are full of them."

"Oh, that will soon be over," said Uncle Liu. "The Communists are finished, that is certain. There are only a couple of bandits down in Hunan. I believe one is called Chu Teh, the other Mao something or other. They are bandits of no importance at all, and will soon be eliminated. Why, they have only a few hundred men with them, less than the White Wolf bandit gang in our northern provinces here."

Papa then turned the conversation to Yusiang, Uncle Liu's eldest son. Uncle Liu was pleased. He gazed fondly at the young man, who wore glasses, had a scholarly face and was dressed in European clothes with a tie. Yusiang spoke some words of English to Mama, who could not understand what he said.

"My daughters are studying English," she replied, "but I have not used it for some years."

Uncle Liu then told Papa what he already knew, that Yusiang was going to the United States to study Political Science. "It is expensive, but worth while. America is the country of the future. The government officials round Chiang Kaishek are most of them returned students from America. Why, his wife only speaks American, she was educated there, she can't speak Chinese. Now the American-educated clique is coming to power. No one has any use for us, poor Belgian-returned or French-returned graduates. If you are trained in America," said Uncle Liu judiciously, "you are sure of a good job in the government today. After all, we have to change with the times."

"That is why my daughters are studying English," said Mama.

First Aunt said not a word, she could not understand either English or French. She crossed her thin small hands over her stomach, and burped, and smiled. Under the skin of her temples the veins stood out very blue.

After the Liu family left, Mama said: "There you are. What did I tell you? At least Uncle Liu can see ahead. If you don't know English, you can't get a good job in China."

"American," said Papa mildly.

Mama retorted: "English or American, it is the same thing, only the accent is different. Yentung, I may not be a clever woman I know, but I have a good instinct. I always told you not to build too many houses. Now my dowry has gone into these bricks and stones, and if everybody leaves Peking and we cannot rent out our houses, how shall we live? It costs a lot, all this education."

Actually Mama had never said anything about not building houses. But she had been right about studying English. And after that Papa also began to study English, fearful that the

Americans might take over the railway, and then, if he did not know English, he would lose his job.

To cram that year of 1927 many other things happened.

First Aunt died in childbirth of too much bleeding only two months after the visit, and for a few days Papa seemed to be running in and out of the house, never at home for meals. Mama debated whether her children should wear black for the funeral or not, but then decided it was too expensive, and sewed black bands round their left sleeves.

It was a prickly day when First Aunt was buried, prickly because the children wore their new cold-weather underwear of thick flannel; both Tiza and Rosalie were growing fast, but Tiza faster than Rosalie.

The coffin in which First Aunt was put sat in the middle of the courtyard of Uncle Liu's house. White strips of cloth hung on every room door. The amahs wore white bands round their heads, and wailed. Uncle Liu had removed his glasses, and his face looked very large, with rare but very big pock marks astray upon it, and two eyes suddenly small, sleepy looking, quite unlike his bespectacled ones. Yuchen, the eldest daughter, was kept shut up in her room as she had started to vomit and to scream when her mother had died, and was now delirious with a high fever. One could hear her moaning in the inner room.

"It is sorrow for her mother," said Uncle Liu. So no one called a doctor for some days. And then, a week later, Papa came back with the news that Yuchen had meningitis, and the doctor had at last been called.

Five or six days after the funeral, at four o'clock in the afternoon, as Rosalie was practising the piano, the light changed: Elder Brother stood in the parlour doorway, blocking it. He had on a grey coat, a beige scarf round his neck, and his felt hat in his hand. Mama was in the kitchen, and Rosalie turned on her stool and shouted: "Mama! Mama!" across the living-room.

Mama came out of the kitchen saying: "What is it? Why do you call?" And then: "Oh, my God," as she saw her son standing there.

Elder Brother walked towards her. Later, Mama was to describe this as "the walk of a ghost, pale as death", although it was nothing of the kind; but he did walk as if his feet were heavy, and he came up to Mama and said: "Mother, I want to apologize."

"Oh, my God," said Mama, "I have had so much pain, so much pain." She was holding a pudding basin in her hand, making a paste which smelt good, and she shifted the bowl on to her left hip as her right hand clutched Elder Brother's overcoat. "So much pain," she repeated. And her face twisted to cry, and Elder Brother put his arm and the hand clutching the felt hat round her shoulders. "If you knew how much . . ." said Mama.

"Yes, I know," said Elder Brother. "I am sorry. You are my mother. I do love you, you know."

And that evening the family ate together, and Elder Brother had two helpings of Mama's pudding. Afterwards in the garden darkness, Papa, inspecting his early chrysanthemums, said as if addressing the wall: "I told him to come back, I wrote to him. I said: Do not make your mother grieve."

Rosalie knew he was speaking to her, for she too made her mother grieve, giving her harshness and rude replies all the time.

But Elder Brother was not returning to live with them, he now had a job in Tientsin, the city port five hours away by railway. It was a good job, teaching mathematics at a college. The college was run by Jesuits, and Elder Brother was happy in Tientsin. He spoke of Tientsin as a big city, where everything was better than in Peking. He had a room in a boarding-house run by a German couple. After supper he began to speak English to Rosalie, and he laughed at her. He said:

"You speak very badly. You don't know how to speak. You are not getting a proper education here."

"But what shall we do?" said Mama. "She has to earn a living, and we don't have so much money to send her to the American school here."

"Send her to the Tientsin Grammar School," said Elder Brother. "It is a good English school, she will learn much quicker."

"It would be too expensive," said Mama, "and who would look after a girl of ten?"

Elder Brother left on the third day, and everyone went to see him off at the station, waving goodbye. Rosalie also waved her handkerchief at him, but she did not look at him as the train carried him away.

It was also in the autumn of 1927 that Rosalie met Joseph Hers for the first time, at a reception organized by Mr. Pinshee, who although Chinese was employed as a Counsellor at the Belgian Legation in Peking. The reception was held at the Returned Students Club, of which Papa was a member. The Returned Students Club had been the palace of a Manchu noble before the 1911 Revolution, when it was turned into a club for graduates like Papa, engineers, doctors, professors, returned from studies abroad. Papa went to the Club on an occasional Sunday afternoon to meet his friends, and sometimes he took his family and then they all watched the bowling alleys inside the Club, and the people weighing those cannon-ball spheres of wood and flinging them at the ninepins. Mama liked the Club because there were magazines from Europe to look at, and sometimes she copied a dress fashion and had it cut out and made up at home by our own Chinese tailor.

The reception was for French and Belgian returned students. Papa took Rosalie, as Mama was not well. She had been suffering from varicose veins, and now had some inflamation of the leg. "You will represent me," she said to Rosalie.

When the two hundred or so men, all at one time students in France or Belgium, queued up as the Belgian dignitary went down the line shaking hands, Papa muttered: "This is my daughter. My wife excuses herself, she could not come."

Rosalie felt so important, representing Mama, that she forgot to curtsy as Mama had told her to do, but shook hands, looking up at the same time, up and up and up at the immensely tall man with the bald head and striking blue eyes, the large nose and small beard, towering above her.

"Your daughter, Mr. Chou?" she heard a voice say. "But your son, Mr. Chou, where is he now?"

As Papa explained the man passed on, not even listening, and Rosalie knew he was important because Papa spoke so differently, laughing a little between sentences, so that his explanation about his son came too slowly and already the important Mr. Hers had passed him. And round Mr. Hers they crowded, those like Papa, all laughing and smiling, smiling smiling all the time, smiling as if afraid that if they stopped smiling their faces would drop off.

About twenty round tables were set in the large dining-room of the Club, all covered with white table-cloths. Ten guests sat at each table, and Rosalie was squeezed in, next to Papa and between him and Mr. Poh. Rosalie sometimes played with his elder son, but not frequently; they were at different schools, and Rosalie did not like boys who did not read space fiction.

Mr. Hua sat at another table, and came round to blink at Rosalie. "Where is your mother, eh?"

There were a few women there, European women, as all the Chinese wives had stayed at home, as Mama had done, but for different reasons. Rosalie counted not more than twenty women, out of whom she only had to say good afternoon to six whom she knew. Mrs. Hua was also absent.

"She is very busy, she is writing a book, a novel," said Mr. Hua.

After the dinner Mr. Hers stood up and made a speech. He was at the head table, and a vase of flowers reached up at his midriff from the white table-cloth, and as he talked he played with his glass. Rosalie, to represent adequately, gave him her attention, but it lasted only for half the speech. She could make out that Mr. Hers was pleased to be with them, and congratulated himself on the brilliant successes achieved by Belgian and French returned students. China was now engaged in a good road, he said, and a brilliant future was ahead under the able new government and its leader, Chiang Kaishek. And to show their confidence in China's future, Belgium had voluntarily given up her Belgian concession in Tientsin, vo-lun-ta-ri-ly, said Mr. Hers, detaching the syllables. This showed the excellent, the deep friendship, between the two countries. Everyone then clapped again.

After that, Rosalie lost track of the speech. There was much more clapping, and then people raised glasses and drank.

After dinner they all trooped to another room, and arranged themselves in rows, to be photographed. As there were many of them, the photographer behind his velvet-hooded tripod had the camera-box on a revolving arrangement, so that it swept the assembly, from right to left, going whirr whirr softly as it moved, and they all stiffened at the glare of the lens. Some days later Papa brought home the photograph, a long one, and there was Rosalie, in her white dress with the long scarf round her neck which Mama had made her wear because it was "more dressy", with the cloche hat right down upon her eyes, standing by Papa; and in the centre

Mr. Hers, overtopping them all by a head, his beard and his eyes very clear and visible among the two hundred or so faces on the photograph.

THIRTY-THREE

IN the spring of 1928 Papa's younger brother, Third Uncle, made the long journey from Szechuan to Peking. He sent a telegram to Papa announcing his train from Hankow, and Papa went to the railway station to meet him.

For two days before his arrival Mama had the house scrubbed clean, and Papa bought food to prepare for him, and pickles at the Szechuanese food store in the East Market, as the last jar of pickles made by Papa had been emptied some weeks before. At that time there were two servants in the house, the cook, Old Hsiung, who had a shaven head, and a young rickshaw man who helped to clean the house and to run errands, whose name was Yang. Yang came from Honan, but had emigrated to Manchuria with his parents when a great drought in his province had driven a million famished peasants northwards to Manchuria. He told Rosalie how his two sisters had been sold, and also his mother; and two younger brothers had died of eating mud which had swelled their bellies until they suffocated. In his province this mud was called the mercy earth, because it filled the belly for a while when there was a famine and thus staved off the torture of hunger, but in the end one died of it. And now his father was still in Harbin in Manchuria, spitting blood, and he could not work, though he still tried, carrying sacks of coal along the streets to sell. Because he was strong, Yang had been press-ganged into service by Chang Tsolin's army, had run away to pull a rickshaw, later found work at the railway station in Peking carrying luggage; now he was happy, with work and lodging, and eight dollars a month, of which he saved almost four to pay his father's fare to come to Peking. Yang washed down the wooden floors, once so bright and shiny, with two pails of water and a mop, but the paint was already coming off in parts; Mama said Papa had been cheated by the contractor who had used poor quality paint. Yang never took any notice of anything Mama said to him, because he could not understand her Chinese pronunciation, all the tones were wrong, so that she often screamed at him as people do when they only know a few words of a language. Yang then stood still and laughed, and said: "It is my fault, I am stupid," beating his own head with his fists. He had learnt to do this, when press-ganged into the warlord's army, to pacify whoever bullied him, but it did not pacify Mama, and one day he was sacked. But that was not before the summer, when Mama took the family to the seaside, and long after Third Uncle had come and gone, and not before Rosalie had taken a snapshot of Yang holding a broom, and Hsiung the cook holding a ladle, in front of the veranda door, both smiling at her in a shy, withholding way, not quite certain that it was right to be photographed.

In the scrubbing and scouring of the house Rosalie also helped, it being so important to make a good impression on Third Uncle. The parlour was aired, the mosquito nets over the beds washed and then put back, the big wardrobe polished; the cheval-glass Mama wiped herself. On the evening of Third Uncle's arrival, which was a Saturday, Rosalie, Tiza and Marianne wore their Sunday dresses of grey serge with black buttons, and their leather shoes which Yang cleaned, and Mama got out the spittoon of pink enamel with a spray of daisies and forget-me-nots which she kept in the store room, because she remembered everyone in Szechuan spat a lot, and she was not going to have Third Uncle spit on her clean floors.

As evening was starting its grey shiver, like hands putting out the sunlight in the garden and making the white-and-red tiles of the veranda fade, the knocker slapped twice at the gate and Mama said: "There they are," straightening the white lace collar on her grey dress, putting back a coil of greying hair behind her ear, and pulling Tiza's skirt even; but it was Papa alone. The train was late, it was said some bandits had derailed the line to the south, and Third Uncle would not arrive until the next day.

Mama took off her lace collar and the children put on their house aprons, and Mama said: "I hope he arrives tomorrow, the food will not keep," and they sat down to eat the chicken which had been prepared for Third Uncle.

Just as they were ending, the knocker clapped, and Yang came in, saying: *"Lao yeh, Taitai,* the Third Venerable Gentleman has arrived."

"He is mad," said Mama, but Papa went to the door, turning on the electric lights on the veranda as he walked by the knobs. Rosalie followed him, and indeed it was Third Uncle, at first only a moving sombreness in the dark, and then emergent, swimming out at her, out of the darkness picked out by the light, a smooth face, a pale-grey long dress, a dark silk jacket, black cotton shoes, advancing and bowing with both hands raising his long sleeves, calling: "Second Sister-in-Law, I apologize for being late. My regrets."

And then it was as if they had all turned into goldfish in a jar, swimming smoothly about, gliding next to each other, and never jarring or bumping as humans did, all eased into the golden-brown light from the electric lamps, because as Papa said the electric power was not strong enough.

They went back to sit round the table, the white cloth upon it had not been removed, and Third Uncle bowed as Mama put chicken on his plate.

"Yes," he said, "the train was late, derailed at Lukouchiao, some tens of miles from Peking." But a friend of his had placed a car at his disposal, and he had come with this friend, who was General Ku. At this name Papa looked surprised, and Mama said:

"But how do you know this general?"

"My chief, General Liu Hsiang, who is the governor of Szechuan Province, has business dealings with General Ku, who is in the Finance Ministry of the Kuomintang government," said Third Uncle, smoothing his white silk cuffs over his hands. The grey cloth of his gown fell in easy folds about him.

When he had left, Mama said: "Well, he has made money, hasn't he, your brother? Financial secretary to the Warlord Liu Hsiang. He must be making millions. And did you see his gown? Pure English wool."

Third Uncle talked, in a voice that was never high, and he laughed, the same laugh as Papa. He was staying with General Ku, at his mansion, and the General had put a car at his disposal, but Third Uncle had refused. "I might be criticized for riding in a car at the present moment," he said.

Of his first and later conversations, the main theme, as Rosalie remembered, was money, money and business. He spoke of the erosion of the dollar. "We in Szechuan were reduced to baking coins of clay. We have had war after war, my brother. And even now, the silver dollars we have are only haf the weight they should be. Clever men pare smoothly their edges, paring away perhaps one-tenth, one-fifth of the dollar, and after a time the round coin shrinks to half its size."

"They have done the same here," said Papa. "For years I have watched, every time a silver coin goes through my hands, to see that it is not a shaven one."

That night Papa and Mama talked in bed. Rosalie craned above the blanket to listen, and she heard Mama say: "You want nothing to do with this, do you hear, Yentung? Your place is here, with your wife and children."

And the next day, while Third Uncle talked with Papa, saying: "I have forty thousand in this company, and twenty thousand more in the steamers. General Teng and General Liu are both well disposed towards our family ... I think they will be interested in building the railway. We want to do it on our own, we want nothing to do with the Nanking government ..."

Mama interrupted to say: "But we have our houses here, and we are content."

And the two men did not look at her, but they stopped talking.

Mama told Rosalie: "Speak to your uncle, tell him you are studying English."

Rosalie did, and Third Uncle looked past her and said: "Good, good," in a way that showed he did not mean it at all.

And every night Mama and Papa talked until Rosalie was too drowsy to strain to listen, and sometimes Mama cried, and Papa would say: "You take everything so hard. I tell you, I shall not go back. I will tell him so tomorrow."

At the end of five days Third Uncle left, and no one but Papa went with him to the railway station. Rosalie and Tiza and Marianne were at school, and then they returned Mama was putting away in silk paper the silks that Third Uncle had brought, rolls of heavy blue silk and lighter grey silk, and very heavy pure white silk sold by weight; and two large plates of filigree silver with ten small plates, two with a design of peonies and humming-birds upon the diaphanous silver lace background, and these also Mama wrapped up to place in safety, with her jewels.

"Does Third Uncle want Papa to go back to Szechuan, Mama?" asked Rosalie, and Mama said:

"Be quiet, or I won't take you to the seaside this summer."

Thus Third Uncle came and went, as Joseph Hers had come and gone, as Elder Brother had returned. All came swimming out of the strange tremulous darkness of this twilight time,

time of in-between childhood and adolescence, goldfish-jar sombre, tangleweed submerged forest of green dark water-slime.

And now Rosalie was nearly eleven, a peevish, irritable eleven, overworked, overtired, no blossom-fragrant youth but a crippled vigour propelled into the already futured though unknown ingrate years that were coming, the years of growing up; and in and out in awkward, ungainly strength that loses before it wins, when the seeing childhood eye and ear abdicate, and this change was terror. "The inside of things is taken out of them, and people become semi-automatic happenings in an amorphous surround, as impotent to cleave as water, become sinister with water-loneliness, with the terror of submerged incomprehensible suffocation. Who am I, what am I, what shall I do, what is this life, why am I as I am, why is Elder Brother thus changed? There is now no more than a wall, paper pasted on the wall, Elder Brother, as existent as a newspaper. Papa says I must be nice to Hers, he gives scholarships, but who is Hers? Why is everything gone? I cannot reach and grasp any longer but all is unsubstantial, so that I am not sure at all. All appear and vanish, flit in and out of a darkness ... Am I going mad?"

The notion that she was going mad terrified Rosalie, and mainly because now she heard Mama say that Yuchen was insane. The girl had fallen ill when her mother, First Aunt, died. Four months later Uncle Liu the Lolo had married again, but without ceremony, a young woman of twenty, twenty years younger than he, but worst of all her surname also was Liu and she had been employed in his household as a servant, and to marry someone of the same surname in China was against tradition and custom, almost incest. Papa said that Uncle Liu needed someone to look after all his children, and particularly after Yuchen, who was now quite abnormal after her meningitis and soiled her bed at night. Rosalie became frightened that she would soil the bed at night, and this kept her awake so that her eyes were dark-ringed.

Elder Brother wrote to her: "It is evident that it will be difficult for you to marry, and therefore with your brains, you should aim at a profession. To become a teacher is a satisfying profession for a woman ..."

"The child is working too hard," said Mrs. Blievermann, who came to see Mama one afternoon.

"She has to work, she is taking an examination in English at the end of the year," said Mama.

In that spring Rosalie caught a bad cold and coughed for weeks. Then one day her ear began to ache. For a week it hurt, and at night she lay in bed listening to a drumming in her ear. "I can hear my heart in my ear."

Mama put hot oil into the ear. But still at night the steady beat went on, thump thump thump, in her ear, keeping her awake. And the child became more frightened. Everything became more and more unreal, withdrawn, separated. Language, names, began to fail, and the fear of madness made her weep.

"Heavens, how clumsy you are."

She was clumsy. Everything dropped from her hands. She bumped into furniture.

Then Mama took her to the doctor, and it was the same Greek doctor who had been at Marianne's birth.

"She has pus in her ear," he said, and her drum was lanced, and then the heart no longer beat at night.

But another terror took its place, clutching her in the nightmare-filled nights: that she would not pass the examination at the end of the year.

"I am becoming stupid, I am becoming stupid."

Terror drove her all through that warming season, and as if the strangling ring round her was not gathering close enough, a surfeit was added by seeing a boy kill a dog by breaking its backbone against a stone wall. And so into a torrid early summer.

Then the last week of school, when the result of the tests would decide whether she would take the examinations at the end of the year or not. And Mama did all she could so that Rosalie might do well in the examinations; Mama made chicken soup, and creme caramel, easy to digest. But now the sight of Mama drove Rosalie to rage, and she turned round viciously and spat out the creme caramel.

"Her nerves are bad, like yours, Madame. She is a bundle of nerves," the doctor said.

"We are going to the seaside for the summer," said Mama.

And then the tests were over, and Rosalie had passed, and now the family would be going to the seaside, Mama and the children. They would be leaving in a week, in only four days, and then it was: tomorrow ...

And a small rain came the morning before they were to leave for the seaside, and it dropped upon the garden; the vine leaves, dust scored, made a deep patter sound, and in the dust road outside the carters shouted with joy, for there had been little water, and much dust into their eyes, powdering their faces and garments.

Rosalie opened the street door with the lions' heads mouthing their rings, and opposite the house, at the well, was the woman of the well-owner, nursing her baby, and the well made the same wailing sound as the baby did, and the water came out, clear and cold, splashing in the wooden buckets.

The rain switched itself off, and the earth began to smell new. Rosalie turned around the house and came to the earth bank by the old disused canal, now going dry, walked by its fainting willows, and remembered the beggar boy who had pursued them with curses here, here, just here. A scavenger dog barked stiffly at her, then fled as she bent to mimic the picking up of a stone. There was a last spurt of rain, and the sun was out before the last drops had fallen, and Rosalie opened her mouth to taste the sun, to chew the honey and date, round cake of the sun. "I am eleven years old, and what shall I do with myself? And who am I?" Walk, walk, walk, Rosalie, and look your fill, even if now your eyes can no longer see with the punctilious passion of childhood; for you are growing up, childhood is going from you, and you are not yet that other you waiting for you, the other, waiting just round the street corner, hiding behind that crooked willow, seized in that dreadful hide-and-seek perhaps at the end of the hutung, or hanging out there at the horizon, still diaphanous, like a dust storm not yet gathered together. Walk, walk towards the horizon, and do not stop, Rosalie, even if your nights are full of terror and you can tell no one.

And now she bent to clutch the earth, the kneaded dust and water, to fling a handful in the canal's thick green water, and watch the ripples go streaming out. And there was no answer anywhere, since everything had to be learned anew.

Walk, walk to Papa's office, where now the portrait of Sun Yatsen hangs above the entrance, in every room, with next to it the portrait of Chiang Kaishek in his uniform and his white gloves, his medals and his sabre. And now the streets are bespattered with slogans calling for a New Life Movement, praising the Leader, and promising to crush the Communists.

Peer at the portraits, Rosalie, read the words, painfully, clutching at them, for they too are vanishing from you, as is your calligraphy, because now you are made to practise the piano and not the brush strokes.

Papa is there, and Mr. Hua, and they are talking as usual, but nothing is the same, for Mr. Hua also is half shadow, you no longer hear his words, they go from you before they have come to you. So do not go in, do not bother to listen, watch them through the dusty window, from the courtyard, and walk away, walk among the strangers in the street, no stranger than your own brother, sisters, parents. Slip quietly among strangers, walking at the same pace, their backs kind to you, deliberately unknowing, and lose your terror into the unknowing indifference of the street, until terror slips off you like a raincoat slipped off after the rain.

Now comes the warm smother of night, taking over the streets of once-Peking, now renamed Peiping, no longer capital but Northern Peace, taking over its million people, taking over the great plain of China, and preparing the bed of steadfast night. "Tomorrow, perhaps, I shall have grown up. Perhaps I can wait till tomorrow."

In front of the East Market there is a sudden scuffle, an uproar, policemen shouting, and dragging a boy, a girl, out of the market into the dim fumous sparse electric light, flinging them into a black car which then drives away. A small crowd, stopped in its walking, congeals at one side, but two plain-clothesmen, in gowns with felt hats, shout: "What are you standing for? Go, walk, walk!"

And Rosalie, who is there too, walks away.

"Perhaps they will be shot tomorrow. I wonder how old they are?"

But tomorrow might forget them. Tomorrow would find herself, Rosalie, again. "If only it happens before going to the seaside." Meanwhile, here one was, walking time away in its four-square box within the four-square city. Tomorrow would come the sea.

·